Staël's Philosophy
of the Passions

TRANSITS:
LITERATURE, THOUGHT & CULTURE

Series Editor
Greg Clingham
Bucknell University

Transits is the next horizon. The series of books, essays, and monographs aims to extend recent achievements in eighteenth-century studies and to publish work on any aspects of the literature, thought, and culture of the years 1650–1850. Without ideological or methodological restrictions, *Transits* seeks to provide transformative readings of the literary, cultural, and historical interconnections between Britain, Europe, the Far East, Oceania, and the Americas in the long eighteenth century, and as they extend down to present time. In addition to literature and history, such "global" perspectives might entail considerations of time, space, nature, economics, politics, environment, and material culture, and might necessitate the development of new modes of critical imagination, which we welcome. But the series does not thereby repudiate the local and the national, for original new work on particular writers and readers in particular places in time continues to be the bedrock of the discipline.

Titles in the Series

The Family, Marriage, and Radicalism in British Women's Novels of the 1790s: Public Affection and Private Affliction
Jennifer Golightly

Feminism and the Politics of Travel After the Enlightenment
Yaël Schlick

John Galt: Observations and Conjectures on Literature, History, and Society
Regina Hewitt

Performing Authorship in Eighteenth-Century English Periodicals
Manushag N. Powell

Excitable Imaginations: Eroticism and Reading in Britain, 1660–1760
Kathleen Lubey

The French Revolution Debate and the British Novel, 1790–1814: The Struggle for History's Authority
Morgan Rooney

Rococo Fiction in France, 1600–1715: Seditious Frivolity
Allison Stedman

For a complete list of titles in this series, please visit http://www.bucknell.edu/university press.

TRANSITS

Staël's Philosophy
of the Passions

SENSIBILITY, SOCIETY,
AND THE SISTER ARTS

Edited by Tili Boon Cuillé
and Karyna Szmurlo

Lewisburg
BUCKNELL UNIVERSITY PRESS

Published by Bucknell University Press
Copublished by The Rowman & Littlefield Publishing Group, Inc.
4501 Forbes Boulevard, Suite 200, Lanham, Maryland 20706
www.rowman.com

Unit A, Whitacre Mews, 26-34 Stannery Street, London SE11 4AB

Copyright © 2013 by Rowman & Littlefield Inc.
First paperback edition 2014

British Library Cataloguing in Publication Information Available

Library of Congress Cataloging-in-Publication Data
The hardback edition of this book was previously catalogued by the Library of Congress as follows:

Staël's philosophy of the passions : sensibility, society, and the sister arts / edited by Tili Boon Cuillé and Karyna Szmurlo.
        Pages cm. — (Transits literature, thought & culture)
    Includes bibliographical references and index.
1.   Staël, Madame de (Anne Louise-Germaine), 1766-1817— Criticism and interpretation. 2.   France—Intellectual life—19th century.   I. Cuillé, Tili Boon editor of compilation. II. Szmurlo, Karyna editor of compilation.
    PQ2431.Z5S64 2013
    848'.609—DC23

                                                                      2012040987

ISBN 978-1-61148-472-4 (cloth : alk. paper)
ISBN 978-1-61148-636-0 (pbk. : alk. paper)
ISBN 978-1-61148-473-1 (ebook)

To our mentors (our source of inspiration)
and our children (our hope for the future).

CONTENTS

Figures

W E ARE INDEBTED TO Madelyn Gutwirth and our anonymous readers for their invaluable insights. The Dean of Arts and Sciences at Washington University in St. Louis generously granted us a publication subsidy. Special thanks are due to Kate Parker for her careful reading of our volume and her expert guidance throughout the revision process.

The Editors

Women endeavor to model themselves on novels, and men on history; but the human heart is still far from being penetrated in its most intimate relations. Someday perhaps someone will tell us sincerely all that he has felt, and we shall be surprised to learn that most maxims and observations are mistaken, and that there is an unknown soul beneath the one we have described.

—Germaine de Staël

IN HER INFLUENTIAL ACCOUNT OF German philosophy and aesthetics *De l'Allemagne* (*On Germany*, 1810/13), Germaine de Staël depicts the human heart as the new frontier, one that the eighteenth century had aspired to fathom but was far from having fully understood. Yet the heart had been at the center of discourse about the novel ever since Richardson, Rousseau, and Goethe started to move their readers not to laughter but to tears. In recent years the passions—sometimes referred to as the language of the heart—have become a subject of renewed critical interest, perceived as pertaining to subjects as varied as natural philosophy, natural law, natural rights, slavery, empire, economics, aesthetics, ethics, sexuality, and gender relationships, particularly in Britain, France, Germany, and Italy. Educated in the intellectual milieu of her mother's Parisian salon, widely read and traveled and an aspiring author in her own right, witness to the ravages of the French Revolution but exiled by Napoleon for meddling in public affairs, Germaine de Staël was ideally situated at the turn of the nineteenth century to chronicle Europe's literary, philosophical, and political past and to envision and influence its future. This volume proposes to examine the nature and extent of

Staël's participation in what Karyna Szmurlo recently termed the "affective revolution" in Europe.[1]

Though moral philosophers considered sensibility to be an instinctive property with which all humans are endowed, the term was also used to designate a sort of sixth sense that enabled certain individuals to experience a greater range and intensity of passion than others,[2] as the following citation from Prévost's *Manon Lescaut* reveals:

> Few can know the full power of these afflictions of the soul. Most men are touched only by five or six passions, and their whole life, with all its storms and stresses, moves round within this circle. Take away love and hatred, pleasure and sorrow, hope and fear, and there is nothing else they feel. But characters of a more delicate texture can be tossed about in a hundred different ways; they seem to have more than five senses, and to be a prey to ideas and sensations surpassing the ordinary limits of nature. And being conscious of this refinement which raises them above the ordinary run of men, they cherish this sensibility of theirs more jealously than anything else. That is why scorn or laughter tortures and exasperates them, that is why shame is one of their most violent emotions.[3]

This sensibility, or heightened awareness of more than the usual range and intensity of sensations or passions, can be either physiological or moral in nature, according to Diderot and D'Alembert's *Encyclopédie ou Dictionnaire raisonné des sciences, des arts, et des métiers* (*Encyclopedia or Classified Dictionary of Sciences, Arts, and Trades*). In the past fifteen years, scholars have paid increasing attention to the relationship between the *Encyclopedia*'s definitions of physiological and moral sensibility and their role in the medical, philosophical, and literary discourse of the Enlightenment. Yet the critical tendency, evident in John O'Neal's *The Authority of Experience: Sensationist Theory in the French Enlightenment* and Anne Vila's *Enlightenment and Pathology: Sensibility in the Literature and Medicine of Eighteenth-Century France*, is to conclude studies of sensibility in eighteenth-century France with its subversion in Sade rather than its culmination in Staël. Several significant studies of sensibility, along with the related terms of sympathy, sentimentalism, and sensationism,[4] have thus omitted Staël entirely, from David Marshall's groundbreaking *The Surprising Effects of Sympathy: Marivaux, Diderot, Rousseau, and Mary Shelley* to Philip Stewart's recent *L'Invention du sentiment: Roman et économie affective au XVIIIe siècle*.[5] Even David Denby, who asserts that "an analysis of the work of Madame de Staël through the prism of sentimentalism would be useful and instructive" in *Sentimental Narrative and the Social Order in France, 1760–1820*, phrases the title he dedicates to the subject in the form of a question: "Beyond Sentimentalism? Madame de Staël," inviting further specula-tion.[6] The following pages comprise a brief overview of the role sensibility and its related terms played in the sciences, social sciences, and the arts in eighteenth-century France, situating Staël with respect to her Enlightenment heritage in order to bring her more fully into this critical conversation.

The investigation of sensibility in the natural sciences in the 1740s to 1760s led Enlightenment vitalists from Montpellier to Paris to question the accuracy and sufficiency of Descartes's mind/body divide as they sought to identify the property (whether physiological or psychological) that facilitated communication between the two.[7] Voltaire's *Lettres philosophiques* (*Philosophical Letters*) of 1734 and Condillac's *Essai sur l'origine des connaissances humaines* (*Essay on the Origin of Human Knowledge*) of 1746 and *Traité des sensations* (*Treatise on Sensations*) of 1754 introduced the French, moreover, to Locke's conviction that the source of our knowledge is not the mind but the senses and to Newton's empirical method, based no longer on deductive reasoning but rather on observation and experi-ence.[8] With this shift, reason and sensibility, which had previously been opposed, increasingly became associated. This association is visible in Jaucourt's definition of moral sensibility in the *Encyclopedia* as a "delicate and tender disposition of the soul that makes it easily moved, touched. The sensibility of the soul . . . goes farther than the penetration of the mind alone . . . Reflection can make a man of honor; but sensibility [the mother of humanity and of generosity] makes a man virtuous."[9] It is also visible in Du Marsais's definition of the philosopher in the *Encyclopedia* not as the "insensitive sage of the stoics" but as a humane member of society who "makes no claim to the chimerical honor of destroying the passions" but rather "works at not being dominated by them . . . and at making reasonable use of them."[10]

Around mid-century, philosophers on both sides of the channel came to perceive sensibility as the property that facilitated communication not only between mind and body or between body parts but also between individuals, fostering community. Jean-Jacques Rousseau takes Condillac's association between reason and sensibility as his point of departure in his *Discours sur l'origine de l'inégalité* (*Discourse on the Origin of Inequality*) of 1754, where he affirms: "Human un-derstanding owes much to the passions, which, by common consensus, also owe a great deal to it. It is by their activity that our reason is perfected."[11] He pauses, however, to consider with awe the vast distance that separates reason from the passions, and contends that the relationship between the two is inconceivable without the notion of communication: "The more one meditates on this subject, the more the distance from pure sensations to the simplest knowledge increases before our eyes; and it is impossible to conceive how a man could have crossed such a wide gap by his forces alone, without the aid of communication."[12] Communication, accordingly, becomes the watchword of Rousseau's idyllic description of the birth of society around a well in his *Essai sur l'origine des langues* (*Essay on the Origin of Languages*, 1761, published 1781), the moment when both language and music arose simultaneously from the pure expression of passion.[13] The communicable passion that Rousseau most closely identifies with the origin of society is not love, however, for its corollary, jealousy, does as much to divide as to unite.[14] Instead he identifies pity, often glossed as sympathy or sensibility, as the primordial social sentiment.

Pity is the natural, instinctive passion that proves mankind harbors an inherent potential for virtue and renders reason more humane in the state of society, replacing self-love, self-interest, and the drive for self-gratification with a spirit of mutual understanding and mutual conservation.[15] It is also the cornerstone of Adam Smith's *Theory of Moral Sentiments* of 1759. In his opening chapter entitled "Of Sympathy" Smith defines his terminology as follows: "Pity and compassion are words appropriated to signify our fellow-feeling with the sorrow of others. Sympathy, though its meaning was . . . originally the same, may now . . . denote our fellow-feeling with any passion whatever." Sympathy, in other words, refers to the *communicability* of passion or our ability to identify with it. Casting beyond Rousseau, Smith locates the mechanism of sympathy, in which we "change places in fancy with the sufferer" in both society and the theater. Likening our response to our fellow citizens to our response to the characters in a play, he extends the language of community to the relationship between stage and audience. This relationship, Smith reminds us, is a reciprocal one, for "as nature teaches the spectators to assume the circumstances of the person principally concerned, so she teaches this last in some measure to assume those of the spectators."[16] As the onlooker places himself in the position of the victim he becomes capable of empathy; as the victim places himself in the position of the onlooker he becomes capable of moral judgment.[17] The role of pity, sympathy, or sensibility in creating social bonds via communication between individuals thus rendered it a crucial element in the nascent social sciences with implications for the arts.[18]

In his *Salon de 1767* (*Salon of 1767*), Denis Diderot attributes the same faculty that Smith had identified in the spectator and citizen to the artist and art critic, the faculty that enables the beholder first to empathize with the plight of the characters on stage (or one's fellow human) and later to judge their performance (or actions) impartially.[19] He thus reinforced and extended the domain of Smith's analogy to the arts and joined Rousseau in his project of aesthetic and social reform. In his *Entretiens sur le Fils naturel* (*Conversations on the Natural Son*) of 1757 and his *De la poésie dramatique* (*On Dramatic Poetry*) of 1758, Diderot proposed a reform of the theater in the guise of a new genre, the bourgeois drama, in which the distinction between actors and audience would essentially be elided, placing the citizen and the drama of daily life on stage in order to appeal to his sympathies. The antidote to the state of society depicted in *Le Neveu de Rameau* (*Rameau's Nephew*)—in which the world is a stage, men and women merely posturing, and sincerity and authenticity nowhere to be found—is therefore a vision of society modeled so closely upon Diderot's reform theater that the difference between art and life becomes imperceptible. Similarly, in his *Lettre à D'Alembert sur les spectacles* (*Letter to D'Alembert on Spectacles*) of 1758, Rousseau proposed that open-air festivals take the place of theater in Geneva in an effort to conceive of an aesthetic form that would have a favorable moral impact on society and facilitate, rather than impede, the communication of sentiment and formation of community.[20]

Staël participated in this philosophical project of aesthetic and social reform, taking the passions as the object of her contemplation and the subject of her writing. In her *De l'influence des passions sur le bonheur des individus et des nations* (*The Influence of the Passions upon the Happiness of Individuals and of Nations*) of 1796 Staël discusses passion with respect to the happiness of the individual, the fate of women, and the future of France. Though inclined to be passion's apologist, Staël seeks to attenuate the effects of passions that, if unmitigated, may prove detrimental to the happiness of the individual and the well-being of the nation. She would spare women in particular the agony of unrequited love, for she identifies love as the passion to which women are most susceptible and the one least likely to lead to happiness. Though wary of the risks, Staël was also aware of the benefits of sensibility to society. While she lauds Smith's *Theory of Moral Sentiments*, she questions his association of sympathy with both emotion and judgment, suggesting that it must be freed of the latter if we are to empathize with someone else's plight irrespective of our own situation. As Denby has noted, this enhanced definition of sympathy, or what Staël calls good will or "bienfaisance," constitutes a third means of attenuating the passions, along with philosophy and fiction.[21] If pity takes the place of virtue in the state of nature, as Rousseau argued in his *Second Discourse*, then it must also take the place of law in a state of revolution, Staël asserts.[22] She therefore recommends that the French have recourse to philosophy and fiction to attenuate the passions in time of peace but cultivate sympathy in time of war, advice that she both gave and followed.[23]

Yet theater and war were not the only venues in which the passions were likely to be unleashed, rendering them apt subjects of study. In his *Éloge de Richardson* (*In Praise of Richardson*) of 1762, Diderot envisioned the new (sentimental) novel as the reflection, or portrait, of the human heart, language that the Marquis de Sade would echo in his *Idée sur les romans* (*An Essay on Novels*) of 1799, in which he recognized Richardson, Prévost, and Rousseau as his predecessors. Diderot and Sade both likened novelists' powers of observation to those of philosophers and ranked them above historians in their ability to convey the truth. Staël makes similar claims in her *Essai sur les fictions* (*Essay on Fictions*) of 1795, as evident in the following passage:

> Novels give a false idea of mankind, it has been said. This is true of bad novels, as it is true of paintings which imitate nature badly. When novels are good, however, nothing gives such an intimate knowledge of the human heart as these portrayals of the various circumstances of private life and the impressions they inspire. . . . Memoirs would be able to do this if their only subjects were not, as in history, famous men and public events. . . . The greatest power of fiction is its power to touch us; almost all moral truths can be made tangible if they are shown in action. . . . Some severe philosophers condemn all emotions, wanting moral authority to rule by a simple statement of moral duty. Nothing is less suited to human nature. Virtue must be brought to life if she is to fight the passions with any chance of winning . . . But the more real power there is in fiction's talent for touching us, the more important it becomes to widen its influence to the passions of all ages, and the duties of all situations.[24]

The role of the novel is thus to depict, convey, and stir the passions, and to enable us to live and learn from them more fully than in life. Yet in *De la littérature considérée dans ses rapports avec les institutions sociales* (*On Literature Considered in Its Relationship to Social Institutions*) of 1800, Staël makes the crucial link between sensibility and observation, or cognition, stating: "No one but Rousseau and Goethe has ever been able to portray self-reflecting passion, the passion that judges itself and understands itself without being able to conquer itself."[25] Like Sade, she thus inscribes herself in a literary tradition, for she endows her heroine Corinne with precisely this combination of faculties, characteristic of sentimental fiction.

Staël's *Corinne ou l'Italie* (*Corinne, or Italy*) of 1807 in many respects epito-mizes the genre of sentimental fiction.[26] Rather than belonging to the sentimental novel that predated the investigations of the property in philosophy and the natu-ral sciences, *Corinne* bears all the earmarks of what Anne Vila dubs the *new* novel of sensibility, pioneered by Diderot and Rousseau, subverted by Laclos and Sade.[27] As in the texts of her predecessors, most notably Richardson, Rousseau, Diderot, and Goethe, Staël initially casts sensibility in a favorable though suspect light. It is the source of Corinne's talent, to which Oswald must become reconciled; enhanc-ing her salon conversation, giving rise to her improvisations, and enabling her to initiate Oswald into a greater appreciation of the Italian language, character, and arts. It also renders her capable of both love and supreme sacrifice, ceding Oswald to her sister Lucile. Yet Staël remains intensely aware of sensibility's physiological repercussions. When too acute, sensibility inevitably leads to sickness and suffering (witness Rousseau's Julie, Diderot's Suzanne, and Goethe's Werther). Staël's novel is thus replete with sensibility's symptoms: from blushes, pallor, tears, fainting, and convulsions, to the memorable scene in which Oswald insists upon nursing Corinne back to health when she contracts a contagious fever in Rome that is so reminiscent of Saint-Preux's attempts to contract his lover's malady with a kiss in Rousseau's *Julie*.[28] Physical ailment gives way to moral suffering leading from eloquent silences to the breakdown of language—no longer adequate to convey her passion—and the attendant melancholy that leads to the loss of life. Staël's novel thus constitutes the logical extension of Vila's influential study of Rousseau and Diderot in *Enlightenment and Pathology*—a more logical extension, to some extent, than Laclos and Sade, for Vila acknowledges the antithetical nature of their stance towards the socio-moral enterprise of their predecessors, whereas Staël up-holds the Enlightenment project to reform society and the arts in light of a revised notion of human nature.[29]

The political message of Staël's *Corinne* differs from that of her predecessors, however, for she also adopts a critical stance towards her Enlightenment heritage, particularly where women are concerned. Cognizant of the mechanism of sensibil-ity at work in society and the arts, Staël's heroine proves capable of manipulating that mechanism, or staging sensibility after the fashion of the characters included in Marshall's perceptive study *The Surprising Effects of Sympathy*.[30] Both Italian and English, native and foreign, Corinne is ideally situated to view her country both from without (critically) and from within (sympathetically). She is also ideally equipped to lead an outsider on the journey from prejudice to tolerance. Corinne displays her sensibility not only by shedding tears herself, but also through her awareness of and ability to trigger the mechanism of sensibility in others. This she does altruistically when she enables Oswald to mourn his dead father by showing him George Augustus Wallis's painting of a scene from Ossian in which a young man is seated on his father's tomb, catalyzing his tears by playing the Scots airs that seem to issue forth from the lyre of the bard in the background.[31] Yet she also does so vindictively when she teaches her niece Juliette, Corinne's spitting image, to repeat this performance every year on the anniversary of the day that Oswald abandoned her. Corinne thus displays the same internal rift that Marshall identifies in Diderot's nun, Suzanne Simonin, whose powers of observation equal her powers of empathy and render us distrustful of a portrait of the heart that is somewhat discolored by an insidious strength of intellect. The duality of being endowed with sensibility on the one hand and the ability to feign, analyze, or catalyze it on the other is characteristic of the sentimental novel.[32] Like Suzanne, however, Corinne ultimately rises above any personal desire to settle her accounts and dedicates her ability to manipulate her audience to a greater social cause: the critique, not of cloistering, but of the equally confining or exclusionary notion of domestic happiness. Far from reconditioning her heroine and her lover in order to render their sensibility more suitable for society—as does Rousseau's Wolmar in the carefully constructed house and gardens of Clarens and the Elysium—Staël capitalizes upon Corinne's mastery of the mechanism of sensibility, using it to ensure that Oswald will never forget her otherwise ephemeral art and that the next generation of women will learn to integrate the artistic talent often attendant upon women's sensibility into Rousseau's domestic arrangement.

Inseparable from Staël's social critique is her aesthetic innovation, which in turn gives rise to a new vision of society.[33] Corinne considers the critical distance that Diderot identified as an intrinsic part of artistic production and reception to be deleterious to artistic inspiration. Her performances are designed, accordingly, to allow complete identification, or the collapse of critical distance. We have already noted how Corinne brings Wallis's painting of a scene from Ossian to life for Oswald by enhancing the similarity between the situation of the subject and the viewer. Similarly, when Staël stages Corinne's performance of Shakespeare's *Romeo and Juliet* in Italian, she positions a column so as to hide the actor playing Romeo from Oswald's view, giving him the impression that Corinne is speaking to him directly at the very moment when she most means what she is saying. The performance is thus reminiscent of the ideal theater Diderot envisions in his *Conversa-*

tions on the Natural Son, in which Dorval acts the part of himself in his own salon before the other members of his household, effectively eliminating the distinction between character and actor, stage and audience, truth and fiction. Corinne's improvisations, which recreate Rousseau's ideal of declamation, likewise eliminate the critical distance that leaves room for duplicity, which Rousseau decried in his *Letter to D'Alembert*. Inspired by the emotions of her audience, the *improvisatrice* rises above her own concerns to embrace those of others in a supreme act of empathy, transcending the divide that potentially separates the performer from her role and her audience. Staël's novel thereby signals not the failure of the Enlightenment project, but its inflection into a Romantic ideal.

Staël's writings thus constitute the culmination of a century's reflection on the relationship between the passions, philosophy, politics, painting, and the performing arts. Unlike Mary Wollstonecraft, who continued to oppose sensibility and reason, billing the one as feminine and the other as masculine, Staël considered the two qualities to be complementary, and their combination to be an essential attribute of all citizens—men and women alike—if the republican ideal was to become a reality.[34] Just as her understanding of sensibility is inseparable from reason, so her reflections on the passions, aesthetics, and the arts (coded feminine) are inseparable from her understanding of politics, international relations, and history (coded masculine). Our volume emphasizes the interdependence of these traditionally gendered domains. In Eric Gidal's words:

> A true disciple of the French Enlightenment, [Staël's] fictional, theoretical, autobiographical, and historical writings all profess a faith in rational progress guided by moral sentiments as means for overcoming political repression and spiritual degradation. The role of the artist and the philosopher in Staël's thinking is to cultivate the emotional and intellectual dispositions most conducive to such progress and to thereby aid in the expansion of political liberty and moral justice.[35]

We have therefore consistently sought to address the relationship between emotion and cognition that William Reddy recently identified as part of our Enlightenment heritage, acknowledging Staël as the precursor of current investigations in the fields of anthropology and psychology in *The Navigation of Feeling: A Framework for the History of Emotions*.

Staël questioned not only the separation of the sexes and the opposition of sensibility and reason, but also the perceived limitations of national art. In *On*

Literature, she envisions the sentimental novel as giving rise to a community of readers that transcends both time (previous and current generations) and space (national divides).[36] In recent years, critics have begun to corroborate Staël's vision, calling attention to the sentimental novel's creation of an inter- (or trans-) national community of readers.[37] This volume explores the aesthetic innovations that enabled Staël to overstep national and generic boundaries and the nature of the sentimental communities to which her writings gave rise. We perceive Staël's role with respect to each of our areas of investigation—the passions, aesthetics, and the arts—to be that of revisionist historiographer, for she both embraces and actively rethinks past models in light of recent political events: in the words of Virginia Woolf, she is "an inheritor as well as an originator."[38] Thoroughly steeped in the aesthetic models and philosophical convictions of her forebears, yet with the hindsight of having witnessed the failure of the republican ideal of communication and community in the worst phases of the French Revolution, Staël sought not to discard but to recast these molds, envisioning a future predicated on conjunctions rather than disjunctions: sensibility *and* reason, politics *and* passion, philosophy *and* art—cosmopolitan, hybrid, and polyglot.

Part I, "The Politics of the Passions," takes Staël's treatise of 1796, *The Influence of the Passions*, as its point of departure. Catherine Dubeau locates the origins of Staël's treatise in her resistance to her mother Suzanne Necker's *Réflexions sur le divorce* (*Reflections on Divorce*) of 1794. She thus shifts the emphasis from the relationships for which Staël was most famed—those with her father, Jacques Necker, her father figure, Rousseau, and her nemesis, Napoleon—towards the far more ambivalent yet equally formative relationships with her mother, her lovers, and the French Revolution. Dubeau then considers the significance of Staël's decision to excise her novella *Zulma* from her treatise and the role of the fictional references that live on in its pages. Each of the ensuing chapters focuses upon Staël's engagement with one passion in particular, relating her treatise on the passions to her other political, philosophical, and fictional works. Nanette Le Coat investigates the crucial role of pity, dubbed the "reasonable passion," in Staël's concept of personal and civic virtue, exposing it as a locus of resistance to the factionalism she had witnessed during the ravages of the Revolution and considering its relationship to her 1793 *Réflexions sur le procès de la reine* (*Reflections on the Trial of the Queen*). Christine Henderson then explores Staël's quest for personal and political happiness, proposing two routes to its realization, via philosophical moderation or the modern novel, as revealed in her analysis of Staël's 1795 *Essay on Fictions*. Karen de Bruin turns from Staël's treatise on the passions to *On Literature*, which Reddy has called "a veritable history of emotions in Europe," to demonstrate how the quest for happiness becomes infused with melancholy, a necessary attribute of the *femme supérieure*, who is willing to sacrifice personal interest for the greater good of the nation.[39]

Part II, "International Aesthetics," explores Staël's persistent interrogation of the limits of nation, gender, and genre in the context of her novel-travelogue. Disclosing the startling similarities between Sydney Owenson's *The Wild Irish Girl: A National Tale* of 1806 and Staël's *Corinne, or Italy* of 1807, M. Ione Crummy demonstrates how Staël arrogated the genre of the novel-travelogue from a peripheral Celtic tale into a mainstream European genre. Jennifer Law-Sullivan then draws upon narratology and post-colonial theory to read the alternation between the voices of Corinne, the narrator, and the author as a dialogue between ethnography and auto-ethnography inherent to Staël's cosmopolitanism. Moving from the significance of voice to the aesthetics of listening in the novel, Lauren Fortner Ravalico emphasizes the importance of non-verbal communication, particularly tears, in establishing a sentimental community within the text and an emotional bond with the reader. Invoking the Aeolian harp as metaphor for the translator, Charles Wharram then investigates the aesthetics of mediation at work in *Corinne* and Staël's 1816 treatise *De l'esprit des traductions* (*The Spirit of Translation*). Turning from Staël's appropriation of English melancholy to German enthusiasm, Kari Lokke exposes the process of acculturation through which women writers of the British regency Letitia Landon and Maria Jane Jewsbury sought to reconcile Staël's aspirations with the subsequent commercialization and commodification of art.

Part III, "Philosophy and the Arts," explores the implications of Staël's politicization and theorization of the passions for painting and the performing arts. Susan Tenenbaum opens the discussion by revealing a fundamental duality in Staël's characterization of the fine arts in *On Literature*, associating them both with *le beau idéal* and its ability to elevate the soul and with *la belle nature* and its propensity to seduce the senses. The remaining chapters move seamlessly from Neoclassicism to Romanticism, from painting to music, and from Staël to her successors, disclosing both the tensions and the affinities between the two. Mary D. Sheriff takes us on a guided tour of Staël's portraits, four of which figured prominently in the 2009 Juliette Récamier exhibition in Lyon, drawing a striking parallel between Elisabeth Louise Vigée Le Brun's and Staël's conceptions of the woman as artist. Juxtaposing the literal space of Staël's art gallery at Coppet with the literary space of Corinne's art gallery at Tivoli, Heather Belnap Jensen likens their collecting practices to those of the Bonaparte women, including Napoleon's first wife, Josephine, and his sisters, Pauline Borghese and Caroline Murat. Music gradually displaced painting as the art form emblematic of Romanticism, as Fabienne Moore demonstrates in her study of Staël's interest in the glass harmonica as an instrument capable of crossing the threshold between pleasure and pain, transcending the dichotomies that riddled Enlightenment discussions of music. Finally, Julia Effertz turns from the dynamic between women artists and collectors to that between women performers and their audiences, examining Corinne's legacy in singer narratives of the 1830s by George Sand, Sophie Ulliac, and Mme R. R. de Thellusson, and once again exposing the commercialization of Staël's ideal.

Like the salons of the Old Regime that were hosted by women (including Necker, Récamier, and Staël)—fostering the rise of public opinion and counterbalancing the monarchy as Dena Goodman has argued—Staël's artistic communities created a semi-private, semi-public forum for women's voices that counterbalanced the Napoleonic regime.[40] Staël's literary heritage therefore consists both in her creation of an inspirational portrait of the artist as a young woman and in forging communities through tears and other non-verbal means of communication, including exchange among women models, artists, and patrons. The term "sister arts" thus comes to refer not only to the age-old relationship between poetry, painting, and music that figures so richly in Corinne's talents and salon conversations, but also to the artistic communities of cosmopolitan women that Staël fostered, communities that, as April Alliston has argued, constituted viable "*alternatives* to nations."[41] Despite critical concerns about the strength of Staël's female solidarity expressed by women authors from the eighteenth century to the present, her lasting contribution consists in having fully grasped the relationship Enlightenment philosophers sought to establish between sensibility, society, and the sister arts and in having taken advantage of the opportunity it afforded women to contest the perceived opposition between reason, virtue, and the passions that prevented them from pursuing their education and deploying their artistic talents.

Notes

1. Karyna Szmurlo, "Pour un état des lieux de la recherche américaine: Germaine de Staël dans le discours de la modernité," *Cahiers staëliens* 57 (2006): 15–34.

2. Both Rousseau and Smith consider pity or sympathy (synonyms for sensibility) to be an instinctive property common to all, though in varying degrees. Yet the sentimental literature of the eighteenth century singled it out as a property that identified a social elite, stronger than blood and akin to merit.

3. L'Abbé Prévost, *Manon Lescaut*, trans. Leonard Tancock (New York: Penguin Books, 1949), 59.

4. In *The Politics of Sensibility*, Markman Ellis notes that "the terms 'sensibility' and 'sentimental' denote a complex field of meanings and connotations in the late eighteenth century, overlapping and coinciding to such an extent as to offer no obvious distinction. Despite the attempts of some recent critics, it is not possible to legislate between the closely allied terms 'sensibility' and 'sentimental' in the mid eighteenth century, especially as they are used in novels. However, though sensibility and sentimental may not be separated, that is not because they share a single unitary meaning, but rather, they amalgamate and mix freely a large number of varied discourses" (Markman Ellis, *The Politics of Sensibility* [Cambridge: Cambridge University Press, 1996], 8).

5. Periodization may, to some extent, be responsible for Staël's exclusion from this corpus, as her writings, published at the turn of the nineteenth century, are too late to be considered part of the Enlightenment and too early to be considered part of French Romanticism.

6. David Denby, *Sentimental Narrative and the Social Order in France, 1760–1820* (Cambridge: Cambridge University Press, 1994), 194.

7. Anne C. Vila, *Enlightenment and Pathology: Sensibility in the Literature and Medicine of Eighteenth-Century France* (Baltimore: Johns Hopkins University Press, 1998). See chapters 1–3 and 7.

8. On this subject, see John O'Neal, *The Authority of Experience: Sensationist Theory in the French Enlightenment* (University Park, PA: Penn State University Press, 1996).

9. Chevalier Louis de Jaucourt, "Sensibility," in *The Encyclopedia of Diderot & d'Alembert Collaborative Translation Project*, trans. Christelle Gonthier (Ann Arbor, MI: Scholarly Publishing Office of the University of Michigan Library, 2004), http://hdl.handle.net/2027/spo.did2222.0000.295 (accessed January 16, 2011). Originally published as "Sensibilité," *Encyclopédie ou Dictionnaire raisonné des sciences, des arts et des métiers*, 15 (Paris, 1765): 52.

10. César Chesneau Du Marsais, "Philosopher," in *The Encyclopedia of Diderot & d'Alembert Collaborative Translation Project*, trans. Dena Goodman (Ann Arbor, MI: Scholarly Publishing Office of the University of Michigan Library, 2002), http://hdl.handle.net/2027/spo.did2222.0000.001 (accessed January 16, 2011). Originally published as "Philosophe," *Encyclopédie ou Dictionnaire raisonné des sciences, des arts et des métiers* 12 (Paris, 1765): 509–11.

11. Jean-Jacques Rousseau, *Discourse on the Origin of Inequality*, trans. Donald A. Cress (Indianapolis: Hackett Publishing Company, 1992), 26.

12. Ibid., 27.

13. "There were formed the first ties between families; there the first meetings between the two sexes took place. Young girls came to fetch water for the household, young men came to water their herds. . . . The heart was moved by these new objects, an unfamiliar attraction made it less savage, it felt the pleasure of not being alone. . . . There the first festivals took place, feet leaped with joy, eager gesture no longer sufficed, the voice accompanied it with passionate accents, pleasure and desire made themselves felt at the same time. There, finally, was the true cradle of peoples, and from the pure crystal of the fountains came the first fires of love" (Jean-Jacques Rousseau, *Essay on the Origin of Languages and Writings Related to Music*, in *The Collected Writings of Rousseau*, eds. Roger D. Masters and Christopher Kelly, trans. John T. Scott, vol. 7 [Hanover, NH: University Press of New England, 1998], 314). This scene recognizably anticipates the open-air festivals in Rousseau's *Letter to D'Alembert*.

14. Rousseau, *Discourse on the Origin of Inequality*, 39–40.

15. Ibid., 37–38.

16. Adam Smith, *Theory of Moral Sentiments*, ed. Robert Heilbroner (New York: W. W. Norton and Company, 1986), 75.

17. I use the masculine pronoun here in order to emphasize that until Staël enters the critical conversation the performer and beholder are, by and large, presumed to be men by the philosophers who theorize them (Diderot, Rousseau, and Smith).

18. For the anthropology of sensibility see Vila, *Enlightenment and Pathology*, chapters 7 and 8.

19. Diderot explains how one can both judge the quality of a play and be moved by its contents to the Abbé in the context of their discussion of Vernet's art in his *Salon de 1767*. See *Ruines et paysages: Salons de 1767*, eds. Else Marie Bukdahl, Michel Delon, and Annette Lorenceau (Paris: Hermann, 1995), 197–200.

20. Jean-Jacques Rousseau, *Lettre à D'Alembert*, in *Ecrits sur la musique, la langue, et le théâtre*, in *Œuvres complètes*, 5 vols., eds. Bernard Gagnebin and Marcel Raymond (Paris: Gallimard, 1995), 114–20.

21. Denby, *Sentimental Narrative and the Social Order*, 197.

22. "Pity is what, in the state of nature, takes the place of laws, mores, and virtue" (Rousseau, *Discourse on the Origin of Inequality*, 38).

23. For an investigation of the relationship between Staël's treatise on the passions and her novels, *Delphine* and *Corinne*, see Denby's chapter "Beyond Sentimentalism? Madame de Staël," in *Sentimental Narrative and the Social Order*, 194–239.

24. Germaine de Staël, "Essay on Fictions," in *Major Writings of Germaine de Staël*, ed. and trans. Vivian Folkenflik (New York: Columbia University Press, 1992), 73–74.

25. Staël, "On Literature," in *Major Writings*, 183.

26. It thus facilitates the transition from the novel of sensibility of the eighteenth century, which is by and large in the form of the memoir or epistolary fiction, to the novel *tout court* of the nineteenth century, with its characteristic third-person narrator.

27. While Sade's libertine character Dolmancé dismisses moral sensibility out of hand in *La Philosophie dans le boudoir* (*Philosophy in the Bedroom*, 1795), professing his exclusive interest in enhancing its physiological manifestations, moral sensibility is clearly of greater interest to Staël. She nonetheless seems just as aware of the medical discourse on sensibility as her predecessors.

28. Denby notes the clear reference to the "inoculation scene" in Rousseau's *Julie* in his analysis of Staël's *Corinne* (Denby, *Sentimental Narrative and the Social Order*, 230).

29. Vila, *Enlightenment and Pathology*, 292.

30. The mechanism of sensibility structures the relationship between victim and onlooker in Rousseau and Smith and between stage and audience, tableau and beholder in Smith and Diderot. See Toril Moi, "A Woman's Desire to Be Known: Expressivity and Silence in *Corinne*," *Bucknell Review* 45, no. 2 (2002): 143–77, for Staël's use of tableaux in general and Tili Boon Cuillé, *Narrative Interludes: Musical Tableaux in Eighteenth-Century French Texts* (Toronto: Toronto University Press, 2006) for Staël's use of musical tableaux in particular.

31. In his analysis of this tableau, Denby notes the intentional nature of Corinne's act, stating "Corinne . . . appears quite self-conscious in her use of the work of art as a detonator of the emotional explosion" (Denby, *Sentimental Narrative and the Social Order*, 236).

32. Consider Samuel Richardson's *Pamela* vs. Eliza Haywood's *Anti-Pamela* or Richardson's Clarissa and Lovelace as well as Pierre Choderlos de Laclos's Présidente de Tourvel and Valmont.

33. As travel literature, Staël's novel *Corinne* is informed by the empirical method of Condillac's *Treatise of Sensations* and entails what John O'Neal calls "sensationist aesthetics," including cultural relativism, the necessity of decoding the world, and of undergoing a sentimental education, making it the logical extension of his work *The Authority of Experience*. O'Neal's study ends with the Idealogues but includes no mention of Staël, possibly because Staël fundamentally disagreed with the Idealogues's radical interpretation of sensationism as a purely physiological phenomenon.

34. Lori Jo Marso, "Defending the Queen: Wollstonecraft and Staël on the Politics of Sensibility and Feminine Difference," *Eighteenth Century: Theory and Interpretation* 43, no. 1 (Spring 2002): 43–52. See also on this subject Florence Lotterie, "Madame de Staël. La Littérature comme 'philosophie sensible,'" *Romantisme* 34, no. 124 (2004): 19–30.

35. Eric Gidal, "Mme de Staël and the Sociology of Melancholy," in *The English Malady: Enabling and Disabling Fictions*, ed. Glen Colburn (Newcastle, upon Tyne: Cambridge Scholars Publishing, 2008), 24.

36. Cited in Denby, *Sentimental Narrative and the Social Order*, 204.

37. Thus distinguishing between the "*national scale* of the communities theorized by [Benedict] Anderson and the first modern imagined [*transnational*] communities catalyzed by sentimental texts" (Margaret Cohen, "Sentimental Communities," in *The Literary Channel: The Inter-National Invention of the Novel*, eds. Margaret Cohen and Carolyn Dever [Princeton, NJ: Princeton University Press, 2002], 107, original emphasis). See also April Alliston's article "Transnational Sympathies, Imaginary Communities," 133–49, in the same volume; and Lynn Festa's *Sentimental Figures of Empire in Eighteenth-Century Britain and France* (Baltimore: Johns Hopkins University Press, 2006, 108).

38. Virginia Woolf, *A Room of One's Own*, annotated and intro. by Susan Gubar (New York: Harcourt, 2005), 108.

39. William Reddy, *The Navigation of Feeling: A Framework for the History of Emotions* (Cambridge: Cambridge University Press, 2001), 144.

40. See Joan DeJean's "Portrait of the Artist as Sappho," in *Germaine de Staël: Crossing the Borders*, eds. Madelyn Gutwirth, Avriel Goldberger, and Karyna Szmurlo (New Brunswick, NJ: Rutgers University Press, 1991); and Dena Goodman's *The Republic of Letters: A Cultural History of the French Enlightenment* (Ithaca, NY: Cornell University Press, 1994).

41. Alliston, "Transnational Sympathies," 133–48 (emphasis Alliston's). Alliston discusses Corinne's Italy in the section entitled "Utopias of Sympathy," 138–40.

THE POLITICS OF THE PASSIONS

THE MOTHER, THE DAUGHTER, AND THE PASSIONS

Catherine Dubeau

T HE PROBLEM OF THE PASSIONS lies at the center of the writings and the relationship of Suzanne Necker and Germaine de Staël. While a number of critics have examined the presence of passion in several studies concerning both these authors, few have been interested in its role as a source of the mother-daughter conflict that Béatrix D'Andlau and Jean-Denis Bredin have analyzed in detail, and that I have examined at length elsewhere.[1] No one has carried out parallel readings of the individual solutions imagined by the mother and the daughter to control these impulses of the soul that threaten domestic as well as social equilibrium. Much more remains to be said, therefore, regarding the relation to the *savage* and *untamed* part of the self that shaped the interaction between Mme Necker and her daughter and that influenced Staël's own concept of the passions.

From her earliest childhood on, Germaine Necker was subjected to the apprenticeship of her mother's morality and ethics, which were founded on virtue, scrupulous obedience to duty, and self-control. Mme Necker raised her child alone. One has only to read her personal writings as well as the fragments in the *Mélanges extraits des manuscrits de Madame Necker* (*Various Extracts from Madame Necker's Manuscripts*, 1798) and the *Nouveaux mélanges* (*Further Extracts*, 1801) to understand that discipline's strict austerity is equal to the force of the passion that must be suppressed: anger, self-love, overly strong feelings, among others.[2] Along with the development of the intellect, Mme Necker's program of education was deliberately directed towards self-control and the attempt to appease the soul's affects. But the daughter could not submit to the mother's wish that she follow in her maternal footsteps.

Germaine Necker, future baroness de Staël, continually incurred blame for the excesses of her passionate character, as can be seen in the letters from her earliest childhood.[3] What was the attitude of the author of *Corinne* regarding the passions that compromised her relationship with Mme Necker? I will attempt to answer this question by paying particular attention to the works written during the 1790s, specifically the works authored simultaneously from 1792 on: the *Réflexions sur le divorce* (*Reflections on Divorce*, 1794) by Mme Necker and *The Influence of the Passions on the Happiness of Individuals and Nations* (1796) by Staël.[4] I have chosen to focus on these two texts because of the very particular context in which they were written, and because of the crucial importance of the passions: the French Revolution was at its height, Staël was having a passionate affair with Louis de Narbonne in a notorious extra-conjugal relationship that definitively affected the mother-daughter relation, and Mme Necker was dying without attempting to reconcile with her daughter.[5] The social and political upheavals, as well as the fact that Louis de Narbonne left Staël, have often been considered as the sources of these two treatises, but it is essential to give the mother-daughter relationship its due and consider it as central to these two works.[6] While Mme Necker rails severely against the partisans of divorce, and states her disapproval of the morals and the temperament of her daughter, Staël tries both to justify herself and to amend her character by temporarily adopting her mother's stoic perspective. This attitude, no doubt inspired by the fear of the loss she would soon suffer, did not last, and would result in her adoption of fiction as a legitimate outlet for the passions, a choice also confirmed by the publishing of *Zulma* (1794) and the *Essay on Fictions* (1795) during the same period.

Reflections on Divorce (1794): The Break Up of Mother and Daughter

Throughout Mme Necker's work, passion appears as threatening and even destructive: "A great passion always leads to grave errors unless one fights against it"; "one always hears that men need great passions in order to be happy; this reminds me of the plants called false dittany that must be set afire twice a week to make them grow, but that is not the way to make roses and lilies grow."[7] This is not very surprising, coming from a writer deeply attached to stoic philosophy as well as the Calvinist faith. But it is interesting that Mme Necker gives personal writing a redemptive function. Indeed, the journal she keeps functions less as a healthy outlet than as a means to examine and correct herself, as a space where, by dint of maxims and precepts, she fashions for herself a new persona ("Every man capable of firmness finally becomes the master of his ideas and his passions"), an endeavor in which she is, however, continually disappointed.[8] The writer is following a tradition of self-reformation and self-examination typical of ancient philosophy. What is striking here is the persistence and the uneasy rigor with which Mme Necker conducts this introspection. Informed by her reading of Cicero, Seneca, Marcus Aurelius, Epictetus, and Calvin, she tracks down passion (especially, in her case, anger and self-love) like an enemy that must be destroyed. To do so she makes rules of conduct for herself:

> Maintain self-control, accustom oneself to a great presence of mind, do not get carried away by one's ideas, but follow them, anticipate them, listen to them, direct them; frequently repress the most innocent fantasies, counter one's habits, reflect on everything, distrust one's first thoughts, stay in a kind of permanent war with oneself, these are the true moral precepts.[9]

Passion is at the center of Mme Necker's *Various Extracts* and *Further Extracts*, but it is no less central in her *Reflections on Divorce*, since it is considered implicitly to be an integral part of the character of the people having recourse to the new law authorizing divorce (enacted September 1792) and, in a more general manner, as a sign of an unfortunate development for the French people, specifically for French women. This text, edited by Jacques Necker, was published posthumously in 1794. Mme Necker had begun writing it at least two years earlier, when the new revolutionary legislation was being written: "So the new law authorizing divorce has just been published, a dangerous law that authorizes and favors divorce; divisions between political parties were not enough; it seems that it was necessary to separate spouses, isolate children, and fight against all natural bonds of affection."[10] The divorce law reduced marriage to the status of a "civil contract" and permitted separation on various grounds, including "the simple allegation of incompatibility of character or humor."[11] The aim of the *Reflections on Divorce* is clear: to stand up against popular opinion and promote the return to an unalterable union. In order to do this, the happily married Mme Necker introduces a dichotomy that runs through her entire work, between "sentiment" and "passion":

> May I be permitted to plead the case for the indissolubility of marriage. I know that the language of sentiment weakens and yields in the presence of the passions; but despite these obstacles I wish to follow the impulses of a tender soul, not yet touched by our moral upheavals,

that would like to render desirable and have others savor the kind of happiness that it enjoys, in order to enjoy it even more.[12]

This excerpt must be read alongside the definition of sentiment in the *Various Extracts*: "Sentiment is almost always very moderate, but one can see that it is deep; one can also see that it does not go beyond the boundaries of reason; because reason and sensibility are two natural faculties related to each other."[13] What is interesting to note in this passage is the co-existence of depth with a certain moderation. The latter endows feeling with a reasonableness that distinguishes it from passion, which always seems to be an invincible force and which will continue to be considered wild, despite the Romantics' attempts to view passion in an increasingly positive light. Feeling remains a matter of the soul, of the heart, and of sensibility, as it is deployed and promoted throughout the eighteenth century, particularly in literature. Feeling leads to virtue and is one of those human qualities that make relationships easier (along with compassion and generosity) and that make love more like tenderness, more like a communion of souls than a purely carnal attraction. These ideas are what Mme Necker wishes to suggest to the reader's imagination when she refers to feeling, a key notion in her defense of marriage:

> This theory of happiness [founded on virtue and the permanence of bonds], that establishes such a great distance between the person who experiences pleasure weakly and feebly through sensations and the person who experiences pleasure fully and strongly through feelings, provides a foundation for the principles of kindness, humanity, in a word all the moral laws; and if the primary goal of marriage as well as that of life is the happiness of the individual, and not the multiplication of the species, then sterility can no longer be used as an argument in favor of divorce.[14]

Thus the *Reflections on Divorce* constitute a clear response to the republican law that would, according to the writer, replace the permanence of tender attachments with the instability of powerful but ephemeral, passionate bonds.

Mme Necker's text is a series of "objections" she makes to the recently enacted law, organized in four parts that study the effects of divorce on "the happiness of the spouses taken individually in their youth [first part] and in their old age [fourth part]; on the happiness of the children [second part]; and finally on maintaining general morality [third part]."[15] The arguments proposed here reproduce the shape of her own marriage that she hopes is indestructible, favoring mutual support and perfectibility, a mirroring on earth of the union between man and his

Creator.[16] As I mentioned above while discussing the question of feeling: the ideal marriage that she defends is profoundly abstract and accompanied by a great distrust of everything bodily and physical.[17] Marriage for her plays an essential role in providing happiness, controlling the soul's inclination by concentrating affection on one person, and binding the person to faithfulness as well as to observance of duty. Hence, the possibility of getting divorced leads to a whole range of misfortunes, a troubling loss of bearings, especially for women. The sexual, domestic, and social order is threatened:

> Can one expect women to retain the taste for retreat so necessary to carry out their duties as wives and mothers, if divorce is allowed? If their fate is left undetermined, women will seem to be amphibious beings in society, neither daughters, nor mothers, nor wives; they will be everywhere and will exist nowhere; . . . they will leave their place in the chain of being and disrupt the order of Nature that they disregard.[18]

A woman who yields to her desires, whether concupiscence or anger, takes on the appearance of a denatured, monstrous being, as the comparison to "amphibious beings" indicates, or of Revolutionary women, as the comparison to dangerously armed "Bacchantes" suggests:

> [W]hen women renounce all types of perfection and refinement, which men and Nature have provided as the foundation of morality, the whole structure is shaken and crumbles into ruin; to rebuild it, they assume virile traits that become denatured in this confusion. Thus courage united with weakness produces ferocity; and boldness, arising out of fear, becomes shamelessness; then women, having come down from their pedestal and mingled with the crowd, want to play a role on the world's stage; soon they imitate men in their frenzy; soon they become drunken with the passions they ought to moderate; finally, in the end, they neglect the graces of their sex: like the Bacchantes they smash Orpheus's lyre and sound drums and trumpets, they mount the podiums armed with bloody spears and thyrses.[19]

Besides the discrepancy between her moral convictions and the revolutionary climate as well as the 1792 law, Mme Necker has some very personal reasons for expressing her opinion, since her own daughter has been engaged since 1788 in an adulterous liaison with the count Louis de Narbonne and hopes to divorce her husband, Eric de Staël.[20] If one believes Staël's letters, Mme Necker's shame and indignation were great, as she apparently attributed her state of health to her daughter's behavior:

> My mother almost died during the night from a horrible suffocation. She asked for me. She said to me: "My daughter, I am dying because of the pain caused by your shameful and public liaison. You are punished by the behavior of the object of your affections towards you: he ended what my prayers could not make you abandon."[21]

While the *Reflections on Divorce* denounce the potential for disorder caused by divorce and the passions it creates, they nevertheless constitute a highly passionate discourse themselves. And if there is one prevailing emotion in this text, it is certainly not love, but anger and the desire for vengeance. While the text is directed against the proponents of divorce, this underlying aggressiveness is undoubtedly directed toward Staël, and consists of three principal aspects.

First, the text of the *Reflections on Divorce* seeks to present Mme Necker's striking success, both moral and conjugal, contrasted with the personal failure of the proponents of divorce in order to highlight the advantages that others lack, primarily her daughter. It is well known that Staël will always envy the love marriage of her mother and father, at least until she meets her second husband, John Rocca.[22] Secondly, Mme Necker's deliberate silence about maternal love can be perceived as aggressive. The press at that time did not fail to notice this silence.[23] The married couple is presented as an exclusive entity, closed in upon itself, where procreation is explicitly treated as optional. There ensues an *exclusion*, or, at least, an implicit distancing of the child: "I will attempt to show that the principal goal of Nature in the institution of marriage is the happiness of the spouses, and therefore reproduction is only a secondary goal that should have no bearing on the law [on divorce]."[24] Finally, Mme Necker's anger is expressed in the depiction of the grave consequences awaiting those who avail themselves of the new law: rivalry among women, the contempt of the abandoned spouse and children, violation of decency and honor, degeneration of morals, solitude in old age, etc. The guilty ones are guilty forever, and forgiveness seems impossible. Mme Necker finds in the ancient Greek philosophers the "deadly consequences of domestic quarrels" and makes women, particularly modern women, one of the parties responsible for misfortune. Although she makes no explicit mention of her daughter, it is highly likely that she is thinking about her when she describes this new kind of woman, who resembles a terrifying Galatea.[25]

Mme Necker reaches the climax of this argument in the second part, where she invokes Medea's infanticide, inviting the proponents of divorce to consider how the new law threatens married couples, and especially new mothers, with uncertainty and tragic consequences:

> Come closer, defenders of divorce, come closer to the bed so well named by the people, the bed of misery, but which hope and love hasten to crown with flowers; take away from the one who gives life in pain her courage and, I would almost say, her joy in suffering; utter the fatal words that make divorce possible . . . Oh! Who would want to give life at such a price! Medea stabbed her children in front of Jason who was leaving her for Creusa; this is a terrible image of the effects of divorce and of the indifference and even the hatred that it can inspire for the fruits of a love that no longer exists.[26]

This vibrant appeal to Medea is no doubt the most spectacular and violent example of a depiction of divorce as a source of devastating, even criminal, passions. This passage illustrates that, for Mme Necker, the status of the child is that of mirror and mediator of the parental union and not that of a distinct being having any personal value.

In sum, under the guise of virtue, Mme Necker employs a combative rhetoric in her *Reflections on Divorce*, fueled by anger, that glorifies spouses in their respect for the most austere virtue and denies any advantages to the defenders— especially female ones—of passion, ambition, and autonomy.[27] Her text uses an offensive strategy that will not leave her daughter indifferent and will visibly affect the latter's treatise on the passions. For Mme Necker, there is little or no place for a different kind of woman who wants to be independent and is inspired by goals other than maternal, societal, or charitable ones. Let us not misunderstand: it is not that Mme Necker never felt the desire to be independent; rather, she gave that up, under the pressure of her temperament and her times. She made too many sacrifices in her life for her to consent to alter, without pain, the social order to which she submitted: "Liberty, a dangerous word for all ages, for all stations, for all genders; but especially for ours, whose strength lies in dependence; feelings, abandoning one's will; tastes, the desire to please; pleasures, relationships with the happiness of others."[28]

Staël no doubt felt the blame hiding under the maternal ethics, and it is possible to see how she answered the *Reflections on Divorce* in her writings. Janet Whatley proposes that we read *Delphine* (1802) in this light, especially the letter from the protestant philosopher Henri de Lebensei (Fourth Part, Letter XVII), a veritable pleading in favor of divorce. Whatley insists on the ambiguity of Staël's response, for even when a philosopher provides encouragement and civil law allows divorce, Léonce and Delphine refuse to go through with it. Public opinion, a fictional substitute for maternal law (Madame de Mondoville's as much as Mme Necker's), is stronger than anything else.[29] But there is another text that can be read profitably in light of the *Reflections on Divorce*: *The Influence of the Passions* offers a no less ambiguous response to maternal criticism. Staël speaks as an accused person in pain and vanquished by revolutionary furor, by Narbonne's abandonment, and perhaps, above all, by the loss of her mother.

The Influence of the Passions (1796): Morality, Mourning for the Mother, and the Power of Fiction

Staël's correspondence is very eloquent about her mother's work, begun the same year as the treatise on the passions and presented as the cause for a duel of the two works. To Narbonne, she writes on July 16, 1793:

> By the way, my mother is writing a work, seriously a work to be published, and guess on what: against divorce. It is being hidden from me because virtue must distrust crime, but I learned from my father that it is quite spirited. That will hinder me from publishing mine: that would seem too much like one of those many battles, including the one between passions and virtue.[30]

As soon as Staël became aware of the book's content, she expressed her concerns about a simultaneous publication and the interpretation it would provoke in the public arena. We know that Staël had access to the published text and read it (in whole or in part) soon after her mother's death in summer 1794. Her own treatise appeared in 1796. The fact that there was a two-year delay between the publication of these texts does not diminish the perception that the project was initially the result of a conflict, of a family "battle." Also, while *Reflections on Divorce* has a combative tone, *The Influence of the Passions* assumes a defensive posture:

> [B]ut it may also be true that, since I am condemned to celebrity without being understood, I feel a need to make myself be judged through my writings. Constantly slandered, and finding myself so unimportant that I cannot resolve to talk about myself, I have given in to the hope

that by publishing the fruit of my meditations I could offer some true notion of the habits of my life and the nature of my character.[31]

Condemnation, judgment, truth: how can one overlook the judiciary tone of this beginning? Throughout the treatise, the moralizing narrator's attempts at analysis are interrupted by the guilt-ridden narrator's regrets and appeals to the reader's indulgence. This double motivation—judgment and guilt—seems invisibly linked to the mother figure, a co-existence that lies at the heart of Staël's correspondence, for example when Staël describes for Narbonne the circumstances under which she undertook the composition of her treatise:

> To many other inconveniences my mother adds a kind of fear that you cannot imagine, and when one leaves Paris, it is hard to think of Coppet as a dangerous place, which appears unnatural. In order to take my mind away from the multitude of worries that would kill me if you were not there to support me, I am writing a treatise on the influence of the passions on happiness.[32]

In July 1794, Staël used the *Reflections on Divorce* as a basis for self-judgment, at the same time that her love relationship with the count Adolphe-Louis Ribbing began: "All these wild dreams that I have had for the past few days are quite contrary to the principles in my mother's book. I do not know what will come of that, but on this earth at least, for me the vague idea of happiness will have been quite precise."[33]

Within the framework of this treatise, Staël seeks forgiveness for her passionate nature as well as some form of remedy. The objective, Staël specifies, is not to "destroy all the passions," but to find instead a "system of life" specially designed for "naturally passionate characters." She strives for a universal discourse, but there is the suggestion in this text and elsewhere that the danger is even greater for women (especially for superior women) because of the overwhelming importance of the sentimental sphere, the fact that there are few places where women can exercise their talents, and the sternness of public opinion. But the author also distances herself explicitly from the tendency to endow what she defines as an "impulsive force . . . sweeping man away quite independently of his own will" with a positive value.[34] She agrees that there is indeed "something great in passion; that passion enhances, as long as it lasts, man's superiority; that with passion man accomplishes almost all that he wishes, because firm and determined will power is such an active force in the moral order." But the inability to motivate oneself in any other way, she adds, leads to all sorts of misfortunes and atrocities, and the "movement," the "impulse," necessary for "virtue" as well as for "social existence," should be able to exist without "this destructive motivation."[35] Since passion "exists only by dominating," there is no use attempting to direct it; one can only avoid it as much as possible:

> [T]here are only two states in man: either he is sure that he is the master of his inner self, and then he has no passions; or he feels that there is a force within him stronger than he, and then he is entirely dependent on it. All these accommodations with passion are purely imaginary; passion, like all true tyrants, is either on the throne or in chains. . . . [O]ne can see that passion is the enemy of man in all its forms, and that passion alone is the grave difficulty of human destiny.[36]

The tone of these excerpts, and especially the belief that one can find a solution to this "grave difficulty," might seem surprising on the part of a writer whose fictions and correspondence have expressed something else: namely, an acceptance of the inevitability of the passions. For Corinne, as for Narbonne's correspondent, passion is an irresistible attraction that leaves one helpless, even if these women have to pay for it with their serenity, their talents, even their life. But here, Staël affirms a very stoic conception of the soul's affects and hopes to find a new "system of life" that would lead her to an essential self-mastery. In this she agrees with Mme Necker's position and, like her, states that "there is no happiness without virtue."[37] The author proposes a typology of the passions by stating that the affects of the soul deserve this name only if "they crush everything that is not them, and one dominant idea absorbs all the others": love of glory (chap. 1), ambition (chap. 2), vanity (chap. 3), love (chap. 4), gambling, greed, and drunkenness (chap. 5), envy and vengeance (chap. 6), partisanship (chap. 7), and, finally, love of crime (chap. 8).[38] Why is passion so dangerous that one must avoid it? Above all, according to the philosophy of Epictetus, because passion creates a certain dependency on circumstances that are beyond one's control: the body, wealth, celebrity, power. For Staël, dependency on others becomes singularly important. Because desires and feelings always imply in some way the existence of *others* (with the exception of the "selfish" passions connected with gambling, greed, and drunkenness), passionate people find themselves subjected to external circumstances, others' personalities and willpower, that lie completely outside their control and thereby jeopardize their happiness. After outlining a typology of the passions in the first part, and after discussing the "feelings that are intermediate between the passions and one's inner resources" (friendship, fatherly, filial, and conjugal tenderness, religion) in the second part, Staël therefore proposes in the third and last part an inventory of "one's inner resources" in order to combat the passions of the soul. These resources are philosophy, study, and charity, which are effective because they rely on the principle of the autonomy of the subject. But strangely the efficacy of this system is put into question at the end of the treatise, where Staël states her own doubts: "I am not sure I succeeded in this first attempt to try my doctrine out on myself. Am I the best person, then, to affirm its power?"[39]

This excerpt calls for a few remarks. First, as previously stated, it is essential to analyze Staël's choice to write a treatise on morals at this particular juncture in her life. Critics have rightly noted the influence of the Revolution and the end of her relationship with Narbonne in the genesis of *The Influence of the Passions*, which was written over a period of at least four years (1792 to 1796), yet it also coincides with the illness and the death of Mme Necker, which Staël witnesses with great grief and powerlessness.[40] "Fear of losing her always makes me forget all the pain she gave and will give me," she writes to her husband as early as 1790.[41] No real reconciliation between mother and daughter will come before this death. Staël's choice of genre seems to play a compensatory role and duplicates the maternal gaze. It is as though she slips for a while into her mother's stoically inspired philosophy, perhaps in order to forestall the coming loss: as if the writer sought to look at the world and herself through her mother's eyes in order to know the enemy and combat it more effectively. The essay thus can be read as a *mother-book* that will replace the person who is about to pass away. This position, as will become clear, did not agree for very long with the baroness of Coppet. Yet her disavowal of the very essay that sought an answer to the problem of the passions does not, I think, indicate its failure or incoherence, but rather obliges us to seek the answer in other writings of the same period: specifically, the novella *Zulma*, and the *Essay on Fictions*.

Zulma was originally intended "to take the place of the chapter on love" in the first part of *The Influence of the Passions*. Staël explains her motivations for the change:

> As I then decided to keep that whole book analytical, I am printing this piece separately. I tried, in portraying love, to present the most terrifying picture possible, the most passionate in character. It seemed to me that this emotion could possess the maximum energy imaginable only in the combination of a savage soul and a cultivated mind, because the faculty of judging increases unhappiness greatly, when it has not reduced one's ability to feel.[42]

The eponymous heroine of this novella, set in a faraway and primitive land, is undergoing a trial for the murder of her lover, Fernand, caught at the feet of another woman, Mirza. The majority of the text consists of the accused's self-defense, whose main argument is the recounting of her increasing passion for Fernand and the description of her murderous act as the necessary outcome of her love that was so exclusive and pure that it could not tolerate betrayal. Moved by the heroine's story, the jury acquits her but soon afterwards witnesses the suicide of the heroine, who pierces her breast with one of her own arrows: "'Did you think I would let Fernand's murderer live?' she asked, with a last effort. 'If I had been able to exist without him, his unfaithfulness would have been justified.'"[43]

Zulma is the most representative Staëlian model of a person dominated by passion. The brutality and the self-destructive gesture in this novella can either be read as the sign of Zulma's adherence to the logic of passion ("If I had been able to exist without him, his unfaithfulness would have been justified"), or, to the contrary, as a sign of her disapproval ("Did you think I would let Fernand's murderer live?"). In any case, the character appears divided, obviously torn between the expression and the repression of her affects. Staël was always very attached to this novella ("this piece of writing, which belongs to my soul more than anything else I have done"); nevertheless, she does not include it in *The Influence of the Passions* in order not to compromise the essay's integrity.[44] The choice to remove the novella permanently interests us less than the spontaneous emergence of fiction as means of discussing the passions, which arguably play a primordial role in the imagination as well as in the life of Staël. Why does she have recourse to fiction here and not elsewhere? What is fiction able to do that a moral treatise cannot? I propose that in the 1790s the author experiments with genres, which leads her to privilege fiction over the moral essay as a legitimate and effective outlet for passion. The treatise on the passions is therefore an essential, but temporary, stage en route to formulating a personal response to the problem posed by the affects of the soul.

Fiction reveals itself to be a formidable ally for both its reader and its creator, because it has an inestimable "talent to touch," described in the *Essay on Fictions* as its "greatest power":

> Virtue must be brought to life if she is to fight the passions with any chance of winning; a sort of exaltation must be aroused for us to find any charm in sacrifice; misfortune must be embellished for us to prefer it to the great charm of guilty enticement; and the touching fictions which

incite the soul to generous feelings make it unconsciously engage itself in
a promise that it would be ashamed to retract in similar circumstances.[45]

For Staël, fiction cannot be separated from a moral and philosophical aim, and
emotion is an integral part of education. From her *Lettres sur les écrits et le caractère
de J.-J. Rousseau* (*Letters on the Works and Character of J.-J. Rousseau*, 1788) to *On
Literature* (1800), the writer affirms the superiority of works of imagination over
philosophical discourse or moralizing maxims for the purpose of educating readers about virtue, expressing a particular fondness for the novel. With the ability to
depict nuances of character and feeling, novels have the right, according to her, "to
offer the severest morality without revolting our hearts; they have captured feeling, the only thing that can successfully plead for indulgence."[46] This observation
is particularly dear to Staël who, in her *Essay on Fictions,* contrasts moralizing and
novelistic forms of writing. The critical and disapproving analysis of the maxim, a
form emblematic of classical discourse and of her mother's writing, is a common-
place in Staëlian texts. This kind of brief and incisive writing does not have the
strength, the delicacy, and the persuasive power of fiction—a proposition repeatedly stated in the *Essay on Fictions*, revealing its crucial importance for the author.[47]

In her reflections on the usefulness of the literary work as well as in other
parts of her life, Staël favors those forms that allow for natural impulses. She
prefers the form that can carry away rather than dominate the reader, prefers to
delight rather than to constrain, thus differentiating herself once again from Mme
Necker. Both mother and daughter endow reading with moral value, both have
the same literary tastes for Milton, Richardson, Rousseau, and Marmontel, but
mother and daughter disagree about the means of moral education on the one
hand, and about their relationship to reading on the other, which can be defined
(quite schematically) as follows: as a means to perfect oneself for the former, as a
cathartic outlet for the latter. Mme Necker obviously does not ignore the power
of fiction to console, but in her inclination towards controlling passion, stoic
teaching, and the Calvinist faith, she wants to use reading above all as a means to
achieve a happiness based on quietude and personal edification. One has only to
read her essays on the topic, where she shows much more mistrust and severity
than her daughter regarding the dangers of works of imagination that are likely
to fire up the passions and find reality distasteful.[48] Let us compare, for example,
their critiques of Rousseau's *Nouvelle Héloïse* (*New Héloïse*)—in particular, their
judgment of Julie: a monstrous creature for Mme Necker, a passionate woman for
Staël.[49] Mother and daughter are diametrically opposed regarding the morality of
the novel: whereas Mme Necker, like Marmontel in *Essai sur les romans, considérés*

du côté moral (*Essay on Novels*, 1787), insists that the example of the fault and the unhappiness that ensues are dissuasive, Staël, like Diderot in his *In Praise of Richardson* (1762), turns her attention away from the *outline* and the *events* in order to situate the agents of moral edification in the *effects of reading* (ideas, feelings).[50] By this means, she advances the ideal of an education founded on the intelligence of the heart rather than on the severity of sanctions. As she states in her *Essay on Fictions*: "Fictions do not find obstacles in passions: they make use of them. Philosophy may be the invisible power in control of fictions, but if she is the first to show herself, she will destroy all their magic."[51] Uniquely capable of describing intimate feelings and personal stories, the novel can reveal individuals to themselves and say the unsayable, thus giving some space to singular personalities that would otherwise be left aside, particularly by History, which does not have the time to penetrate the inner workings of the heart and exceptional motivations. In summary, fictions know how to speak the "language" of "ardent, sensitive souls."[52] The transfer of intimate emotions to writing and their discovery by the reader put into play movements of identification and distanciation that allow the reader sometimes to lose herself, sometimes to see herself reflected in the mirror of the work.

The *Essay on Fictions* thus takes a position opposed to the rationalist and philosophical one proposed in the treatise, defining imagination as "man's most valuable faculty" and more useful than "philosophical force" in the struggle with the pains of existence.[53] But upon closer examination, while *The Influence of the Passions* does not seem to address the use of fiction, it nevertheless resorts to it constantly. One has only to notice the contextual use that Staël makes of figures taken from novels, plays, and poems, here as in her other essays: she abandons her argumentative mode of discourse in passages that are filled with painful emotions and memories, and turns instead to literary references. She then focuses entirely on one figure, a symbolic double whose task it is to express a situation, a feeling, a state of mind with much more immediacy than any long description could. Virgil's Dido appears as an emblematic figure of her whole work, and is inscribed at the head of the chapter on love and quoted at its beginning; Bernardin de Saint-Pierre's Pariah transmits the analogy between the fate of the excluded and that of sensitive souls.[54] Her habit of referring to characters and works cannot be reduced to a mere rhetorical device: for Staël the fictional is interwoven with evasions from reality for the sake of healing. Fiction, both read and written, is a refuge and a receptacle for the passions, distilling on paper the delicate transformation of the self, achieving a salvational *catharsis*; fiction provides innumerable places where affects, images, and reminiscences can find a home: in a word, all the intensity of the passions, the moments of pure feeling that cannot fit into moralist and essayistic prose. These places that a title or a name is able to evoke with as much presence as if they were real are emblematic of Staëlian writing and constitute its very essence.

Fictional writing assists Staël in her struggle with the ravages caused by the passions because it provides a more or less lasting relief from her internal division. Better than philosophical reflection, the creation of fictional figures—Zulma above all—allows the author to interact with her dual internal selves, one who *suffers* and is tragically overwhelmed by her demons, and one who *listens* and dispenses pity. By representing "the passion that judges itself and understands itself without being able to conquer itself," she is one of the masters of "self-reflecting passion" along with Rousseau and Goethe.[55] She thereby belongs to that restricted group of authors that best represent literary modernity, defined by the sensibility and melancholy that she values so much in *On Literature*.

–Translated by Sylvie Romanowski, Northwestern University

Notes

1. See Béatrix D'Andlau, *La Jeunesse de Madame de Staël, de 1766 à 1786, avec des documents inédits* (Geneva: Droz, 1970); Jean-Denis Bredin, *Une singulière famille: Jacques Necker, Suzanne Necker et Germaine de Staël* (Paris: Fayard, 1999); and Catherine Dubeau, "La Lettre et la mère: Roman familial et écriture de la passion chez Suzanne Necker (1737–1794) et Germaine de Staël (1766–1817)," (PhD diss., Université Laval, 2007). For a study of the passions in Germaine de Staël's works, see in the bibliography the contributions by Madelyn Gutwirth, Biancamaria Fontana, Jean Starobinski, Michel Delon, and Marie-Laure Girou Swiderski, as well as my article on *On Literature*. Regarding Mme Necker, apart from my doctoral dissertation and articles, no work has yet focused specifically on the role of passion in her writings. However, some observations can be found in the works of the count of Haussonville, Valérie Hannin, Geneviève Soumoy-Thibert, Dena Goodman, and Sonja Boon.

2. Suzanne Necker's *Mélanges extraits des manuscrits de Madame Necker*, ed. Jacques Necker, 3 vols. (Paris: Pougens, 1798); and *Nouveaux mélanges extraits des manuscrits de Madame Necker*, ed. Jacques Necker, 2 vols. (Paris: Pougens, 1801). Most of the personal writings of Suzanne Necker are kept in the private holdings of the Coppet estate, as well as in the Bibliothèque de Genève, the Institut Voltaire (Geneva), the Bibliothèque Cantonale et Universitaire de Lausanne, and the Archives cantonales vaudoises in Lausanne.

3. Mme Necker replies to her daughter's overflowing enthusiasm: "Your letter is that of a good child; I can see that you are satisfied with yourself, and so I am satisfied too, because neither you nor I need any other judge except your own heart; but your style is a bit excessive. Do not go overboard in order to praise or please me. This is a frequent lapse in good taste at your age. After one has lived longer, one realizes that the best way to please and hold someone's interest is to convey one's thought

in a precise and unadorned manner; in this way, one's thoughts seem original and true, more than if they contain far-fetched comparisons. The letter to your father was simple and good. Farewell, my child; tell me that you love me and prove it to me by improving every day your heart and your reason" (Mme Necker to her daughter [Paris] May 15, 1779, in *Madame de Staël, ses amis, ses correspondants: choix de lettres (1787–1817)*, ed. Georges Solovieff [Paris: Klincksieck, 1970], 30). In order to understand the passionate temperament of Germaine in her youth, see the first volume of the general correspondence, especially the "Letters of 'Minette' Necker; The Child," in *Correspondance générale de Madame de Staël*, 4 vols., ed. Béatrice W. Jasinski (Paris: Pauvert, 1960–78), 1, 1:3–14.

4. The exact dates when these two works were begun are unfortunately not known, and the manuscript of the *Reflections on Divorce* remains lost. However, there are indications that the manuscript was probably begun around 1792 at the latest. In her *Reflections on Divorce*, Mme Necker mentions the new law enacted on September 20, 1792, and I agree with Jasinski that this project was certainly undertaken "as early as the fall" of that same year (see Staël, *Correspondance*, ed. Jasinski, 3, 1:73, n9). Also Staël's correspondence confirms that the treatise on the passions was begun by September 24, 1792 (2, 1:28–29), that by July 16, 1793, at the latest (2, 1:140) the author knew that the text of the *Reflections on Divorce* was being written, and that she had read it in part or in its totality before July 31, 1794 (3, 1:73), soon after Mme Necker's death (May 1794) and the work's publication (summer 1794).

5. Mme Necker died on May 15, 1794, in the Beaulieu château in Lausanne. During her agony she refused to see her daughter.

6. In addition to the references given in note 1 on Staël's treatise, see also Janet Whatley, "Dissoluble Marriage, Paradise Lost: Suzanne Necker's *Réflexions sur le divorce,*" *Dalhousie French Studies* 56 (2001):144–53; Sonja Boon, "Does a Dutiful Wife Write; or, Should Suzanne Get Divorced? Reflections on Suzanne Curchod Necker, Divorce, and the Construction of the Biographical Subject," *Lumen* 27 (2008):59–73. Louis de Narbonne (1755–1813), a French count and general, was known for his luxurious tastes and his ability to seduce that made him one of the great libertines of the period. According to Jasinski, Mme Necker is said to have formally forbidden her daughter to see him. Staël, however, was charmed by him and started a liaison in fall of 1788 (or at the latest at the beginning of winter 1789) that lasted till the beginning of 1794. One can see the passionate nature of this liaison and the immense grief that followed in the letters of the second volume (part 1) of Staël's *Correspondance*, ed. Jasinski, that is composed entirely of the *Lettres inédites à Louis de Narbonne*.

7. Necker, *Mélanges*, 2:97 and *Nouveaux mélanges*, 1:201.

8. Necker, *Mélanges*, 2:56. See also the *Nouveaux mélanges*, "Passions do not belong to man's nature; one finds only tendancies and inclinations, and virtue can always stop their fermentation and exaltation" (1:39) and my article, "Mrs. Spectator: Journal, comptes moraux et tyrannie de l'introspection dans les *Mélanges* et les *Nouveaux mélanges* de Suzanne Necker," in *Influences et modèles étrangers sous l'Ancien Régime*, ed. Virginie Dufresne and Geneviève Langlois (Québec: Presses de l'Université Laval, 2009), 145–48.

9. Necker, *Mélanges*, 2:112. See the example of anger in *Mélanges*: "When one is on one's guard, one is able to speak calmly; anger spreads only if one lets it, or it stops: it seems that it is a faucet that is opened or closed completely at will. So one must close it completely; because even the most moderate and justified anger stirs up the blood, makes one ugly, produces distractions in society

and in business, awakens nervous aches, and makes one lose that serenity of the soul that is the true jewel of virtue" (3:45).

10. Necker, *Réflexions sur le divorce*, 5.

11. "Loi qui détermine les causes, le mode & les effets du Divorce [Loi du 20 semptembre 1792]," cited in Francis Ronsin, *Le Contrat sentimental: Débats sur le mariage, l'amour, le divorce, de l'Ancien Régime à la Restauration* (Paris: Aubier, 1990), 110.

12. Necker, *Réflexions sur le divorce*, 5–6.

13. Necker, *Mélanges*, 1:255–56.

14. Necker, *Réflexions sur le divorce*, 14. For a detailed analysis of feeling in France and England in the eighteenth century, see Philip Stewart's *L'Invention du sentiment: Roman et économie affective au XVIIIe siècle* (Oxford: Voltaire Foundation, 2010).

15. Necker, *Réflexions sur le divorce*, 6.

16. Ibid., 16.

17. "Thus through efforts opposed to those of the wise ancient philosophers, [eighteenth-century French philosophers] want to bring man down to the level of animals. . . . Let us then shield marriage from the deadly magic of Circe's wand; and through a contrary influence, may all tender and pure souls find in such a well ordered association, one so necessary given our weakness, the means to perfect themselves and approach the nature of angels" (ibid., 15–16).

18. Ibid., 75–76.

19. Ibid., 56–57.

20. See Staël, "To M. de Narbonne, Rolle, 13 October [1792]," *Correspondance*, 2, 1:45, where she writes "Marriage is a deadly institution! . . . But seriously, I would like to ask you to find out discreetly what the laws on divorce are in Sweden. I don't dare ask myself, but it is important for me to know, in order to either use them or threaten to use them: the laws regarding separation of possessions and people."

21. Staël, "To M. de Narbonne, Lausanne, 22 March [1794]," *Correspondance*, 2, 1:253.

22. Albert Jean Michel de Rocca (1788–1818), known as John Rocca, was born in Geneva, and was a lieutenant in the French army during the Napoleonic wars. Germaine de Staël met him in Geneva in 1810. Love overcame the difference in age (twenty-two years), and a son, Louis-Alphonse Rocca, was born on April 7, 1812. They married secretly on October 10, 1816.

23. "Following the invocation . . . dictated to the author by her feelings as a spouse and as a child, one would have expected to see yet a third feeling, but it is not there." (*Journal littéraire de Lausanne*, II, 205-06, Sept. 1794), in Staël, *Correspondance*, 3, 1:73, 9n.

24. Necker, *Réflexions sur le divorce*, 13.

25. Ibid., 54. "If, according to the aim of their existence, women of our time had become used to knowing only the happiness that they give, to giving order and logic to their lives, to respecting the past and considering it as a factor in their misfortune or their felicity, they would never have been able to bear the idea of divorce; but their new morality teaches them to pay attention only to the present; they separate the present from the past and the future, so that they can free themselves from gratitude, do away with sacrifices, and deliver themselves both from the counsel of experience

and the lessons of wisdom; thus they reduce eternity to one day, and one day to an instant. Eve was not more fatal to the human race in depriving it of immortality; but at least Eve was hiding in the woods from the angels' gaze, whereas in our era's mindset women are always ready to show themselves and argue for paradoxes that go against honor and appropriate conduct; feeble and miserable, combining all the defects of strength, they no longer belong to nature, they are a product of our rationalizers, for whom I predict a fate opposite to that of Pygmalion: the knife will fall from their hands and they will be frightened by their own work" (ibid., 72–73).

26. Ibid., 33–34.

27. Let us note that Mme Necker does not allow any exception to the indissolubility of marriage, not even in cases of spousal violence: "It would be desirable, I know, for women who are really unhappy because of their husbands' actions and vices to remove themselves from their tyranny; but laws are not made to have exceptions; and such is the imperfection of human institutions that modifying them, even with the utmost care, always demands sacrifices. Experience . . . shows us that victims of duty are always crowned with a few flowers: but these victims are very few, while the number of women who seek divorce today are very numerous" (ibid., 61).

28. Ibid., 28.

29. Whatley, "Dissoluble Marriage, Paradise Lost," 151.

30. Staël, "To Mr. de Narbonne, Coppet, July 16 [1793]," *Correspondance*, 2, 1:140.

31. Germaine de Staël, *The Influence of the Passions upon the Happiness of Individuals and of Nations*, in *Major Writings of Germaine de Staël*, ed. and trans. Vivian Folkenflik (New York: Columbia University Press, 1992), 151.

32. Staël, "To M. de Narbonne, Coppet, September 24 [1792]," *Correspondance*, 2, 1:28–29.

33. Staël, "To Ribbing, Thursday evening [July 31, 1794], Mézery," *Correspondance*, 3, 1:73. Adolphe-Louis, Count Ribbing (1765–1843) is a young nobleman of Swedish origin, who was a career officer in the army and in particular was a captain of the royal guards of the King of Sweden, Gustav III. A fierce opponent of despotism and defender of liberty, he was favorable to the French Revolution in its first years. Because of his role in the conspiration leading to the assassination of Gustav III, he was exiled (March 1792). He was warmly welcomed in France, and he left soon afterward for Switzerland where he met Germaine de Staël (1793).

34. Staël, *The Influence of the Passions*, in *Major Writings*, 153.

35. Germaine de Staël, *De l'influence des passions*, in *Œuvres complètes, Œuvres critiques, Lettres sur Rousseau, De l'influence des passions et autres essais moraux*, ed. Florence Lotterie, series 1, vol. 1. (Paris: Honoré Champion, 2008), 154–55.

36. Ibid., 155, 258.

37. Ibid., 155.

38. Ibid., 225.

39. Staël, *The Influence of the Passions*, in *Major Writings*, 170.

40. Not only have critics neglected to study the influence of the mother-daughter conflict on the writing of the treatise on the passions, but they mostly ignore the passing of Suzanne Necker, an event whose importance cannot be denied. Albertine Necker de Saussure surprisingly makes no mention

of it, while she foregrounds mourning for the father (see Germaine de Staël, *Œuvres complètes de Mme la Baronne de Staël, publiées par son fils, précédées d'une Notice sur le caractère et les écrits de Mme de Staël, par Madame Necker de Saussure*, 17 vols. (Paris: Treuttel et Würtz, 1820–1821), 1:j-ccclxxiij), just like David Glass Larg does in *Madame de Staël: La vie dans l'œuvre 1766–1800* (Paris: Champion, 1924).

41. Staël, "To Mr. de Staël, Coppet, October 29 [1790]," *Correspondance*, 1, 2:381.

42. Staël, "Foreword," *Zulma, A Fragment*, in *Major Writings*, 139.

43. Ibid., 150.

44. Ibid., 140.

45. Staël, *Essay on Fictions*, in *Major Writings*, 74.

46. Ibid., 76. See also: "The novel as we conceive of it, however—as we have a few examples of it—is one of the most beautiful creations of the human mind, and one of the most influential on individual morality, which is what ultimately determines the morality of the public" (71).

47. "We can glean a morality purer and higher from novels than from any didactic work on virtue; didactic works are so dry that they have to be too indulgent. Maxims have to be generally applicable, so they never achieve that heroic delicacy we may offer as a model but cannot reasonably impose as a duty" (ibid., 75), and "Pity for misfortune or interest in passion often win the struggle against books of morality, but good novels have the art of putting this emotion itself on their side and using it for their own ends" (76).

48. See "On reading: on choosing what one reads, according to one's age," "How to judge books and their authors," and "A method to make reading more useful; concerning its influence on happiness" (Necker, *Mélanges*, 1:167–83); "On books in general, and on which books suit diverse kinds of minds" (*Nouveaux mélanges*, 2:150–58). See also *Mélanges*: ". . . this relation [between what we read and the soul] is that of our tastes, our faculties, not of our fantasies and our passions. Thus a young girl who allows herself to read novels will feel sad when going forth in society, because she will not find anything there resembling her chimeras; while a reasonable woman who has lifted up her soul to the Creator, studied her duties, and cultivated her reason, will be able to use in the social world the salutary reflections that have already preoccupied her" (1:180).

49. See Suzanne Necker: "Nothing is less moral than the *New Héloïse*; it is an edifice of virtue built on the foundations of vice. . . . Nothing is as immoral as an exception quoted as an example: using the delirium of one's faults to turn it into enthusiasm for virtue, that only confuses them both, and makes one forever incapable of distinguishing between them" (*Mélanges*, 3:106). Let us note that this criticism, similar to Marmontel's in his *Essay on Novels*, does not prevent Suzanne Necker from recognizing the superior value of a work that she praises elsewhere (see "To M. Moultou," in *Mélanges*, 1:147). See Staël, "On the *New Héloïse*" in *Letters on Rousseau*: "Rousseau may have given in to the impulse of his soul and talent. He had something very violent to express: passion and virtue, in contrast and in combination. But look at his respect for conjugal love! He may have meant to use Julie's misfortunes and her father's inflexible pride as an example to attack social prejudices and institutions, following his usual line of thought. But he has such reverence for the tie to which nature has destined us! He tried so hard to prove that it is capable of making people happy, even people whose hearts have known other delights! Who would dare resist his morality? Is he a stranger to the passions? Does he fail to recognize their power? Hasn't he earned the right

to speak to the tenderhearted, and teach them the sacrifices which lie within their power? Who would dare call such sacrifices impossible, when Rousseau teaches us that Julie, the most passionate of women, was capable of them, finding her happiness in the fulfillment of her duties without deviating from them again until the very last moment of her life?" (*Major Writings*, 47)

50. See Necker: ". . . if Rousseau put any morality in his work, it was above all when he made Julie guilty; thus he showed that a great passion always leads to great vices when it is not resisted" ("Fragment on the New Héloïse," in *Nouveaux mélanges*, 2:97). See also Staël, "On the *New Héloïse*" in *Letters on Rousseau*: ". . . a novel's real usefulness lies in its effect rather than its plot, in the feelings it inspires rather than the events it narrates" (in *Major Writings*, 45); Staël, *Essay on Fictions*: "The morality of novels belongs more to the development of the internal emotions of the soul than to the events they relate. We do not draw a useful lesson from whatever arbitrary circumstance the author invents as punishment for the crime; what leaves its indelible mark on us comes from the truthful rendition of the scenes, the gradual process or sequence of wrongdoing, the enthusiasm for sacrifices, the sympathy for misfortune" (*Major Writings*, 73) and Staël, *De l'Allemagne*, ed. Simone Balayé, 2 vols. (Paris: Flammarion, 1968): ". . . the morality of a novel thus consists in the sentiments that it inspires" (2:47).

51. Staël, *Essay on Fictions*, in *Major Writings*, 61.

52. Ibid., 72–73, 77.

53. Ibid., 60.

54. "I keep rereading a few pages from a book entitled *The Indian Cottage*; I can't think of a more profound treatment of sensitive morality than the depiction of the Pariah's situation, a man of a cursed race, abandoned by the whole universe, wandering in cemeteries during the night, who terrifies his fellow man without having committed a single sin; rejected by the whole world where the gift of life thrust him. There one can see a man struggling with his own strengths. No living being offers him help, no living being is interested in his existence; he can only contemplate nature, and she is enough for him. Such is the sensitive man's life on earth; he too belongs to a cursed race, his language is not understood, his feelings isolate him, his desires are never fulfilled, and what surrounds or abandons him, approaches only to wound him" (Staël, *De l'influence des passions*, 281).

55. Staël, *On Literature*, in *Major Writings*, 183.

2

THE VIRTUOUS PASSION: THE POLITICS OF PITY
IN STAËL'S *THE INFLUENCE OF THE PASSIONS*

Nanette Le Coat

It is during the crisis of the revolution that our ears are incessantly compelled to hear that pity is a puerile sentiment; that it impedes every necessary action, and obstructs the general interest; and that it ought consequently to be banished, together with those effeminate affections which let down the dignity of statesmen and unnerve the vigour of party leaders. The contrary, however, is the truth: it is amidst the disorder of a revolution that pity, which, under every other circumstance, is an involuntary emotion, ought to become the rule and guide of our conduct.

—Germaine de Staël

THERE IS A PARADOX AT THE HEART of Germaine de Staël's *The Influence of the Passions upon the Happiness of Individuals and of Nations*. Having persuasively argued that the passions are the principal source of human unhappiness, Staël concludes her essay with a paean to pity. Pity—not quite a passion but something like one—is, she declares, "The only sentiment that can serve as a guide to us in all situations, and that may be applicable to all circumstances."[1] Pity is "that divine sentiment which transforms sorrow into a human bond, [. . .] that instinctive virtue which preserves the human species, by preserving individuals from the effects of their own ferociousness, [which] the spirit of party has alone succeeded in erasing from the soul, by shifting concern from individuals in order to focus it on nations and future generations."[2]

Staël and Rousseau

Rousseau, more than any other literary figure, shaped Staël's writing and thought. From her early *Letters on the Works and Character of J.-J. Rousseau* to works of maturity such as *On Germany*, Rousseauian passions, themes and preoccupations resonate persistently in Staël's oeuvre. While this influence is indisputable, it is equally true that, even in her early works, Staël was divided between her admiration for her mentor's genius and style and her abhorrence of certain troubling aspects of his thought.[3] One of these was his misogyny; another the disturbingly authoritarian cast of his political thought. In *The Influence of the Passions* one finds both fidelity to and independence from Jean-Jacques. Resonances with Rousseau's characterization of pity in his *Discourse on the Origin of Inequality* are unmistakable.[4] Pity, Rousseau had pronounced in his prize-winning essay, is the "principle" given to man "in order to mitigate, in certain circumstances, the ferocity of his egocentrism or the desire for self-preservation before this egocentrism of his came into being, [which] tempers the ardor he has for his own well being by an innate repugnance to seeing his fellow men suffer."[5] Both Staël's and Rousseau's definitions describe a psychological dynamic in which pity counters the brutal tendencies in human nature. For Rousseau this tendency is expressed in human *amour propre*. For Staël, however, one of the most ferocious human inclinations is political fanaticism: that is, the capacity to be consumed by abstract ideas of the good. This tendency, Staël maintains, is opposed to *amour propre* or self-interest.

Like Rousseau, Staël believed that only an instinctual and pre-reflective feeling would be strong enough to counter selfish or destructive human impulses. Rousseau had famously asserted that pity was "prior to all reflection."[6] Pity, or the repugnance inspired by the suffering of one's fellows, was the only impulse in natural man capable of countering his powerful instinct for self-conservation. Pity's primal origin qualifies it as a virtue—"the only natural virtue"—and guarantees man's prelapsarian innocence.[7] Staël's characterization of pity in *The Influence of the Passions* echoes the definition of pity Rousseau first enunciated in the *Second Discourse*. For Staël, as for Rousseau, pity is a natural virtue; it is "the only primitive idea" associated with human nature. Pity is primitive both in terms of coming first and in terms of its physical nature:

> Can there be a finer final cause in the moral order of the world, than the prodigious influence which pity exercises over every heart? It seems as if our very physical organization was intended to receive its soft impression. A voice that begins to falter, a countenance that is suddenly changed, operate directly upon the soul like our sensations. Thought

does not intervene between them, they are like blows or wounds to the heart: there is nothing intellectual about these impressions.[8]

This characterization of pity as an immediate, pre-reflective response to the spectacle of suffering recalls the primal scenes imagined by Rousseau when he describes a mother spontaneously rescuing her endangered child, or a horse refusing to trample a wounded animal. For Staël, as for Rousseau, pity is aroused by physical sensations: the sound of a faltering voice or the sight of an altered face have a direct effect on the spectator's psyche. So rapid and forceful is this effect, there is no time for thought to intervene.

In order to underscore the primacy of pity as an unmediated, involuntary response, Staël draws on the physiological lexicon favored by eighteenth-century theorists of sensibility. She speaks of "physical organization" and invokes the role of sensation and the combinatory role of the various faculties in the evolution of complex feeling. But Staël's recourse to the language of sensation does not mean that she was tempted by a materialist explanation of moral feeling. Here she parts company with her Swiss compatriot. For Rousseau, pity was essentially a biological feeling. At one point in his career he envisioned writing a treatise to be titled *La Morale sensitive, ou le Matérialisme du sage* (*Sensitive Morality or the Wise Man's Materialism*), in which he would develop his thoughts on the complex interplay between passive physical and organic sensibility and an active moral sensibility.[9] Staël, on the other hand, believed that moral feelings were triggered by, but never fully reducible to, sensation. If she emphasizes the physical nature of pity she does so in order to stress the priority of moral feeling over rational thought. Pity is a "spontaneous impulse of the heart" [*élan d'âme*] that manifests itself *before* sensations combine to form ideas and *before* the reasoning process begins. It is thus uncontaminated by a sophisticated, but potentially morally problematic, form of reason she calls "calcul." Staël uses the term variously to signify mathematical reasoning, a methodical approach to a social problem, or cold political calculation. In its manifestation as political calculation, "le calcul" is a form of thought that is antithetical to pity. I shall return later to the importance of "calcul," but first I should like to discuss some of the political stakes attached to the notion of pity in the aftermath of the French Revolution.

Reclaiming the Notion of Pity

Staël originally intended her treatise on the passions to have two parts: a first part that would discuss the destructive effects of the passions on individual lives, and a second that would discuss the passions' deleterious effects on the commonweal. Martha Nussbaum's account of the emotions and their relevance to political theory in *Upheavals of Thought: The Intelligence of the Emotions* is useful in helping us to appreciate the political ramifications of Staël's moral reflection, for she did not immediately complete the political section of her essay on the passions. The first part demonstrates repeatedly how personal and political passions are intertwined and how, during the French Revolution, leaders were so blinded by passion they caused suffering to themselves and brought about the agony of the nation. What leaders lacked in the civil conflict and what was required to bring an end to the Revolution was pity.[10] Distilling several strands in a classical philosophical tradition, Nussbaum identifies three cognitive conditions for pity or compassion and teases out some of their political implications: "The first cognitive requirement of compassion is a belief or appraisal that the suffering is serious rather than trivial. The second is the belief that the person does not deserve the suffering. The third is the belief that the possibilities of the person who experiences the emotion are similar to those of the sufferer."[11]

The fratricidal violence of the French Revolution provided a surfeit of opportunities for these cognitive conditions to be tested. Commentators as divergent as Staël and Burke concurred that the first condition that Nussbaum would later describe had been met. Civil strife had indisputably inflicted serious and general suffering. At the time, however, revolutionary actors disagreed considerably about what conditions ought to inspire pity. Staël clashed with Rousseau—and the Jacobin leaders who hailed him as their mentor—on the question of who merited sympathy or compassion. Rousseau had argued in *Émile, ou De l'éducation* (*Emile, or On Education*, 1762) that inasmuch as nobles and kings sever themselves in thought from the people, and thereby fail to have compassion, they are themselves undeserving of pity or compassion.[12] Staël, on the other hand, appealed to the second and third cognitive conditions of compassion in her effort to engage readers from all reaches of the political spectrum. If, she argued, we are all vulnerable to serious suffering, then we all merit compassion for our suffering regardless of our class or circumstances. Explaining pity in terms of identification, she appealed to what Nussbaum would later term *eudaimonistic* judgments. In order to feel compassion for the other, we must not only be able to imagine that we might at some time be forced to undergo similar suffering, we must also see the other as "an important part of [one's] own scheme of goals and projects."[13] Mere recognition of our shared vulnerability does not in itself oblige us to be compassionate; we must also share a common goal. We might add another requisite to Nussbaum's three conditions. For spectators to feel compassion for others, it is imperative that they not be blinded by their own passions.

Staël's account of the passions, like the philosophical lines of thought Nussbaum reviews, is fairly traditional. Yet while Staël discusses a range of passions—love, envy, desire for vengeance—a few take on a special coloration as seen through the lens of recent revolutionary upheaval. Such is the case for ambition, vanity and greed, to which she devotes successive chapters. But there is one passion—perhaps the most subtle of them all—to which she gives particular attention, and that is factionalism or "l'esprit de parti."[14] In the chapter of that name she explains that "the spirit of party is a kind of frenzy of the soul, which does not depend upon the nature of its object. It sees but one idea."[15] The paradox of "l'esprit de parti" is that while it may be inspired by lofty ideals, it frequently deploys ruthless and intolerant methods to realize them. Thus, in Staël's view, radical republicanism may have been inspired by enlightenment ideas, but *philosophie*, like the "cult of prejudices" the *philosophes* campaigned against, had degenerated into a new fanaticism. Enlightened men [hommes d'esprit] were, she believed, particularly subject to this kind of passion. That is why "l'esprit de parti" was not always recognizable as a vice. It is one of the ironies of this passion that it turns idealistic principles towards cruel ends: "The spirit of party is the only passion which erects the destruction of all the virtues into a virtue."[16] Factionalism is the opposite of self-love, and those who were inspired by it are willing to sacrifice everything to an apparently disinterested goal. They may even take a particular point of pride in doing so and persuade themselves that they alone are virtuous. But though guilty acts may be committed by virtuous men, the ends can never justify the means. So while the source of factionalism might be philosophically comprehensible, its effects are unacceptable: "This passion annihilates in superior men the talents they received from nature."[17] The first natural faculty that factionalism perverts is reason itself. The factionalist is opposed to rational deliberation and the detached comparison of ideas; he sees only one idea and one abstract goal, which he champions in the name of reason, justifying any sacrifice in its pursuit. Maximilien de Robespierre's remorseless fanaticism embodied this will to favor abstract ideas over individual lives. He did not shirk from depopulating France in the name of purging the body politic of its corrupt elements, and Staël credits him with the brutal dictum: "There are two million men too many in France."[18]

Thus compassion was stifled during the revolutionary conflict not only by blind passion, but by an excessive, perverted reason. Political calculus blinded legislators to "the unique characteristics" [les singularités particulières] of individual human experience. "Legislators . . . often govern with the help of ideas that are too general" and "general ideas are cruel for the person who suffers."[19] Extreme factionalists sought to govern according to abstract political calculations. In its most extreme form this mentality led to Robespierre's "system":

> It is said that during the French Revolution, barbarous speculators used mathematical calculations as the basis of their bloody laws to coldly sacrifice the lives of several thousand individuals, which they regarded as the happiness of the majority.[20]

This tension between reason and pity was a problem with which Rousseau had grappled in his *Contrat social* (*Social Contract*, 1762). Philip Knee has articulated the tension that Rousseau never fully resolved:

> The sentimental impulse combats cold reason, which always privileges particular interests, but reason combats the impulse towards pity by generalizing what is too particular. It is through such generalization that pity can become a social virtue. Yet one sees the risk of such generalization, for by extending pity beyond particular cases, one risks emptying morality of the sentimental impulse and transforming it into a cold love of humanity in general.[21]

Eudaimonistic judgments were at the heart of the Jacobin politics of pity, for they only deemed the people with whom they could identify to be deserving of compassion. The Jacobins insisted, for political reasons, on identifying themselves with an abstract political entity—"le peuple"—and this rendered them cruelly indifferent and indeed hostile to those who they felt did not belong to this human category.[22] On the one hand, the Jacobin leaders insisted that their compassion for the people was proof of their virtue. On the other hand, they derided pity as a puerile and effeminate affection and claimed that by displaying pity toward minorities, individuals and governments risked being unjust to the majority.[23]

Staël felt compelled, therefore, to redefine the politics of pity. If she used the term "pity" rather than the more general term "sympathy," it was in order to reclaim a moral sentiment appropriated and inverted by the Jacobins. The logic by which the interests of "le peuple" demanded revolutionary retribution had begun to assert itself during the trial of Louis XVI, when two of the Revolution's most forceful orators—Robespierre and Saint-Just—argued relentlessly that the king had, by his own misdeeds, separated himself irrevocably from the people and thus deserved to die. Ironically, Robespierre invoked the same Rousseauian text that had inspired Staël's reflection on pity. While Rousseau had identified pity as the original impulse that constituted a natural preventative against human violence,

Robespierre appealed to public sentiments of pity in order to sanction a violent act. In his *Lettres à ses commettans* (*Letters to His Constituents*, 1792) Robespierre invoked pity only to turn it on its head. Far from inspiring clemency, pity demanded that the king be punished. By breaking his pact with the people, Louis XVI had placed himself under the aegis of natural law and had to be punished accordingly:

> Yet what does this law prescribe? It imposes a double duty: the first is to attend to their own conversation, from which results the right to punish all those who attack their liberty or their safety; the second is to assist our oppressed fellows, from which results the right to punish their oppressors. For alongside the penchant that leads us to defend our existence, nature placed the imperious sentiment of compassion, which is but an emanation of the first penchant, and that serves as an internal warning to fear the repercussions of the outrage made to our neighbor.[24]

Saint-Just, too, insisted that punishment of the king was necessary to preserve the nation. Any inclination to pity the king or to detect in him compensatory goodness was a weakness. The king's "false sensitivity" [fausse sensibilité], he warned, masked the calculated cynicism with which he had systematically deceived the people and taken advantage of their fundamental goodness. The same mystification that had legitimized tyranny was now at work exploiting the people's spontaneous natural feeling. The people must be wary: "This conduct makes you feel compassion, which involuntarily corrupts your energy, rather than a feeling of persuasion."[25] Misplaced pity was not only a weakness: it was a derogation of civic duty. "You have neither the right to be merciful, nor the right to be sensitive towards treason," Saint-Just warned his fellow legislators. "You do not work for your own sake, but for that of the people."[26] In the minds of the Revolution's most extreme factionalists, republican virtue required the transcendence of compassion and the transformation of pity into its opposite: "For pity, for love of humanity, be inhuman."[27]

Women and Jacobin Politics of Pity

The Jacobin politics of pity was not only the expression of class warfare, it had gender implications as well. Jacobin vindictiveness was not directed exclusively towards aristocrats: bourgeois women were also targets. Violent public expression of hostility towards upper-class women—already evinced during the September massacres of 1792—reached its apogee during the period André Malraux described as the "plutarchian era," that is to say, the exclusively masculine moment in the Revolution during which a horde of brothers rose up against the father, punished the mother, and excluded the sisters.[28] The year 1793 alone saw the execution of Mme du Barry, Marie-Antoinette and Mme Roland. If the punishment of aristocrats and upper-class women was motivated by class envy, humiliation of women in general was motivated by pure misogyny. Jacobin orators invoked their female victims' supposed depravity and their manipulative appeals to pity in order to justify their degrading treatment of these victims. Yet women were not innocent in the persecution of other women. As Lori Jo Marso has pointed out, though the Revolutionary Criminal Tribunal that condemned Marie-Antoinette to death consisted of a male jury and nine male judges, "lower-class women of Paris were among her most notorious and vicious enemies."[29] Exiled by the Jacobin government and the target of relentless calumny, Staël was all too familiar with the experience of degrading treatment. She recognized, however, that the Queen's trial represented much more than the persecution of one woman. She saw in it nothing less than the "immolation" of all women. In her *Réflexions sur le procès de la reine par une femme* (*Reflections on the Trial of the Queen, by a Woman*) of 1793, she undertook to defend Marie-Antoinette both as a woman and as a political being, for "she sensed that with the end of the reign of Louis XVI, women's aspirations for political life were being condemned to death."[30] Staël came to the queen's defense not as sympathetic court member, but as a politically astute defender of her sex. Marie-Antoinette had been put on trial because she was an important public and visible woman and her trial coincided, significantly, with women's bid to fully engage in revolutionary politics. To quote Marso again: "Staël worried if women failed to defend the queen, the most prominent and visible woman in France, women's future in the Revolution would be forever compromised."[31] Whether or not Staël's strategy achieved its end, the decision to portray Marie-Antoinette as a devoted mother was a shrewd approach. First, by appealing to shared maternal feelings, Stäel made a eudaimonistic appeal to women of the popular class thereby transforming—or at least attempting to transform—their hostility into identification. Secondly, by appropriating the Rousseauian rhetoric of femininity according to which women as mothers and spouses would regenerate the nation through their self-sacrificing and lactating generosity, Staël sought to counter Jacobin accusations of the queen's maternal dereliction and sexual depravity. As Madelyn Gutwirth put it: "For the Revolution, maternity redeemed female sexuality."[32]

Staël's strategy in her *Reflections on the Trial of the Queen*, many critics have pointed out, was not without its contradictions. First, to defend Marie-Antoinette as an essentially private and apolitical being denied her real status as both the queen of France and an Austrian princess.[33] Secondly, by basing her defense of the queen on her maternity, Staël risked falling into an essentialist argument whereby women are fundamentally emotional and performative beings rather than persons capable of being motivated by reason and transparency.[34] This position concurs with an anthropological perspective whereby women are confined to a never-never land outside of both nature and culture—a perspective that Staël seemingly confirmed later in *On Literature* when she observed that "women, for the most part, belong neither to the order of nature nor to the order of society."[35] Whatever the weaknesses of Staël's *Reflections on the Trial of the Queen*, it is a piece that should not be disregarded, for here she is emboldened to develop discursive moves that would characterize her writing and thought for years to come and set her apart as a truly original thinker.

The Alliance of the Passions

Staël's *Reflections on the Trial of the Queen* and *The Influence of the Passions* are highly polemical essays. While nominally addressed to women of the popular class, the target audience of the *Reflections on the Trial of the Queen* was doubtless the court of public opinion, which alone could have been brought to bear pressure on the political camp favoring the execution of the queen. *The Influence of the Passions*, with its goal of promoting national reconciliation, sought to persuade extremists at both ends of the political spectrum that the Revolution needed to be brought to an end. A rhetorical strategy common to both essays is the borrowing and redefinition of key terms in the opposing side's lexicon. In the *Reflections on the Trial of the Queen*, Staël had countered the misogynist arguments used by the Jacobins by appropriating their rhetoric of maternity; in *The Influence of the Passions*, she refuted the Jacobin stigmatization of pity as a puerile and effeminate emotion by redefining pity as the premier emotion capable of inspiring moral human behavior. Reversing the Jacobin dictum whereby citizens were required to stifle their pity for the undeserving or risk becoming themselves enemies of the nation, Staël insisted that failure to show compassion and to succor those in need would condemn the whole nation to unspeakable barbarism.

Staël's rhetorical strategy was not only to appropriate her opponent's vocabulary, but to reconfigure the semantic field. She redefines pity as a feminine, morally elevating passion. "Calcul," on the other hand, and the fanaticism it enables, while never explicitly characterized by Staël as male characteristics, are in

The Influence of the Passions exclusively associated with masculine figures. One such figure is Robespierre; the other, surprisingly, is Nicolas de Condorcet. According to Staël, it was precisely Condorcet's taste for abstraction and "calcul" which predisposed him to fanaticism or "l'esprit de parti":

> His friends declare, that he would have written against his own opinion, that he would have disavowed and openly attacked it, without confiding to any one the secret of his exertions, if he had imagined that this expedient could contribute to the triumph of the opinion he supported.[36]

In the introduction to her treatise on the passions, Staël had spoken in optimistic terms of the beneficial potential of "positive calculation" [*le calcul positif*]. Statistical analysis of social trends seemed to offer a way of predicting and rationalizing human behavior. At an historical moment characterized by political instability and partisanship, the "geometrical evidence" of science had the appeal of a serene philosophical detachment and mathematical certainty. Writing four years later, in *On Literature*, Staël reaffirmed her cautious optimism that Condorcet's "calculation of probabilities" would provide a method for articulating a moral science.[37] Yet in her overview of contemporary philosophy in its relationship to literature and social institutions, Staël expresses doubts about the degree to which the moral domain was intelligible by mathematical means:

> In the exact sciences, all the premises are invariable; in moral ideas, everything depends on the circumstances. One cannot decide without taking a multitude of considerations into account, among which there are some that are so fugitive, that they frequently defy speech itself, let alone calculation.[38]

Understanding human psychology required the analysis of a far greater number of variables than might be accounted for in a purely statistical approach. Furthermore, the level of generality required to analyze broad social phenomena was ill suited to understanding individuals for, Staël contended: "[m]orality, each time it is applied to someone in particular, can be entirely mistaken in its assumptions."[39]

"Le calcul" was double-edged, too, when applied to the political side of the moral/political equation. On the one hand, social institutions founded in "le calcul positif" would ensure the Republic's adherence to its basic philosophical principles; on the other, reliance on principles that were too abstract or general blinded legislators to "the unique characteristics" of individual human experience.[40] "Legislators . . . often govern with the help of ideas that are too general" and "general ideas are cruel for the person who suffers," Staël writes.[41] Those who sought to govern according to abstract political calculations frequently prevailed by demanding enormous sacrifices from the minority. Taken to an extreme, this mode of political calculation led to Robespierre's "system."

Staël's thinking challenged other key concepts in the political/philosophical lexicon of her day. If she associated "calcul" with "fanatisme" in her treatise on the passions, later, in *On Literature*, she would also come to link this capacity for abstraction with "la raison politique" [political reason] to which she opposed "la raison morale" [moral reason]: "Morality should dictate our calculations and our calculations should dictate politics."[42] As Suzanne Guerlac has argued, Stael's notion of "la civilisation universelle" [universal civilization] breaks with the earlier discourse on perfectibility, imagining instead a phase in human thought anchored in a concrete universality.[43] In this concept of civilization, thought and feeling are intertwined: "Feeling's purpose is not to dismiss reason, but to complement it, to serve as its witness and guarantor: 'the proof of the mind's inventiveness is in experience and feeling.'"[44]

We observe a similar challenge to the reigning political discourse in *The Influence of the Passions*. Here, Staël uncouples enthusiasm from terror, linking it instead with pity: "A spontaneous impulse of the heart, mixing enthusiasm and pity, alone puts an end to internecine wars."[45] Addressing the moderates and conservatives who, with the fall of Robespierre, had triumphed, she asks: "Your enemies are vanquished: they no longer oppose resistance: they no longer minister to your glory by their defeats: would you still continue to astonish us? Pardon, for you are the conquerors."[46] But pity was not, in Staël's view, simply an option: it was a moral imperative. One could not fail to act:

> Woe to a nation that having heard cries of despair repressed its natural feelings: liberty is not promised to such a nation, and other nations, who had held high hopes for France's future after this enormous effort would no longer be able to imagine a promising future nor any redeeming event that could restore that devastated generation.[47]

This conviction, as Staël repeatedly demonstrated, was not merely theoretical. Staël was much admired in her day for her energetic intervention on behalf of numerous individuals threatened by exile, financial ruin and death.[48] But as horrified as she was by Jacobin behavior during the Terror, she was also aware that the violence was not the exclusive preserve of one camp. Aristocrats and Jacobins, alike, spoke the same political language and were guilty of the same fanatical intolerance. That was because they were governed by the same passion which—like a fever—produced the same effects on people of the most disparate temperaments.

Staël's understanding of the universal effects of the passions is essential to her rhetorical mission. Political reconciliation required the recognition of the reversal of power relations. The victors would have to treat the vanquished with respect. Conversely, those who had displayed little pity or compassion when in power must now express remorse. To understand is to forgive; providing, that is, that the vanquished show remorse. Pity alone would enable us to imagine the suffering of those whose characters, physical constitutions, and social circumstances are markedly different from our own:

> If, by the help of abstraction, you should figure to yourself a kind of pain which required, in order to be endured, an organization wholly different from your own, you still would feel pity for that painful situation. Indeed, *the most opposite dispositions* must necessarily be impressed with pity at sufferings *which they themselves could never have experienced.* In a word, the spectacle of misfortune must move and melt mankind by means of commotion, or, as it were, by a talisman, and not by examination or combination.[49]

Pity's reliance on imagination is key to the way Staël links private experience with the happiness of the nation. In the new, political world Staël envisages, our aptitude for imagining the sufferings of those whose characters and experiences are radically different from our own would allow legislators to enact laws and governmental structures that would renounce the old enmities. That is why, at the risk of appearing to make excuses for criminal behavior, Staël emphasized that fanaticism was the only feeling that could provoke an honest person to commit crimes: "It requires some effort to make the confession, lest it should tend to moderate the horror which guilt ought to inspire; yet there have been men, in the course of the French revolution, whose public conduct has been detestable, and who, in their private relations, have shown themselves highly virtuous."[50] She paints a vivid psychological portrait of a factionalist whose principles have driven him to perpetrate inhumane acts. Like the hero of antique tragedies, the factionalist is brought down by his own obsessions. Once his political goals have been accomplished and the enthusiasm of the moment has subsided, the factional leader is wracked by guilt, regret, and self-contempt. As his followers return to their lives eager to forget the past, the factionalist finds himself isolated and despised, but the contempt others feel for him is nothing compared to his own self-contempt for having stifled his pity. Staël presents this portrait of the remorseful factionalist in order to remind warring factions on both ends of the political spectrum that their political enemies are individuals who, like themselves, are capable of suffering and remorse. Only those who fail to show remorse should not be shown pity. If, on the other hand, the perpetrator of political crimes displays the least glimmering of remorse, this sentiment must be seized upon as an opportunity for a personal transformation. The personal transformation of both the victims and perpetrators of revolutionary violence alone could bring about the forgiveness necessary to heal the nation's wounds and, since it was "contrary to the nature of things that a nation should pardon," reconciliation could only be achieved by many private acts of forgiveness.[51]

There remains a final connection to which we must call attention in discussing Staël's reconfiguration of the semantic field of the passions, and that is the relationship between pity, enthusiasm and moderation. If fanaticism is the enemy of pity, it is also the enemy of moderation. Here again Staël's boldness is in evidence, for she succeeds in redefining both enthusiasm and moderation and bringing them together in an unforeseen alliance. Virtually all Staël's writings reflect on and express enthusiasm: it is as if she were watching herself write. From her early *Letters on the Works and Character of J. J. Rousseau* to her *Essay on Fictions* to the later *Réflexions sur le suicide* (*Reflections on Suicide*, 1813) it was important to Staël to gauge, self-consciously, her response to the world and the emergence of her own aesthetics. As her philosophy developed, Staël continued to think more deeply about the nature of this passion. Kari Lokke sees enthusiasm as a core concept that explains not only *On Germany*, but Staël's entire oeuvre.[52] Staël's originality consists in her insistence that enthusiasm was not, as the majority of Enlightenment thinkers would have it, a passion divorced from reason. In *On Germany* she comments on the mistaken understanding of the nature of feelings. "Is it possible," she asks, "to see as opposed two characteristics of the soul that are like two flames in the same hearth? When one claims that reason is incompatible with enthusiasm it is because one substitutes calculation for reason and madness for enthusiasm." Feeling and passion were not incompatible with reason: "Feeling's purpose is not to dismiss reason, but to complement it."[53] The affinities Staël reveals in this work between enthusiasm and mysticism do not undermine the relationship between enthusiasm and reason, nor do they cast the former in a passive role. Rather, the enthusiasm imagined by Staël was a higher order of thinking that, like meditation, demanded detachment and complete self-mastery. One understands then, that the enthusiastic moderation envisaged by Staël is not quite what one would suppose.

Enthusiasm was neither overwrought nor strictly dominated by the emotions. Similarly, moderation was not the milk milquetoast "middlingness" of the political coward. This alliance of passions was strong, assertive and energetic. As Aurelian Craiutu has elegantly demonstrated, Staël's moderation was of a unique sort for it was "inseparable from her passion for ideas, her romantic thirst for adventures and glory, and her defense of enthusiasm in the service of liberty."[54] Pity, that virtuous passion, partook of both moderation and enthusiasm and promised a measure of that illusive ideal of happiness that Stael described as "the union of all contrary things."[55]

Notes

1. Germaine de Staël, *A Treatise on the Influence of the Passions upon the Happiness of Individuals and of Nations*, anonymous translation (London: Gale ECCO print editions, 2010), 330.

2. Ibid., 191–92. Translation modified.

3. See Madelyn Gutwirth, "Madame de Staël, Rousseau, and the Woman Question," *PMLA* 86, no. 1 (1971): 100–09.

4. Jean-Jacques Rousseau, *Du contrat social, écrits politiques*, in *Œuvres complètes*, eds. Bernard Gagnebin and Marcel Raymond, vol. 3 (Paris: Gallimard, 1964); and *Discourse on the Origin of Inequality*, trans. Donald A. Cress (Indianapolis: Hackett Publishing Company, 1992). It should be stressed that pity is not a fixed concept in Rousseau's writing. Rousseau had already maintained in *The First and Second Discourses*, eds. Roger D. Masters and Judith R. Masters (New York: St. Martin's, 1964), that pity degenerated in civilized society. In *Émile* and *Lettre à D'Alembert*, pity serves less as a counter to self-interest than an expression of it.

5. Rousseau, *Discourse on the Origin of Inequality*, 36.

6. Ibid., 37.

7. Ibid., 36.

8. Staël, *The Influence of the Passions*, 335.

9. Victor Goldschmidt discusses the biological aspects of Rousseau's notion of pity in *Anthropologie et politique: Les principes du système de Rousseau* (Paris: Vrin, 1974). In *Enlightenment and Pathology: Sensibility in the Literature and Medicine of Eighteenth-Century France* (Baltimore: Johns Hopkins University Press, 1998), Anne Vila draws out the parallels between Rousseau's *morale sensitive* and materialist theories of moral hygiene of contemporary *médecins philosophes* in her chapter "The Moral Hygiene of Sensibility," 182–224.

10. Martha C. Nussbaum notes that "there is more than the usual degree of verbal confusion concerning what to call" pity. In English, the term "pity" has "recently come to have the nuances of condescension and superiority to the sufferer that it did not have when Rousseau invoked *pitié*" (*Upheavals of Thought: The Intelligence of the Emotions* [Cambridge: Cambridge University Press, 2001], 301). For this reason Nussbaum avoids using it. I, on the other hand, have chosen to use

the term "pity" because, despite its modern connotations, it is the word used by Staël and because it is the word that is contested in Revolutionary discourse.

11. Ibid., 306.

12. In presenting his "Second Maxim" in vol. 4 of his *Émile*, Rousseau designates clearly who is undeserving of pity (Rousseau, *Émile, Education, Morale, Botanique*, in *Œuvres complètes*, eds. Bernard Gagnebin and Marcel Raymond, vol. 4. [Paris: Gallimard, 1969], 507–8).

13. Nussbaum, *Upheavals of Thought*, 322. The term *eudaimonistic* is from the Greek *eudaimonia*, commonly translated as "human flourishing." *Eudaimonia* is linked in Aristotelian ethics and political philosophy to the notion of *areté* or virtue and is thus quite relevant to Staël's understanding of pity as a political virtue that promotes social well-being. Nussbaum uses the term to describe a specific type of judgment that evokes pity. In this judgment the sympathetic individual is moved to feel pity for another because of a perceived sense of shared goals and projects (see 321–32).

14. I have used the English term "factionalism" to translate Stael's "esprit de parti." The latter, in Stael's mind, is closely associated with "fanatisme" which is "l'esprit de parti" at its most intolerant: "The spirit of the party must, of all the passions, be that which is most hostile to the developement [*sic*] of thought, since, as we have already observed, the fanaticism it inspires does not leave any choice in the means of securing victory" (Staël, *The Influence of the Passions*, 189).

15. Ibid., 185.

16. Ibid., 191.

17. Ibid., 189.

18. Ibid., 165.

19. Ibid., 250.

20. Germaine de Staël, *De la littérature considérée dans ses rapports avec les institutions sociales*, eds. Gérard Gengembre and Jean Goldzink (Paris: Garnier-Flammarion, 1991), 374; my translation.

21. Philip Knee, "Les Mésaventures politiques de la sympathie chez Rousseau," in *Les Discours de la sympathie: Enquête sur une notion de l'âge classique à la modernité*, eds. Thierry Belleguic, Eric Van der Schueren, and Sabrina Vervacke. (Quebec: Les Presses de 'Université de Laval, 2007), 423–41.

22. In her essay, *On Revolution*, Hannah Arendt identifies the emergence of a modern form of sensibility—the Jacobin "politics of pity." This notion, inspired by Rousseau, was a perversion of compassion. Pity was "talkative," self-interested, a delightful sentiment that could be enjoyed for its own sake. It had "as much vested interest in the existence of the unhappy as thirst for power has a vested interest in the weak" (*On Revolution* [New York: Viking Press, 1963], 83–85).

23. Staël, *The Influence of the Passions*, 249.

24. Maximilien Robespierre, *Lettres à ses commettans*, in *Œuvres de Maximilien Robespierre*, eds. Albert Laponneraye and Armand Carrel (New York: B. Franklin, 1970), 222.

25. Louis Antoine de Saint-Just, *Second discours concernant le jugement de Louis XVI*, ed. Charles Vellay, vol. 1 (Paris: Charpentier et Fosquelle, 1908), 388.

26. "[V]ous ne travaillez pas pour votre compte, mais pour le peuple," Robespierre, *Rapport de ventôse*, Year 2, quoted by David Denby in *Sentimental Narrative and the Social Order in France, 1760–1820* (Cambridge: Cambridge University Press, 1994), 158.

27. Petition from Parisian Commune to the National Convention, quoted in Arendt, *On Revolution*, 85.

28. Jean-Marie Roulin, "Réflexions sur le procès de la Reine: Du procès d'une femme au procès de la Révolution," *Cahiers staëliens* 57 (2006): 89–102.

29. Lori Jo Marso, "Defending the Queen: Wollstonecraft and Staël on the Politics of Sensibility and Feminine Difference," *Eighteenth Century: Theory and Interpretation* 43, no. 1 (Spring 2002): 43.

30. Catriona Seth, *Marie-Antoinette: Anthologie et dictionnaire: Textes choisis, présentés et annotés par Catriona Seth* (Paris: Editions Robert Laffont, 2006), 150.

31. Marso, "Defending the Queen," 53.

32. Madelyn Gutwirth, "Nature, cruauté et femmes immolées: Les *Réflexions sur le procès de la reine*," in *Le Groupe de Coppet et la Révolution française*, eds. Etienne Hofmann and Anne-Lise Delacrétaz (Paris: Touzot, 1988), 130.

33. Ibid., 128.

34. Marso, "Defending the Queen," 57.

35. "Les femmes ne sont pour la plupart, dans l'ordre de la nature, ni dans l'ordre de la société," cited in Roulin, *Réflexions sur le procès de la Reine*, 101.

36. Staël, *The Influence of the Passions*, 176.

37. Staël, *De la littérature*, eds. Gengembre and Goldzink, 372.

38. Ibid., 367.

39. Ibid., 61.

40. Germaine de Staël, *Des circonstances actuelles qui peuvent terminer la Révolution et des principes qui doivent fonder la république en France*, ed. Lucia Omacini (Geneva: Droz, 1979), 96.

41. Staël, *The Influence of the Passions*, 250.

42. Staël, *De la littérature*, eds. Gengembre and Goldzink, 375.

43. Suzanne Guerlac, "Madame de Staël et le discours féminin de la 'civilisation naturelle,'" *Cahiers staëliens* 57 (2006): 77–88.

44. Ibid., 83.

45. Staël, *The Influence of the Passions*, 253.

46. Ibid., 341.

47. Staël, *Réflexions sur le procès de la Reine*, 167.

48. On Staël's role rescuing Lafayette, see Paul Spalding, "Germaine de Staël's Role in Rescuing Lafayette, 1792–1797" in *Germaine de Staël: Forging a Politics of Mediation*, ed. Karyna Szmurlo (Oxford: Voltaire Foundation, 2011), 35–46. He lists at least twelve other individuals besides Lafayette on behalf of whom Staël intervened with considerable risk to herself.

49. Staël, *The Influence of the Passions*, 331. Emphasis mine.

50. Ibid., 199.

51. Ibid., 208.

52. Kari Lokke, "L'Enthousiasme, l'éternité, et les 'armes du temps' chez Madame de Staël," *Cahiers staëliens* 57 (2006): 63–76.

53. Germaine de Staël, *Œuvres complètes de Mme la Baronne de Staël*, ed. Auguste de Staël, vol. 3 (Paris: Treuttel et Wurtz, 1820–1821), 352.

54. Aurelian Craiutu, *A Virtue for Courageous Minds: Moderation in French Political Thought, 1748–1830* (Princeton, NJ: Princeton University Press, 2012), 160.

55. Staël, *The Influence of the Passions*, 8. Translation modified.

3

PASSIONS, POLITICS, AND LITERATURE:
THE QUEST FOR HAPPINESS

Christine Dunn Henderson

T HROUGHOUT HER CAREER, Madame de Staël made appeals to both reason and the imagination, the two faculties she understood as distinctively human.[1] Politico-historical analyses like her posthumous *Considérations sur la Révolution française* (*Considerations on the Principal Events of the French Revolution*) are clearly aimed at man's rational faculties, while her work as the author of novels such as *Delphine* and *Corinne* reminds us of her awareness of the power of man's imaginative capacity. Whether appealing to reason, to the imagination, or to both, Staël's goal remained the same: "to struggle against unhappiness in all its forms, to study the thoughts, feelings and institutions which make men unhappy and to try to discover the reflection, the impulse, the combination, which could diminish something of the intensity of the soul's torments."[2]

Obstacles to happiness can arise from reason and from the passions. So, too, can solutions to the problem of unhappiness. While Staël's magnum opus, *Considerations*, offers one perspective on the political problem of happiness, this chapter will investigate two early works—*The Influence of the Passions on the Happiness of Individuals and Nations* (1796) and her *Essay on Fictions* (1795)—as supplements to that political work, particularly considering the place of the passions, and the connections between political happiness, personal happiness, philosophy, and literature. The argument for reading *The Influence of the Passions* and her *Essay on Fictions* in the context of the *Considerations* is that just as *Considerations* tutors reason, fiction can tutor the emotions or the passions. Right reason and properly ordered passions are equally necessary for happiness, whether we understand that happiness on the political or the personal level. Some of these arguments are pursued in mature works such as *On Literature Considered in Its Relationship to Social Institutions* and *On Germany*. In the fourth volume of *On Germany*, for example, Staël underscores the desirability of enthusiasm, which she casts as a moderate passion inspiring individuals to rise above selfish goals of health, wealth, and power. Enthusiasm is an essential supplement to calculation and reason, promoting happiness more than any other sentiment and elevating the souls of both individual and nations.

Thus, while these themes figure in the mature works, Staël's initial articulations of them in her early works are particularly interesting, as they reveal a shift in her approach to the passions. In the treatise on the passions' influence, she appears to consider the idea of a quasi-stoical negation of the passions as the path to human liberty. Ultimately, however, this idea is rejected in favor of the solution first developed in her *Essay on Fictions*: rendering the passions less dangerous to individuals (and to regimes) by moderating and shaping them, via the reading of a certain type of fiction. Staël's rejection of the stoic ideal is also a rejection of a certain view of philosophy. Thus, the solution she crafts to the problem of the passions is also a new understanding of the role of philosophy, a new understanding, especially, of the relationship between the philosopher and the poet.[3]

The inspiration for linking the political, the personal, and the literary begins with Staël herself, whose own work is emphatically interdisciplinary and who repeatedly stresses that her interest as a thinker, theorist and writer is in both the political and the personal.[4] She tells readers that the French Revolution—its movement from reform to Terror to the dictatorship of Napoleon—had created a special need for humans to reflect more deeply upon "the nature of individual and political happiness, on the way to achieve it, on its limitations, on the rocks separating us from such a goal."[5] Any discussion of the routes and obstacles to happiness must, however, be preceded by some exploration of happiness itself. At the beginning of the essay on the passions, Staël offers this lengthy definition of happiness:

> Happiness, as people wish for it, is the union of all contrary things. For individuals, it is hope without fear, activity without anxiety, glory without calumny, love without inconstancy, imagination to embellish our possessions in our own eyes and fade the memory of what we have lost; the intoxication of moral nature, the good side of all conditions, talents, and pleasures, without all their accompanying evils. For nations, happiness would also be a reconciliation of republican liberty with monarchical calm, the emulation of talents with the silence of factions, a military

spirit abroad and respect for laws at home. Happiness, as one imagines it, is the impossible in every genre.[6]

If the "imagination" or the ideal of happiness is "the impossible in every genre," the reality of happiness consists in something more concrete: "the assurance of never being disturbed or dominated by any force stronger than the self."[7] Philosophically, this definition of happiness prefigures later liberals like Benjamin Constant or even F. A. Hayek, both of whom emphasize freedom from domination and coercion as the core of liberty. Politically, the definition translates into the blend of liberty and order Staël admired in the English Constitution. Following this definition's political side, we are able to trace any number of her liberal principles, including her advocacy of constitutionalism, rule of law, representative government, and political moderation, as well as her deep distrust of unbridled power of whatever form. We can also understand her emphasis on individual liberty in its various forms—thought, speech/press, religion, even economic activity. On the personal or interior level, the idea of not being disturbed or dominated by any force stronger than one's self elevates the virtue of self-command. In its most extreme form—and Staël articulates this position in *The Influence of the Passions*—self-command requires the complete conquest of the passions. A less extreme form of self-command approaches a modified stoicism of the sort endorsed by thinkers such as Adam Smith. I would argue that, despite the explicit teaching at the end of *The Influence of the Passions*, Staël, like Smith, does not ultimately aim for the rejection of emotion entirely, for that would dehumanize us. Human existence is passionate, yet it is also rational, and when the passions attempt to usurp and dominate reason's realm, they must be brought back to their proper limits, or appropriately re-directed. The *Essay on Fictions* reveals Staël's call for a particular tutelage of the passions, one which would moderate them and direct them toward suitable ends.[8]

Staël's attention to the passions is not merely focused on the individual, and she observes that whether happiness is viewed from the political or the individual perspective, its main obstacle is the same: passion, or—more precisely—excessive and misdirected passions. Such disorderly passions are capable of overcoming the individual's reason and, significantly, the rationally constructed political system. Just as James Madison drew attention to the frailties of human nature and the corresponding need to protect against the concentration of political power in *The Federalist Papers*, Staël is also keenly aware of the human element of the political.[9] Government is indeed a reflection on and of human nature; "without the passions," she observes, "government would be as simple a machine as any lever the force of which is proportional to the weight it has to lift."[10] Yet eliminating the passions entirely from public affairs is neither possible nor desirable. Not only do the passions add color to life, but they also augment reason's force, insofar as most men are incapable of being devoted pursuers of virtue without passion lending its force to reason's arguments.[11] Staël's awareness of passion's role as reason's handmaiden—"men cannot be moved without the stimulus of passion"—recalls platonic reminders about reason's need for reinforcement from the soul's irrational elements as well as Jaucourt's entry for "sensibility" in the *Encyclopedia*, in which he sketches a similar connection between reason and the passions, asserting, "The sensibility of the soul . . . goes farther than the penetration of the mind alone."[12]

Wise governments recognize both that passion cannot be eradicated and that it can be a useful tool. Thus, in their pursuit of public happiness, governments must understand which passions ought to be encouraged and which constrained. This, in turn, demands a thorough knowledge of the passions and their workings. The art of governing—either the *polis* or the self—requires cultivating those passions and passionate (i.e., irrational) actions in manners that are conducive to freedom, while avoiding passionate responses that lead to the enslavement of a people or an individual.[13] Thus, government should not look to remake human nature by removing the passions, nor should it engage in moral judgment about "bad" and "good" passions. Rather than seeking to eliminate the vicious in human nature, the science of politics is neutral, aiming at understanding human nature *as it is* and using its knowledge of our nature to steer humans away from despotism and toward liberty.

Molding the Passions: The Case of Vanity

Understanding and instructing the passions is, then, a project with both political and personal implications. Staël's treatment of vanity in *The Influence of the Passions* is interesting not merely because it offers an excellent illustration of her dual goals of taming and directing the passions, but also because it indicates that vanity, traditionally thought of as a bad or at least morally ambiguous passion, can be put to good use in politics. Her exploration of vanity begins with the observation that vanity and the love of glory are both passions which emerge fully only within society. At first glance they seem to be polar opposites: love of glory is "the most commanding" passion and "the most beautiful of the principles capable of moving our souls,"[14] whereas vanity attaches itself to the "leftovers" of glory and ambition—to petty objects with no intrinsic value—with the sole desire of creating an effect in the eyes of other men.[15] Despite its petty scope, however, vanity's force is as strong as any of the other passions, and in an analysis which owes much to Jean-Jacques Rousseau's penetrating treatment of vanity (or *amour propre*) in his *Discours sur les sciences et les arts* (*Discourse on the Sciences and the Arts*) and his *Discourse on the Origins of Inequality*. Staël observes that the student of the passions can discern in vanity the "concomitant miseries in the servile way this feeling makes you dependent on the circle of those around you."[16] Her discussion of vanity encompasses this passion's role in the French Revolution, emphasizing the manner in which it contributed to the Revolution's increasing radicalization and accompanying bloodiness. Staël does not, however, judge vanity to have caused the Revolution's early phases—the revolt of the many against the privileges of the few was merely an assertion of fundamental equality and the reclamation of natural rights. Nor does she permit herself to attribute aristocratic resistance to the Revolution to vanity. Rather, she emphasizes vanity's workings among the revolutionaries, particularly in their public debates, attributing to this passion the increasing radicalization of the Revolution. Many opinions, Staël notes, were put forth in more radical forms merely in the hopes of surpassing other orators, and allowing audiences to witness the Revolution's debates and proceedings "was enough to change the direction of public affairs in France."[17] Describing the self-fulfilling and violent cycle caused by the passion of vanity, she writes, "Before long, however, they were giving up principles, proposing decrees, even approving of crimes, to get that applause. In a reciprocal and disastrous reaction, everything done to please the crowd made its judgments even wilder, and this wilder judgment then demanded new sacrifices."[18] Had vanity been moderated or better directed, the Revolution's slide into Terror might have been averted.

It is important to remember that Staël treats vanity neutrally, presenting it as a natural passion that is not necessarily destructive and whose workings can be shaped to serve the cause of liberty. She asserts that, with proper guidance, vanity can be shifted from the desire to elevate oneself in the opinion of other men to the desire to prevent any single individual from gaining undue precedence or privilege. So directed, vanity will work in the service of liberty, making the rule of one man detestable and also supporting "the constitutional laws which make the most powerful men soon return to private life."[19] Staël claims, moreover, that the vanity-inspired jealousy of their own equality can make citizens vigilant for liberty, thus thwarting those who seek to satisfy their ambitions through public life. She even goes so far as to hope that properly directed vanity might eventually prevent all those but the patriotic and humanitarian from seeking political office.

Staël herself admits, however, that this vision of well-directed vanity may be utopian, and indeed it does seem simplistic in several ways. First, although she reckons with the vanity's force and its potential to enslave both individuals and citizens, she overlooks another strong passion—the love of equality—which is similarly ambiguous. Although not part of the Staëlian analysis, Alexis de Tocqueville offers a brilliant account of equality's growing strength in the heart of modern man which points to the dangers Staël does not see. Man, says Tocqueville, naturally loves both liberty and equality, but he feels the passion for equality more strongly than the passion for liberty. Unless his interest and his heart are aligned, modern man will find the unequal results produced by liberty to be intolerable: when the passions of liberty and equality conflict, he will prefer equality, even if that equality is the equal enslavement of all under a single tyrant.[20]

Staël's accounts of vanity and the love of honor also seem to underestimate the persistence of the desire for distinction in the human soul, and the potential for that desire to turn destructive. Those belonging to what Abraham Lincoln later called "the family of the lion, or the tribe of the eagle" seek distinction at any cost—such examples of "towering genius" are insatiably and amorally ambitious.[21] While these individuals may seek political office, they are not naturally suited to be caretakers of existing political orders. The fame they crave depends on singular deeds, and in that quest for distinction, it does not matter to them whether they are the founders or the destroyers of civilizations. Staël's solution of harnessing citizens' vanity to guard against such individuals seems inadequate, perhaps because, while she is aware of love of honor's strength in the human heart, she underestimates its potentially destructive side. This naiveté is particularly striking, coming after the French Revolution and coming from a thinker generally attuned to cautionary lessons drawn from the Revolution's course. Perhaps Staël really did believe human nature could be changed, though her discussions of Napoleon certainly merit further attention in light of this question.[22] Perhaps her inattentiveness to the problem of the grandly ambitious is due to her belief that certain constitutional structures could place effective institutional checks upon ambition's destructive side. If this last is the case, then properly tutored vanity—by which the citizens would jealously guard their own rights—can only be a secondary defense, while the institutional structures she lauds in her political writings must serve as liberty's primary safeguards.

Over-optimism aside, Staël does hold out the possibility that passions such as vanity can be moderated and properly channeled to function as positive rather than detrimental forces in free political life. Moving from the political perspective to a purely individual one, however, the situation becomes more complex. Staël notes this complexity in the opening section of *The Influence of the Passions*, which announces the most important difference between political governance and self-governance. She presents a contrast between political and individual happiness, noting that the former takes for granted that the passions cannot be extinguished and therefore focuses on how to harness the people's passions in the name of a healthy regime, while the latter strives for "the most perfect moral independence" [*l'indépendance morale la plus parfaite*].[23] In both the political and the personal cases, "independence" does indeed mean freedom from domination, but Staël seems to argue that—in the case of the passions within individuals—freedom from domination can only be achieved by eliminating the passions themselves, because passion, by definition, is a controlling force whose workings dominate the rational: "I do not understand how one can manage that which exists only in dominating; man has but two conditions: either he is certain of being the master of himself and there is, thus, no passion; or he feels reigning in him a power stronger than himself, upon which he is entirely dependent."[24] In order to resist dominating forces such as the passions—those storms that shake the individual's soul—one must overcome the passions through one's own resources, most specifically, by attaining a type of self-mastery through philosophy.

Philosophy's Task

The idea that philosophy is among the internal resources for combating the domination of the passions is developed in the penultimate section of *The Influence of the Passions*. By philosophy, Staël means the ability to rise above the demands of both ourselves and others, to step back from our natural myopia and, by adopting a broader or more long-range viewpoint, to gain a moderating perspective on our all-consuming, yet momentary, passions. Ironically, given its purpose as an antidote to domination of the passions, philosophy is described as seizing control over the soul and *by its domination*, making the soul "place less value on everything it possesses and hopes for."[25] It is striking that philosophy does not appear to change the soul's desires, which are perhaps natural and, in some fundamental sense, unalterable. Rather, philosophy instructs the soul on the correct valuation of those desires. Philosophy helps human beings find the proper mean between loving life too much and disdaining it, apparently restoring a natural balance that has been distorted by the passions.[26] Philosophy's method of restoring balance to the disordered and passionate soul is to deflate the value the passions have set on their various objects by teaching the individual to detach him or herself from those objects. The kind of philosophy Staël recommends seems, on the one hand, an echo of Epicureanism's carpe diem, and on the other hand, an echo of Stoicism's detachment and apathy.

The Staëlian understanding of philosophy emphasizes freeing oneself from the domination of the passions by acquiring detachment and self-control. It involves placing "ourselves above ourselves in order to control ourselves, and above others in order to expect nothing of them."[27] A long struggle with the passions is the precondition for learning this detachment; indeed, only when one gives up on the quest for happiness is the attainment of happiness or something close to it possible. The process works in the following manner: by conceding that perfect happiness (or "the imagination of happiness") is an impossible quest, the individual renounces his pursuit of it; with this renunciation, the other passions no longer dominate the individual; he is thus freed to begin philosophizing. The philosophic life requires us to "learn to conceive of life passively, to suffer its uniform flow, to make up for everything by thinking, to find in our thoughts the only events which depend on neither fate nor men."[28] This view of philosophy owes much to the Stoics, as we shall see, but its departures from the Greeks are worth a passing mention. As articulated by Staël, philosophy is the renunciation of a certain type of desire, rather than the fulfillment of a desire (i.e., the desire for wisdom) or the replacement of a destructive desire with a productive one. Her admission that freedom from the passions helps us attain "something like" happiness indicates that philosophy does not necessarily produce individual happiness in and of itself. Rather, philosophic renunciation is a tool, which seems to secure two goods for the philosopher: (1) the elimination (or at least the diminution) of daily anxiety, and consequently, (2) the enhancement of incidental and actual pleasures. Interestingly, neither of those goals approaches the *telos* of classical Greek philosophy, which aims at understanding the whole and acquiring knowledge of the good.

The renunciation of the passions Staël advocates is clearly indebted to Stoicism's emphasis on the free individual as having liberated his soul from enslavement by the passions and by vices. The Stoics believed that vanquishing the passions restores the proper order to the soul, by allowing the highest part of the soul—the rational element—to govern. Self-control, absence of anger and desire, and endurance help free the soul from anxiety and fear, and developing the classical virtues of prudence, justice, courage, and moderation leads the individual into harmony with the rational governance of the universe. The Stoic individual attains an end Staël would endorse: the ability to withstand Fortune's blows with patience, and nobly to endure whatever befalls him.[29]

Staël's emphasis on the philosophic individual's self-command or self-overcoming is consistent with her elevation of courage as the prime philosophic virtue. Despite the importance of self-command and self-overcoming—and despite remarks at the close of *The Influence of the Passions* that approach an endorsement of Stoic apathy or the absence of passion as the path to mental tranquility or happiness—Staël remains adamant that the passions have a role in human life, and she insists that "philosophy is not insensitivity."[30] Her resistance to defining philosophy in Stoic terms may be indebted to Du Marsais's definition of the philosopher in the *Encyclopedia*, which begins by noting that, while reason is the philosopher's dominant quality, reason is always accompanied by morality and sociability.[31] Du Marsais continues,

> From this idea it is easy to conclude how far removed the insensitive sage of the stoics is from the perfection of our philosopher: such a philosopher is a man, and their sage was nothing but a phantom. Humanity would make them blush, and he glories in it; they wished foolishly to deny the passions, and to raise us above our nature by means of a chimerical insensitivity: as to him, he makes no claim to the chimerical honor of destroying the passions, because that is impossible; but he works at not being dominated by them, at benefiting from them, and at making reasonable use of them, because that is possible, and because reason directs him to do so.[32]

Philosophy may offer the individual a buffer against Fortune's winds, but it is impossible to do away with those winds entirely. The human condition is inherently precarious and therefore anxious. Staël's awareness of the anxiety within the human condition seems distinctly modern, reminding us of thinkers such as Thomas Hobbes, John Locke, and Jean-Jacques Rousseau, who characterize the human condition as naturally desirous, with one desire inevitably producing another in an endless and restless cycle, famously characterized as the "joyless quest for joy."[33] Rousseau's analysis of the loss of man's natural happiness and of his growing vanity, dependence, and insecurity as society develops is graphically portrayed in his *Discourse on the Origin of Inequality*. Rousseau's depiction—with its discussion of how luxuries become needs, of how "people were unhappy to lose them [luxuries] without being happy to possess them," and of the anxiety produced by needing the others' good opinion—was well-known to Staël, and surely influenced her own thinking.[34] But perhaps the deepest analysis of this malaise in modern, democratic society comes from de Tocqueville, writing some forty years after Staël. Writing of the restlessness [inquiétude] characterizing American life, Tocqueville paints more clearly what Staël but sketches, capturing the frenetic pace, the anxiety and the tragic nature of an endless cycle in which the thirst to satisfy the passions (particularly the passion for well-being) can never be quenched. Describing man's fear-driven rush to grab each pleasure and the almost immediate dash to the next one, Tocqueville comments, "one would say he fears at each instant he will cease to live before he has enjoyed them. He grasps them all without clutching them, and he soon allows them to escape from his hands as to run after new enjoyments." The cycle is endless, stopping only when "death finally comes to him, and it stops him before he has grown weary of this useless pursuit of a complete felicity that always flees from him."[35] The phenomenon Tocqueville describes is essentially the same cycle of passionate anxiety described by Staël. Whereas Tocqueville indicates this cycle is essentially unbreakable and therefore the tragic dimension of modernity, Staël suggests philosophic detachment can put an end to this tragedy.[36]

If philosophy is capable of freeing the individual from the fears and anxieties that necessarily accompany the passions, Staël also argues (perhaps paradoxically) that this same quasi-Stoic philosophy opens the individual to additional pleasures. She points out that when in the grips of strong passions, the individual feels only those desires and the accompanying fear of not attaining his object; he is thus completely unaware of other pleasures. Once free from strong passion's tyranny, however, the individual is able to experience the "thousand fragmentary delights in existence" which present themselves "to anyone with a soul at peace and ready to savor them." Couching her discussion in explicitly philosophic terms, Staël describes how the philosopher liberates his thoughts from a single passionate desire: "He now no longer focuses them on a single object, and enjoys the pleasant impressions each of his ideas can provide for him in turn and individually." In passing, it is worth noting Staël's reworking of philosophy from the erotic desire for a single object—the good—into a de-eroticized (perhaps de-fanged), chance series of passing enjoyments through which the philosopher drifts "at the will of the wind."[37]

With this discussion of the passing pleasures to which philosophy opens the individual, Staël retreats from the Stoic ideal, again considering the possibility of something other than the eradication of the passions. Within her discussions of philosophy, there is a tension between the Stoic detachment from (or eradication of) the passions and this "live in the moment" approach to moderating them. Considered within the broader context of her work, however, the flirtation with Stoic apathy at the end of her essay on the passions seems just that—a passing exploration. A rejection of Stoic apathy is not a new position for her: not only does the essay on the passions begin by acknowledging a human (and passionate) element in all political life, but her *Essay on Fictions*, penned just a year earlier, is also sharply critical of the inhumanity of "severe" philosophy (Stoicism) which sought to completely subject the passions to moral duty's dictates. The *Essay on Fictions* echoes the moderation emphasized in Staël's political works and argues that because the passions are a fundamental part of human nature, attempts to remove them would be unsuccessful and, ultimately, undesirable. Accepting the impossibility of eliminating the passions and adopting a more reasonable stance vis-à-vis the passions, the *Essay on Fictions* thus advocates the moderation or tutelage of the passions in a manner beneficial to both the individual and society. We have seen that institutional design can help channel and even shape the passions in political life, but perhaps the most effective tool for reshaping and moderating them is literature: particularly, "natural fiction," or the modern novel.

A Novel Idea

With a nod to Rousseau, the *Essay on Fictions* acknowledges the dangers of the imagination and of the passions inflamed by the imagination. Nevertheless, properly directed or properly moderated imagination—like passion—has utility, for the passions and the emotions are powerful forces in shaping the individual's moral behavior.[38] Man has two distinctive capacities, and fiction uses one of them (imagination) to bring the passions under the control of the other (reason). "Fictions do not find obstacles in passions; they make use of them," Staël writes; by engaging the emotions, imaginative works augment their force. In the best fictions, however, the reader's emotional engagement is genuine, and yet it is instrumental to the goal of developing a love of virtue and a hatred of vice, for these are the keys to a personal—and, ultimately, a public—morality that is rooted in reason.[39]

The modern novel holds the greatest potential as a vehicle to harness and educate men's emotions, for as opposed to histories and mythology, this genre most accurately and fully depicts the spectrum of human passions and sentiments.[40] Indeed, the modern novel's prime advantage over stories of the fantastical and the marvelous is its ability to present the complete range of interior emotions in a believable manner. Despite its imaginative character, the novel depicts feelings "so natural[ly] that the reader often believes he is being spoken to directly, with no artifice but the tactfulness of changing the names."[41] This verisimilitude increases the novel's affective force, heightening the reader's sympathetic engagement with the characters and their plights, and consequently augmenting the force of the moral lessons imparted by the novel. Staël, whose analysis of the novel is, in all likelihood, indebted to Diderot's redefinition of the novel in his essay *In Praise of Richardson*, emphasizes that the novelist's art lies in his or her ability to engage the reader's sentiments and passions with embodied principles.[42] Through this emotional engagement, the novelist makes moral truths—particularly the love of virtue and duty—"tangible" to the reader in an especially forceful way.[43] Because of its superior ability to ally the reader's sympathies with the virtuous and against the vicious, the novel surpasses all other methods of instilling morality and the love of virtue in the reader's soul.[44] Novels cultivate sensibility—in Staël's language, they nurture the "internal emotions" of the reader's soul—and these internal emotions are better developed when imagination is allied with reason than when reason must work alone. The novelist's art thus consists not only in painting the imaginary as real and creating the real from the imaginary, but also in his or her talent for arranging this material so that the philosophic truths emerge logically, without the reader becoming aware of the novelist's pedagogical intent.[45]

But if the novelist is to instill a genuine love of virtue and hatred of vice, he or she must understand the nature of these things—including human nature, of which the passions are an inescapable part. It would seem that the novelist must be a philosopher, yet a philosopher engaged with the emotions, as opposed to the Stoic ideal fleetingly embraced in *The Influence of the Passions*. Reason is superior to the passions, but the passions are necessary to render reason effective and to humanize its precepts.[46] In this sense, then, fiction also functions as a corrective to the over-rationalism of the age, for it is a reminder that all systems—no matter how beautiful in their abstraction—are peopled with individuals. Such a reminder is consistent with the emphasis on the individual, which runs throughout Staël's writings in both the political and the non-political works.[47] Yet the novel remains a work of art or artifice, adding "a kind of dramatic effect to the truth; not deforming it, but condensing it to set it off."[48] Merely presenting true events is insufficient, in that simply mirroring events risks burying the significant in a sea of details. A "genuine" representation of nature reveals nature's moral truths as well; in the service of this end, the novelist must highlight some events, downplaying the others. The novelist's art is like the painter's: "Far from distorting objects, it represents them in a way that makes them more immediately apprehended."[49]

Rather than being a deficient reflection of nature, the novelist's ability to present a tableau which fully engages the reader's imaginative sensibilities or capacity for sympathy is an *improvement* upon nature. Staël notes that "if we copy her [Nature] too slavishly, we become incapable of portraying her. The most truthful account is always an imitative truth."[50]

With this understanding of literature as philosophic imitation, Staël enters into the ancient quarrel between the poets and the philosophers. In Plato's *Republic*, Socrates had criticized the poets on political grounds—for teaching unsalutary doctrines—and on philosophic grounds—for making beautiful images which are defective insofar as they do not reflect the truth of the objects they represent.[51] Staël's articulation of the modern novel's possibilities establishes her as firmly on the side of poetry in the ancient debate, but a philosophically informed poetry, freed of the tensions between philosophy and passion she discusses in *The Influence of the Passions*, and a philosophically informed poetry which is productive of both individual and political happiness.

Notes

1. Germaine de Staël, *Essay on Fictions*, in *Major Writings of Germaine de Staël*, ed. and trans. Vivian Folkenflik (New York: Columbia University Press, 1992), 61. Unless otherwise specified, quotations from Staël's works are drawn from this volume.

2. Germaine de Staël, *The Influence of the Passions on the Happiness of Individuals and Nations*, in *Major Writings*, 155–56.

3. Here, I use the term "poet" rather loosely, to designate all creators of imaginative works.

4. On the simultaneous advance of literary endeavors (including history, fiction and philosophy) and of liberal, democratic politics, see also Simone Balayé, *Madame de Staël: Lumières et liberté* (Paris: Éditions Klincksieck, 1979), 85.

5. Staël, *The Influence of the Passions*, in *Major Writings*, 152.

6. Ibid., 154.

7. Ibid., 153.

8. Whether the goal of educating the passions is to orient them toward proper ends or to orient them away from improper ends is an open question. Staël's language emphasizes the former, but the latter—in which individuals freely choose among a wide variety of appropriate ends—seems more fully consistent with her own classical liberalism. If the ends to which Staël urges orienting the passions are, however, things like propriety, moderation, etc., then they are sufficiently broad, speaking more of an orientation than a specific goal, and would allow the individual a wide range of particular options from which to freely choose, in a manner consistent with classical liberal ideas.

9. Madison writes, "But what is government itself, but the greatest of all reflections on human nature? If men were angels, no government would be necessary. If angels were to govern men, neither

external nor internal controls on government would be necessary. In framing a government which is to be administered by men over men, the great difficulty lies in this: you must first enable the government to control the governed; and in the next place oblige it to control itself." See James Madison, "Federalist No. 51" in Alexander Hamilton, John Jay, and James Madison, *The Federalist Papers*, ed. George W. Carey and James McClellan (Indianapolis: Liberty Fund, 2001), 269.

10. Staël, *The Influence of the Passions*, in *Major Writings*, 153.

11. See Staël's letter, "On the *New Héloïse*": "But if it is true that men cannot be moved without the stimulus of passion—if few of them are set on fire by thought, or rise through enthusiasm for virtue by thought alone without any foreign sentiment giving charm and life to such an abstract love of perfection. . . ." (*Major Writings*, 45). On life's drabness without passion, Madison's "Federalist No. 10" argument about the undesirability of controlling factions by eliminating the cause of faction, liberty, comes to mind. Such a drastic remedy, writes Madison, would be "worse than the disease. . . . But it could not be less folly to abolish liberty, which is essential to political life, because it nourishes faction, than it would be to wish the annihilation of air, which is essential to animal life, because it imparts to fire its destructive agency." (Madison, "Federalist No. 10," in Hamilton, Jay, and Madison, *The Federalist Papers*, 43).

12. Jaucourt's complete entry reads: "Delicate and tender disposition of the soul that makes it easily moved, touched. The sensibility of the soul, as the author of *les moeurs* accurately puts it, imparts a kind of wisdom about propriety, and it goes farther than the penetration of the mind alone. Exuberance may prompt sensitive souls to make mistakes that men of reason would never commit; but they gain so much through the abundance of goodness they generate. Sensible souls get more out of life than others; good and bad multiply to their benefit. Reflection can make a man of honor; but sensibility makes a man virtuous. Sensibility is the mother of humanity and of generosity; it increases worth, it helps the spirit, and it incites persuasion" (Chevalier de Louis Jaucourt, "Sensibility," *The Encyclopedia of Diderot & d'Alembert Collaborative Translation Project*, trans. Christelle Gonthier [Ann Arbor: Scholarly Publishing Office of the University of Michigan Library, 2004], http://hdl.handle.net/2027/spo.did2222.0000.295 [accessed August 13, 2010]).

13. J. Christopher Herold argues that despite the intertwined nature of the personal and the political, the political ideas of the essay are "far more original and fruitful" than the attempts to theorize about personal happiness, for while individual happiness aims at mastery of the passions, political happiness accepts a certain amount of passion as a given. Passion is highly unpredictable in individual cases, but with a larger aggregate (i.e., on a national scale), it is more easily predicted and, thus, more easily managed by the artful statesman. See Herold, *Mistress to an Age: A Life of Madame de Staël* (New York: Grove Press, 2002), 202–3.

14. Which also includes the love of literary glory.

15. Staël, *The Influence of the Passions*, in *Major Writings*, 156, 158–59.

16. Ibid., 158.

17. Ibid., 163.

18. Having described the workings of vanity during the Revolution, Staël continues, "There is no doubt that the rule of fear followed the emulation of vanity, but it is vanity that created this power which destroyed all the spontaneous impulses of men for some time" (ibid., 164).

19. Ibid., 165.

20. "I think that democratic peoples have a natural taste for freedom; left to themselves they will seek it, they will love it, and they will see themselves parted from it only with sorrow. But for equality they have an ardent, insatiable, eternal, invincible passion; they want equality in freedom, and, if they cannot get it, they still want it in slavery" (Alexis de Tocqueville, *Democracy in America*, trans. Harvey C. Mansfield and Delba Winthrop [Chicago: University of Chicago Press, 2000], 482).

21. Abraham Lincoln, "Address to a Young Men's Lyceum of Springfield, Illinois," in *Speeches and Writings, 1832–1858* (New York: The Library of America, 1989), 34.

22. Staël's preface to the 1814 edition of her *Letters on Rousseau* suggests that perfectibility is a process (*Major Writings*, 39–59). See also Aurelian Craiutu, "Moderation and the Groupe de Coppet," in *Germaine de Staël: Forging a Politics of Mediation*, ed. Karyna Szmurlo (Oxford: Voltaire Foundation, 2011), 109–24.

23. *De l'influence des passions sur le bonheur des individus et des nations*, in Germaine de Staël, *Œuvres complètes, Œuvres critiques*, série 1, vol. 1 (Paris: Honoré Champion, 2008), 139.

24. "Je n'entends pas comment on dirige ce qui n'existe qu'en dominant: il n'y a que deux états pour l'homme, ou il est certain d'être le maître au dedans de lui, et alors il n'y a point de passion; ou, il sent qu'il règne en lui-même une puissance plus forte que lui, et alors il dépend entièrement d'elle" (ibid., 155).

25. Staël, *The Influence of the Passions*, in *Major Writings*, 167. The alternative would, of course, be a balance within the soul, of the passions or appetites, and the rational element.

26. Staël does not explicitly state that the natural condition is a balanced one, and the alternate reading—that we are not naturally balanced—is both possible and plausible.

27. Staël, *The Influence of the Passions*, in *Major Writings*, 165.

28. Staël continues, "As soon as we have told ourselves that happiness is unobtainable, we are a good deal closer to reaching something like it" (ibid.).

29. See, for example, Philo's *Every Good Man Is Free*, in *Philo*, trans. F. H. Colson, vol. 9 (Cambridge, MA: Harvard University Press, 1941), 3–4, 22.

30. Staël, *The Influence of the Passions*, in *Major Writings*, 167.

31. How close Staël comes to endorsing Stoic apathy is contested. Morroe Berger, for example, contends that Staël "never advocated their absolute restraint in the name of order, happiness, or anything else," while Angelica Goodden reads Staël as arguing that "the passions ought simply to be neutralized." See Morroe Berger, "Introduction," in *Politics, Literature, and National Character*, by Germaine de Staël, ed. and trans. Morroe Berger (New Brunswick, NJ: Transaction Publishers, 2000), 57; Goodden, *Madame de Staël: The Dangerous Exile* (Oxford: Oxford University Press, 2008), 75. This issue reveals an important difference between Staël and eighteenth-century advocates of Stoicism (or moderated Stoicism) such as Adam Smith. While part 7 of Smith's *Theory of Moral Sentiments* also favors a modified Stoicism, Smith takes explicit issue with Stoic apathy and with a complete renunciation of the passions (*Theory of Moral Sentiments*, ed. D. D. Raphael and A. L. Macfie [Indianapolis: Liberty Fund, 1984]). The contrast between Smith and Staël is particularly interesting for its civic implications: what types of citizens do Stoics (or philosphers) make?

32. César Chesneau Du Marsais, "Philosopher," *The Encyclopedia of Diderot & d'Alembert Collaborative Translation Project,* trans. Dena Goodman (Ann Arbor: Scholarly Publishing Office of the University of Michigan Library, 2002), http://hdl.handle.net/2027/spo.did2222.0000.001 (accessed August 13, 2010).

33. Leo Strauss, *Natural Right and History* (Chicago: The University of Chicago Press, 1953), 251. Strauss is referring to Locke.

34. Jean-Jacques Rousseau, *The First and Second Discourses,* ed. Roger D. Masters and Judith R. Masters (New York: St. Martin's Press, 1964), 147. See also, 149, 156, 179.

35. Tocqueville, *Democracy,* 512. This explains why American souls (or modern souls, more generally) are simultaneously violent and enervated.

36. Though her famous characterization of herself to Chateaubriand as "always alive and sad" ("J'ai toujours été la même, vive et triste") might call into question the possibility of such detachment and its ability to secure happiness. Quoted in Lady Charlotte Blennerhassett, *Madame de Staël: Her Friends and Her Influence in Politics and Literature,* vol. 3 (London: Chapman and Hall, Ltd., 1889), 575.

37. Staël, *The Influence of the Passions,* in *Major Writings,* 166.

38. Staël also notes that imagination's ability to distract us from troubles is a source of happiness, though this seems a less significant aspect of its utility than its ability to influence moral behavior.

39. Staël, *Essay on Fictions,* in *Major Writings,* 61, 71.

40. Mme de Staël acknowledges that the modern novel's reputation has suffered because of its exclusive focus on love. To serve the purposes she envisages for them, novels must move beyond love and depict the range of human emotions, doing for the other emotions what they have done for love— i.e., presenting them in their roundness, giving the readers a complete sense of the other passions' objects, workings, excesses, costs, etc. *On Literature* and *On Germany* offer other suggestions for literature's development. See, for example, the discussion of the "new hero" which *On Literature* sketches in John Clairborne Isbell's *The Birth of European Romanticism: Truth and Propaganda in Staël's De l'Allemagne, 1810–1813* (Cambridge: Cambridge University Press, 1994), 107. Interestingly, however, Herold comments that Mme de Staël's own novels are not of the new form for which she calls (Herold, *Mistress,* 236–37), while Balayé offers an analysis of Mme de Staël's novels in the context of her own theories (Balayé, *Madame de Staël,* chapter 4).

41. Staël, *Essay on Fictions,* in *Major Writings,* 71.

42. See *In Praise of Richardson,* in Denis Diderot, *Selected Writings on Art and Literature,* trans. Geoffrey Bremner (London: Penguin, 1994).

43. Duty is, of course, a social or political concept. Lori Jo Marso develops a pity- (or sympathy-) based account of "alternative politics" in Staël's thought. Susan Tenenbaum also notes sentiment's superiority to self-interest in providing an "inherently ethical faculty as the foundation of modern virtue." See Lori Jo Marso, *(Un)Manly Citizens: Jean-Jacques Rousseau's and Germaine de Staël's Subversive Women* (Baltimore: Johns Hopkins University Press, 1999), 9; and Susan Tenenbaum, "Liberal Heroines: Mme de Staël on the 'Woman Question' and the Modern State," *Annales Benjamin Constant* 5 (1985): 48.

44. Not merely all other literary methods, but all other methods, with no further qualification (Staël, *Essay on Fictions*, in *Major Writings*, 73).

45. See Lady Blennerhassett's discussion of fiction's method of moral instruction: "The outward circumstances must have been taken into account, the motives and intentions watched, the conditions of the mind observed, the impulses comprehended which are to be described. Only at this cost can a work of art be produced, the highest aim of which is to teach and elevate, and, from the height of its powerful influence, to solve for us a moral problem" (*Madame de Staël*, 2:285).

46. Mme de Staël describes the relationship between philosophy and fiction (or between the philosopher and the poet) in the following manner: "Philosophy may be the invisible power in control of fictions, but if she is the first to show herself, she will destroy all of their magic" (*Essay on Fictions*, in *Major Writings*, 61).

47. See Berger, "Introduction," 45.

48. Staël, *Essay on Fictions*, in *Major Writings*, 73. Cf. Machiavelli's description of his own artistry in the Dedicatory Epistle to *The Prince*, trans. Harvey C. Mansfield Jr. (Chicago: University of Chicago Press, 1985).

49. Staël, *Essay on Fictions*, in *Major Writings*, 73.

50. Ibid.

51. See Plato's *Republic*, trans. Allan Bloom (New York: HarperCollins Publishers, 1991), bks. 2, 3, and 10.

4

MELANCHOLY IN THE PURSUIT OF HAPPINESS:
CORINNE AND THE *FEMME SUPÉRIEURE*

Karen de Bruin

I N *ON LITERATURE*—a work that could have been entitled *On Melancholy* with its over thirty references to the "melancholy of northern people"—Germaine de Staël creates a hierarchy of the freest and happiest nations and epochs.[1] In this hierarchy, contemporary England, its regime of political liberty, and its melancholic people rank as superior. With a nod to the humoral theory of climates so prevalent during her time, Staël argues that the natural melancholic temperament of the English, catalyzed by the advent of Christianity, led to their political freedom and relative national happiness because English melancholy naturally begot serious reflection and the resignation of the pain-filled soul to civil service.[2] Staël warns, however, that whereas political freedom begets national happiness, individual happiness "is the impossible in every genre."[3] Hoping to put post-Revolutionary France, which was under the repressive politics of Napoleon, back on the path to freedom and happiness—and ultimately on a path superior to that of England—Staël argues for the cultivation of melancholy on French soil, similar to that of the English.[4]

Ten years later, after the discovery of the "new school" of Germanic thought, Staël elevates melancholy to one of the two components that together comprise "true superiority":

> Sentiment is melancholic, the mind audacious: sentiment looks to the past, the mind to the future; the veritable superiority of man is born from this reverie and this impulse. This mix of contemplation and of activity, of resignation and will, allows man to link to the heavens his life in this world.[5]

The "melancholic sentiment" to which Staël refers in the above passage from *On Germany* is no longer merely a natural sentiment specific to the English, just as the "superiority" to which she refers is no longer comparative. It is this shift from superiority as a relative concept to superiority as an ideal that forms the subtext of Staël's second novel *Corinne, or Italy*, a novel that has as its philosophical bookends *On Literature* and *On Germany*. I will argue that between *On Literature* and *On Germany* Staël succeeds in locating a new philosophical origin of melancholy to help the French—a so-called non-melancholic people—to harness melancholy's impetus toward freedom. I will furthermore argue that she seeks to promote the improvement [*perfectionnement*] of the soul through this philosophical melancholy.[6] To do so, however, Staël needs an individual who can serve as a model of emulation for the nation, and this model is Corinne, *femme supérieure*. Contrary to the vast majority of studies on *Corinne, or Italy* that either see Corinne as "superior" at the beginning of the novel or see her as a (vengeful) failure at the end of the novel, I argue that Corinne's shadow of her former self must be seen as the embodiment of superiority and the most advanced stage of the perfectibility of the human species.[7] Before I trace how Staël came to represent Corinne, at her dénouement, as the model of moral emulation for a nation seeking freedom, however, let me make a few brief remarks about why Staël concluded that France had deviated from the path of the perfectibility of the human species in the first place.

When the French Revolution erupted, Staël was jubilant. Finally, France had the opportunity to throw off the yoke of absolutism in the name of liberty. After the overturn of the first revolutionary constitution, the death of the royal couple, the advent of the Reign of Terror, and the coup d'états of 18 Fructidor and 18 Brumaire, however, Staël realized that a population who doesn't know freedom cannot respect freedom or the institutions conceived to protect it.[8] This conundrum explained, at least in her mind, the successive reversals of institutions conceived to protect France's nascent free republic. Though traumatized by the revolutionary events, Staël refrained from judging the people and the violence they committed. She understood that, for the most part, the French people believed they were responding to calls to virtuous action. The problem, as she saw it, was that the notion of virtue had been hijacked by a few dangerous men who manipulated their factions through fanaticism [*l'esprit de parti*], the most dangerous of passions.[9] This corruption of virtue, Staël believed, was responsible for the moral disorientation of the nation that persisted throughout the Revolution, a disorientation that diverted France from the path of freedom, and put it on course for Napoleon's authoritarian rise to power. A more universal morality had to be defined in order for France to become a free nation.

For Staël, the chaos into which France descended resulted in part from true feelings anchored to false virtue, and in part from false virtue anchored to an expectation of absolute conformity. Consequently, to lead France out of the Revolution would necessitate that moralists and philosophers unhitch feelings like generosity and pity from false virtues like duty toward "public salvation." It would also require that moralists and philosophers ground these feelings in a more universal morality that allowed for resistance and independence of judgment. While Staël understood the problem of political repression to be essentially a moral one, she nevertheless spent many years reflecting on the solution to this problem.

Though in her later discovery of German philosophy, Staël would stumble upon moral liberty as the means of grounding feeling and political and social freedom, in her early years she looked for answers both in moral history and across the Channel, since England appeared to have at last acquired freedom. The solution she proposed in her early nonfiction work, *On Literature*, was the fruit of these reflections. Staël deemed it necessary to try to foster a culture of melancholy in France similar to that in England. By grounding sentiment in a history of moral progress, and by demonstrating that melancholy fueled this movement, as Florence Lotterie points out in her erudite study of progress and perfectibility in eighteenth-century France, Staël hoped to purge from sentiment the tragic connotations derived from the Jacobins.[10]

True to her Enlightenment roots, Staël defines the melancholy of Northern people as that which "inspires the suffering of the soul" and that stems from both "the emptiness that sensibility finds in existence" and "reverie that incessantly makes thought meander from the fatigue of life to the unknown of death."[11] Similar to her French contemporaries, she furthermore associates this natural melancholy with civic virtue or, as Eric Gidal explains, with a "tradition [that] understands melancholy as the dark undercurrent of political identification, removing the individual from vain aspirations and luxurious self-indulgence while simultaneously promoting civic ideals and public engagement."[12] This civic melancholy, inspired by the suffering of the soul and the promotion of civic ideals and public engagement, led the English to political freedom, in her opinion:

> One wonders why the English, who are happy by their government and
> their morals, have an imagination that is much more melancholic than

that of the French. It is because liberty and virtue, the two great results of human reason, require meditation, and meditation leads necessarily to serious objects.[13]

In the passage above, Staël demonstrates her Enlightenment belief in "rational progress guided by moral sentiments."[14] She also infers that, if France is seeking this same political freedom, French writer-philosophers would do well to adopt and propagate a similar reflexive melancholy. In this, Staël, in effect, elevates melancholy to what Julia Kristeva calls the "soul of the elite."[15] If Staël sought, however, to inspire melancholy in the merry French, the question was how to "transplant" this melancholy, since—according to the humoral theory of climates—morosity did not come as naturally to the French as to the English.

In her attempt to transplant melancholy, with the overarching goal of grounding feeling in a universal morality, Staël traced the history of moral progress from Antiquity through the Revolution in *On Literature*. In this analysis, Staël aimed to demonstrate the perfectibility of the human species: namely, the movement of morality, recorded and transmitted through literature, and catalyzed by the advent of Christianity, which tends toward the ideal of liberty, equality and happiness for all.[16] She also sought to prove the existence of a non-humoral melancholy that served as an impetus to the gradual perfection of the human species since the advent of Christianity. While this "great cumulative work of moral nature," as Staël explains, began during Antiquity, it only gained its full momentum when Christianity sanctioned men and women's free choice in marriage and their moral equality before God.[17] This sanction inaugurated woman's moral equality with man, which—in turn—gave rise to domestic love and the possibility of domestic happiness, equality and freedom: "When women became half of the human association is when veritable domestic happiness became known."[18] Staël continues:

> The felicity of man grew from all the independence that the object of his tenderness obtained. He could believe himself loved; a free being was choosing him, a free being was obeying his desires. The glimpses of the mind, the nuances felt by the heart multiplied with the ideas and impressions of these new souls, who were trying on a moral existence after having for a long time languished in life.[19]

In addition to increased domestic happiness, Staël posits that the feeling of love, stemming from the moral equality between men and women, gave rise to a whole new "moral existence" rooted in other feelings, specifically feelings of generosity and pity, which come more naturally to women: "The Moderns, influenced by women, easily gave into the bonds of philanthropy, and the mind became more philosophically free."[20] Following Staël's logic, the taste of *domestic* happiness, freedom and equality initiated by love furthermore allowed both men and women to understand the presence of *universal* happiness, freedom and equality, and to know that universal freedom, equality and happiness were divine, for, as Corinne exclaims, "to love, to go on loving, is what is left to us of our divine heritage."[21]

Tracing the rise of an era of sentiment, so to speak, Staël surgically removes the radical republican referents from feelings of generosity and pity, and substitutes for them the divine origin of love. But, far from giving us a glimpse of human nature through rose-colored glasses, she quickly submits both sentiment and the taste for universal values to melancholy and suffering. While Staël argues that moral equality before God gives rise to the possibility of increased domestic happiness, equality and freedom, she also warns that society is slow to inaugurate these values as governing principles. Consequently, if domestic freedom, equality and happiness find themselves challenged by societal norms and conventions that don't allow for them, the individual and/or couple will inevitably experience a fall from grace that gives rise to melancholy. Whereas Staël recognizes that most individuals will then submit to the greater societal norms with the goal of lessening their suffering, Staël entreats the writer-philosopher to recognize the productive force behind the resulting melancholy and suffering. In other words, Staël calls on the writer-philosopher to recognize this melancholy as a call to throw off all forms of repression—political, social and moral—and to propagate a cult of freedom, equality and happiness for all, reminding her that "man owes his greatest achievements to his aching sensation of unfulfilled destiny."[22] To echo Lotterie's conclusion, it follows then that, for Staël, it is the writer-philosopher's duty to sacrifice herself to the ideals of freedom and equality for as long as moral, social or political repression exists.[23]

Staël represents the writer-philosopher as willing to resist political tyranny and to fight for liberty, equality, and happiness for all in order to promote the perfectibility of the human species. She does not, however, resolve the issue of how to help the writer transcend the suffering of melancholy. She also does not fully answer the question of how to harness melancholy's philosophical power in order to propagate a cult of freedom in France. It is through her novel *Corinne, or Italy* that Staël presents to her readers for the first time the solution of moral freedom, a solution that she will elaborate in much more detail in *On Germany*, her philosophical *exposé* of the "new school" of German thought. She furthermore presents

Corinne to her readers as a woman who, by the end of the novel, transcends her melancholy through her commitment to moral freedom and the propagation of a cult of conscience, thus representing (at least for Staël) the embodiment of the most advanced stage of the perfectibility of the human species. Let us now turn to the novel itself for an illustration of how Staël presents to her readers a new moral model for a nation seeking freedom.

Corinne, or Italy opens in Edinburgh in November 1794, just two weeks after the dissolution of the Jacobin Club in France and four months after the fall of Robespierre. Against the backdrop of the fallen Jacobin sentimentalist regime stands Lord Oswald Nelvil, the melancholic Englishman, who embodies the very pain of an incomplete destiny characteristic of the Northern melancholy of which Staël speaks in *On Literature*: "At twenty-five, he had wearied of life; his mind prejudged everything, and his wounded sensibility no longer had any taste for the illusions of the heart."[24] Poised as the captain of the vessel that will take him across the English channel en route to Rome, the narrator describes Oswald as a man with a great name, a superior mind, a sensitive character, a melancholic disposition, a profound respect for English mores and political liberty, and a sense of sacrifice to both patriotic and patriarchal duty. In a few short opening pages, Oswald cares for a child on the ship, shelters an old man from gale-force winds, and saves ostracized Jews and the sequestered mentally handicapped from ravaging fire despite cries to "let them burn." Though these acts are indeed noble, the narrator informs the reader that "[t]ime and again he effortlessly sacrificed his own preferences to those of others, but generosity alone could not explain such completely disinterested abnegation."[25] Motivated by civic melancholy, a temperament natural to the English, such selfless acts stand in stark contrast to Jacobin executions of enemies of the republic in the name of moral virtue. They also lead the reader to believe that Oswald's civic-minded melancholy could be the very temperament that Staël seeks to cultivate in France. This belief becomes quickly complicated, however, when Oswald falls in love with Corinne.

Oswald first witnesses Corinne at a coronation held to honor "the most celebrated woman in Italy . . . poet, writer, *improvisatrice*, and one of the most beautiful women in Rome."[26] Shortly, she will be crowned in the male tradition that also crowned Petrarch and Tasso. With Oswald at the coronation are throngs of Romans from all social ranks. With each moment that passes, the curiosity of the Italian people transforms into jubilant enthusiasm. They applaud at every opportunity, at which point the narrator exclaims: "In their present situation Italians are allowed but one glory: the fine arts. Their vivid sense of this form of genius should give rise to many great men, yet mere acclaim is not enough to bring them forth; only intense life, lofty concerns, and an independent existence can nourish thought."[27] Through the inference that Italy has never been able to equal politically, socially or morally the greatness of Rome, the narrator echoes Staël's judgment of modern-day Italians: "In their political and moral situation, the soul cannot develop entirely. Their sensibility is not serious, their greatness is not imposing, and their sadness is not somber."[28] When Corinne finally speaks, she seems to mirror this lack of "serious sensibility," greatness and "somber sadness" that Staël attributes to the Italians.[29] During her improvisations she sings the praises of Ancient Rome, and of Renaissance poets, artists and savants, the great men that Staël herself criticizes for their poetic exaggerations and lack of serious sensitivity.[30]

For the moment, Corinne, heralded by the Romans as one of their own, does not seem to offer a serious alternative to the civic melancholy that Oswald has already demonstrated. Indeed—despite the rich imagery and symbolism surrounding Corinne and her coronation—Corinne, "dressed like Domenichino's Sibyl," offers no prophetic message, nor does she offer any real superiority over her predecessors, Petrarch and Tasso.[31] By no means should the crowned Corinne be taken to represent a "superior woman" worthy of emulation. (In fact, symbolically, Corinne's crown falls after her eloquent improvisations.) At this beginning point of the novel, Corinne can be said to embody an Italy who, because limited by political repression, can do no more than to retrace the same path as her predecessors.[32] As the embodiment of a culture, Corinne thus represents the state of the perfectibility of the human species in its early years, namely before the advent of Christianity and the introduction of love. It is to the shadow of her former self at the end of the novel that the reader must look for Corinne's real superiority.

In this early stage of the novel, it is Lord Oswald Nelvil of Scotland who better represents the "somber sadness" that Staël deems necessary to the philosophical and moral development of a nation. Before Corinne's improvisations, the melancholic Oswald remains skeptical and unmoved: "His gaze, fixed on her, seemed to chide her gently."[33] However, when Corinne lays eyes on him for the first time, recognizes his features as English, and sees his skepticism, she quickly empathizes with his melancholic disposition: "Divining the thoughts going through his mind, she was impelled to meet his need by talking of happiness with less certainty, by devoting a few verses to death in the midst of the celebration."[34] Able to perform such a quick transition to a more romantic discourse on sentiment and death, Corinne—of English patrilineage herself—wins over Oswald, who finds himself delighted by these last verses. Quite predictably, Oswald seeks out Corinne who, mutually charmed, offers to take him on a journey through the masterpieces of Rome and the beauties of Roman culture.

Throughout the tour, although enamored of his guide, Oswald can neither suppress his skepticism of her fascination for the masterpieces of Rome nor his discomfort with Corinne's social independence. To begin with an example of Oswald's skepticism towards the beauties of Roman culture: when Corinne brings him before St. Peter's Basilica she exclaims, "When a monument symbolizing so many noble and generous ideas is given to the nation, it is even a service to public morality."[35] Oswald responds: "Yes . . . the arts are magnificent here; the imagination shows genius; but what about human dignity, how is that protected? What institutions, what weakness in most Italian governments! And even in their weakness, how they enslave the spirit!"[36] Suggesting that England has succeeded, at least politically, in founding its society upon the universal values of liberty and equality, Oswald cannot overcome his disdain for the lack of gravity and philosophy in Italy. He remains convinced that the English are more virtuous than the Italians because they are more attached to "the cult of sorrow," a cult that defines virtue as the resignation of the pain-filled soul to public service.[37] Oswald's second discomfort—Corinne's social independence—is best exemplified in the scene where Corinne and Oswald are at a Roman ball that "Lord Nelvil still bitterly resented."[38] Oswald is concerned about compromising Corinne by spending so much time alone with her in the presence of the Roman social elite. Corinne responds: "There is no reason to worry. . . . No one will pay any attention. It is common practice here to do as you please in society; there are no set standards, nothing to take into consideration . . . Liberty, as you understand it in England, is certainly not to be found in this land, but we do enjoy perfect social independence."[39] To which Oswald replies non-interrogatively: "That is to say there is no respect for morals."[40]

This exchange highlights the beginning of a fissure that will, by the end of the novel, transform into a rift between Corinne and Oswald, namely around the subject of how to define liberty. For Oswald, any society that would give as much social independence to women would be antithetical to a society in which real political freedom can exist, and thus he dismisses the very notion of social independence. Instead, Oswald argues for a society that defines the individual as *he* who obeys all laws and who submits entirely to his duty toward convention and public opinion, even if this definition rejects women as both citizens and individuals (thus relegating them entirely to the domestic sphere). Corinne disagrees. Rejecting the definition of English political liberty that requires absolute conformity of all—and especially the women—to very specific social conventions and morals,

Corinne chooses Italian social independence, which allows for a certain amount of social freedom within a larger context of political absolutism. This choice is not surprising since Corinne left England after realizing that her enthusiasm, imagination and highly-developed faculty of reason—all developed during her youth in Italy—could never be integrated into the "systematized regularity" of English domestic life.[41] In fact, in a later letter to Oswald, she asks him: "Is not every woman, as much as every man, obliged to make her way according to her own character and talents? And must we forever imitate the instinct of the bees, one swarm following another, without progress and without change?"[42]

At this stage of the novel, Oswald and Corinne do not realize that they are slaves to their respective ideas of freedom. Since neither has experienced what Staël considers to be the first true moment of freedom—that is, freedom in the choice of love—both remain slaves to their respective conventions. They do not yet recognize that it is at the conjuncture of personal freedom and political liberty that true freedom can exist. Consequently, neither Corinne nor Oswald yet embodies the liberal thinker that Staël believes should serve as moral compass for a future free French republic.

Despite his discomfort with her social independence and his skepticism of the greatness of Roman culture, Oswald continues to let himself be led through Rome by the enchanting Corinne. Faster than he can realize, Oswald falls in love. Curiously, at the moment when he declares his love for her, his skepticism of the Roman arts transforms temporarily into the very appreciation for what he had before disdained: "But who knows whether it is not really the deep tenderness you are stirring up in my heart that makes me sensitive to everything I see?"[43] For the first time since his arrival in Italy, Oswald admits that "nature sets you dreaming more in Italy than anywhere else . . . she is more in touch with man here and . . . the creator uses her like a language between His creatures and Himself."[44] At least for several moments, Oswald's preponderant faculty of reason gives way to love, as he experiences for the first time the feeling of total freedom from society, convention and propriety.

When Corinne first experiences the feeling of love, she too feels freedom for the first time. With tears in her eyes she declares to Oswald: "I am free and I love you as I have never loved."[45] Freed from convention and societal norms, Corinne exclaims, "Unquestionably, it is through love that we can understand eternity! Love muddles all sense of time; it erases the notion of beginning and end."[46] Thanks to the feeling of love, Corinne and Oswald experience freedom. However, as both Corinne and Oswald's trajectories will demonstrate, this moment of freedom is ephemeral. Very quickly Oswald becomes subsumed by English convention, and Corinne falls victim to the tyranny of the passions. Neither, however, escapes the debilitating melancholy that ensues from this first experience of freedom, equality and happiness.

Soon after he experiences love and freedom for the first time, Oswald begins to worry about how Corinne, a woman of superior mind and independence, could fit into his life defined by the morals and social conventions of England: "But even though he admired Corinne, even though he loved her, he remembered how little such a woman fit in with the English way of life, how different she was from his father's idea of a suitable wife for him."[47] The feeling of love proves not to be strong enough to combat the rigid moral and social order to which Oswald belongs. As a consequence, Oswald decides to abandon the state of personal harmony whereby his amorous feelings free him to think outside of the box of moral convention, deciding instead to fulfill the will of his deceased father who reminds him: "A man born in our fortunate country must be English first and foremost: he must fulfill his duties as a citizen since he has the good fortune to be a citizen. And in countries whose political institutions give men honorable occasions to act and prove themselves, women should remain in the background."[48] Oswald chooses to return to England to follow his passion for glory in battle as the French count Erfeuil predicts: "Lord Nelvil is a man like any other. . . . He will go back to his country, pursue his career: in a word, he will be reasonable."[49] This decision to return to England to pursue his military career should not be construed as a self-sacrificing act in the name of English political liberty, however. On the contrary, Oswald's choice to return to England is motivated by a desire to attenuate the emotion he sustains when he learns that his love defies his father's patriarchal English wishes. In a symbolic decision that pits "natural" northern melancholy against the philosophical melancholy that results from the conflict between true love and social convention, Oswald chooses to uphold repressive social convention instead of resisting such convention in the name of liberty, equality and happiness for all, including women.[50] In doing so, he deviates from the perfectibility of the human species in order to privilege his *amour propre*, his own self-interest. Consequently, he loses what Staël calls his "moral dignity," which she defines in *Reflections on Suicide* as follows:

> What characterizes the true dignity of man is devotion. . . . The elevation of the soul tends incessantly toward our liberation from what is purely individual in order to unite us with the great visions of the Creator of the universe. Love and thought only relieve and exalt us through their

capacity to lift us up from selfish impressions. Devotion and enthusiasm are what cause a purer air to enter our bosoms. *Amour propre*, irritation and impatience are the enemies against whom our conscience requires us to fight, and the fabric of a moral being's life is composed almost entirely of action and reaction of our inside forces against outside circumstances. . . . [Conscience] is the true measurement of man's greatness, but it only merits our admiration in the generous being who turns it toward himself, and who knows how to sacrifice himself when conscience commands.[51]

While Oswald chooses the route of submission to English norms and conventions—conventions that consider the masculine passions of glory and honor to be admirable—Corinne quickly realizes that she is losing the object of her love. As Oswald begins to show signs of understanding that a marriage with Corinne would not only go against the will of his father but also against English public opinion, Corinne's love transforms into blinding passion. With the goal of holding on to the object of her devotion, Corinne renounces her independent life as poetess, and simultaneously her commitment to her superior intellect [*esprit supérieur*] in order to try to fit the mold of the subservient English woman: "I am leaving to follow Oswald, without even knowing what fate he plans for me, him whom I prefer to the independent lot that has given me so many happy days!"[52] At this moment when Corinne chooses to give up her social independence and life as a crowned poetess in order to follow the object of her love and to conform to Oswald's set of social conventions, Corinne experiences melancholy for the first time:

> Breaking with all her customary practices gave Corinne a melancholy feeling: for several years she had created an enjoyable style of life for herself; she was the center for all there was in the way of famous artists and enlightened men; perfect independence in ideas and practices lent great charm to her existence. What was to become of her now?[53]

Aware that she can no longer follow the path trodden by her male predecessors, the "celebrated artists and the enlightened men" of Rome, and no longer able to ignore her feelings, Corinne describes her newfound melancholy to Oswald: "There are only two distinct ways of feeling nature: animate it like the ancients . . . or, like the Scottish bards, yield to mystery's terror, to the melancholy prompted by the uncertain and the unknown. Since I have known you, Oswald, the northern way appeals to me."[54]

However, what Corinne does not yet realize is that this newfound melancholy is, in reality, a product of having experienced freedom, equality and happiness through love, and then experiencing the fall from freedom and happiness. Much like Oswald who submits to his *amour propre*, Corinne tries to chase the individual feeling of happiness by chasing the object of love: Oswald. However, the more she pursues the object, the more her divine love transforms into tyrannical passion. Corinne deviates, like Oswald, from the universal and the path of the perfectibility of the human species. This explains why she confusedly declares:

> Astonishing mystery of love! A splendid or worthless feeling! Religious as the martyrs of old or colder than the most elementary friendship. Does what is most involuntary in the world come from heaven or from earthly passions? Must we yield to it or struggle against it? Ah! what storms take place in the depths of our heart![55]

Contrary to Oswald (who has an array of socially revered passions that he can choose to follow in order to muffle the melancholy in his heart), Corinne (who had once single-mindedly dedicated herself to the arts of poetry and improvisation as well as to the masculine pursuit of glory) is left alone with the passion of love. By virtue of relegating herself to the socially repressive private sphere, reserved for women, Corinne has no other socially acceptable passions that she can indulge. Consequently, she finds herself alone with her suffering and melancholy. In contrast to Oswald, who has the option of forever silencing his conscience through conformity to social convention and socially acceptable passions, Corinne is left alone with her suffering. It is, perhaps, this proximity to her feelings that allows her to be more susceptible to rediscovering the divine whisper of conscience. Despite her devotion to him, when she realizes that Oswald is entertaining thoughts of marrying her half-sister Lucile, a traditional young English woman, Corinne commits the ultimate act of "moral dignity": she sacrifices her love. Instead of deciding to pursue her individual happiness, she decides instead to obey her conscience and to follow the path of "elevation of the soul." The narrator describes this scene:

> As she made this vow, supreme effort of her soul, Corinne drew from her breast the letter with Oswald's ring. . . . Lucile's innocence, her youth, her purity exalted Corinne's imagination, and for a moment at least, she was proud to sacrifice herself so that Oswald might be in peace with his country, with his family, with himself.[56]

This ultimate act of self-sacrifice places Corinne on the path of moral freedom, for she resigns herself to "abdicating personality in order to be reabsorbed in the universal order."[57] Henceforth, she enters into direct communication with her conscience as she explains to Oswald in a letter to him five years later:

> And what was left for my conscience if I wanted one last day, one last hour? Because I have managed to give up seeing you, perhaps I will be more confident now when I appear before God. This fine resolve will bring peace to my soul. The happiness I felt when you loved me is not in harmony with our nature. . . . But regular prayer—religious reverie whose goal is self-perfection and decisions made solely through the sense of duty—is a sweet state of mind.[58]

Corinne finally finds peace in the abdication of her desire's object and in devotion to her conscience. As such, she experiences the reformation of her soul through moral liberty, a liberty that Staël will define in *On Germany* as an individual's duty to act in accordance with her conscience.[59] It is, furthermore, her self-sacrifice to divine will that puts her on the path to martyrdom:

> Every heroic action is inspired by moral liberty: the act of devotion to divine will. This act that all sensations combat and that enthusiasm alone inspires is so noble and so pure that angels themselves, virtuous by nature and without obstacle, could envy it in man.[60]

Corinne's newfound sense of sacrifice leads her to devote herself to the moral education of future generations of women, represented by the education that she provides to her niece, Juliette. Corinne teaches Juliette that *perfectionnement de soi* [self-improvement] consists in one's continued commitment to the perfectibility of the human species, a view that Staël shares when she writes: "Since happiness is not the goal of human life, man [or in this case woman] must tend to *perfectionnement*."[61] For Corinne, true perfection lies in the relationship between a woman of superior mind and the Divine, and it is this relationship that women must cultivate. The *femme d'esprit supérieur* must not let herself be guided entirely by her reason, swept away by passion, nor subjugated by societal norms for, as Corinne exclaims, "Men do not know the harm they do, and society persuades them that it is a game to fill a heart with happiness, only to follow up with despair."[62] She must let herself be guided uniquely by her conscience and her commitment to freedom. Corinne warns, however, that marginalization, suffering, and melancholy are permanent components of the lives of women who sacrifice themselves to the universal values of liberty and happiness through devotion to their conscience. These few true female martyrs must transcend their suffering and melancholy to trace a path superior to the only two paths open to women of superior mind: the masculine intellectual tradition or the subservient domestic role. Women of superior mind must tread a new moral path both for other women and for humanity. As Staël writes in "On Women Writers":

> Enlightening, teaching and perfecting women together with men on the national level: this must be the secret for the achievement of . . . the establishment of any permanent social or political relationships.
>
> . . . And indeed, by developing their rational minds one might well be enlightening them as to the misfortunes often connected with their fate; but that same reasoning would apply to the effect of enlightenment on the happiness of the human race in general, a question which seems to me to have been decided once and for all.[63]

At the end of the novel, Corinne truly becomes a martyr for both the women's cause and for freedom. Rather than contemplating suicide, which Staël considers to be a selfish act, Corinne is motivated by a newfound sociability that can be defined as devotion to women, to freedom and to humanity. She sacrifices herself to the cult of conscience, thus embodying the definition of martyr as defined by Staël:

> In effect, isn't the greatest example of the sacrifice of life the basis of Christian beliefs? and doesn't this example bring out the contrast that exists between martyrdom and suicide? The martyr serves the cause of virtue through the letting of her blood for the teaching of the world. . . . The martyr teaches men what force exists in conscience. . . .[64]

Though her melancholy was acquired and not "natural," Corinne attains moral superiority through her complete devotion to the divine ideals for which conscience serves as medium. She exclaims in her last writing before her death:

> There is nothing narrow, nothing slavish, nothing limited in religion: she is boundless, infinite, eternal. Genius is far from turning us away from her, for imagination passes beyond life's boundaries at first flight, and in every form the sublime is a reflection of the divine.
>
> Ah! had I loved only her, had I set my head in the heavens, safe from the stormy affections, I would not be broken before my time. . . .

My genius, if it still survives, can be sensed only through the strength of my sorrow. . . .[65]

To which one could imagine Staël responding as she does in *On Germany*:

> Religious *mysticité* brings with it a light that shines so far, that it gives a very decided moral superiority to those who hadn't received it through nature. They apply themselves to the study of the human heart . . . and go through as much trouble to know passions in order to better appease them as men of the world do to use them. Of course it is possible to find great faults in the characters of those in whom the doctrine is the purest: but should one attack their doctrine?[66]

This last question anticipates the objections that critics of Corinne would raise throughout the centuries. Despite her faults and her lack of "natural melancholy," Corinne nevertheless demonstrates courage and dedication to the perfectibility of the human species. As such, she is indeed a model of superiority for the "great men" of France who neither objected to the Terror nor stood up to Napoleon.[67] Benjamin Constant, one of Napoleon's greatest detractors and arguably Staël's best friend, only began to publish his criticisms of Napoleon after his fall. Staël, to the contrary, who upheld the ideal of moral liberty, and whom many generations of female writers came to conflate with her heroine, never faltered in her resistance to political oppression.

Notes

1. This word count was run on Germaine de Staël, *De la littérature considérée dans ses rapports avec les institutions sociales*, eds. Gérard Gengembre and Jean Goldzink (Paris: Garnier-Flammarion, 1991), in the ARTFL-FRANTEXT database, using the terms "mélancolie" and "mélancolique." All translations are mine unless otherwise indicated. I would like to thank the Dean and Provost's Office of the University of Rhode Island for their generous support as well as the University of Rhode Island Council for Research and the URI Interlibrary Loan Office.

2. Eric Gidal, an authority on the representations of melancholy in eighteenth- and nineteenth-century Europe, calls this melancholy to which Staël refers "civic melancholy," as I shall highlight later in the chapter. See Eric Gidal, "Civic Melancholy: English Gloom and French Enlightenment," *Eighteenth-Century Studies* 37 (2003): 23–45.

3. Germaine de Staël, *The Influence of the Passions on the Happiness of Individuals and Nations*, in *Major Writings of Germaine de Staël*, ed. and trans. Vivian Folkenflik (New York: Columbia University Press, 1992), 154.

4. Here I echo Gidal's claim in "Civic Melancholy," wherein he states that Staël sought to "transplant" the English melancholic temperament to France.

5. Germaine de Staël, *De l'Allemagne*, ed. Jean de Pange, intro. by Simone Balayé (Paris: Hachette, 1958–1960), 5:75.

6. Thus echoing Gidal's conclusion that by the end of Staël's life, she is attempting to reform the European soul (Gidal, "Madame de Staël and the Sociology of Melancholy," in *The English Malady: Enabling and Disabling Fictions*, ed. Glen Colburn [Newcastle upon Tyne: Cambridge Scholars, 2008], 33). For an excellent study of how Staël seeks to reform the European soul through German pre-Romantic philosophy, see John Claiborne Isbell's *The Birth of European Romanticism: Truth and Propaganda in Staël's* De l'Allemagne, *1810–1813* (Cambridge: Cambridge University Press, 1994).

7. There are many studies that see Corinne's trajectory as that of failure or of revenge. Most pertinent to this article are Anne Amend-Söchting's analysis of Corinne's vengeful and veiled suicide in "La Mélancolie dans *Corinne*," in *Madame de Staël*, Corinne ou l'Italie, "*l'âme se mêle à tout*," ed. José-Luis Diaz (Paris: SEDES, 1999), and most recently, Souad Bouhouch's analysis of Corinne's fall from sublimity to tragedy in "*Corinne ou l'Italie*: Une esthétique d'un savoir tragique," *Cahiers staëliens* 61 (2011): 165–95. For an extensive list of additional studies on Corinne's trajectory as failure, see chapter 4 of my dissertation entitled "'La Femme supérieure': L'individu, le roman et la république de Germaine de Staël" (PhD diss., University of Chicago, 2007).

8. For more on Germaine de Staël's direct political involvement in the aftermath of each one of these reversals, see the chapter entitled "La Révision de la constitution" in Patrice Gueniffey's *Le Dix-huit brumaire: L'épilogue de la Révolution française* (Paris: Gallimard, 2008).

9. Germaine de Staël, *De l'influence des passions et autres essais moraux*, in *Œuvres complètes*, série 1, *Œuvres critiques*, ed. Florence Lotterie, vol. 1 (Paris: Champion, 2008), 225.

10. Florence Lotterie, *Progrès et perfectibilité: Un dilemme des Lumières françaises (1755–1814)* (Oxford: Voltaire Foundation, 2006), 140.

11. Staël, *De la littérature*, 203.

12. Gidal, "Civic Melancholy," 25. For more on Gidal's concept of civic melancholy, see also his more recent study, "Melancholy, Trauma and National Character: Mme de Staël's *Considérations sur les principaux événements de la Révolution française*," *Studies in Romanticism* 49 (2010): 261–92.

13. Staël, *De la littérature*, 241.

14. Of Staël's belief in the perfectibility of the human species as a movement that should guide rational progress toward political freedom, Gidal writes: "A true disciple of the French Enlightenment, [Staël's] fictional, theoretical, autobiographical, and historical writings all profess a faith in rational progress guided by moral sentiments as means for overcoming political repression and spiritual degradation" ("Mme de Staël and the Sociology of Melancholy," 24).

15. Julia Kristeva, "Gloire, deuil et écriture. Lettre à un 'romantique' sur Mme de Staël," *Romantisme* 62 (1988): 12.

16. Rousseau invents the neologism "perfectibility" in his *Discourse on the Origin of Inequality*. See Jean-Jacques Rousseau, *Discours sur l'origine et les fondements de l'inégalité parmi les hommes. Discours sur les sciences et les arts*, ed. Jacques Roger (Paris: Flammarion, 1992). For a detailed analysis

of the concepts of progress and perfectibility in the eighteenth century, see Lotterie's *Progrès et perfectibilité*.

17. Staël, *De la littérature*, 87.

18. Ibid., 171.

19. Ibid.

20. Ibid., 181.

21. Germaine de Staël, *Corinne, or Italy*, ed. and trans. Avriel Goldberger (New Brunswick, NJ: Rutgers University Press, 1987), 183. Staël is undoubtedly making reference to passages in the New Testament such as Galatians 3:28: "There is neither Jew nor Greek, there is neither bond nor free, there is neither male nor female: for ye are all one in Jesus Christ."

22. Staël, *On Literature*, in *Major Writings*, 177.

23. See Florence Lotterie, "Madame de Staël. La Littérature comme 'philosophie sensible,'" *Romantisme*, 34, no. 124 (2004): 27.

24. Staël, *Corinne, or Italy*, 3.

25. Ibid.

26. Ibid., 19.

27. Ibid., 20.

28. Staël, *De la littérature*, 201.

29. In *De la littérature*, Staël explains that, at least in her opinion, the Italians never succeeded in surpassing their Ancient Roman predecessors in literature, philosophy and the arts, and thus have not evolved as have the northern countries. See her chapter entitled: "De la littérature italienne et espagnole" in *De la littérature*.

30. See her critiques of Petrarch and Tasso, for example, in her chapter entitled "De la littérature italienne et espagnole" in *De la littérature*.

31. Staël, *Corinne, or Italy*, 21.

32. Staël writes, "The Italians, prevented by their governments and their priests from exploring anything having to do with philosophical ideas, have only been able to retrace their same steps, and as a consequence weaken" (*De la littérature*, 200).

33. Staël, *Corinne, or Italy*, 30.

34. Ibid.

35. Ibid., 59.

36. Ibid.

37. Ibid., 58.

38. Ibid., 94.

39. Ibid., 95.

40. Ibid.

41. Ibid., 259.

42. Ibid., 255.

43. Ibid., 87.

44. Ibid.

45. Ibid., 80.

46. Ibid., 141.

47. Ibid., 89.

48. Ibid., 329.

49. Ibid., 188.

50. For a Freudian analysis of how Oswald's melancholy causes him to desire initially to reproduce the social order of the father, see Margaret Cohen's "Melancholia, Mania and the Reproduction of the Dead Father," in *The Novel's Seductions: Staël's* Corinne *in Critical Inquiry*, ed. Karyna Szmurlo (Lewisburg: Bucknell University Press, 1999), 95–113.

51. Staël, *Réflexions sur le suicide*, in *Œuvres complètes*, 370.

52. Staël, *Corinne, or Italy*, 287.

53. Ibid., 190.

54. Ibid., 301.

55. Ibid., 369.

56. Ibid., 357.

57. Staël, *Reflections on Suicide*, in *Major Writings*, 352.

58. Staël, *Corinne, or Italy*, 408.

59. Referring to conscience as the foundation of feeling, and inspired by Kant, Staël writes in *On Germany*: "Feeling is what assures us of our freedom, and this freedom is the foundation of the doctrine of duty. If man is free, he must create his own all-powerful motives to fight the influence of the outside world, and disengage our will from egoism. Duty is the proof and guarantee of man's metaphysical independence" (*Major Writings*, 309).

60. Staël, *De l'Allemagne*, 4:50.

61. Staël, *Réflexions sur le suicide*, in *Œuvres complètes*, 363.

62. Staël, *Corinne, or Italy*, 418.

63. Staël, *On Literature*, in *Major Writings*, 205.

64. Staël, *Réflexions sur le suicide*, in *Œuvres complètes*, 365.

65. Staël, *Corinne, or Italy*, 416.

66. Staël, *De l'Allemagne*, 5:108.

67. For more on the history of this "great man," see the article by Jean-Claude Bonnet, "Le Culte des grands hommes en France au XVIIIe siècle ou la défaite de la monarchie," *MLN* 116 (2001): 689–704. See also my article entitled, "The Helm and the Compass: The Great Man and the Superior Woman in Germaine de Staël's Republic," in *Héroïsme et Lumières*, ed. Sylvain Menant and Robert Morrissey (Paris: Honoré Champion, 2010), 235–50.

II

INTERNATIONAL AESTHETICS

5

THE PERIPHERAL HEROINE TAKES CENTER STAGE: FROM OWENSON'S NATIONAL TALE TO STAËL'S EUROPEAN GENRE

M. Ione Crummy

ERMAINE DE STAËL'S *Corinne, or Italy* (1807), in which the eponymous heroine, the archetypal woman of artistic genius, introduces her Scottish lover to Italian civilization, is credited with demonstrating "how the characteristic social relations of a nation nurtured its distinctive cultural productions."[1] Textual evidence, however, suggests that Staël's *Corinne, or Italy* was inspired by *The Wild Irish Girl: A National Tale* (1806) by Sydney Owenson (later Lady Morgan), in which the intelligent, talented heroine instructs her English admirer about Irish culture. The fame of Staël's text has overshadowed Owenson's immensely successful national tale, despite the fact that, as Geneviève Gennari noted in 1947, the Irish novel predated the French one—by eight months.[2] During Owenson's lifetime she was called "the Irish Corinne" and the "Irish de Staël," which Claire Connolly considers Owenson's "greatest public relations triumph."[3] Most scholars who have noted similarities between the two texts assume that the more famous French novel influenced the Irish one.[4] Caroline Franklin has remarked that Staël reemploys in *Corinne* Owenson's tactic in *The Wild Irish Girl* of using "a heroine embodying the colonized nation, to charm the British traveler and the reader at the same time within a travelogue framed by a courtship narrative," but does not examine Owenson's influence on Staël.[5] Deirdre Lynch makes her claim a little bolder, stating that by "explicitly imitating" Macpherson's *Ossian* and Owenson's *The Wild Irish Girl* in *Corinne*, Staël "renders the bardic generic."[6] In this chapter I investigate how Staël transformed Owenson's national tale into a European genre, first establishing the similarities between the texts that suggest Owenson's tale served as a source of inspiration for Staël's novel, then emphasizing the key differences that rendered Staël's novel of more universal application and appeal.

When Sydney Owenson published *The Wild Irish Girl* in August 1806, "her aspiration was to make her native country better known and to dissipate the political and religious prejudices that hindered its prosperity."[7] Before the publication of her *National Tale*, Owenson asserts, no "fictitious narrative, founded on national grievances, and borne out by historic fact, had yet appealed to the sympathies of the general reader"; the novel-travelogue's "subtle political argument" riveted even "masculine minds," thus blurring lines between genres and genders.[8] *The Literary Journal* of November 1806 criticized Owenson's "very singular work" because "Scenes of love and courtship . . . are intermixed with long antiquarian discourses" that attempt "to prove that Ireland was once the Athens of the world." The reviewer mocked the Irish princess whose "accomplishments in all kinds of learning, her sense, eloquence, sensibility, . . . and all the virtues and charms of body and mind, are of the first order and transcend every thing heard of."[9] A poem in the *Monthly Magazine* on September 1, 1806, extolled Owenson's national mission, evoking a woman of genius crowned with a laurel wreath—the object of a nation's gratitude, who reclaims national cultural pride through her works of imagination and public musical performances.[10] Staël, who may have read this praise of Owenson in the *Monthly Magazine* (to which she subscribed), lauds these qualities in her heroine Corinne, who is honored by her compatriots for using her genius to enhance the glory of her native Italy.[11] Another review in the *Monthly Magazine*, January 25, 1807, praised Owenson's "knowledge of the literature and antiquities of her native country," admired her "genius and taste" and claimed that her "delineations of the Irish customs and manners . . . rectify the judgment of the reader."[12] Mirroring Owenson's project for the Irish in her national tale, in *Corinne* Staël's goal was to help her readers truly discover Italians, "to give them back the reputation for sincerity and wit."[13]

Staël's text also embodies the novel-travelogue pioneered by Owenson. Although Staël originally conceived of *Corinne* merely as a novel set in Italy, by mid November 1806 she was privileging Italy in the work, and by early February 1807, she called it a *roman-voyage* that she hoped would interest both the intellectual Dr. Louis Odier and his daughters.[14] Staël's remarks bespeak a literary project like Owenson's to blur lines of genre and gender. The transformation of Staël's novel into a novel-travelogue coincides with her mid-September to late-November 1806 stay at Rouen—a stop on the route to England, from whence she corresponded with literary anglophile friends in Paris.[15] Journalist J.-B.-A. Suard, who assiduously read the *Critical Review*, may have seen its November 1806 review of Owenson's novel.[16] That periodical's criticism of her copious "disquisitions on the manners of the Irish," and her "lengthened argument on the comparative antiquity of the Scotch or Irish poetry,"[17] would have piqued Suard's interest, given the recent republication of his translations of Ossian.[18] Staël shared Suard's interest in Ossian, having discussed the chants of the "fourth-century bard" in *On Literature* as the earliest example of Northern poetry.[19] During August and September 1806 in Paris, Suard enjoyed the society of his friend Dugald Stewart, who had accompanied Lord Lauderdale, head of the British peace delegation.[20] Stewart entrusted to Suard, as the man who first introduced the poetry of Ossian in France, a paper on its authenticity for the Celtic Academy of Paris from the Highlands Society of London.[21] In mid-September, Staël, through her friend de Gerando, corresponded with Professor Stewart about sending her son to Edinburgh University.[22] Thus, through her friends in Paris, Staël was in contact with British intellectuals immediately following the publication of *The Wild Irish Girl*—as her text became a novel-travelogue. Staël entitled the work *Corinne, or Italy* to create a double expectation of a work on both a woman and Italy, and sought to have publicity advertise it as "a travelogue and not a novel."[23]

Several key aspects Owenson had emphasized in *The Wild Irish Girl* are stressed in Simonde de Sismondi's July 1807 article on Staël's *Corinne*: The author's "new ingenious way" of using a patriotic heroine to extol her homeland's natural beauty, cultural productions, and the lively poetic imagination of all classes of its people, despite political repression.[24] Sismondi praised in *Corinne* "a noble vindication [*apologie*] in favor of a people that all others have long treated with ingratitude" and judged her depiction of Italy "equitable, exact and true in the slightest details," able to "excite for them the affection of foreigners."[25] The *Edinburgh Review*, in October 1807, noted her text's intermixing of "a fictitious narrative" with descriptions of Italian points of interest, and underlined the key role of "the difference of national character" between Great Britain and Italy that is "personified and contrasted in the hero and heroine."[26] It was Owenson, however, who first combined descriptions of Irish culture with the romance of protagonists who personify their respective nations.

Ina Ferris considers what Owenson dubbed the national tale to be an explicit critique and rewriting of the Irish tour genre and its civic assumptions, for through the romance plot of encounter it subjects the metropolitan traveler to a "disorientation that alters his center of personal and national being."[27] Ferris also notes that due to the national tale's address to an English reader, it was dismissed as a "naïve colonialist genre."[28] Yet in *Corinne* Staël used the "performative" national tale to praise the cultural riches of Italy (a politically disenfranchised country like

Ireland), thereby transforming bardic nationalism from a genre of the Celtic peripheries to one of the European center.[29]

Let us now examine the textual similarities between the two travel-novels
to ascertain how Staël transforms Owenson's national tale into a European genre.
Each text begins with a young Englishman who travels abroad due to filial remorse. The patronymic of Owenson's Glorvina O'Melville is even echoed in Staël's
hero Lord Nelvil. Her male protagonist was still called Lord Sydney in February
1807 and, as Geneviève Gennari attests, the change to Nelvil only occurred in the
final manuscript version of *Corinne*.[30] Gennari considers Staël's choice of the patronymic Nelvil an allusion to Admiral Nelson, while James Marshall suggests that
Staël sought to avoid confusion with Sir Sidney Smith. I posit that Staël's initial
choice of the name Sydney points to her Irish model, and that she finally opted
for Nelvil as a more discrete acknowledgment of her debt to Owenson's novel.
The epistolary *Wild Irish Girl* opens with the arrival in Ireland of Horatio M—,
banished by his father for having neglected his legal studies and having been drawn
in by a married woman, whose complicit husband has taken legal action against
him. His gullibility in the affair with Lady C—, "equally victim to the husband's
villany as the wife's artifice," resembles Oswald's manipulation by Mme d'Arbigny,
for whom he ignored his father's pleas to return to England.[31] Thus both heroes
fail to live up to paternal moral standards, expressed in each novel through letters
of fatherly disapproval or moral dicta.

When he arrives in Ireland, Horatio has "a decided prejudice" against the
country, which he considers "semi-barbarous, semi-civilised," an attitude echoed
in Oswald's "prejudice" against Italians and Italy.[32] Before meeting Glorvina,
Horatio hears her "great learning" lauded by Irish peasants, just as Oswald hears
the people of Rome praise Corinne as "the most celebrated woman in Italy . . .
poet, writer, improvisatrice."[33] Both texts stress the heroine's uniqueness and mystery; an elderly peasant tells Horatio that Glorvina "is like nothing upon the face
of God's creation but herself," while a lower class Roman calls Corinne "a goddess
amid the clouds."[34] Told that the Wild Irish Girl reads Greek and Latin, the English hero disparages her as "a pedant, and a romp," in order to sooth his conscience
for his Protestant ancestor having taken her Catholic family's lands during the time
of Cromwell.[35] Whereas Owenson underlines the religious and political division
between her English Protestant hero and Irish Catholic heroine, Staël stresses the
gender politics, for her Italian poetess's public acclaim is contrary to her English
hero's notions of feminine modesty.[36] Each hero sees the heroine initially in a
crowd of her devoted admirers. To satisfy his curiosity, Horatio observes Glorvina

at vespers in her family chapel, his "ardent glance" trying in vain to pierce the veil hiding her face.[37] Staël, to the contrary, brings her heroine out into the public sphere. Oswald, attends Corinne's public crowning at the Capitol, where he witnesses the display of her talents and beauty, and is even able to speak to her. Thus Staël transforms Owenson's veiled, silent, devout heroine, who is glimpsed in the private, paternal space, into a publicly acclaimed heroine, without patronymic or paternal control, who exhibits her face, form, voice and ideas.

In each initial description, the heroine's attire has a distinctive, antique quality; the Irish princess's is "singular and characteristic," that of the Italian poetess is "colorful" [*très pittoresque*].[38] Both are dressed in empire style gowns and shawls: Glorvina in "a robe of vestal white, . . . enfolded beneath the bosom with a narrow girdle," draped with "a mantle of scarlet silk"; Corinne in "a white tunic with a blue drapery fastened beneath her breast."[39] The heroines are also coiffed similarly; a jeweled "diadem" secures Glorvina's veil, and an Indian shawl binds Corinne's hair until she is crowned with a laurel wreath.

In addition to their similar garb, the heroines are characterized in a like manner. Each is presented as an otherworldly being with special powers. Owenson's hero describes Glorvina as "the incarnation of some pure ethereal spirit" and Corinne is likened to a Sybil, "an inspired priestess."[40] In each heroine, however, are combined the qualities of an exceptional and an ordinary woman. As Glorvina's behavior bespeaks both "the native woman" and "the *ideal* princess," Corinne appears at once a "perfectly simple" woman and "a priestess of Apollo."[41] Glorvina's "superior and original character," Horatio proclaims, "is both *natural* and *national*."[42] This linking of the natural and national is evident in Staël's heroine as well, whom her compatriot proclaims "a gift of our felicitous nature" and "the image of our beautiful Italy."[43]

Corinne's devotion to Apollo is not surprising given her country's fondness for the arts. Coincidentally, however, Owenson's text posits Apollo as "the tutelary deity" of Ireland, "[f]or surely no nation under Heaven was ever more enthusiastically attached to poetry and music than the Irish."[44] Staël's text makes a similar claim for Italy: "For centuries, Italians have loved music rapturously."[45] The "true ancient Irish character" underlines Owenson's antiquarian priest, features an "enthusiastic love of talents," and Staël's narrator notes "the Italian enthusiasm for all the gifts of the imagination."[46] As Horatio observed that "the most courted objects" in Dublin society were "those whose talents alone endowed them with distinction," Staël's text stresses Oswald's surprise in Rome at "such homage paid a woman, . . . renowned only for the gifts of genius."[47] Each author thus presents her heroine as a modest priestess of the arts in a country that highly values artistic and intellectual gifts.

Both texts attribute a key role to the voice of the inspired heroine who sings of her country's glories. The "low wild tremulous voice" of Glorvina, whose name means "sweet voice" in Irish, bewitches Horatio.[48] Oswald is enchanted by the "movingly sensitive voice" of Corinne, whose name shares assonance with Glorvina.[49] Horatio falls under the spell of "the independent witchery of the lovely minstrel," which he initially mistook for the "professional exertions of the bard of Inismore."[50] He climbs a parapet wall and literally "crashes" the secluded Irish heroine's family circle. To meet Staël's public heroine, Oswald has merely to gain an invitation to her salon, and he questions whether to attribute her charm to Armida's magic or Sappho's poetic inspiration.[51]

Each heroine plays a stringed instrument associated with bards or poets. The harp eases the protagonists' awkwardness at their first tête-à-tête; Glorvina masks her confusion by "running her finger carelessly over the chords of the harp," and Corinne "absentmindedly fingered the harp . . . playing several chords at random," while a disconcerted Oswald, like Horatio, suddenly rises and walks to the window.[52] Owenson's hero learns "that Ireland, like Italy, has its *improvisatorés*, . . . highly estimated by their rustic compatriots."[53] Glorvina's harp improvisations may have inspired Staël's *improvisatrice* heroine, for both authors, remarks Claire Connolly, "shared an interest in the idea of female genius, especially the figure of the *improvisatrice*."[54] Corinne, who accompanies her Capitol performance on a lyre, an instrument much like a harp, often ends her improvisations by playing "simple national melodies."[55] Significantly, in 1805, Owenson had published *Twelve Hibernian Melodies from the Works of the Ancient Irish Bards*, traditional Irish airs to which she set words. Staël's decision to make her heroine an *improvisatrice* came some time after her Italian trip, for her notebooks indicate no such intention. Simone Balayé speculates that after hearing Signora Mazzei improvise in Florence, Staël decided to give Corinne that talent, making her even more a sibyl and priestess of Apollo.[56] The improvisational talents of Owenson's Glorvina could also have contributed to Staël's formulation of Corinne as an *improvisatrice*, however.

Both texts link the heroine's voice and instrument to the sound of nature: specifically, to wind on an Aeolian harp. When Horatio first hears Glorvina's harp it is "as if the breeze of midnight stillness had expired . . . on the Eolian lyre"—his every nerve thrills with emotion, and he wonders whether it is an "illusion" of his "fancy."[57] Returning to the deserted castle near the novel's end, Horatio hears the sound of Glorvina's harp, "breathing its wild melody," "the gale of the ocean . . .

sigh[ed] on the chords of the harp, and its plaintive tones went to his very soul."[58] Similarly, at Corinne's Tivoli villa, "Aeolian harps" she has placed in grottos around the garden make "the sound of the wind melodious" and "lend nature a voice."[59] Both authors associate the sound of wind on harp strings with poetry. Glorvina compares her "sweet melancholy" while reading Ossian to her sensation when "the passing breeze . . . faintly breathing on the chords [of her harp] seems to call forth its own requiem."[60] Corinne, too, links the wind on harp strings to poetry, imagining that "it is as if the pure breath of heaven and sea act on man's imagination like the wind on Aeolian harps, and as if poetry—like those chords—echoes nature."[61]

In both texts the heroine's performance of national music expresses the voice of nature and elicits deep emotion in the hero. Glorvina's tearful voice, "'low and mournful as the song of the tomb,'" sighed over the chords of her national lyre, as she faintly murmured Campbell's beautiful poem to the ancient Irish air of "Erin go Bragh" moves Horatio to tears.[62] Before a painting of Ossian's Caïrbar asleep on his father's tomb, Corinne, taking up her harp, sings "Scottish ballads whose simple notes seem to keep pace with the sound of the wind moaning in the valleys," and Staël's protagonists weep together.[63] Each heroine performs a national melody that expresses a political exile's emotional attachment to his native land: Glorvina sings Thomas Campbell's *The Exile of Erin* (1801), about an Irish patriot banished after the United Irishmen's rebellion of 1798, while Corinne renders Allan Ramsay's *Farewell to Lochaber* (1724), about a Scottish fugitive after the Jacobite Rebellion of 1715.[64] The national nostalgia conveyed through the refrain of Erin go bragh—Ireland forever—echoes in the Scottish ballad's refrain of "Lochaber No More." Whereas Owenson's Irish heroine laments her own nation's thwarted struggle for self-determination, Staël, in having her Italian heroine empathize with a failed Scottish rebellion, internationalizes the lament.

The portrayal of the heroine's character in these two texts is remarkably similar. The noble princess of Inismore, who first appears supporting the dignity of her infirm father, seems modest, tender, and sweet to Horatio, while Oswald notices Corinne's manner "so noble and modest, so sweet and dignified."[65] The authors each use a close, older, male friend of the heroine to expose her exceptional talents and character; Glorvina's tutor Father John extols his pupil's "rare endowments," "her versatile genius," and "exquisite sensibility," and Corinne's devoted friend Prince Castel-Forte praises her "impassioned sensibility" and "inventive mind."[66] Each heroine excels in verbal expression; of Glorvina, Horatio remarks, "the fertility of her imagination supplied incessant topics of conversation, always new, always original," while Corinne's conversation combines "enthusiasm for the arts," "subtle ideas and deep feeling" with vivacity.[67] Castel-Forte notes "the originality of Corinne's language," as Horatio did "the force and energy" of Glorvina's expressions.[68] Each heroine's mind combines complexity and depth with simplicity and lightness. In the Irish girl, Horatio finds a "union of intelligence and simplicity, infantine playfulness and profound reflexion," while in the Italian woman are united "imagination and simplicity, sound judgment and rapturous emotion."[69] Horatio signals Glorvina's "evident feelings," "the enthusiasm of her disposition, the uncontrollable smile, the involuntary tear, the spontaneous sigh."[70] Corinne's major attraction is her "spontaneity and absence of restraint," and she moves "almost instantaneously from melancholy to gaiety."[71] Horatio appreciates the "playfulness" and "original whimsicality" of Glorvina's humor, as Corinne's gaiety has its source in her "lively mind and radiant imagination."[72] Due to "the vivacity of her genius," her "natural impatience and volatility," Horatio remarks, Glorvina's "ever active mind requires incessant exercise," and a talented woman such as Corinne needs "diversion" and "variety" to avoid boredom.[73] Thus both heroines are described as intelligent, enthusiastic, vivacious, passionate, imaginative, sensitive, and natural, but at the same time as noble, sweet, and modest, deep thinkers.

Both authors establish the heroine as the national inspiration or muse. Horatio considers Glorvina to be "the ministering angel of thy poor compatriots, who look up to thee for example and support—thy country's muse, and the bright model of the genuine character of her daughters."[74] Castel-Forte calls Corinne "the image of our beautiful Italy" and of its possibilities, "an offspring of the past, prophet of the future," for "Italians are far more remarkable for what they once were and what they could be than for what they are at present."[75] Horatio first imagines that his father's remote Connacht Lodge is "the *harem* of some wild Irish *Sultana*" only to discover that the "fancied *harem*" is a study containing books on the "language, history and antiquities of Ireland," and that his father's *Sultana* is the *Irish Muse*.[76] Staël's text, in turn, develops this allusion to the national muse as Scheherazade, for Corinne teaches Oswald about Italian culture to forestall his departure, "like the sultana of Arabian tales who sought to captivate the interest of the man she loved by a thousand different stories and thus to put off his decision on her fate until the moment the charms of her mind stood victorious."[77] Yet, whereas Owenson's Irish muse succeeds in captivating her hero, the creative charms of Staël's heroine do not triumph over national and gender prejudices.

Just as the heroines play similar roles, so several scenes in Staël's *roman-voyage* bear a striking resemblance to those in Owenson's novel-travelogue. Each heroine performs her national dance with a countryman while her foreign lover looks on, admiring her movements and envying her partner. Glorvina, "won unsought," dances with a peasant at a rustic May Day celebration; Corinne, without having "to be persuaded," performs with a prince at a grand Roman ball.[78] Glorvina's dance, the Irish jig, "leaves the most to the genius of the dancer" and is performed "as if bit to merry madness by a tarantula," while Corinne's dance is the "very original and graceful" Neapolitan Tarentelle or spider dance.[79] While dancing, Glorvina's eyes express "the wildest exhilaration of pleasure," and Corinne's exhibit "joyous pleasure" [*un plaisir vif*]; the Irish girl glows with "the spirit of health, mirth, and exercise," and the Italian seems animated by "an enthusiasm for life, for youth, and for beauty."[80] In Glorvina's dancing, Horatio admires "the swimming languor of the most graceful motion," and calls dance "the *Poetry of Motion*." Oswald praises in Corinne's dancing "a graceful litheness, mixing modesty and sensual delight," like Bayadères, "poets of the dance." Owenson compares her heroine's dance to "an Egyptian *alma*" or Aspasia, who performed privately.[81] Staël, in contrast, likens her heroine's performance to "Bayadères," public temple dancers, and to "the women dancers of Herculaneum," sculptures that originally graced an entrance portico and inspired her contemporary Emma Hamilton's publicly performed "attitudes."[82] Although Staël claimed Mme Récamier's dancing inspired Corinne's Tarantella performance, her travel notebook records seeing the dance performed in Naples, where Lady Hamilton had recently been ambassadress. Geneviève Gennari believes Staël's depiction of the Tarantella owes more to Lady Hamilton's performance of the dance than to Mme Récamier's.[83] Comparing Corinne's dance with Staël's travel notes of the Tarantella's vivacity, Italian passion, gaiety and lightness, Simone Balayé remarks a key difference: unlike the dance Staël witnessed in Naples, Corinne dances with only one partner.[84] This is significant, for Glorvina dances alone with a young peasant, the "King of the May," before an admiring village throng. Nor does Staël's notebook mention the hero's jealousy while observing his beloved dance with another man—this is an element in Owenson's scene that recurs in Staël's novel.

Both novels enact a touching love scene in a cemetery, although Staël's is more public. In a rural Irish graveyard, seeing a young woman strewing flowers on the fresh grave of her father, Glorvina sadly wonders, "what affectionate hand will scatter flowers over *my* solitary tomb" after her own father's death. In response, Horatio declares his desire to share with her "a closer kindred . . . than even parental affinity can assert," then presses her hand to his heart and sums up their tender exchange, saying, "A glance was all I required—a glance was all I received."[85] Staël transfers Owenson's rural scene to Rome's celebrated Apian Way, where, at the famous tomb a bereaved father has erected to Cecilia Metella, the protagonists agree that lucky children die before their parents. When Corinne declares her love for him, Oswald imitates Horatio's gesture: "Taking her hand, saying nothing, promising nothing, he gazed at her with a love that justified every hope" [*Il prit sa main, la serra contre son cœur . . .*].[86] Staël's scene, like Owenson's, ends with a meaningful glance and no spoken promise, but reverses the respectively active and passive roles of Owenson's male and female protagonists. In Staël's text, it is the heroine who declares her love and her hero who responds passively with a loving look.

Though the hybrid genre of Staël's novel-travelogue, her main characters, and certain key scenes suggest beyond a doubt that Owenson's tale served as a source of literary inspiration, I will now turn my attention to some crucial differences that modified the import and application of Staël's work. Staël's Italian heroine is more experienced and worldly than Owenson's Irish Girl. Glorvina at nineteen has never loved before Horatio. Corinne at twenty-six has many admirers, believes she was in love before, and knows Oswald's father did not choose her for his son. The reasons why Oswald's father preferred Corinne's half-sister Lucile as his son's fiancée are precisely, in the eyes of Lord M—, the merits of Miss D—, the bride he intends for Horatio: "her personal charms, and the simplicity of her unmodified character." Lord M— declares:

> How delightful . . . to form this young and ductile mind, to mould it
> to your desires, to breathe inspiration into this lovely image of primeval
> innocence, to give soul to beauty, and intelligence to simplicity, . . . and
> finally clasp to your heart that perfection you have your-self created.[87]

Lord M— has to some extent formed the mind of Glorvina, whom he hopes to wed (unbeknownst to his son). To the thoughtless, pleasure-seeking Miss D—, Horatio prefers the Irish Girl, in whom genius and sensibility are united with beauty and innocence, for he has found "a mutual intelligence of mind and feeling with her, which a look, a sigh, a word is sufficient to betray—a sacred communion of spirit."[88] Oswald shares a similar bond with Corinne alone, "this harmony of soul" and "close understanding of mind and heart," that Prince Castel-Forte describes as "the creative soul that shared and multiplied your feelings and your thoughts."[89] Whereas Father John extols Glorvina's "shining abilities that would equally enrich the solitude of their possessor, or render her an ornament to that society she may yet be destined to grace," Corinne's extraordinary talents disqualify her for marriage: "*[w]hat do you do with that at home?*" her kinsman Mr. Edgermond wonders ruefully, declaring: "I would like to see her on the throne of England, but not under my humble roof."[90] Oswald, jealous of the public, would prefer that Corinne save "her eloquence and genius for him alone."[91] Although Glorvina's artistic gifts enrich her private social circle, Corinne's genius propels her into the public sphere and excludes her from domestic happiness. Taking leave of Glorvina, Horatio silently wishes that she be "veiled from the rude intercourse of th[e] world . . . : long amidst the shade of the venerable ruins of thy forefathers mayest thou bloom and flourish in undisturbed felicity!"[92] The Irish muse, unlike the Italian one, does not defy propriety or upset the patriarchal order. Glorvina is chaperoned by her nurse, but Corinne travels alone with Oswald and damages her reputation.[93] Owenson's heroine, unlike Staël's, is willing to sacrifice her happiness by marrying her father's choice, although she is finally able to marry her beloved Horatio. Staël is thus rewriting Owenson's narrative as a critique of a society that cannot reconcile the notion of domestic happiness with a woman of Corinne's (or Glorvina's) talents. Staël's text also calls for a reconciliation of the British value of domestic happiness with the Italian appreciation of artistic talent in the figure of Corinne's niece and protégée, Juliette, whom the dying heroine teaches to perform the Scottish ballad "Lochaber No More" on the harp to remind Oswald of her talents every year on November 17th (the date he left her to return to England.)[94]

Through these novel-travelogues, both authors combine the private entertainment of a love story with a public political message. Each narrative considers the complications attendant upon the union of a Protestant hero of a dominant culture and a Catholic heroine of a subjected one. As Owenson's writings supported the British Whig's parliamentary push for Catholic emancipation, Staël's "liberal vision" of religious tolerance, notes Avriel Goldberger, echoes throughout *Corinne*.[95] Although Owenson's Protestant hero first imagines Glorvina to be "bigoted and illiberal," like the "Jesuitical priest" who raised her, Horatio comes to admire the "dignified simplicity" of her venerable chaplain Father John, whom he later describes as "the embodied spirit of philosophy moralizing amidst the ruins of empires, on the instability of all human greatness."[96] Attending vespers in the prince of Inismore's ruined chapel, Horatio exclaims of the Catholic religion: "How seducingly it speaks to the senses; . . . how strongly it seizes on the imagination; . . . how graceful its ceremonies; how awful its rites.—What a captivating . . . faith!"[97] Staël's narrator similarly remarks that religion in Italy "captures the imagination by its practices and ceremonies" and finds it impossible not to feel "a deeply religious emotion" during the Stations of the Cross in the Coliseum, or to be "moved" in darkened St. Peter's Basilica at the sight of the pope and cardinals prostrate before the illuminated cross on Good Friday.[98] Referring to the pope's Holy Thursday ritual of washing the feet of twelve "apostles," however, the Staëlian narrator cautions: "Worship brilliant and stately in its external forms is surely calculated to fill the soul with the most exalted feelings; but care must be taken that the ceremonies not degenerate into a show."[99] Oswald, who prefers the simplicity of Anglican rites, explains, "Dogma that offends my reason also chills my enthusiasm," as before him Horatio rejected the "captivating" Catholic faith due to "the stern opposition of reason."[100] Both Protestant heroes thus stress the seductiveness of Roman Catholic ritual and the irrationality of its dogmas. As Frank Bowman has shown, Staël, through her protagonists, seeks to reconcile Protestantism—the masculine religion of the North, focused on reason, sacrifice to moral duty, and to paternal law—and Catholicism—the feminine religion of the South, linked to enthusiasm, passion, joy, divine beauty, and consolation. Displaying ecumenical openness to the Protestant and Catholic religions, her text calls for the coexistence of reason and feeling.[101]

Yet while Staël examines Catholic practices in Rome, the religious center of Catholicism, Owenson describes them in Ireland, the isolated, persecuted periphery. Her Protestant hero observes Catholic rites at the "parish masshouse," a simple cabin with a rough stone cross, in a scene that contrasts the actual primitive conditions of Irish religious practice with grand Roman Catholic tradition. Owenson's description of Irish peasants "praying over their beads with as much fervour as though . . . in the golden-roofed temple of Solyman," and of the parish priest "in pontificalibus, . . . with as much self-invested dignity as the *dalai lama*" associates Catholicism with Islam and Buddhism, religions that to her were exotic and foreign.[102] Owenson criticizes the Catholic clergy for trading prayers for money, as Horatio describes the priest "addressing each of his flock by their name and profession, and exposing their faults and extolling their virtues, according to the nature of their contributions," and remarks the mendicant friar "turning his beads to two accounts . . . making intercession for the souls of his good subscribers, and . . . diligently keeping count of the sum total of their benefactions."[103] In comparing this parish priest to Father John, who refuses to live off his impoverished parishioners, Horatio cannot avoid thinking: "It is the *man* who must give dignity to the situation."[104] Just as Owenson's text criticizes the financial motivation of Catholic sermons (and indirectly the obligatory tithes Irish Catholics paid to support Anglican ministers),[105] Staël's narrator faults the lack of ideas and "Christian philosophy" in Italian religious oratory.[106]

A reference to the Italian shrine of Our Lady of Loreto in Owenson's novel even resurfaces in Staël's. Witnessing an elderly woman circle a sacred well three times on her knees, Father John calls the most celebrated Irish holy well, Lough Derg, the "*Loretto* of Ireland," which the Protestant hero dismisses as a "shrine of Christian superstition."[107] At the Apennine shrine of Loreto, where pilgrims "on their knees" have worn a path around the sanctuary, Oswald, upon discovering Corinne "prostrate," wonders how "a person of such superior mind might follow such popular practice."[108] Staël's text thus echoes Owenson's description of the supplicant's kneeling posture and the Protestant hero's rejection of superstitious religious rituals; yet, as Bowman states, through her heroine Staël validates the communal aspect of Catholicism, its ability to participate in the psychology and emotions of the masses.[109]

In response to Horatio's query as to whether Glorvina receives "all the doctrines of [her] church as infallible," the Irish heroine's "strong mind" proves "an emanation of . . . divine intelligence" as she proclaims that the removal of the remaining Penal Laws against Catholics will give them a common investment in British society:

> Of the many who are the inheritors of *our* persuasion, *all* are not . . . influenced by its superstitions. If its professors are coalesced, it is . . . not in the dogmas of their belief . . . it is by the tie of temporal interests . . . ; and once incorporated in the great mass of general society, their feelings will become diffusive as their interests; their affections, like their privileges, will be in common; . . . their hearts . . . will then be animated to the nobler pulsation of universal philanthropy.[110]

Staël's narrator expresses a similar desire for religious understanding. Through shared emotion at the pope's Easter blessing from Saint Peter's, her Protestant and Catholic protagonists feel "that all forms of worship are alike. Religious feeling binds men close when pride and fanaticism do not make it an object of jealousy or hate."[111] Similarly, through the marriage of her heroine of the Old Irish Catholic nobility to an Anglo-Irish Protestant landlord, Owenson creates a "family" solution (the "Glorvina solution") to end centuries of cultural and religious division and forge a united Irish identity. Her text expresses hope that such family alliances will bring national unity.[112] Although both authors call for religious tolerance, therefore, Owenson seeks an end to specific legal and civil restrictions on Roman Catholics in Protestant Great Britain, whereas Staël eliminates religious divisions in general, dreaming of ecumenism and reconciliation.[113]

Owenson's text pleads for a revaluation of Irish national culture, degraded by English hegemony. The prince of Inismore attributes the disappearance of the Irish fame for "patriotism, . . . love of letters, skill in arms and arts, and refinement of manners" to their connection to England; the loss of national freedom destroyed national virtues.[114] In *The Wild Irish Girl* the priest posits that "it is always the policy of the conqueror . . . to destroy those mementi of ancient national splendour which keep alive the spirit of the conquered."[115] Owenson exposes the practice of cultural warfare in which a dominant culture seeks to supplant a subjected one. Like the Irish author, Staël criticizes the contemporary situation of Italy and links civic virtues to freedom: "Deprived of independence . . . by unfortunate circumstances, Italians have lost . . . the very possibility of speaking [truth]."[116] If the Italian nation is no longer known for its military valor, love of liberty, and illustrious literature, science and art, as it was in past ages, Corinne accuses its political situation. She links the Italian people's lack of dignity to their not being "allowed to be a nation," but suggests that "traces of ancient grandeur" in the Italian character "could rise to the surface" in happier times, thereby implying that Italians could regain their national dignity by gaining political autonomy.[117] Lord M— entrusts his Irish estates to his son, placed "by Providence over . . . the descendants of a brave, a free and an enlightened people," and charges him to nurture "those national . . . virtues blighted . . . by the fatality of circumstances."[118] Thus whereas Owenson seeks the improvement of conditions in Ireland but not Irish independence, Staël calls for more than better treatment by the overlords—nothing less than Italian self-determination. Staël thus broadened the application and appeal of Owenson's tale from the specificity of the Irish heroine's domestic situation, religious beliefs, and national concerns to the more universal subject of the politics of gender, religion, and nation.

Owenson's "passionate defense of her 'unhappy country,'" Marcel Moraud writes, "The evocation of Ireland's glorious past and allusions to the injustices suffered from England, made a national heroine of the novel's Glorvina and of the author who was identified with her."[119] Owenson was invited to play her harp in Dublin and London salons as Glorvina, assuming the role of Irish national genius.[120] In a pose strikingly similar to John Comerford's undated miniature of Owenson at the harp (figure 5.1), Staël had herself painted in September 1807 by Elizabeth Vigée-Lebrun as Corinne performing on a lyre.[121] Yet Staël never acknowledged her debt to Sydney Owenson's *The Wild Irish Girl*, which finally appeared in France in 1813 as *Glorvina, ou la jeune irlandaise*. The two authors never met, for Staël was in Geneva when the Irish author first visited France in

1816–1817 to write on the state of the nation after Napoleon's fall. Yet in the resulting book, *France* (1817), Lady Morgan paid tribute to Mme de Staël as "a Delphic oracle" and expressed her wish "that she were less inspired, or we more intelligent."[122] Morgan's *France*, which was immediately translated, created an enormous sensation, for her democratic spirit, liberal conception of political rights, and moving depiction of the lower classes provoked a furor among Conservatives.[123] Morgan's national tales were admired in France, claims Patrick Rafroidi, for their descriptions of Ireland's "picturesque of unknown regions and primitive traditions"—a regionalism he considers nationalist.[124] The Irish author was gratified to learn from Staël's son during her second French sojourn of 1818–1819 that his mother had *France* read to her during her final illness.[125] The fertile literary exchange between these two gifted and politically engaged authors thus continued beyond *Corinne, or Italy*, for Sydney Owenson Lady Morgan in turn published a travel book on Italy in 1820.

Figure 5.1. Samuel Freeman, 1846, engraving of Sydney Owenson after a painting by John Comerford. Courtesy of the Master and Fellows of Trinity College Cambridge.

Figure 5.2.   John Lavery, 1928, portrait of Lady Lavery as Kathleen Ní Houlihan depicted on the Irish pound.

Owenson's fictional creation Glorvina and her public appearances as her heroine perpetuated the image of the "Genius of Ireland" as a lady with a harp,[126] notably in John Lavery's 1928 painting for the Irish pound (figure 5.2), which aptly illustrates Deirdre Lynch's claim that Staël's imitation of *The Wild Irish Girl* in *Corinne* "renders the bardic . . . the currency of transcultural exchange."[127] By using "bardic nationalism" to revalue Italian culture and call for Italian political self-determination, Staël transformed the peripheral national tale into a major European genre. In emulating Owenson's pioneering literary form of a novel-travelogue, Staël—like her precursor—redefined both the novel and the woman writer's social role in forming national identity for lands struggling against foreign rule. Yet Staël moves Owenson's paradigmatic national heroine in a new direction; the cosmopolitan Corinne challenges fantasies of national union and points to an alternative social order in a new Europe.[128]

Notes

1. Clarissa Campbell Orr, "Mary Shelley's Rambles in Germany and Italy, the Celebrity Author, and the Undiscovered Country of the Human Heart," *Romanticism on the Net* 11 (August 1998): 2.

2. Geneviève Gennari, *Le Premier voyage de Madame de Staël en Italie et la genèse de Corinne* (Paris: Boivin, 1947), 139–40.

3. Marcel Ian Moraud, *Lady Morgan, une Irlandaise libérale* (Paris: Marcel Didier, 1954), 55; and Claire Connolly, "Introduction: The Politics of Love in *The Wild Irish Girl*," in *The Wild Irish Girl*, by Sydney Owenson (London: Pickering and Chatto, 2000), lxvi.

4. Clíona Ó Gallchoir has examined the influence of Staël's *On Literature* on *The Wild Irish Girl* in "Germaine de Staël and the Response of Sydney Owenson and Maria Edgeworth to the Act of Union," in *France-Ireland: Anatomy of a Relationship*, eds. Eamon Maher and Grace Neville (Frankfort, Germany: Peter Lang, 2004), 69–82.

5. Caroline Franklin, "Romantic Patriotism as Feminist Critique of Empire: Helen Maria Williams, Sydney Owenson and Germaine de Staël," in *Women, Gender and Enlightenment*, ed. Sarah Knott and Barbara Taylor (Basingstoke: Palgrave Macmillan, 2005), 556–62.

6. Deirdre Shauna Lynch, "The (Dis)locations of Romantic Nationalism: Shelley, Staël, and the Home-Schooling of Monsters," in *The Literary Channel: The Inter-National Invention of the Novel*, ed. Margaret Cohen and Carolyn Dever (Princeton, NJ: Princeton University Press, 2002), 199, 202.

7. W. Hepworth Dixon, ed. *Lady Morgan's Memoirs: Autobiography, Diaries and Correspondence* (London: W. H. Allen & Co., 1862), 1:284.

8. William J. Fitzpatrick, *Lady Morgan: Her Career, Literary and Personal* (London: Charles J. Skeet, 1860), 110–14.

9. *Literary Journal: A Review of Domestic and Foreign Literature*, series 2 (November 1806): 582–83.

10. *Monthly Magazine* (September 1, 1806): 154.

11. Victor de Pange and Norman King, "La Bibliothèque anglaise de Mme de Staël," *Cahiers staëliens* 14 (September 1972): 67.

12. *Monthly Magazine* (January 25, 1807): 643.

13. Germaine de Staël, *Correspondance générale de Madame de Staël*, ed. Béatrice W. Jasinski (Paris: Klincksieck, 1993), 6:572. All translations are mine unless otherwise indicated.

14. Staël, *Correspondance générale*, 6:155–56, 189; J-D. Candaux and N. King, "Théâtre et société, la correspondance des Staël et des Odier, 1806–1817," *Cahiers staëliens* 38 (1987): 8.

15. Comtesse Jean de Pange, *Auguste-Guillaume Schlegel et Mme de Staël* (Paris: Éditions Albert, 1938), 177.

16. Alfred Collinson Hunter, *J. B. A. Suard, un introducteur de la littérature anglaise en France* (Paris: Champion, 1925), 52–53, 167.

17. *Critical Review* 9 (November 1806): 327–28.

18. Hunter, *J. B. A. Suard*, 92, 137.

19. Staël, *Major Writings of Germaine de Staël*, ed. and trans. Vivian Folkenflik (New York: Columbia University Press, 1992), 174–75.

20. Sir William Hamilton, ed., *The Collected Works of Dugald Stewart* (Edinburgh: Thomas Constable, 1863), 10:lvii, lxxix–lxxx.

21. Robert MacFarlan, *The Poems of Ossian, in the Original Gaelic, with a Literal Translation into Latin* (London: W. Bulmer, 1807), 3:483.

22. Jean-Daniel Candaux and Norman King, "La Correspondance de Benjamin Constant et de Sismondi, 1801–1830," *Annales Benjamin Constant* 1 (1980): 99–100; and Staël, *Correspondance de Madame de Staël*, 133–34; Victor de Pange, "Madame de Staël and her English Correspondents," DPhil thesis, (University of Oxford, 1955), 2:297.

23. James F. Marshall, *De Staël–Du Pont Letters: Correspondence of Madame de Staël and Pierre Samuel Du Pont de Nemours and of Other Members of the Necker and Du Pont Families* (Madison: University of Wisconsin Press, 1968), 324; Staël, *Correspondance de Madame de Staël*, 6:249.

24. Simone Balayé, "Madame de Staël et Sismondi ou un dialogue critique," *Cahiers staëliens* 8 (April 1969): 44–45.

25. Ibid., 41–42.

26. *Edinburgh Review* 11 (October 1807): 183; quoted in Robert Calvin Whitford, "Madame de Staël's Literary Reputation in England," *University of Illinois Studies in Language and Literature* 4, no. 1 (February 1918): 17.

27. Ina Ferris, *The Romantic National Tale and the Question of Ireland* (Cambridge: Cambridge University Press, 2002), 11–12.

28. Ibid.

29. "Katie Trumpener has argued that travel writing on Ireland in the Romantic period typically crossed the rational discourse of the Enlightenment survey with a counter-strain deriving from a 'bardic nationalism' developed in the Celtic peripheries" (ibid., 20–21).

30. In a letter to Staël dated February 22, 1807, Du Pont referred to her hero as "Lord Sydney" (Marshall, *De Staël–du Pont Letters*, 320–21; Gennari, *Le Premier voyage de Madame de Staël en Italie*, 148–49).

31. Sydney Owenson, *The Wild Irish Girl* (Oxford: Oxford University Press, 1999), 9.

32. Owenson, *Wild Irish Girl*, 10; Germaine de Staël, *Corinne, or Italy*, ed. and trans. Avriel Goldberger (New Brunswick, NJ: Rutgers University Press, 1987), 17.

33. Owenson, *Wild Irish Girl*, 41; Staël, *Corinne, or Italy*, 19.

34. Owenson, *Wild Irish Girl*, 41; Staël, *Corinne, or Italy*, 21.

35. Owenson, *Wild Irish Girl*, 41–42.

36. Staël, *Corinne, or Italy*, 19.

37. Owenson, *Wild Irish Girl*, 42, 48–49.

38. Owenson, *Wild Irish Girl*, 60; Staël, *Corinne, or Italy*, 21; Staël, *Corinne ou l'Italie* (Paris: Gallimard, 1985), 52.

39. Owenson, *Wild Irish Girl*, 48; Staël, *Corinne, or Italy*, 21.

40. Owenson, *Wild Irish Girl*, 48; Staël, *Corinne, or Italy*, 21, 32.

41. Owenson, *Wild Irish Girl*, 68; Staël, *Corinne, or Italy*, 21.

42. Owenson, *Wild Irish Girl*, 120.

43. Staël, *Corinne, or Italy*, 25.

44. Owenson, *Wild Irish Girl*, 138.

45. Staël, *Corinne, or Italy*, 165.

46. Owenson, *Wild Irish Girl*, 64; Staël, *Corinne, or Italy*, 19.

47. Owenson, *Wild Irish Girl*, 17; Staël, *Corinne, or Italy*, 22.

48. Owenson, *Wild Irish Girl*, 52.

49. Staël, *Corinne, or Italy*, 31.

50. Owenson, *Wild Irish Girl*, 52–53.

51. Staël, *Corinne, or Italy*, 39.

52. Owenson, *Wild Irish Girl*, 68–69; Staël, *Corinne, or Italy*, 42.

53. Owenson, *Wild Irish Girl*, 22.

54. Claire Connolly, "'I accuse Miss Owenson': *The Wild Irish Girl* as Media Event," *Colby Quarterly* 36, no. 2 (2000): 110.

55. Staël, *Corinne, or Italy*, 59, 45.

56. "Le Premier Voyage en Italie," in *Les Carnets de voyage de Madame de Staël: Contribution à la genèse de ses œuvres*, ed. Simone Balayé (Genève: Droz, 1971), 113–14.

57. Owenson, *Wild Irish Girl*, 52.

58. Ibid., 234.

59. Staël, *Corinne, or Italy*, 152.

60. Owenson, *Wild Irish Girl*, 116.

61. Staël, *Corinne, or Italy*, 44.

62. Owenson, *Wild Irish Girl*, 74.

63. Staël, *Corinne, or Italy*, 157.

64. Robert Ridell, "Lochaber," in *Scots Musical Museum*, pt.1, no. 95 (1787). http://chrsouchon.free.fr/lochaber.htm.

65. Owenson, *Wild Irish Girl*, 48, 61; Staël, *Corinne, or Italy*, 22.

66. Owenson, *Wild Irish Girl*, 77; Staël, *Corinne, or Italy*, 23–24.

67. Owenson, *Wild Irish Girl*, 82; Staël, *Corinne, or Italy*, 38.

68. Staël, *Corinne, or Italy*, 23; Owenson, *Wild Irish Girl*, 119.

69. Owenson, *Wild Irish Girl*, 92; Staël, *Corinne, or Italy*, 24.

70. Owenson, *Wild Irish Girl*, 119.

71. Staël, *Corinne, or Italy*, 74, 38.

72. Owenson, *Wild Irish Girl*, 103; Staël, *Corinne, or Italy*, 23.

73. Owenson, *Wild Irish Girl*, 86; Staël, *Corinne, or Italy*, 202.

74. Owenson, *Wild Irish Girl*, 123.

75. Staël, *Corinne, or Italy*, 25, 17.

76. Owenson, *Wild Irish Girl*, 34, 37.

77. Staël, *Corinne, or Italy*, 81.

78. Owenson, *Wild Irish Girl*, 145, 147; Staël, *Corinne, or Italy*, 91–92.

79. Owenson, *Wild Irish Girl*, 29; Staël, *Corinne, or Italy*, 91.

80. Owenson, *Wild Irish Girl*, 146; Staël, *Corinne*, 92–93; *Corinne ou l'Italie*, 149.

81. In Egypt the 'Awalim (Alma singular) were learned women, who wrote poetry, composed music, sang, played musical instruments, and danced, but only for a female audience. If men were present, the 'Awalim would sing from behind a screen or lattice. "These educated 'awalim were highly appreciated for their art and probably respected as well, since they . . . did not break any rules of propriety" (http://www.living-belly-dance.com/egyptian-belly-dance.html).

82. Chloe Chard, *Pleasure and Guilt on the Grand Tour: Travel Writing and Imaginative Geography, 1600–1830* (Dublin: Gill and MacMillan, 1992), 147 cited in Connolly, "'I Accuse Miss Owenson,'" 110.

83. Gennari, *Le Premier voyage de Madame de Staël en Italie*, 147–49.

84. Balayé, "Le Premier voyage en Italie," 141–42.

85. Owenson, *Wild Irish Girl*, 185–86.

86. Staël, *Corinne, or Italy*, 81; *Corinne ou l'Italie*, 132.

87. Owenson, *Wild Irish Girl*, 226–27.

88. Owenson, *Wild Irish Girl*, 83, 226–27.

89. Staël, *Corinne, or Italy*, 311, 25.

90. Owenson, *Wild Irish Girl*, 77; Staël, *Corinne, or Italy*, 133.

91. Staël, *Corinne, or Italy*, 124.

92. Owenson, *Wild Irish Girl*, 123.

93. Ibid., 96.

94. Staël, *Corinne, or Italy*, 411, 413, 305. Louis de Narbonne, the father of Staël's sons, died on November 17, 1813.

95. Avriel Goldberger, "Introduction" in *Corinne, or Italy*, xlvi.

96. Owenson, *Wild Irish Girl*, 43, 47, 74.

97. Ibid., 50.

98. Staël, *Corinne, or Italy*, 175, 176, 180.

99. Ibid., 177.

100. Staël, *Corinne*, 185; Owenson, *Wild Irish Girl*, 50.

101. Frank Paul Bowman, "*Corinne* et la religion," in *L'Éclat et le silence:* Corinne ou l'Italie *de Madame de Staël*, ed. Simone Balayé (Paris: Honoré Champion, 1999), 145–60.

102. Owenson, *Wild Irish Girl*, 134.

103. Ibid., 134–35.

104. Ibid., 135.

105. Lady Morgan Sydney Owenson championed the anti-tithe cause in her *Patriotic Sketches of Ireland* (London: Phillips, 1807).

106. Staël, *Corinne, or Italy*, 175.

107. Owenson, *Wild Irish Girl*, 153.

108. Staël, *Corinne, or Italy*, 290.

109. Bowman, "*Corinne* et la religion," 151.

110. Owenson, *Wild Irish Girl*, 187.

111. Staël, *Corinne, or Italy*, 186.

112. Owenson, *Wild Irish Girl*, 250.

113. Bowman, "*Corinne* et la religion," 160.

114. Owenson, *Wild Irish Girl*, 176–77, 178.

115. Ibid., 174–75.

116. Staël, *Corinne, or Italy*, 113.

117. Ibid., 101, 36–37.

118. Owenson, *Wild Irish Girl*, 250–51.

119. Moraud, *Lady Morgan*, 54.

120. Lionel Stevenson, *The Wild Irish Girl: The Life of Sydney Owenson, Lady Morgan (1776–1859)* (London: Chapman & Hall, 1936), 102–05.

121. For the artistic, intellectual, and social links between Owenson and Staël and for Staël's desire to style herself as Corinne see my essay, "Le Barde féminin comme génie national: *The Wild Irish Girl* de Sydney Owenson, un modèle de *Corinne, ou l'Italie* de Mme de Staël," *Cahiers staëliens* 59 (2008): 79–95.

122. Moraud, *Lady Morgan*, 107.

123. Elizabeth Suddaby and P. J. Yarrow, eds. *Lady Morgan in France* (Newcastle upon Tyne: Oriel Press, 1971), 12. Patrick Rafroidi, *L'Irlande et le Romantisme* (Lille: Éditions Universitaires, 1972), 75.

124. Rafroidi, *L'Irlande et le Romantisme*, 304, 151–52.

125. Dixon, *Lady Morgan's Memoirs*, 1:86; Suddaby and Yarrow, *Lady Morgan in France*, 193.

126. Mary Helen Thuente, "Liberty, Hibernia and Mary Le More: United Irish Images of Women," in *The Women of 1798*, eds. Dáire Keogh and Nicholas Furlong (Dublin: Four Courts Press, 1998), 12.

127. Lynch, "(Dis)locations of Romantic Nationalism," 202.

128. Esther Wohlgemut, "'What Do You Do with That at Home?': The Cosmopolitan Heroine and the National Tale," *European Romantic Review* 13 (2002): 192.

6

ETHNOGRAPHY AND AUTOETHNOGRAPHY: COSMOPOLITANISM IN *CORINNE OU L'ITALIE*

Jennifer Law-Sullivan

G ERMAINE DE STAËL has been called a woman of genius, literary critic, novelist, and historian. This analysis will focus on her role as a traveler. I will argue that, in this role, Staël is best able to combine all of her talents and illustrate her ultimate goal of cosmopolitanism. Since her novel *Corinne, or Italy* was first classified by the author herself and by the Bibliothèque Nationale de France as a work of travel literature, it is a fitting source for this study. Corinne's tour of Italy with Oswald reads as ethnography, autoethnography, architectural and literary criticism—even, some would argue, as autobiography. The multiplicity of genres present in this work mirror the multifaceted nature of its author, and yet this multi-genre work would not be such a rich well of possibilities were it not for its overarching theme of travel. The hybrid genre of *Corinne* has prompted me to examine the text using both post-colonial theory and narratology. I will demonstrate that this novel strikes a balance between ethnography and autoethnography, allowing Staël to demonstrate her hopes for a world that values multiple perspectives, hopes that can only be realized via cosmopolitanism. I employ terms of post-colonial inquiry in conjunction with narratology in an attempt to further elucidate what I have previously labeled a "novelogue," a combination of both novel and travelogue.[1] Whereas the role of Corinne's voice and its significance have been thoroughly examined, this study will investigate the role of the narrator's voice instead, one that has so often been called that of Staël herself.[2] It is my contention that the narrator's voice is of equal significance to that of the heroine and furthers Staël's attempt to create a cosmopolitan community.

As has already been very well documented, travel is intrinsically linked with the question of nation so prevalent in *Corinne* and plays an important role in Staël's own life.[3] In her collection *Les Carnets de voyage de Madame de Staël*, Simone Balayé discusses Staël's desire to travel when she writes: "Madame de Staël has an insatiable curiosity about other nations, people, and ideas. She thinks that one cannot speak about a country without knowing it in its physical existence."[4] There are several reasons for this interest, the first of which is Staël's own national identity. As someone who was born in Geneva, banned from Paris, lived in Germany, and traveled extensively throughout Europe, Staël suffered from her own identity crisis. To which nation did she belong? She was not considered to be French since she was not married to a Frenchman.[5] Additionally, Napoleon forced an almost nomadic existence on her by exiling her from Paris. As Balayé has noted, "Bonaparte's harshness would have the unexpected consequence of opening Europe up to Madame de Staël and provoking the birth of two of the major works composed during the Empire, *Corinne* and *On Germany*."[6] Staël's numerous voyages to England, Germany, and Italy took place both before and during her exile. These journeys and her observations of the political and social structures and problems of other countries would become the inspiration for some of her most important works.

The concept of cosmopolitanism in Staël's works has also been amply studied. Esther Wohlgemut, relying on Immanuel Kant and Bruce Robbins, defines the term thusly: "Cosmopolitanism subordinates the historical inescapability of place to a trans-historical, trans-national ethical constant, creating a form of nationness [. . .]. Understood in a Kantian sense, cosmopolitanism does not mean the absence of all national attachment or the elimination of national boundaries in the creation of a single world state. Rather, it involves the co-existence of national demarcations and universal belonging, of form and freedom."[7] Jill Heydt-Stevenson and Jeffrey Cox explain what I view to be the crux of the cosmopolitan question specifically as it is seen in *Corinne*: "From the start, cosmopolitanism raised the question of whether it provided one with a wider vision than that afforded within the restricted interests of home or city or nation or whether it loosened the ties that bind only to leave the cosmopolite unbound wandering in the no man's land of exile."[8] For Corinne, that question of "wider vision" or condemnation to exile is not an either/or option, but both. Her "wider vision" leads to the loss of her love affair with Oswald and, eventually, the loss of her life. Heydt-Stevenson and Cox go on to state that "cosmopolitanism eschews binaries in favor of subject positions that strive toward the flexible."[9] The flexibility upheld by the novel arguably leads to Corinne's undoing, but also creates a sense of community among her readers. Staël activates what April Alliston has termed an "idealized interpersonal bond of sympathy" that is used "to represent utopian imaginary communities that transgress the limits defining nations."[10] Staël intentionally tugs on her readers' sympathetic heartstrings, demanding that we sympathize with Corinne's plight in order to make us imagine with her the idyllic community she envisions.

The categorization of Staël's *Corinne, or Italy* as a novel-travelogue invites us to examine the work from an ethnographical as well as a narratological standpoint. Before proceeding, however, I wish to define the terms *ethnography* and *autoethnography*. According to Paul Atkinson:

> [Ethnography] displays not merely the sequential order of social life, but also its consequentiality. Through narrative the ethnographer—like the historian, the biographer, or the novelist—shapes individual and collective action, character, and motive. The ethnography embeds and comments on the stories told by informants, investing them with a significance often beyond their mundane production. It includes the ethnographer's own accounts of incidents, "cases," and the like. They too are transformed and enhanced by their recontextualization in the ethnography itself. These narrative instances are collected and juxtaposed in the text so that their meaning (sociological or anthropological significance) is implied by the ethnographer and reconstructed by the reader.[11]

Atkinson goes on to highlight what we could call the literary aspects of ethnography, explaining that an ethnographic text "can set up a reader's expectations only to deny them. It can transform the reported events of everyday life into the heroic, or endow them with weighty significance. The ethnography can become a morality tale, a high drama, a picaresque tale of low-life characters, a comedy of manners, a rural idyll."[12] James Clifford similarly explains that there are numerous ways to determine ethnographic writing and that the end result is what he calls "ethnographic fictions." He justifies the term as follows:

> It suggests the partiality of cultural and historical truths, the ways they are systematic and exclusive. Ethnographic writings can properly be called fictions in the sense of "something made or fashioned," the principal burden of the word's Latin root, *fingere*. But it is important to preserve the meaning not merely of making, but also of making up, of inventing things not actually real. (*Fingere*, in some of its uses, implied a degree of falsehood.)[13]

When the ethnographer compiles observations into a meaningful context, a fictional element is introduced into the ethnography. Fact and fiction merge, therefore, resulting in a final product that aggregates multiple genres.

"Autoethnography," a term coined by Mary Louise Pratt, is the response of the object of ethnography. In her article on transculturation, she defines an autoethnographic text as one "in which people undertake to describe themselves in ways that engage with representations others have made of them . . . autoethnographic texts are representations that the so-defined others construct *in response to* or in dialogue with those texts."[14] Those being studied answer and often counter their observers.

The tour of Italy—at the time a grouping of city-states on the cusp of nationhood—lends itself perfectly to the post-colonial concepts of ethnography and autoethnography. The novel woven around and through the travelogue is a third-person narration, however. Moreover, the information given by the narrator is not merely the framework of a travelogue, but rather stories that move the plot forward and are intertwined with the fate of the work's heroine. As Madelyn Gutwirth so aptly explained, "So it is that places are to some extent integrated with the plot, but no outline could pretend to contain the travelogue, because it is everywhere in the work."[15] Thus these two apparently unrelated tools of literary analysis—post-colonial theory and narratology—come together quite harmoniously to help elucidate this discussion. Genette himself seems to justify this marriage of travel and the novel when he explains that "written narrative exists in space and as space, and the time needed for 'consuming' it is the time needed for *crossing* or *traversing* it, like a road or a field."[16] Although Genette's metaphor is intended for the reader, the author, one could argue, is the one who, like the narrator of *Corinne*, leads the reader through the journey's text. Genette also specifically references (albeit in a footnote) what he calls "travel narratives," citing Stendhal's *Mémoires d'un touriste* (*Memoirs of a Tourist*, 1838) and Victor Hugo's *Le Rhin* (*The Rhine*, 1845). He uses these two Romantic texts as examples of geographical syllepsis, "the principle of narrative grouping in voyage narratives that are embellished by anecdotes."[17] While Genette's brief discussion of geographical syllepsis highlights the importance of narrative in a travel text, *Corinne* is better characterized by thematic syllepsis, "with its numerous insertions of 'stories,' justified by relations of analogy or contrast."[18]

I would first like to demonstrate that the narrator in *Corinne* is an ethnographer and that the ethnography takes place at the extradiegetic level of the narrative, whereas the narration provided by Corinne is an autoethnography and takes place at the diegetic level. At the beginning of the work, Corinne shows Oswald around Rome, pointing out her favorite places, artwork, and architecture. The narration here switches between Corinne's voice and that of the narrator. First, Corinne explains why she has chosen to organize their tour as she has, preferring to show Oswald the best of Rome first so that he will be prepared for and open to the other wonders of the city:

> "Perhaps *I* should have had you see our most beautiful buildings last," *Corinne said,* "but that is not my method. *I* think you have to begin with things that inspire deep and lively admiration if you want to develop sensitivity to the arts. Once experienced, this feeling reveals a new sphere of ideas, so to speak; the result is that you develop a greater ability to love and judge everything that recalls your first impression, even if it is of a lesser order."[19]

At St. Peter's, the narrator then takes over and elaborates on the physical aspects of the monument, its columns, its history, the obelisques, the fountain. Corinne interrupts the narrator's ethnography, however, to give her own autoethnography of the site, elaborating on how one *should* respond to the magnitude and solemnity of this place: "'Stop here for a moment,' said Corinne to Lord Nelvil who was already under the portico of the church . . . 'does not your heart beat faster as you draw near the sanctuary? And as you are about to enter, do you not feel all the expectation a solemn event would inspire?'"[20] Corinne cannot let St. Peter's speak for itself, as it were. She is so eager to have Oswald become a part of her cosmopolitan community that she attempts to inform him of the acceptable reaction to this hallowed place. When Oswald answers by critiquing the lack of "human dignity," Corinne responds with an even stronger autoethnographic response, saying, "There is so much spirituality in our arts that perhaps one day our character will equal our genius."[21] What is problematic here is that this autoethnography is being penned by an ethnographer—Staël is not Italian. The words she places in Corinne's mouth cannot truly be the response of the ethnographic subject and thus any attempt to defend the Italian people and customs comes across as something just short of benevolent pity. Moreover, Corinne is not simply Italian, but also English. Nevertheless, Corinne is an autoethnographer and her autoethnography takes place at the diegetic level of the narrative: it is the story. As Marie-Claire Vallois has pointed out: "Italy is the metaphorical double of the heroine."[22] The entire story is centered on Corinne's response to the way that she is seen by Oswald, or the way that Italy is seen.

Each time that Corinne defends herself or Italy, therefore, she takes part in an autoethnographic response. For example, after Oswald has insulted Italian women, saying that they are incapable of a deep, sincere love, she refuses to see him because "the views he had expressed on Italian women grieved her painfully, and precisely because of those views she made it a rule for the future to hide the feeling that was sweeping her away—if only she could."[23] Her role, then, is rather that of the "go-between" or the "contact zone" between England and Italy.[24] She reacts to Oswald's opinions on women both as a defender of Italian women and *as* an Italian woman herself. As Balayé points out: "Corinne will thus play the role of mediator between Oswald and Italy."[25] The multiplicity present in this and all the other scenes like it illustrates the resonant theme of multiple voices and multiple perspectives that is so central to the work, advancing a utopian vision of a world in which traditional boundaries and limitations are no longer of importance. In other words, Staël's intentions are laudable (in spite of the tone of benevolent pity) in that she is trying to depict such multiplicity and duality in her characters in an effort to broaden her readers' perspectives.

Another ethnographic narration takes place while Corinne and Oswald are in Naples. The narrator provides many details about the people of Naples and the impact the climate has had on their way of life. Describing the Lazzaroni and "their taste for money," the narrator comments: "What is most lacking in *this nation* is the sense of dignity."[26] The use of the words "this nation" underscores the fact that the narrator is viewing Naples—and all of Italy—as a foreigner. The depiction of "this nation," therefore, comes from an outsider, is tinged with exoticism, and thus displays what Atkinson calls the consequentiality of social life as seen in an ethnography.[27] The narrator does not merely describe social life, but rather imbues the social life with a meaning and significance.

The narrator's ethnography is also seen, near the end of the work, when Oswald returns to Italy with his wife, Lucile, and their daughter, Juliette. The absence of Corinne the autoethnographer, here, is profound and creates a vacuum for both the reader and Oswald and his new family. They arrive in Bologna, and they both look in vain for what they believe to be the "real" Italy. For Oswald, Italy is only incarnated by Corinne herself, whereas Lucile relies on preconceived notions of what Italy is. Yet they are both sorely disappointed by what they find. "Bologna is one of the cities where you find the greatest number of men learned in all disciplines, but its people make an unpleasant impression. Lucile had heard about the harmonious language of Italy, and the Bolognese dialect must have proved a painful surprise, for there is none harsher in the countries of the north," the narrator states, reiterating that "indeed, everything in this place gave the impression of a people without dignity."[28] The narrator presents a picture both of Bologna itself and how Bologna impacts the characters in the story.

Not only does the narrator serve as a guide through the Italian countryside, but she also serves as a guide into the thoughts and emotions of Lucile and Oswald. This narrator is the classic third-person omniscient narrator and yet is also the text's ethnographer. The narration continues:

> Italy can be judged in many different ways, according to circumstances. Sometimes what you see corresponds to what people say when they speak ill of her, and at other times they seem supremely unjust. In a country where most governments were without safe-guards and the authority of public opinion almost as inconsequential for the highest classes as for the lowest, in a country where religion is more concerned with ceremony than with morality, there is little to be said for the nation considered in a general way, and yet many private qualities are to be found. Thus chance relationships inspire mockery or praise in travelers, and the people we know individually determine our judgment of the nation as a whole, a judgment that cannot be solidly based on institutions, customs, or public spirit.[29]

This description of the shortcomings of Italy is classic ethnography.[30] The ethnographer gives both her observations and interpretations of the culture being observed. What is missing here is an explicit autoethnographic response on the part of Corinne. Without her defense of the people of Bologna, the portrait is incomplete, and Oswald and Lucile are left feeling disappointed and unfulfilled. Instead, the autoethnographic response is implicit: when Italy is viewed through Corinne's eyes, with Corinne acting as Italy's representative, spokesperson, and ideal form, the traveler's opinions of Italy cannot help but be positive. In Corinne's absence, however, Italy is misunderstood and unappreciated.

At one point in the work, the narrator's ethnography is complicated by a narrative switching. While in Naples, we see for the first time that the narrator, previously speaking as the omniscient third person, takes on an invested tone in the telling of the story, using collective personal pronouns instead of the earlier impersonal pronouns. In describing the effect of the heady citrus trees, the narrator states: "In *our* climate, there is nothing like the southern perfume of lemon trees in open country."[31] With this one (perhaps intentional) slip of the pen, the narrator reveals that s/he is not Italian and is a stranger in this land: "The whole aspect of the countryside is foreign. You feel that you are in another world, in a world known only through the descriptions of the ancient poets, who show so much imagination along with such precision in their portrayals."[32] Clearly, the narrator of this story is not Italian, and the ethnography performed here is cemented with the narrator's own foreignness. In the next paragraph, the narrator again uses the collective pronoun, not only illustrating a perspective of being on the outside looking in to Italy, but also causing the reader a sense of confusion: who is speaking here? The sea is described thus: "This aimless motion, this purposeless force, repeated throughout eternity without *our* having any way to know either its cause or its object; *we* feel somehow terrified and obliged to draw near the waves and let their uproar dull *our* thoughts."[33] This sort of pre-Flaubertian switch between the collective and personal "our/nous" and impersonal "you/on" gives the reader pause. Genette explains that with the use of free indirect speech, "the narrator takes on the speech of the character, or, if one prefers, the character speaks through the voice of the narrator, and the two instances are then *merged*."[34] Who is this "we"? Has Corinne taken over the narration without the aid of quotation marks? The us/them binary mirrored in the ebb and flow of the sea's tides is a powerful metaphor, but the ambiguity of the "us" creates a hybridized narrator that serves to advance Staël's goal of cosmopolitanism. For if the narrator, Corinne, Oswald, and even the readers are implicated in this discussion, then there is a commonality of existence and experience.

A final level of ethnography in the narration of this work can be found in the extradiegetic author's notes, adding an element of authenticity to the text and yet also further problematizing the question of truth. Whose truth is being depicted and through what lens? This extradiegesis, while it does not advance the plot, does clarify the story being told in that it offers yet another perspective on the story's events. These are not the narrator's observations, nor Corinne's, but those of the author herself. Take, for instance, Corinne's improvisation at the Capitol. The narrator points out to us that Corinne's vocal modulations during her improvisations are quite unique: "Most Italians read verse in a monotonous tone called *cantilena* that destroys all feeling. It makes no difference that the words vary; the effect is the same since the tone of voice—more telling than the words—scarcely changes. But Corinne used a variety of tones that did not destroy the sustained charm of the harmony."[35] First, the information the narrator relates here is provided solely through external focalization—these details are not about Corinne's thoughts or feelings, these are simply the facts. The ethnography relays a brief and critical impression of the way in which Italians "normally" deliver their verses and then announces Corinne's uniqueness. Without speaking of her own improvisational style, Corinne is nonetheless afforded the opportunity to give an autoethnographic response with regards to reading poetry: we (Italians) do not all use this unappealing style. Staël, then, in an author's note, goes on to explain that there is indeed one "real" person in Italy who, like Corinne, modulates his voice: "The celebrated Monti, who recites verse the way he writes it is a clear exception to this criticism of the Italian declamatory style. It is truly one of the greatest theatrical pleasures to hear him recite."[36] Staël's insertion of her own comments here serves to justify and validate Corinne's exceptionality as an *improvisatrice*. She uses a contemporary and well-known example (Monti) to support both the narrator's criticism of the usual declamatory style and the possibility of Corinne's unique and rare talent. What's more, Staël furthers her goal of forming a cosmopolitan community of readers by creating a community of viewers in the text itself. The crowd who gathers to hear Corinne's improvisations coupled with the crowd who hears Monti's declamations signifies the importance of community in Staël's cosmopolitan vision.

Another example of authorial narration is found in the famous scene of Corinne dancing the tarantella. The dance is recounted by the narrator, through the eyes of the Comte d'Erfeuil and Lord Nevil, both of whom are surprised by how quickly Corinne accepts the offer to perform this dance. The use of internal focalization in this scene allows the readers a double layer of voyeurism, in that the narrator shows us the audience watching Corinne, and so our reception of this dance is mediated by their reactions. And, like with Corinne's improvisations, a community of viewers comes together. The narrator then explains that Corinne danced so gracefully and well that she "called to life, in succession, a host of new ideas for drawing and painting."[37] The author's note on this scene explains: "It was Madame de Récamier's dancing that suggested the dance I have tried to portray here."[38] The multiple levels of inspiration here are noteworthy: Madame Récamier inspires Madame de Staël to create this dance for Corinne. The narrator then recounts that Corinne inspires her observers to draw and paint. The interruption of the author here, however, raises the question of *why* Staël feels the need to justify including this story in her text. It could be that, like the note on declamatory style in Italy, Staël simply wants to explain how this idea originated and give credit where it is due. In this same note, Staël writes that Récamier "so famous for her grace and beauty, offers in the midst of her misfortunes so touching an example of resignation and total disregard for her own interests, that her moral qualities seem as remarkable as her charm in everyone's eyes."[39] For Madame de Staël, Madame Récamier is, like Corinne, the perfect embodiment of both beauty and talent, both attractiveness and morality. Similar to the improvisation scene, the tarantella scene features a group of people who gather to watch Corinne perform. This group, coupled with the group who had gathered to watch Mme Récamier dance, work together to highlight the role of community viewing, and to activate the sympathetic imagination of the reader.

This authorial intervention is also evident in the scene in which Oswald and Lucile are disappointed by the people of Bologna. The narrator writes, "Sedentary life perfects the social order, but the sun introduces something wild into the practices of the common people by allowing them to live in the street."[40] This ethnographic description evokes the climate theory evident in Staël's *On Literature*, as well as in the writings of her predecessors, Montesquieu, Rousseau, and Smith. The savagery induced by the sun is witnessed in the "beggars who are generally the scourge of Italy" and the prisoners who "took the most unpleasant joy in calling to the passersby in thundering tones, asking help with disgraceful jokes and unrestrained laughter."[41] Staël's authorial note on this scene adds further ethnographic "proof" of the existence of this "people without dignity":

> A solar eclipse had been announced for two o'clock in the afternoon in Bologna. The people gathered in the public square to see it, and impatient when it was late, they summoned it impetuously, as they would an actor who kept them waiting; and when cloudy weather kept it from producing a fine effect, they began to hiss noisily, judging that the show did not live up to their expectations.[42]

Again, the extradiegetic addition here does more than simply justify the scene. What we have is ethnography couched in an amusing travel note. While a comical aside, the story serves to prove that the first impression of the Bolognese is indeed that they are coarse, childish, and uncivilized. Staël's authorial addition acts as an authoritative eyewitness account. More importantly, though, Staël portrays yet another community of viewers—those who have gathered to see the eclipse. Thus, there is once again an extradiegetic as well as an intradiegetic community of viewers present.

Perhaps the most intriguing and poignant use of authorial intervention comes when Corinne reads Oswald's father's words regarding a father's death. The multiple levels of narrative here are rendered even more striking by the author's note. While Corinne reads aloud to Oswald the words of his father, intended for Oswald, Staël herself informs the readers that these are the words of her own father! She writes:

I have taken the liberty of borrowing here several passages from *The Discourse on Death*, which may be found in Monsieur Necker's *Course on Religious Morality*. . . . Without fear that my opinion will be ascribed to my feelings, I will say that among religious writings, this book is one of the first to console the sensitive being and interest minds that reflect on the great questions that soul and thought ceaselessly stir up within us.[43]

Once again, the narration is hybridized. Although Corinne, the spokesperson of Italy, is the actual narrator here (she is the one speaking), the words are those of Oswald's father, which are those of Staël's father—it's enough to make the reader's head spin. The ethnography that takes place in this scene is far more metaphoric than in the other examples. Oswald's father's writings read as an ethnography of the journey from life to death. Referring again to the earlier cited definition of ethnography given by Atkinson, we can argue that Oswald's father does not relay only the "sequential order of social life" with regards to facing death, but also gives it a more profound meaning: he gives instructions on how a man should prepare his family for his death. As with Staël's previous authorial remarks, the comment she makes at this juncture calls to mind a community of viewers or, in this case, readers. In this last instance, however, the sympathies of the reader are brought to the forefront, and the community of viewers does more than simply connect one event to another. Here, the community of viewers is even allowed to connect one era to another, life to death. As Alliston has explained, Staël does not create in this novel an imagined community as Benedict Anderson might suggest, but rather creates a "novelistic sympathetic [community that decentralizes] the nation-state geographically."[44] The focus is not on an imagined community within the nation, but rather on what Margaret Cohen calls an imagined community of sentimentality that is transnational.[45]

While the multiplicity, complicity, and duality that are present in *Corinne, or Italy* can cause a certain amount of ambiguity, the revolutionary message of equality, utopia, and cosmopolitanism prevails. The interplay between ethnography and autoethnography, and between diegetic and extradiegetic narrative, illustrates precisely Staël's cosmopolitan ideology and hope for communication between cultures and between past, present and future. As Jennifer Birkett has explained, "Every word in Staël's text recognizes the constitutive force and the dominant pull of the past, inscribed in that vast sequence of present landscapes over which Corinne travels and whose history both she and the narrative voice evoke . . ., and carried by the individuals of different cultures who make up Corinne's various audiences."[46] A work written in French, with extensive references to the

Italian and English languages, and peppered with quotes from German authors, can certainly be defined as polyglot. Multiple narrative voices lead to a multilingual and polyphonic tone that reflects Staël's cosmopolitanism and her desire to showcase the value of all voices and perspectives.

Notes

1. See Jennifer Law-Sullivan, "Border Crossings as a Gateway to Border Dwellings: The Case of the Novelogue," *Prism(s): Essays in Romanticism* 13 (2005): 47–62.

2. On Corinne's voice see, for example, Marie-Claire Vallois, "Voice as Fossil; Germaine de Staël's *Corinne, or Italy*: An Archaeology of Feminine Discourse," in *The Novel's Seductions: Staël's* Corinne *in Critical Inquiry*, ed. Karyna Szmurlo (Lewisburg, PA: Bucknell University Press, 1999), 127–38. See also Doris Y. Kadish, "Narrating the French Revolution: The Example of *Corinne*," in *Germaine de Staël: Crossing the Borders*, eds. Madelyn Gutwirth, Avriel Goldberger, and Karyna Szmurlo (New Brunswick, NJ: Rutgers University Press, 1991), 113–21. See also Joan DeJean, "Portrait of the Artist as Sappho," in the same volume, 122–37.

3. Avriel Goldberger, in her introduction to *Corinne, or Italy*, gives an excellent account of Staël's travels throughout Germany and Italy and the influences of these visits on *On Germany* and *Corinne* (in Germaine de Staël, *Corinne, or Italy*, ed. and trans. Avriel Goldberger [New Brunswick, NJ: Rutgers University Press, 1987], xxvii–xxxii).

4. Germaine de Staël, *Les Carnets de voyage de Madame de Staël: Contribution à la genèse de ses œuvres*, ed. Simone Balayé (Genève: Droz, 1971), 15.

5. See Pratima Prasad, *Colonialism, Race, and the French Romantic Imagination* (New York: Routledge, 2009).

6. Simone Balayé, *Madame de Staël: Lumières et liberté* (Paris: Klincksieck, 1979), 101.

7. Esther Wohlgemut, *Romantic Cosmopolitanism* (New York: Palgrave Macmillan, 2009), 1.

8. Jill Heydt-Stevenson and Jeffrey N. Cox, "Introduction: Are Those Who Are 'Strangers Nowhere in the World' at Home Anywhere?: Thinking about Romantic Cosmopolitanism," *European Romantic Review* 16, no. 2 (April 2005): 131.

9. Ibid., 135.

10. April Alliston, "Transnational Sympathies, Imaginary Communities," in *The Literary Channel: The Inter-National Invention of the Novel*, eds. Margaret Cohen and Carolyn Dever (Princeton, NJ: Princeton University Press, 2002), 133.

11. Paul Atkinson, *Understanding Ethnographic Texts* (Newbury Park, CA: Sage Publications, 1992), 13.

12. Ibid., 13.

13. James Clifford and George E. Marcus, eds., *Writing Culture: The Poetics and Politics of Ethnography* (Berkeley: University of California Press, 1986), 6.

14. Emphasis is Mary Louise Pratt's in "Transculturation and Autoethnography: Peru, 1615/1980," in *Colonial Discourse, Postcolonial Theory*, eds. Francis Barker, Peter Hulme, and Margaret Iversen. (Manchester: Manchester University Press, 1994), 28.

15. Madelyn Gutwirth, *Madame de Staël, Novelist: The Emergence of the Artist as Woman* (Urbana: University of Illinois Press, 1978), 184.

16. Gérard Genette, *Narrative Discourse: An Essay in Method*, trans. Jane E. Lewin (Ithaca, NY: Cornell University Press, 1983), 34.

17. Ibid., 85.

18. Ibid.

19. Emphasis mine; Staël, *Corinne, or Italy*, 56–57.

20. Ibid., 58.

21. Ibid., 59.

22. Marie Claire Vallois, "Old Idols, New Subject: Germaine de Staël and Romanticism," in *Germaine de Staël: Crossing the Borders*, eds. Madelyn Gutwirth, Avriel Goldberger, and Karyna Szmurlo (New Brunswick, NJ: Rutgers University Press, 1991), 89.

23. Staël, *Corinne, or Italy*, 97.

24. Pratt defines contact zones as "social spaces where disparate cultures meet, clash, and grapple with each other, often in highly asymmetrical relations of domination and subordination . . ." (Mary Louis Pratt, *Imperial Eyes: Travel Writing and Transculturation* [New York: Routledge, 1992], 4).

25. Balayé, *Lumières et Liberté*, 141.

26. Emphasis mine; Staël, *Corinne, or Italy*, 198.

27. Atkinson, *Understanding Ethnographic Texts*, 13.

28. Staël, *Corinne, or Italy*, 399.

29. Ibid., 399–400.

30. Staël has been harshly criticized for her deficient Italianism. For more on this discussion, see Robert Casillo, *The Empire of Stereotypes: Germaine de Staël and the Idea of Italy* (New York: Palgrave Macmillan, 2006); and Joseph Luzzi, "Translator's Introduction: Italy in Translation," *Romanic Review* 97, nos. 3–4 (May–November 2006): 275–78.

31. Emphasis mine; Staël, *Corinne, or Italy*, 194; Staël, *Corinne ou l'Italie*, 286.

32. Staël, *Corinne, or Italy*, 194. The narrator's gender is perhaps a question to be examined in another study. For the purposes of this analysis, suffice it to say that the narrator's gender is not obvious and so I have chosen gender-neutral terms where possible.

33. Emphasis mine; ibid., 194.

34. Genette, *Narrative Discourse*, 174.

35. Staël, *Corinne, or Italy*, 31.

36. Ibid., 422.

37. Ibid., 92.

38. Ibid., 425.

39. Ibid.

40. Ibid., 399.

41. Ibid.

42. Ibid., 434.

43. Ibid., 427.

44. Alliston, "Transnational Sympathies, Imaginary Communities," 142–43.

45. Margaret Cohen, "Sentimental Communities," in *The Literary Channel: The Inter-National Invention of the Novel*, eds. Margaret Cohen and Carolyn Dever (Princeton, NJ: Princeton University Press, 2002), 107.

46. Jennifer Birkett, "Speech in Action: Language, Society, and Subject in Germaine de Staël's *Corinne*," *Eighteenth-Century Fiction* 7, no. 4 (July 1995): 399.

7

LIQUID UNION: LISTENING THROUGH TEARS AND
THE CREATION OF COMMUNITY IN *CORINNE*

Lauren Fortner Ravalico

IN A RECENT BIOGRAPHY of Germaine de Staël, Francine du Plessix Gray paints a portrait of her subject as a fascinatingly unattractive, yet "extravagantly seductive" conversationalist who "even when not talking tended to leave her mouth slightly open."[1] In a review of du Plessix Gray's book, historian Stacy Schiff perfectly (if perhaps unwittingly) reproduces the biographer's tone of snarky admiration to ironize "the first modern woman" as a busybody and plucky troublemaker who "woke with her mouth open" and "fell silent only when asleep." Schiff sums up Staël's biography with a quick series of gossipy insults culminating in an anecdote about the one man who finally silenced her:

> As a woman, she comes off as a mix of self-regard, self-delusion, and raw, overpowering intellect. Her physical charms were less defined, by no means set off to advantage by her wardrobe. She went in for feathered turbans and vibrantly colored décolletés. You know the type; if you grew up in a small town, she taught modern dance. She was speechless on only one recorded occasion, an early meeting with First Consul Bonaparte. "No doubt," he ventured, speaking directly to her formidable bosom, "you have nursed your children yourself?"[2]

This Napoleon "bosom scene" reappears especially in mainstream English-language biographies about Staël to illustrate the animosity between the two historical figures.[3] Schiff seems to take particular delight in portraying Staël as a debased figure whom Napoleon effectively put in her place. And yet, the fact that biographers harp on this specific anecdote in which Staël is shocked into embarrassed silence suggests a more widespread Napoleonesque discomfort in twenty-first-century culture with the combination of her amply visible womanhood and life-long participation in the public sphere of intellectual conversation.

To the contrary, in his complimentary piece on Staël in *Portraits of Women*, nineteenth-century literary critic Charles-Augustin Sainte-Beuve exalts the role of conversation in her life and work. Sainte-Beuve insists on the importance of verbal exchange as the force animating the author's "quick and penetrating [wit]" that sets apart Staël's immensely successful second novel, *Corinne, or Italy*, as an "immortal monument."[4] In the introduction to Staël's *The Influence of the Passions on the Happiness of Individuals and Nations*, Chantal Thomas elaborates on the central role of verbal self-expression in the author's thinking and writing process:

> Both noise and the notion of a public are inherent to the energy of Mme de Staël's writing. The solitude of writing is mitigated in her mind by the multitude of future readers. . . . She is in conversation with generations to come. There is nothing more foreign to her than absolute solitude without sharing, without an interlocutor.[5]

It is not surprising, then, that Staël's seminal work, *Corinne*, is a noisy novel in-sofar as it stages many different speech acts, particularly that of conversation. Set against the historical backdrop of eighteenth-century European tourism, the novel explores the possibilities of dialogue, friendship, and love across cultures. The male protagonist, Oswald Lord Nelvil, departs from Scotland in 1794 on a voyage to Italy that reflects and perverts the upsurge in "travel for health" as a restorative form of tourism.[6] The purpose of his trip is to get beyond the guilt and melancho-lia from which he suffers after the death of his father, a loss the narrator calls "the most personal of all griefs."[7] Upon his arrival in Rome, the beautiful and talented Italian *improvisatrice,* Corinne, quickly consumes his attention as the archetypal "object of idolatry" for young English men abroad.[8] Partly a doomed love story be-tween an artistic woman and a melancholy man and partly a European travelogue, the novel is arranged according to twenty episodes that chart both a spatial and an emotional itinerary. The massive book features scenes of extensive dialogue, episto-lary exchange, poetic improvisation, theatrical performance, and an opinionated, omniscient narrator who mediates the narrative with comments and clarifications.

Corinne and Oswald's battle to love one another and their ultimate inability to find happiness together often find expression in such repetitive and hyperbolic wordiness that the novel can read like a theatrical melodrama in which, as Peter Brooks describes it, "nothing is *under*stood, all is *over*stated."[9] Indeed, Margaret Waller has characterized the protagonists' rocky courtship as "a conversation" in which Oswald "will listen (although he will not always hear)." Further on, Waller uses the metaphor of reading to hint at the mutual problem of deafness or misunderstanding: "Corinne finds that Oswald is *not* an open book for her."[10] Madelyn Gutwirth goes so far as to argue that conversations between the two protagonists suffer from a "static, frozen quality rob[bing] the whole [novel] of forward movement."[11] In the midst of such linguistic immobility—a veritable whiteout of words—where exactly is the conversational effect that Sainte-Beuve senses in his reading of *Corinne*?

Though the practice of conversation certainly implies illocution, equally important to its functioning is the *reception* of language in which we silence our voices in order to listen, to digest meaning, and to produce some kind of response—whether verbal or gestural—that implies absorption of the other's words. In *On Germany*, Staël characterizes the reciprocal energy of conversation as "a sort of electricity that makes sparks fly," and she criticizes the Germans as bad conversationalists primarily because they are overly literal listeners lacking in a sense of playfulness.[12] Catherine Rilliet Huber's account of having dinner at the Necker household when she was thirteen and Germaine was eleven suggests that active listening was in fact constitutive of Staël's development as a brilliant thinker:

> We weren't allowed to talk during dinner; we were listening, but you must understand how Mlle Necker would listen! Her eyes followed each speaker's movements and seemed to be jumping in front of their ideas. She never opened her mouth, and yet her body was so expressive that she seemed to speak in turn. She was following everything, grasping everything, understanding it all.[13]

Set against the backdrop of conversation in Madame de Staël's life and in her writing, this chapter aims to amplify the understated, yet integral role of listening in *Corinne*. Recall Thomas's assertion that both noise *and* the notion of a public are native to Staël's writing.[14] Similarly, Karyna Szmurlo identifies *Corinne* as a type of "relational writing" that implies a "dynamic exchange between reader and text."[15] While scholars acknowledge that the notion of reception is fundamental to Staël's construction of narrative, no one has used the basic intersubjective structure of conversation to probe the question of how her writing might go about relating the relational in terms of *aural* receptivity. In other words, does Staël go beyond just thinking about a public that will receive her work in order to creatively theorize *within her writing* what it means to be in a position of receptivity? Can we thus find figural traces of listening amidst all the noise of *Corinne*?

I set about locating those traces in a discussion that unfolds in two parts and follows the flow of conversation. I begin with a story of deep listening to suggest that the effect of "frozen" language we sense when reading *Corinne* is due to a dynamic of verbal manipulation that stagnates conversational communication between the protagonists. Corinne and Oswald's story would be unreadable, however, if their interactions were entirely frigid. I then pinpoint a sudden thawing, as it were, in instances of extra-linguistic communication that occur when the characters cry together. Tears communicate through a body language of psychic anguish that, I argue, can be wordlessly shared to represent reciprocal listening as the experience of understanding without relying on verbal communication. Listening through tears functions in the text to advocate sympathy as a mode of living outside the self that initiates a communal bond among individuals.

Historians and literary scholars of the eighteenth century have aptly interpreted the representation of tears and listening (specifically to music) in art as fostering a sense of emotional community among readers and spectators. I problematize this notion by studying the phenomenological substance at the root of both of these physical actions of human receptivity that makes them such powerful signifiers of community. The conclusion I reach is that crying and listening are both involved in a kind of metaphysical border crossing: they are bodily and yet something else at the same time. It is in their overlap, as transcendent experiences in everyday embodied life, which allows us to better understand the potential within the affective and the sensorial event to create sentimental communities.

Aural Absorption and Verbal Manipulation

During an episode of the radio program *Fresh Air* from 2009, journalist Terry Gross interviewed actor Gabriel Byrne about his role as a psychotherapist on the HBO series *In Treatment*. This exchange between a professional interlocutor and an expert on the character of the attentive analyst provides a vocabulary for thinking about listening and the question of its representation in art that pertains to *Corinne*. Early on in the interview, Byrne talks about developing his television character out of the happenstance experience of observing an interaction between a couple at a café one day while he was having coffee. He describes what he saw:

> And she was so absorbed in everything that he was saying. . . . In the act of engaging with him by listening she was outside herself. And I looked at them and thought: "That is what listening is, when you're absolutely

absorbed in what the other person is saying" . . . Really, truly, profoundly listening is to be unaware of yourself at a deep level.

This description of the act of listening and the kind of generosity it implies brings forth several conceptual issues—to which I will return—concerning the role of bodies and borders in how we imagine the event of successful interpersonal communication. More immediately though, it makes us wonder how one might attempt to represent the complexity of such an experience in art. In fact, Byrne tells his anecdote in response to a comment Gross makes: "Watching somebody listen . . . usually isn't a great visual experience."[16] While she is asking how to make listening look like an action the television camera can pick up, the issue of listening and the possibility of its representation in visual art actually has a rich history in the eighteenth century. In France in the 1750s, artists like Jean-Baptiste Greuze, Carle Van Loo, and Jean-Baptiste-Siméon Chardin led a trend away from the predominantly Rococo aesthetic of decorative art toward a form of genre painting that depicted human subjects in various narrative scenes of mental and emotional captivation, especially in the acts of reading and listening. Art historian Michael Fried has famously analyzed these paintings in tandem with Denis Diderot's art criticism to argue that such works represent states of receptivity that he calls "absorption." Absorptive paintings evoked intense emotional responses in Diderot, and Fried concludes that they entreat the spectator to engage in a kind of mimetic or responsive experience of absorption through viewing; the utter captivation of the depicted subjects to the exclusion of all else makes us feel the reality effect of absorption itself.[17]

Fried is making a case for French Enlightenment painting as an interactive, phenomenological study of receptivity, and throughout he uses the terms "absorption" and *oubli de soi* [forgetting of the self] to define the ontological state of receptiveness. Gabriel Byrne's ekphrastic description of the real scene of listening he witnessed draws on these same key concepts to define the kind of receptivity on which he based his motion picture portrayal of psychoanalytic attention. The overlap between Fried and Byrne's conceptual vocabulary to convey the power of the *visual* spectacle of listening raises the question of whether such representational complexity is possible in literature. How might an art form fashioned through words go about representing the complicated psychic and emotional interiority involved in the wordless act of listening?[18]

As I indicated at the outset, my response is that narrative moments of shared tears in *Corinne* work metaphorically to capture the essence of aural receptivity as a profound and existential experience of exiting the self. This sense of transcendence is only perceptible, however, in contrast with scenes of linguistic communication between Corinne and Oswald. Their dialogue demonstrates the perils involved in giving oneself over to listening: in risking to understand another person through the exchange of words, we also desire to control the other's desire.

Falling in love with Corinne and Italy has been, since the beginning, a gamble for Oswald. Bound emotionally and politically to his father, a deceased role model, Oswald is what Naomi Schor calls "a severely depressed Oedipus."[19] As the story progresses and the noble Oswald agonizes over whether to risk his loyalty to patriarchal tradition in order to marry a liberated, creative, independent-minded woman, Oswald becomes an equally risky prize for Corinne. In the historical scheme of the Grand Tour, young British men were to return home having left the vices of tourism behind.[20] There is no role scripted for Corinne the Famous Poet in Oswald's life after the Grand Tour. Thus, she must use language to convey enough passion for Oswald to stay in the game, for she has wagered her public identity as well as her imaginative talents against becoming the Abandoned Woman or the idol-gone-idle Domesticated Wife.

The manipulation of language becomes a mode of bluffing that Corinne will use to forestall Oswald from making a choice between his father and her: "Corinne was not a frivolous person, but each day she felt increasingly enslaved by her love for Oswald, and she wanted to try to weaken its power."[21] Later on, when Oswald and Corinne pass through Ancona on their way to Venice, Oswald is horrified when Corinne bows down before him with the other villagers who coronate him in a kind of cult-like frenzy for having saved the villagers from a terrible fire. The narrator explains that Corinne's imagination has simply become spontaneously swept up in the intensity of emotion surrounding her, but Oswald is extremely disturbed by this display of excess and submission. Corinne manages to calm his panic by framing her mimetic participation in the fervor as complicity with traditional gender roles:

> Suddenly I was seized with the feeling of respect every woman has for the man she loves. To all appearances we women get the tribute, but in reality—in nature—it is the woman who deeply reveres the one she has chosen to defend her.[22]

Cleverly, she appeals to Oswald's patriarchal desire to protect her in order to keep him feeling as though her enraptured passion is acceptable to his British sense of propriety. Corinne therefore uses socially complicit language in a power play to convince Oswald to transgress the very social institutions with which she verbally complies. For yet another moment the love story survives, albeit held together with a loosely bound discursive suture that only temporarily safeguards the heroine's imagination.

Yet Corinne must eventually end the game and show her hand. She finally reveals that she knew Oswald's father who, in fact, rejected her as a suitable wife for his son. Upon learning the truth, Oswald decides to leave Italy and Corinne for Scotland. Once the story enters this textual space of "Parting and Absence," the unexpected repetition of the verb *entendre* exposes a layer of sentimental sincerity underneath the more cynical and verbally manipulative aspects of the courtship plot. Indeed, *entendre* begins to echo through this psychological state of separation anxiety and nostalgia to evoke the ineffable synergy of communication experienced in reciprocal love. The French word *entendre* derives from the Latin *intendere*, "to tend toward," and it signifies both "to hear" and "to understand." This double meaning highlights that understanding as a cognitive and psychic process is bound up with sensorial experience. As contemporary philosopher Jean-Luc Nancy explains in *À l'écoute* (*Listening*), the verb *écouter* (to listen) is equally deep in meaning and etymologically interchangeable with *entendre*:

> [We find] that kernel of meaning [in the verb *écouter*] where the use of a sensory organ (hearing, the ear, *auris*, a word that gives the first part of the verb *auscultare*, "to lend an ear," "to listen attentively," from which *écouter*, "to listen," comes) and a tension, an intention, and an attention, which the second part of the term marks, are combined. To listen is *tendre l'oreille*—literally, to stretch the ear.[23]

Nancy's evocation of the triad "tension, intention, and attention" further defines the cognitive and psychic stakes of listening; it involves a seemingly contradictory mental movement of both anxiety and care.

Oswald epitomizes the essence of Corinne's love as a kind of telepathic hearing—a deep, almost ineffable form of understanding—until the very end of the novel when he writes to his dying ex-lover: "Corinne, sublime friend, you who read into the heart, guess what I cannot say. Hear me as you used to hear me" [*entendez-moi comme vous m'entendiez*].[24] Meanwhile, the narrator also uses transcendent vocabulary to describe Corinne's overwrought elation in Scotland upon hearing Oswald's voice from the balcony of a ball when she clandestinely follows him after his departure from Italy: "Thus Corinne heard Oswald's voice. The voice of the one we love: indescribable thrill! Chaotic mixture of emotion and terror!"[25] Roland Barthes discusses the phenomenon of voice and the *jouissance* (orgasm/

pleasure/joy) that occurs through the instance of hearing it in his essay "The Grain of the Voice." He defines the grain of the voice as a quality of the human vocal instrument that makes use of language while simultaneously going beyond it toward a visceral and bodily essence to be perceived by the listener.[26] While Barthes is describing the reaction he has specifically when listening to the singing voice, Anne Deneys-Tunney argues that throughout *Corinne* there is no real effort to distinguish between the powerful effects one experiences when listening to speech versus music: "Contrary to Rousseau and Diderot's conceptions, for Madame de Staël the power of music lies more in the sound itself than in the words expressed by the voice."[27] The ineffability of Corinne's feeling certainly invokes orgasmic Barthesian pleasure, especially because it is Oswald's voice itself, rather than his words, that stirs her.

The eavesdropping scene becomes even more provocative as Corinne is filled with happiness when she perceives that Oswald's melancholia seems to persist even though he has returned home: "Corinne rejoiced to hear that sigh and the melancholy tone of his voice: she believed that she could be sure of regaining Oswald's heart, that she could still make him hear her" [*se faire encore entendre de lui*].[28] Corinne's longing to be heard again by her lover brings to mind Barthes's description of what he considers a kind of third level of listening in another essay, *Écoute* (*Listening*). He calls this sort of listening "psychoanalytic" because it is a depth of aural attention that does not seek out the literal meaning of language-content (the plot, so to speak); instead, it pursues "what the speaking-subject does not say," which is located underneath language at a subconscious level.[29] Barthes defines this subliminal level as "the corporeality of speaking, the voice which is at the threshold of body and discourse." Psychoanalytic listening thus seeks to hear the grain of the voice—"this materiality of the body surging forth from the throat"—located "between body and discourse." In order to be able to hear the grain, though, the listener must attempt to become fluent in the language of the other's subconscious. As such, she comes to mediate her own responses according to how she has internalized this new language.[30] Barthes thus theorizes that such deep listening "develops in an intersubjective space where 'I am listening' also means 'listen to me'; this is the game of transference, in which listening takes hold of 'I am listening' to reopen it infinitely."[31] Corinne hears the grain of Oswald's nagging desire and indecisiveness in the mental sickness that has stowed itself away in his soul. The Grand Tour in Italy did not cure him, and so her flame of hope is rekindled that Oswald will seek treatment, so to speak, in the "back and forth" of conversation therapy.[32]

The problem, of course, is that conversation between Corinne and Oswald becomes caught in a cycle of manipulation; the language of love effectively fails to create change—to create happiness between these two people dealing with major emotional pain. In his article "Communication and Power in Germaine de Staël: Transparency and Obstacle," Frank Bowman argues that "a major problem in Staël's writing" is "how communication is impeded or interrupted by silence, lying, hypocrisy, [and] the debasement of language."[33] In reading *Delphine* and *Corinne* through this dialectical approach, he assumes that Staël considers communication through language to be the ideal medium of transparency. If we pose the question of communication differently so as to read these "impediments" and "interruptions" as meaningful and interpretable in and of themselves, *Delphine* begins the deconstructive work that becomes fully realized in *Corinne*: to fracture the ideal of linguistic transparency by privileging the body as a more effective communication system. While the failure of language is an important aspect of the book, there is a level of communication beyond the verbal that gives weight to the protagonists' nostalgia for gracious listening as more than just the hapless idealization of their own love story. An effective, yet silent conversation occurs between two bodies in emotional pain that is expressed through the non-verbal language of tears.

Sharing Tears and Creating Community

Gabriel Byrne uses an intriguing amplification of terms to define the experience of active listening that will deepen our understanding of what is at stake in sharing tears in *Corinne*. He moves from "absorbed" to "outside herself" to "absolutely absorbed" to "unaware of yourself at a deep level." His vocabulary reveals a conception of listening based on the opposition of inside/outside, a binary that Maggie Kilgour reminds us, "as a spatial metaphor . . . has the illusion of stability and substance" and "is based in bodily experience and the sense that what is 'inside' one's own body is a coherent structure that can be defined against what lies 'outside' of it."[34] The woman's act of listening was so powerful for Byrne in the development of his character—the psychoanalytic listener—precisely because it seemed to succeed in dissolving this boundary in order to occupy the mental territory of the man. Such an image calls to mind Baudelaire articulating his insatiable, aching desire to "sortir de soi" [get out of self] in his diaries, and his frustrated awe before "ce noir océan où l'autre est enfermé" [this black ocean where the other is locked away] in the poem "La Chevelure" [The Head of Hair].[35] Indeed, Byrne's repetition of the word "absorbed" also partakes in a metaphor of fluidity and bodily assimilation, from the Latin *absorbere* ("to swallow up" or "to suck in") and synonymous with *imbibere* ("to drink in" or "to soak in").[36] Attentive listening involves a liquefaction of self in which I am drunk in by you by the very act of my own auditory swallowing. Ears become open passageways and the sense of hearing—*entendre*—becomes a metaphor, that is to say a mode of transportation, pouring me out of my me-ness in order to be incorporated into the black ocean of you.

It seems to me, then, that tears are an incredibly rich mode of textual figuration to illustrate the dynamic of listening, this liquefaction of self and the permeability of the (imagined) border between self and other through a kind of aural respiration.[37] Kilgour reminds us that Freud defines the instinctual oral impulses of the infant as either introjection or rejection. That which the infant takes into its body through the mouth is assimilated as "good" and that which the infant rejects is "bad"—bad being synonymous with alien and external.[38] While tears reify this dynamic of introjection and rejection, they also deny its mutual exclusion, which is why I think they are such apt metaphors of listening. As visual signs emanating from within the body—through the tear ducts—they are evidence that a person has taken in or is taking in the outside world, and suggest that bodies are, as Byrne says at one point, "repositories of emotion."[39] Yet simultaneously, as they mark the surface of the face, they show the repository body to be a leaky container; tears bear witness to an overflow of emotion rejected by the body, as it were, and ejected into the exterior world.

The idea that tears actually upset our conventional conceptions of bodily borders and opposites with the in-betweenness of their presence becomes especially pronounced in contemporary psychological and philosophical discourse. Helmuth Plessner, for example, contrasts weeping with "disciplined, articulate speech" to argue that crying "surge[s] up from the depths of life bound to feeling."[40] Like laughing, crying is an "eruption of the body": "Compared with speech, gesture, and mimic expressive movements, laughing and crying attest to an incalculable emancipation of bodily events from the person."[41] The uncontrollability of tears makes our bodies into passive transmitters of emotion, yet such transmission actively produces a connection between the self and other.

The first and the fourth chapters that frame Book VIII, "Statues and Paintings," in *Corinne* form a fascinating and beautiful network of scenes in which tears are interwoven within a discourse that explores human communication by putting into question what it means to come together, to unite. At the center of both chapters is the question of the possibility of a marriage between Corinne and

Lord Nelvil. Chapter i initiates the issue through a chain of linguistic displacements originating in the mouth of a visiting Scottish gentleman, Mr. Edgermond. He offers his opinion about Corinne by way of the words of Thomas Walpole, whose citation originated in English, but in the original French text of *Corinne* is translated into French and italicized with a footnote re-translating the quotation back into English: "What do you do with *that* at home?"[42] Here the institution of marriage is evoked through the synecdoche of home [la maison], while for the remainder of "Statues and Paintings" the topic will be taken up directly by Corinne and Oswald through a gradual metamorphosis of the term *unir* ["to unite"].

Lord Nelvil speaks of marriage twice. First, it is as the verb *unir*, an action to be taken: "But I do not know whether we can join our lives in marriage or whether we should" [*Mais je ne sais pas si nous pouvons, si nous devons nous unir*]. And then it is as the noun "union," a state of being as impenetrable as a brick house: "Oswald was convinced that Corinne . . . kept away anything that might lead to an indissoluble union." While for Oswald the institution of marriage must signify this kind of rock-solid, impermeable bond, Corinne responds by employing the term "unity" passively as an adjective—an attribute—and dislocates *unir* from the linguistic bond of marriage in order to displace the conversation to the realm of pleasing harmonies in art: "Finally, here are the two paintings where, in my opinion, history and poetry are successfully combined [heureusement unies] with the landscape."[43] The question of "union," then, is at the thematic center of "Statues and Paintings." However, as it undergoes this linguistic metamorphosis from verb to noun to attribute, we can read it as a vanishing point—a *point de fuite*—at which the possibility of a viable marital union between Corinne and Oswald all but disappears, yet out of which radiates oppositions between linguistic unifications and tearful unions that are more or less bounded and more or less successful.

The emotional intrigue of Book VIII, chapter i, is plotted through a scene in which Oswald asks Corinne to read his father's diary to him. It reads like a séance: two people conjuring the word of the dead father through the mouth of Corinne and the receptive ear of the son. I am going to analyze two passages now, one from the beginning of the séance and the other from its aftermath. The highly charged scene thematizes the weight of words and the problem of mediation. It redoubles the sense of linguistic poaching from the earlier utterance of the Thomas Walpole quotation and moves toward linguistic trespass and aporia. We will see throughout that the liquidity of crying contrasts with the solid, almost ossified sense of words here.

"Corinne," he said in a low voice, "read to me my father's reflections on death in this collection of his thoughts." Seeing Corinne's fright, he added: "Do not think I feel threatened, but I always read these consoling words when I am ill, and I feel that I can still hear them from his lips. . . ." Corinne took up the book of reflections that Oswald always carried with him, and read several pages in a faltering voice. . . .[44]

Overcome with emotion, Oswald and Corinne interrupted the reading frequently until, at last, they were obliged to give it up. Corinne was afraid for Oswald to weep so freely. Distraught at his state, she did not realize that she was herself as troubled as he.

"Yes, dear friend of my heart," said Oswald reaching out his hand to her, "yes, your tears have mingled with my own [tes larmes se sont confondues avec les miennes]. You weep for him with me, for the guardian angel whose last embrace I still feel, whose noble grace I still see. Perhaps you are the one he has chosen to console me, perhaps. . . ."

"No! No!" Corinne cried out. "No, he did not think me worthy."

"What did you say?"

Alarmed at revealing what she meant to hide, Corinne repeated the words that had escaped her lips, saying only: "He *would* not think me worthy!"[45]

Oswald's desire for "consolation" appears in both passages, and I think that the tension of this scene turns around that idea. Oswald calls his father's words consolations, and then uses the same term to speak of Corinne at the end. He elides the language of a dead man—a man meant to be in the past tense—with the *presence* of this woman before him. This union presents such a problem for Corinne that Oswald's words fall like bricks on her head; you get the feeling with each of her exclamatory "no's" that she is practically ducking a physical onslaught, and consequently she fumbles verb tenses herself, almost giving her secret away.

At the same time, we have a contrasting image of tears practically melting together—*confondues* in the original French—and Corinne who, the narrator tells us, was unaware of herself to such an extent that she didn't even notice her own intense inner pain: ". . . she did not realize that she was herself as troubled as he." This fusion of tears, while momentary, and interrupted by Oswald's immediate interpretation into words, works as what eighteenth-century scholar David Denby calls a "textual *tableau*." Its function is (ironically) to "freeze narrative" "so that the set of forces which the narrative has brought together in a particular moment may be allowed to discharge their full affective power."[46] For me, then, the affective power of the *tableau* of tears in *Corinne* is that it allows the two characters to briefly express and listen to each other's pain as a cry "anterior to language" and "untranslatable," to use two of Elaine Scarry's terms for pain in *The Body in Pain*.[47]

Psychotherapist Paul McGinley opens his paper on "what it means to cry" by marveling at the fact that in his field there is virtually no published research on crying (whereas he locates more than ten thousand articles on fruit fly behavior).[48] He draws from Heideggerian thought ultimately to suggest that Western culture should rethink the importance of crying as a meaningful phenomenon anterior to the Word: "Tears can only be seen directly. Where do tears belong? Are tears something somatic or psychical? There are neither the one, nor the other."[49] Similarly, in her philosophy of intelligent emotions, *Upheavals of Thought*, Martha Nussbaum investigates the phenomenon of disgust to argue that tears occupy a very singular place in the way humans imagine the borders of the body. Disgust appears to relate to the idea that the outside world is contaminated and will contaminate us if incorporated.[50] As such, "one's own bodily products are not viewed as disgusting so long as they are inside one's own body, although they become disgusting when they leave it." Disgust also has a role in "policing the boundary between ourselves and nonhuman animals" and thus reveals shame about our own animalism. However, tears are "the one human bodily secretion that is not found disgusting, presumably because they are thought to be uniquely human, and hence do not remind us of what we have in common with animals."[51]

One aspect of the in-betweenness and uncontrollable essence of tears that is particularly relevant to *Corinne* is their role in artistic expression and reception, especially their ability to permeate the border separating text and reader. Tears, of course, are not unique to Staël; they are a hallmark of both the Enlightenment and Romantic artistic creation. Anne Vincent-Buffault begins her *History of Tears* with the frenzy of crying that drenches the pages of Jean-Jacques Rousseau's *Julie ou la Nouvelle Héloïse* (*Julie, or the New Heloise*, 1761) and sets the tone for Romantic reader-text relations for years to come: characters suffer and weep, and readers are moved to tears to the point that they are emotionally "converted" to Rousseau's moral viewpoint.[52] Jay Caplan's analysis in *Framed Narratives* similarly demonstrates that Diderot's fiction seduces readers to imagine spectacles of suffering and thus to become (unwittingly) beholden to their affective power: "Somatic and semantic, biological and dialogical, the tear at once expresses our universally sensitive nature and addresses itself to our fellows."[53] Indeed, Margaret Cohen argues that in European literature around the time of the French Revolution, the textual spectacle of shared tears becomes the "synecdoche" of what she calls "the sympathetic community." Individual citizen-readers find a sense of collective belonging in their post-aristocratic world through sympathy—an ability to imagine themselves in the place of the victim.[54]

According to Nussbaum's historical and etymological research, "sympathy" is akin to "compassion" as well as to the French *pitié* because all three imaginatively reconstruct another person's experience and "include a judgment that the other person's distress is bad."[55] She contrasts this to empathy, an emotion that engages in the same act of imagining but without reasoning and evaluating. Her characterization of sympathy derives from Jean-Jacques Rousseau's *Second Discourse* as well as that of Scottish philosopher Adam Smith in his *Theory of Moral Sentiments*. Staëlien sympathy works through a dynamic of identification in which the first step is to throw away the mirror. We must, instead, use our imaginations to flee the self and open a mental pathway to the feelings of others:

> Pity is often removed from any sort of return to the self. If you were to abstractly imagine a type of suffering that would demand a completely different constitution than your own in order to bear it, you would still sympathize with that pain. It is essential that people of entirely opposing characters can experience pity for feelings they would never have felt. . . .[56]

The sympathetic response demands the renunciation of control; we engage in the instinctive process of letting go of self, rather than nervously reduplicating it through projection.

Listening, like the sympathetic response, initiates a relationship based on mutual giving and a degree of personal renunciation. Although Nancy does not overtly theorize the communal implications of the listening dynamic in his work, it is quite present in the grain, so to speak, of *Listening*. The overlap between his writing and the theory of tears as crossing metaphysical boundaries provides an inroad through which to better understand affective connectivity and its communal potential in Enlightenment and Romantic thinking. At one particularly poignant moment, Nancy reflects on listening as a spatial event that occurs when it is impossible to be an enclosed being because "self" is opened up in a way that is quite reminiscent of Barthes's "game of transference":

> To listen is to enter that spatiality by which, *at the same time*, I am penetrated, for it opens up in me as well as around me, and from me as well as toward me. . . . To be listening is to be at the same time *outside and inside*, to be open *from* without and *from* within, hence from one to the

other and from one in the other. Listening thus forms . . . the sharing of an inside/outside, division and participation, de-connection and contagion.

Barthes and Nancy both delight in the excitement of this "double, quadruple, or sextuple opening [through which] a 'self' can take place," as though it were an unproblematic process available to everyone.[57] *Corinne* does not, and as such the novel reminds us that openness and border crossing can be painful.

Like listening, the act of sharing tears constitutes fusion through the presence of differences that can be co-existent and irreducible, yet come together: a liquid union. A community built on sympathy initiates a union that allows for personal differences to express themselves even as we imagine what it is like to be someone else, to be completely the same in the space of another person's utter otherness. Such a union is then experienced as an effect, an attribute—like the harmonies Corinne observes in art—rather than a solid system or structure.

Although the tragic ending to *Corinne* perhaps leaves us with a sense of injustice at the heroine's untimely death, I want to conclude by suggesting that Corinne in fact bequeaths a sympathetic strategy for how we can relate to this book. In the final sentence of her last letter to Oswald, Corinne discusses her wish for him after her death: "I want nothing that might grieve you: I want but a tear and a few glances toward heaven, where I shall be waiting for you."[58] Her request for a tear in her own aftermath draws the reader into a position of identification with Oswald, as it asks us to close the book while remembering their love as a kind of *entend(r)ement*. Caplan argues that "when we cry for each other and with each other . . . we sense that the conflict between *ceux qui souffrent* and *ceux qui jouissent* has been lifted. . . . The pleasure of crying is a dialogical one."[59] The writer of *On the Influence of the Passions* would appear to agree, declaring: "Infinite *jouissance* is only to be found outside the self."[60] A good cry, like a good read, allows us to become absorbed in a world of otherness that we may not fully understand. But we dive in to flip and flap in the currents of that "black ocean" where the other floats away. In a word, we are moved.

Notes

1. Francine du Plessix Gray, *Madame de Staël: The First Modern Woman* (New York; London: Atlas, 2008), 33. A chapter entitled "Romancing" directly follows "Conversing," and there is a rather vulgar association intimated between the two: the first modern woman was wholly loose-lipped. This biographer is not alone in showcasing Staël's main characteristics as homely, talkative, and promiscuous. What interests me is that this trinity of traits persists in biographical writing even in the twenty-first century.

2. Stacy Schiff, "The Woman Who Never Stopped Talking: The Secret of Madame de Staël's Success," *Slate*, October 6, 2008, http://www.slate.com/id/2201499.

3. See Gray, 106–07; Maria Fairweather, *Madame de Staël* (New York: Carroll and Graf, 2005), 270; Angelica Goodden, *Madame de Staël: The Dangerous Exile* (Oxford: Oxford University Press, 2008), 143–44, 225; Christopher Hibbert, *Napoleon's Women* (London: W. W. Norton, 2002), 158. In her generally complimentary review of *The Dangerous Exile*, Karyna Szmurlo nonetheless critiques Goodden's choice to once again rehash misogynistic comments about Madame de Staël's body and her loquacity. See Karyna Szmurlo, review of *Madame de Staël: The Dangerous Exile*, by Angelica Goodden, *H France Review* 12, no. 34 (March 2012): 1–2, http://www.h-france.net/vol12reviews/vol12reviews.html.

4. Charles-Augustin Sainte-Beuve, *Portraits of Women*, trans. Helen Stott (London: D. Stott, 1891), 47, 49, translation modified.

5. Chantal Thomas, "Introduction," in *De l'influence des passions sur le bonheur des individus et des nations*, by Germaine de Staël (Paris: Rivages, 2000), 13; my translation.

6. See Jeremy Black, *The British Abroad: The Grand Tour in the Eighteenth Century* (New York: St. Martin's, 1992).

7. Germaine de Staël, *Corinne, or Italy*, ed. and trans. Avriel Goldberger (New Brunswick, NJ: Rutgers University Press, 1991), 3. Occasionally, I will also reference the original French version: Germaine de Staël, *Corinne ou l'Italie*, ed. Simone Balayé (Paris: Gallimard Folio, 1985).

8. Black, *British Abroad*, 191.

9. Peter Brooks, *The Melodramatic Imagination: Balzac, Henry James, Melodrama, and the Mode of Excess* (New Haven, CT: Yale University Press, 1995), 41.

10. Margaret Waller, *The Male Malady: Fictions of Impotence in the French Romantic Novel* (New Brunswick, NJ: Rutgers University Press, 1993), 71, 79.

11. Madelyn Gutwirth, *Madame de Staël, Novelist: The Emergence of the Artist as Woman* (Urbana: University of Illinois Press, 1978), 183.

12. Germaine de Staël, *De l'Allemagne*, ed. Jean de Pange (Paris: Hachette, 1958–1960), 1:161; my translation.

13. Catherine Rilliet Huber, "Notes sur l'enfance de Mme de Staël," *Cahiers staëliens* 60 (2009): 63. In her discussion of the role of listening in salon culture of the Enlightenment period, Dena Goodman notes the recurrence of the word "attention" in the journals of Staël's mother, the great *salonnière* Suzanne Necker. Goodman suggests that Mme Necker's insistence on the importance of attentive listening during intellectual conversation reinforces Michael Fried's theory of absorption in eighteenth-century painting. See Dena Goodman, *The Republic of Letters: A Cultural History of the French Enlightenment* (Ithaca, NY: Cornell University Press, 2002), 79–88.

14. Preface to Staël, *De l'influence des passions*, 13.

15. Karyna Szmurlo, ed., "Introduction," in *The Novel's Seductions: Staël's* Corinne in Critical Inquiry (Lewisburg, PA: Bucknell University Press, 1999), 22.

16. "Gabriel Byrne and the Art of Listening," Narr. Terry Gross, *Fresh Air*, Natl. Public Radio, WHYY, Philadelphia, April 30, 2009, Radio.

17. Michael Fried, *Absorption and Theatricality: Painting and Beholder in the Age of Diderot* (Chicago: University of Chicago Press, 1980).

18. Tili Boon Cuillé has studied this question in her work on representations of musical listening in eighteenth-century literature. She demonstrates the dynamic rather than the static quality of what she calls "musical tableaux," for the literary staging of the acoustic scene emphasizes the emotional engagement of the absorbed listener. See Tili Boon Cuillé, *Narrative Interludes: Musical Tableaux in Eighteenth-Century French Texts* (Toronto: Toronto University Press, 2006), 3–21. In her chapter on *Corinne*, Cuillé argues that the novel's musical tableaux initially function to effect "reconciliation" or "communion" between Oswald and Corinne. But once Corinne has lost Oswald for good, the musical tableau of Corinne's swan song becomes "an instrument of revenge" meant to make Oswald understand his role in causing the heroine's death (192–97).

19. Naomi Schor, "Corinne: The Third Woman," *L'Esprit créateur* 34, no. 3 (1994): 102.

20. The Grand Tour fostered much cross-cultural curiosity, but particularly in Great Britain it also provoked fears that the outside would infiltrate and threaten the British way of life. See Black, *British Abroad*, 287.

21. Staël, *Corinne, or Italy*, 90.

22. Ibid., 292.

23. Jean-Luc Nancy, *Listening*, trans. Charlotte Mandell (New York: Fordham University Press, 2007), 5.

24. Staël, *Corinne, or Italy*, 407; 470.

25. Ibid., 355.

26. Roland Barthes, "The Grain of the Voice," in *Image, Music, Text*, trans. Stephen Heath (New York: Hill-Farrar, 1977).

27. Anne Deneys-Tunney, "*Corinne* by Madame de Staël: The Utopia of Feminine Voice as Music within the Novel," *Dalhousie French Studies* 28 (Fall 1994): 61–62. Deneys-Tunney also reminds us of several points in *On Germany* in which Madame de Staël epitomizes the magnificent essence of painting, poetry, and music as beyond articulate language; as such, they "awaken in us the sense of the infinite." See Staël, *De l'Allemagne*, 3:376; my translation.

28. Staël, *Corinne, or Italy*, 355; 501.

29. Roland Barthes, "Écoute," in *L'Obvie et l'obtus: essais critiques III* (Paris: Seuil, 1982), 217. All translations are my own. While Barthes thinks about this kind of listening through the psychoanalytic experience, it does not mean that one can achieve this sort of depth only by being a professional therapist. In fact, for Jean-Luc Nancy, the very nature of listening, beginning with its etymological history, "is to be straining towards [est tendue vers] a possible meaning, and consequently one that is not immediately accessible." See Nancy, *Listening*, 6; *À l'écoute* (Paris: Gallilée, 2002), 20.

30. Barthes, "Écoute," 226. Jonathan Rée conveys the meaning of voice in a similarly fascinating way by using a child's perspective to pose the question of where voice comes from: "Is it the lips or mouth? Or the throat? The head? The chest? Clearly none of these answers is quite satisfying, so it may be better to accept the mystery of it and say that your voice comes straight from your self,

from deep inside you, from your soul." In *I See a Voice: A Philosophical History of Language, Deafness and the Senses* (London: HarperCollins, 1999), 61.

31. Barthes, "Écoute," 217.

32. Ibid., 225.

33. Frank Bowman, "Communication and Power in Germaine de Staël: Transparency and Obstacle," in *Germaine de Staël: Crossing the Borders*, eds. Madelyn Gutwirth, Avriel Goldberger, and Karyna Szmurlo (New Brunswick, NJ: Rutgers University Press, 1991), 55. For an insightful feminist analysis of Staël's subversions of language, see: Marie-Claire Vallois, "Voice as Fossil: Germaine de Staël's *Corinne, or Italy*: An Archaeology of Feminine Discourse," in *The Novel's Seductions: Staël's* Corinne *in Critical Inquiry*, ed. Karyna Szmurlo (Lewisburg, PA: Bucknell University Press, 1999), 127–38.

34. Maggie Kilgour, *From Communion to Cannibalism: An Anatomy of Metaphors of Incorporation* (Princeton, NJ: Princeton University Press, 1990), 4.

35. Charles Baudelaire, *Œuvres complètes*, ed. Claude Pichois (Paris: Gallimard, 1975), 1:26; all translations from this text are my own.

36. Oddly, Michael Fried never explains or problematizes his choice of the word "absorption" over any number of possible synonyms ("captivation," "riveting," or "immersion").

37. According to Rée's reading of Hegel's *Philosophy of Mind*, "weeping" is based "on the element of air rather than water: inner feelings acquired objectivity . . . primarily through the expulsion of air from the lungs" (*I See a Voice*, 60).

38. Kilgour, *Communion to Cannibalism*, 4.

39. "Gabriel Byrne and the Art of Listening," Radio.

40. Helmuth Plessner, *Laughing and Crying: A Study of the Limits of Human Behavior* (Evanston, IL: Northwestern University Press, 1970), 23.

41. Plessner, *Laughing and Crying*, 31, 33.

42. Staël, *Corinne, or Italy*, 133, 204.

43. Ibid., 140, 237.

44. Ibid., 136.

45. Ibid., 138–39, 211.

46. David Denby, *Sentimental Narrative and the Social Order in France, 1760–1820* (Cambridge: Cambridge University Press, 1994), 76.

47. Elaine Scarry, *The Body in Pain: The Making and Unmaking of the World* (New York: Oxford University Press, 1985), 4. Scarry is theorizing specifically physical pain, but I don't see why the experience of emotional pain would be any more or less hospitable to articulation in language than the physical kind.

48. Paul McGinley, "On Crying," *Existential Analysis* 19, no. 2 (2008): 210. Plessner begins his study by similarly noting the lack of scholarship on crying, and Barthes writes in *Fragments d'un discours amoureux* (*A Lover's Discourse: Fragments*): "Qui fera l'histoire des larmes?" [Who will write the history of tears?]. See Roland Barthes, *Œuvres complètes*, ed. Éric Marty (Paris: Seuil, 1995), 3:627.

There is now a relatively small, yet powerful body of historical and philosophical work on tears. Of note, Catherine Chalier's study of tears in the Old Testament and in Jewish thought, *Traité des larmes: Fragilité de Dieu, fragilité de l'âme* (Paris: Albin Michel, 2003). See also Tom Lutz, *Crying: The Natural and Cultural History of Tears* (New York: W. W. Norton, 1999).

49. Cited in McGinley, "On Crying," 211. From Martin Heidegger, *Zollikon Seminars Protocols-Conversations-Letters*, ed. Medard Boss (Evanston, IL: Northwestern University Press, 2001), 81.

50. Julia Kristeva has argued that the psychosomatic experience of revulsion occurs when we apprehend a lack of distinction between the supposedly enclosed self and the outside world. This moment of self/other blurring constitutes an instance of disruption in the life of the subject that Kristeva terms "abjection." Disgust reveals that the primary oppositional relationship by which we live—inside/outside—is actually unstable and relative. When we recoil upon smelling the sour stench of rotting trash, we are recognizing the fragility of our own embodied existence in the smell of the object's decay. Abjection is then the instance when we unwittingly identify with the other, but the reaction of revulsion constitutes a refusal of identification that simultaneously reifies the self/other border. See Julia Kristeva, *Powers of Horror: An Essay on Abjection*, trans. Leon S. Roudiez (New York: Columbia University Press, 1982).

51. Martha C. Nussbaum, *Upheavals of Thought: The Intelligence of Emotions* (Cambridge: Cambridge University Press, 2003), 202–03.

52. Anne Vincent-Buffault, *The History of Tears: Sensibility and Sentimentality in France* (New York: St. Martin's, 1991), 12.

53. Jay Caplan, *Framed Narratives: Diderot's Genealogy of the Beholder* (Minneapolis: University of Minnesota Press, 1985), 10–11.

54. Margaret Cohen, "Sentimental Communities," in *The Literary Channel: The Inter-National Invention of the Novel*, eds. Margaret Cohen and Carolyn Dever (Princeton, NJ: Princeton University Press, 2002), 112.

55. Nussbaum, *Upheavals of Thought*, 302.

56. Staël, *De l'influence des passions*, 242n1; my translation.

57. Nancy, *Listening*, 14.

58. Staël, *Corinne, or Italy*, 573.

59. Caplan, *Framed Narratives*, 10–11.

60. Staël, *De l'influence des passions*, 115; my translation.

8

AEOLIAN TRANSLATION: THE AESTHETICS OF
MEDIATION AND THE JOUISSANCE OF GENRE

C. C. Wharram

In presenting the sublime in nature the mind feels *agitated*. . . . This agitation (above all at its inception) can be compared with a vibration, i.e., with a rapid alternation of repulsion from, and attraction to, one and the same object.

— Immanuel Kant

In a revealing encounter in her novel *Corinne, or Italy*, Germaine de Staël depicts an expedition of Corinne and her Scottish admirer, Oswald, to Corinne's house near Tivoli. Before allowing them to take a stroll in Corinne's country gardens, Staël situates the couple within an ambient space that accentuates the merging of human and natural or divine forces. The ruins that proliferate in the environs of Corinne's home, Staël comments, "blend with the trees, with nature; they seem in harmony with the lonely mountain stream, image of time which has made them what they are."[1] The ruined temple to the Sibyl likewise provokes a consideration of the permeability of human thought to external stimuli, as Staël's narrator effuses: "Where in Italy could there be a place better suited for Corinne's house than the dwelling consecrated to the Sibyl, to the memory of a woman quickened [une femme animée] with divine inspiration!" The "unusual charm" of the place is intimately connected to an atmosphere that "ennobles the soul, . . . stimulates thought, and sharpens talent."[2] Corinne reflects her surroundings, and her surroundings reflect her. Either Corinne is the apparent product of an animating environment capable of bringing individuals into attunement with itself, or Corinne's surroundings are a fitting reflection of her unique sensibility, her ability to apprehend and merge with external stimuli. The novel's title accentuates the indeterminacy of this reciprocal relationship, holding the heroine and the nation in suspension: *Corinne, or Italy*.[3]

As Corinne and Oswald enter her gardens, Staël enhances the picturesque constituents of the atmosphere with an acoustic overlay:

> Strolling with Corinne, Oswald noticed that the sound of the wind was melodious, scattering chords through the air which seemed to come from the sway of the flowers, from the stir of the trees, and to lend nature a voice. Corinne explained that the wind set ringing the Aeolian harps she had placed in a few grottoes around the garden to fill the atmosphere with sound as well as perfume. Oswald was inspired by the purest feeling in these delightful surroundings.[4]

Just as the neighboring ruins merge with the trees, the "scattering chords . . . seemed to come from the sway of the flowers." The sound, although produced by the Aeolian harps, nevertheless seems without agency, a spontaneous yet melodious invention intended to "fill the atmosphere."

The Aeolian harps are indeed fit instruments for the *improvisatrice*: Corinne, after all, embodies the aesthetics of mediation. She spontaneously transmits her given themes to her auditors, just as the Aeolian harp automatically "lends a voice to nature."[5] Corinne has the facility to gather up the cultural vibrations of her experience—conversational, historical, natural, and literary—and retransmit them in such a way that inspires "purest feeling."

Overwhelmed, Oswald feels compelled to pledge his troth to Corinne. Yet this garden stroll serves as a mere preface to Oswald's tour of Corinne's picture gallery. When the tour comes to a close, the couple find themselves admiring a depiction of a scene from Ossian.[6] At this point Staël recalls the image of the Aeolian harp, thereby stressing the intimate connection between Corinne and the instrument: "Corinne took up her harp, and in front of this painting began to sing Scottish ballads whose simple notes seem to keep pace with the sound of the wind moaning in the valleys."[7] The "simple notes" of Corinne's song that seem to "accompany" the moaning wind create confusion between three different instruments: the harp of Corinne, which produces the notes accompanying the "sound of the wind"; the Aeolian harp, which symbolically "lends a voice to nature" through the "wind moaning in the valleys"; and the voice of Corinne, which seems capable of invoking the Scottish atmosphere.[8] Corinne's breathy repetition of *no more* prompts from Oswald a reciprocal emotional response: "As she gave moving expression to two of the most harmonious and sensitive English words: *no more*, Oswald offered no resistance to the emotion weighing him down, and both of them freely gave way to their tears."[9] Moments of Aeolian transmission, in Staël's work, lead to momentous outpourings of passion.

It is perhaps this intimate proximity between Corinne and the instrument that prompted Felicia Hemans to call on the Aeolian harp when apostrophizing Corinne in her well-known poem "Corinne at the Capitol":

And thy lyre's deep silvery string,
Touched as by a breeze's wing,
Murmurs tremblingly at first,
Ere the tide of rapture burst.[10]

Here, Hemans presents Corinne's lyre through its similitude to Aeolian "murmurs," just as the moaning wind of Scottish valleys mediated through Corinne's harp precipitates the "touching" sound that brings about Oswald's "tide of rapture" in the novel. Corinne herself calls her improvisations "this genre" in which she channels the voices of others, a "lively conversation" comprised of her "impressions" of her auditors, the words and thoughts of her friends, and the "loveliest lines of the different languages."[11] The genre of improvisation sublates the individual into a series of mediated acts and becomes a model for a Romantic subjectivity steeped in polyvalence and multiplicity.[12]

The Aeolian harp has been recognized since at least M. H. Abrams's "The Correspondent Breeze" as "a persistent Romantic analogue of mind," as a representation of the spontaneous conversion of "inner emotion" into "outer motion" or vice versa.[13] A simple wooden box spanned by metal strings that vibrate with currents of air, the makeshift instrument had a surprisingly long run as a fundamental emblem for poetic creativity. Well into the latter half of the nineteenth century, writers such as Thoreau, Emerson, Verne, Melville, and Stevenson would continue to breathe life into the well-worn form of the Aeolian harp, almost a century and a half after the instrument first appeared in English print.[14] I would like to explore the metaphor of the harp in a particularly resonant section of Staël's *De l'esprit des traductions* (*The Spirit of Translation*, 1816) to investigate the relationship Staël perceives between the reverberations of the Aeolian harp and the performance of translation. By foregrounding the affective pleasures of translation through its analogy with the Aeolian harp, Staël posits translation as a "genre" informed by sentimental resonance, a genre capable of transcending its own generic—and, as we shall see, *genetic*—limitations.

Transforming the Aeolian

Staël may well have been aware that Italy and Scotland, the two nations around which so much of the plot of *Corinne* revolves, played formative roles in the creation of the instrument that came to be known as the Aeolian harp. Italy, and specifically, Rome, was home to the first *aeolium instrumentum*, as J. J. Hofmann referred to it in his *Lexicon universale* of 1698, or the first "self-operating harmonic device" (*machinam harmonicam automatam*), as the inventor, Athanasius Kircher, called it in his *Musurgia Universalis* of 1650.[15] Kircher's instrument, he claimed, was greeted "with amazement, [since] no one ever suspects . . . by what hand or pump or artifice it creates its melodious sound," and therefore recommended that it "will be so much the more *recherché* and worthy of wonder to the extent that it is more hidden and concealed," a technique Staël's Corinne retained by placing her Aeolian harps in grottos.[16] Timothy Morton has recently cited "The Aeolian" as a special form of "ambient poetics," one operating seemingly without agency: it "establishes a sense of processes continuing without a subject or an author" and "comes 'from nowhere,' or it is inextricably bound up with the space in which it is heard."[17] From its inception, the *aeolium instrumentum* was also closely tied to feeling—the "anxiety" produced by the obscurity of the sound's source in Morton's analysis, "amazement" and "wonder" in Kircher's.[18]

Despite Kircher's work, it was not until the reappearance of the "Harp of Aeolus" in 1748 that the instrument reached a wider audience. That audience, interestingly, was originally formed by a group of Scottish émigrés to London. After the publication of Scotsman James Thomson's *The Castle of Indolence* and "On Aeolus's Harp" in 1748, other Scottish writers, such as Christopher Smart and Tobias Smollett, mention the Aeolian harp in the 1750s. As Hankins and Silverman recount, the prevalence of the image amongst Scottish writers was no coincidence, as Thomson's explanatory footnotes in *The Castle* and "On Aeolus's Harp" reveal.[19] Thomson attributed the invention of the harp to a "Mr. [James] Oswald," a Scottish composer and music-shop owner, who transformed Kirchner's object of curiosity into a full-fledged consumer commodity.[20] Oswald's pupil, William Jones, wrote "On the Aeolian Harp," a treatise housed within his *Physiological Disquisitions* of 1781, a primary reference point for many scientific works on the wind harp in the coming decades. The treatise provided a detailed account of Oswald's "invention" of the instrument.[21] This initial, short-lived rise of the Aeolian harp to popularity laid the groundwork for its re-emergence in a spate of poems in the late 1780s and throughout the Romantic period.

The very same James Oswald in all likelihood inspired the name of Staël's character. Throughout her literary career, Staël demonstrated profound interest in and knowledge about the Aeolian harp. She concludes the opening chapter of *On Germany* with a description of German gardens: "Often in the center of the superb gardens of German princes Aeolian harps are placed near grottoes surrounded with flowers, so the wind can carry through the air both sounds and perfumes."[22] She refers specifically to Ernst Chladni's experiments in harmonics, which detailed how nodal points in the vibrations of various media, such as the strings on an Aeolian harp, determine the variety and "shape" of harmonic tones.[23] Staël's repeated allusions to the Aeolian harp are unsurprising, considering how attractive the technology became as a metaphor for the receptivity of the mind to external stimuli during the Romantic era.[24] Her linking of the Aeolian harp to the production of strong feelings, or "poetic sensibility," in listeners is equally typical of the period.[25] What *is* unique, however, is Staël's late-career connection of the Aeolian harp both to feeling and to translation.

Staël invokes the Aeolian harp in her treatise *The Spirit of Translation* in the context of what we might call an aesthetics of mediation. Staël defines the work of a good translator: "Translating a poet [. . .] is to animate with the same breath of life a different instrument. One asks still more for a *jouissance* of the same kind [*genre*] than perfect fidelity."[26] Her explicit connection between the Aeolian harp and translation is augmented by her claim that what determines a good rendering from one language into another is a feeling of pleasure, and a facility to transmit feeling ("jouissance") through a transformation in code (a "different instrument"). But before I undertake to address the question of what Staël means by "a *jouissance* of the same kind" [*une jouissance du même genre*], I want to consider the practical and theoretical complexities of "genre" as they apply to translation in general, and to *The Spirit of Translation* in particular.

Mediating Genres

First translated by Pietro Giordani in the Italian literary journal *Biblioteca Italiana* in 1816, Staël's treatise—generally credited with having "launched the Romantic Movement in Italy"—theorizes translation as a complex "genre," one trumping all others: any genre, after all, can be superceded through its translation into another language.[27] *The Spirit of Translation* challenges the traditional taxonomy of literature into national and linguistic groupings, of rigorously parceling literatures according to "nation" and "language." We might call this "gendering" of literature, following Jacques Derrida, "the law" of the national literary genre. Derrida's famous critique of genre—"The Law of Genre"—formulates the phenomenon similarly to Staël's treatise: "As soon as genre announces itself, one must respect a norm, one must not cross a line of demarcation, one must not risk impurity, anomaly, or monstrosity."[28] And, like Staël, Derrida goes on to problematize genre. He defines "the law of the law of genre" as follows:

> It is precisely a principle of contamination, a law of impurity, a parasitical economy. In the code of set theories, if I may use it at least figuratively, I would speak of a sort of participation without belonging—a taking part without being part of, without having membership in a set.[29]

One could intertwine Staël and Derrida in a hybrid formulation: translation, acting as the law of the law of genre (since it functions both as genre and anti-genre), participates without belonging. In "the field of general textuality"—the object submitted to this law, according to Derrida—this genre represents the principle of contamination, of excess.[30] For Staël, translation is an *Über-genre*, for the obvious reason that translation can include all other genres within its territorial regime. Any genre—or any mixture of genres—can be sublated through its translation into another language.[31]

Staël's treatise argues that the Italian literary scene found itself in acute need of regeneration through an influx of the foreign, positing translation as a necessary infusion of the external.[32] Serving to inoculate the nation against literary stultification, Staël's concept of translation—that it delivers the "more original"— underscores its own paradoxical nature: "Translations of foreign poets can, more effectively than any other means, protect the literature of a [host] country from these banal turns of phrase, which are the surest signs of its decline."[33] Her language here evokes a positive immunology of literature: the national literary body introduces foreign elements to forestall its "decline."

Appearing seven times in *The Spirit of Translation*, the word *genre* engenders a myriad of English translations: "form," "type," "kind," "mode," "genus," "species" (as in "the human *genre*"), and "gender" (as in the grammatical *genres* of masculine, feminine, and neutral). Through the etymological punning of *genre* with *generalité*, she observes that the general populace does not comprehend the "genre" of Latin: "several of the riches of Italians, in this genre [of Latin], were unknown even to themselves, because the majority of readers understood nothing but the idiom of the land."[34] The majority, in other words, does not comprehend the genre. The *genre*—in this instance, *un*translated literature—fails to connect to the people [*les gens*].

As slippery as Staël's use of "genre" may be, she clearly argues that translation demands the approximate capture of a work's spirit rather than its technical accuracy: "Translating a poet, is not to take a compass and copy the dimensions of the building: it is to animate with the same breath of life a different instrument.

One asks still more for a *jouissance* of the same kind [genre] than perfect fidelity."[35] Thus, genre for her is to be associated with neither the demarcation of parameters, of "dimensions," nor "perfect fidelity," but rather with pleasure, *jouissance*. I would like to linger momentarily over Staël's preference for pleasure over fidelity. More than simply indexing her refusal to conform to the marital standards of her day, her demotion of *fidelity* from its commanding position as the guiding principle of the translator's work highlights the *genre* (gender) of the translator. As Lori Chamberlain has demonstrated, fidelity's central role in translation theory set the stage for a gendering of original and translated texts as masculine and feminine, respectively.[36] Staël, in challenging the primacy of fidelity in the relationship between translated and original texts, flaunts her disdain of contemporary aesthetic regulations much as her own public disregard for marital conventions flew in the face of social strictures: if translation reproduces, it is not in the service of duplicating conventions.

Staël legislates a new conception for translation in Italy in order to expand its expressive possibilities through an acquaintance with the literatures of different nations: "It would be very desirable that the Italians dedicate themselves to translating with care the diverse new poesies of the English and German; they will thus make their compatriots acquainted with a new *genre*."[37] *Genre*, in this case, embodies both diversity of influence ("diverse attentions") and translation itself: translation becomes the generic mode for the expansion of genre. She goes on to note that the translations of Shakespeare by her long-time companion A. W. Schlegel have become "altogether *national* in Germany" such that "Shakespeare and Schiller have become compatriots."[38]

Staël had already modeled a version of this expansive strategy in *Corinne*. In Book VII, "Italian Literature," representatives of Italy, Britain, and France discuss the relative strengths and weaknesses of their national theaters. Count d'Erfeuil, mouthpiece of French chauvinism, extols the superiority of French theater, claiming that an influx of Greek "inconsistencies" or Shakespearean "monstrosities" would only serve to threaten French élan: "French is too pure for that. Our theatre is a model of refinement and elegance. . . . To introduce anything foreign among us would be to plunge us into barbarism."[39] D'Erfeuil's xenophobia serves as a foil to Corinne's theatrical production of a translation into Italian of Shakespeare's *Romeo and Juliet*, and to Staël's own expressed receptiveness to foreign stimuli. The "mingling" of the North with the South, in Corinne's Italian translation of Shakespeare's play, puts into practice the cultivation of a hybridized sensibility that Staël had previously theorized in *On Literature*.[40] Claiming that "better than any other foreign writer, Shakespeare grasped Italy's national character," Staël recommends the importation of Shakespeare, already practiced in Germany (the famous *unser Shakespeare*), with equal confidence for Italy: "Translated into Italian, *Romeo and Juliet* seems to return to its native tongue."[41] Yota Batsaki has recently argued that the double translation of *Romeo and Juliet*, "infused with a northern sensibility" in Shakespeare's rendering, only to return to its cultural/linguistic point of origin in Corinne's performance, allows the Italians "to transcend their historical predicament."[42] This *sentimental outsourcing*, we might say, models a new way of thinking about translation that, Sherry Simon has argued, emerged around 1800 as a "*horizontal* axis of exchange among national literatures, closely related to the notion of *Bildung*, culture as a movement of self-realization."[43] That is, the apotheosis of Italian national character—"Never had tragedy produced such an effect in Italy"—is an Italian tale infused with English sensibility and rendered in the Italian language.[44]

Similarly, in *The Spirit of Translation* Staël argues that, through a translation of French drama into Italian, "It will be possible in Italy to obtain a result of the same sort [*genre*]" as Germany had undertaken with English. Staël proposes a generic hybrid for Italy, based on a German model of English translation. In Staël's formulation—*un résultat du même genre*—*genre* stresses the *reproductive* capacities, the genetics, of such an undertaking. Splicing these strands of *genre* together, then, we can recognize Staël's command for a reproductive literature based not on fidelity (the traditional trait of the "translatress" *par excellence*), but on *jouissance*. The desire of the translator, so conceived, demands a genetic hybridization towards the national good, towards a breaking free from the strict limitations imposed by "conventional forms."[45] The role of the genre of translation on this literary stage is to interrupt the genetic homogeneity of Italian literature by encoding the foreign into the linguistic parameters of Italian speech, *parole*.

Concerns about genre are inherently taxonomic, inevitably leading to questions of biological species—especially in French, where the notions of "genre" and "species" are fused in the word *genre*. Translation, in Staël's account, genetically alters a former species, thereby creating a new taxonomic category—that is to say, produces a new species, *un genre nouveau*. I want briefly to consider this generic proliferation in the context of late-eighteenth-century and early-nineteenth-century discourse on natural history, and specifically on the problem of species or genera. After Carl Linnaeus's codification of botanical taxonomies based solely on the reproductive organs of plants in the 1740s, botanic discourse became intimately linked with what Theresa Kelley has called the "lawless sexual transactions of flowers" and its "counterpoint," conservative commentators hoping to temper the "promiscuous" language of botany.[46] As Alan Bewell has conclusively shown, discussions of species, genus, and phylum were "so imbued with socio-sexual implications that no botanical description was entirely removed from these concerns."[47] Moreover, with an ever-increasing repository of global specimens in the late 1700s, natural historians were overwhelmed with taxonomic complexity. *Après Linné, le deluge*, we might say: botanical concerns about taxonomic prolifera-tion, especially with respect to hybridization, flooded debates about the zoological classification of species. Of particular interest in this regard was the taxonomy of bird species, which were "more numerous, more multiplied" than other species.[48]

Georges-Louis Leclerc, Comte de Buffon, whom Staël had met in the days of her mother's salon, clearly articulated the propensity of birds for generic pro-liferation, accentuating their inclination toward *jouissance*: "Birds are, in general, more sexually active [plus chauds] and more prolific than quadrupeds. They unite more frequently, and . . . are more willing than quadrupeds to mate with proxi-mate species."[49] The union of two bird species results in "*métis*, who are themselves able, through sexual unions . . . to form new intermediate species." The fecundity of *métis* birds prompts Buffon to meditate on the relation between Nature's facility for species augmentation and what he calls *jouissances illégitimes*: "Who can num-ber the illegitimate pleasures between individuals of different species! Who could ever . . . determine in a word all the effects of the powers of Nature for multiplica-tion, . . . all the supplements that result, and how she goes about augmenting the number of species in filling in the intervals that seem to separate them!"[50] This sort of reproduction without duplication, of propagation based on *jouissance*, however *illégitime*, recalls Staël's playful meditation on the role of translation in the prolif-eration of literary genres. Translation, too, disrupts the perpetual duplication of "conventional forms," in order to facilitate *un genre nouveau* "filling the intervals that seem to separate" nations, or members of the *genre humain*.[51]

Interpreting Cognition

In her elucidation of idealist philosophies and their relation to the "New Sciences" in *On Germany*, Staël notes that German philosophers have "a tendency to dis-cover the resemblance between the laws of human understanding and those of na-ture." She goes on to extol the utility of "those continual metaphors, which aid us in comparing our sentiments with external phenomena. . . . It is the same thought of our Creator, [translated] into two different languages, and capable of reciprocal interpretation."[52] Staël's moment of "reciprocal interpretation"—of translation be-tween "two different languages"—is precipitated by a moment of "comparing our sentiments with external phenomena." Staël's grounding in German idealism—the precise topic she elucidates in this section of *On Germany*—would suggest that when she writes "external phenomena," she refers to "objects of cognition." That is, our emotional responses can be translated into rational concepts, and vice versa. In fact, such interconnections and comparisons are vital.

In his influential work *The Navigation of Feeling*, William Reddy examines the aftermath of the Terror, detailing a tremendous public backlash against the culture of sentiment deemed to have produced the Terror, but not the Revolution. This backlash resulted in the "erasure of sentimentalist origins and of the senti-mentalist idiom" from not only the historical record, but also the public sphere in general. Staël, writing against this backdrop, was highly invested in retrieving "natural feeling" from the grip of a revisionary history that eliminated the role that emotion played in the work of the eighteenth-century French Enlighten-ment. Reddy considers Staël's *On Germany* to be a last-ditch attempt to revive sentimentalist ideals.[53]

Reddy approaches this history through a theoretical reorientation of the study of emotion that emphasizes the relationship between varying kinds of cognition—"codes"—with special attention to cognitive events that convert emo-tions into denotative utterances. Instead of the psychological term "processing," Reddy argues that cognitive events are better understood as acts of "translation": "When an individual correctly identifies an outline drawing as representing a bird, for example, I simply propose that this feat of cognitive 'processing' be regarded as an act of translation from the code of the outline drawing to the code of everyday English categories."[54] By positing cognitive acts as the translation of "thought material" (e.g., sensory inputs, "procedural" memories, emotions) from one code into another, Reddy argues that his schema provides a theoretical grounding for the acknowledgment that "there are kinds of thought that lie 'outside' of language, yet are intimately involved in the formulation of utterances."[55] Reddy reserves a special place in his framework for "emotives," utterances that translate emotional material into descriptions.[56]

These emotional expressions—"emotives"—carry "self-exploring and self-altering effects" and are "like performatives in that they do something to the world."[57] At moments of emotional intensity, a welter of "thought material" comes to our attention, demanding to be processed. Reddy likens cognitive attention to "a translator beset by an extraordinary array of translation tasks. Such tasks, with all their indeterminacy, must be carried out before a person can achieve the coordinated pursuit of a goal, however simple."[58] If moments of high affect can be likened to being pummeled by "an extraordinary array of translation tasks," then it is little wonder that the Aeolian harp should rise to the level of "analogue of mind" during the Age of Sensibility. The harp can translate the slightest movement of the air, the slightest sensation, into audible expression, unfazed by the overwhelming number of "translation tasks" at hand. Human cognition, on the other hand, is not so efficient, as Reddy notes: the tasks presenting themselves to our attention may far outnumber the possibilities for translation, and "translation tasks are always incomplete"[59]—a truism that every translator knows, and that Walter Benjamin made famous in his formulation of the *Aufgabe* ("task" and "surrender") of the translator.

Such an account of cognitive processes reveals an uncanny proximity to one of today's most important writers on translation, Douglas Robinson. Robinson's *The Translator's Turn* presented his somatic thesis of language, that "we have a feeling for words and phrases, registers and styles, . . . either when we are working in a single language or when we are engineering a transfer from one to another; and that all of our decisions about language, including what word or phrase would be best or what would be most 'equivalent,' are channeled through these feelings."[60] A decade after writing *The Translator's Turn*, Robinson recounts his annoyance at repeated "reductionist" readings of his theory: "I kept insisting . . . that the somatics of language use don't take the *place* of reason; they are the necessary ground of reason. It's not that we have a choice between thinking and feeling . . ., it's that there *is* no thinking without feeling." Robinson notes that his suppositions have been borne out by research in cognitive science: neurologist Antonio Damasio's *Descartes' Error*, for example, concludes that "emotion is absolutely essential for reason."[61] Damasio's book stands metonymically for a groundswell of work in cognitive science, developmental psychology, and evolutionary anthropology that has rediscovered emotion as a basis for human reason and achievement, a relationship Staël often conveyed: "We must have a philosophy of belief, of enthusiasm, a philosophy that confirms by reason, what sentiment reveals to us."[62]

The work of Ernst Cassirer in the 1920s provides an historical bridge between Staël's theories on the nature of sentiment, reason, and translation, and modern-day cognitive science. In speculating on the origins of language, Cassirer hearkens back to "[Johann] Hamann's dictum, that poetry is 'the mother-tongue of humanity,'" but only insofar as poetry expresses the "power of subjective feeling." The key to solving how language comes into existence, for Cassirer, is to explain "whereby a sound is transformed from an emotional utterance into a denotative one."[63] The problem, as Staël had recognized, was of translating feeling into concept, which Cassirer resolved somewhat hastily in a bond sealed between affect and word: "As soon as the emotion of the moment has found its discharge in the word . . ., a sort of turning point has occurred in human mentality: the inner excitement . . . has been resolved into the objective form . . . of speech."[64] And yet, in connecting the mother-tongue to poetic expression, emotional intensity, and language acquisition, Cassirer approximates contemporary research into "motherese" or "infant-directed speech" (IDS).

Alan Richardson has recently applied this research on "motherese" to Romantic-era representations of "unintelligible yet alluring female speech." Citing Ellen Dissanayake, Richardson highlights the "special role that a 'high-pitched, undulant, breathy, patterned, repetitive' mode of speech plays, genetically, in introducing the child to spoken language and, in the evolution of human cultures."[65] Although Richardson's focus is on the relation of this highly aesthetized—and often "nonsensical"—speech to male anxieties about the threat of the allure of "female speech" in the Romantic era, in the context of the present discussion I am interested in the "high affect" that child-development and linguistic researchers have determined to be prevalent in IDS, a speech form that sounds closer to the emotive sonorities of the Aeolian harp than to everyday human speech.[66] If it is true—as the researchers cited by Richardson claim—that IDS's highly affective, often unintelligible nature sets the stage for "child language acquisition," then what we witness here is precisely the comparing of two different languages, one highly affected, the other highly denotative, which, according to Staël, should be capable of reciprocal interpretation.

The gulf between sentiment and thought that Aeolian moments in Staël's work so often translate brings us to an unexpected example of the convergence of Staël's sentimental ideals with modern-day aesthetics. Christopher Nolan's recent film *Inception* translates into the twenty-first century Staël's thoughts on the affective power of translation. The premise of the film hinges on a group of "information extractors" hired not to retrieve specific data from someone's brain, but to implant a specific idea into the mind of the heir to a corporate empire. Strangely enough, the difficulty of their mission centers on the prospect of translating between the realms of cognition and sentiment. In order to induce the corporate heir to divide his father's empire, they must find a way to "translate this [idea] into an emotional concept," for "the subconscious is motivated by emotion . . ., not reason."[67] The question is raised—"How do you translate a business strategy into an emotion?"—and answered through a labyrinthine narrative woven through dream architecture, psycho-pharmaceutics, and cognitive-science fiction.[68] The question—"How do you translate a business strategy into an emotion?"—suggests that translating emotions into ideas, and ideas into sentiments, has found its way from the Aeolian harp to the more familiar arenas of cognitive science and translation theory, and into the boardrooms of corporations and the dystopian films that critique them.

Translating Sensibilities

Corinne, like most of Staël's work, is generically complex, bridging the travelogue, the epistolary novel, drama, and Corinne's improvisational form. Batsaki has noted that not only is much of the conversational material of *Corinne* (from English) and the transcriptions of her improvisations (from Italian) translated into French, but also her "ekphrastic" descriptions of Italian art objects "translate works of art into words." As such, translation is the "mode that governs the whole book."[69] I would like to suggest that Staël regarded translation as a "mode" that could legislate well beyond the bounds of *Corinne*. The fact that we can trace Staël's legacy to fields as diverse as philosophical inquiry, cognitive science, translation theory, and film should hardly surprise us: the promiscuity of her thinking has produced a body of work staggering in its generic and theoretical complexity, throughout which her meditations on the genre of translation have been particularly fertile. For Staël, translation is not simply a genre: it is the beyond of genre, genre in excess of genre—genre saturated with *jouissance*.

Staël offers us a model of cognition that recognizes moments of intense emotion—*jouissance*—as participating in the performance of a valuable sort of translation. Such sublime moments hold us in rapt attention, opening up a space, according to Reddy, for the translation of emotional material into expression. They remind us, too, of the vital connection between cognition and sensibility that Reddy claims was broken in the wake of the French Revolution, and that Staël attempted to repair in her writings—a connection that has once again become the focus of critical scrutiny in the fields of cognitive science, psychology, anthropology, history, and literary studies.[70] The Aeolian harp, for its part, shows us that the best model for the connection between cognition and emotion may well be a few metal wires strung between two pieces of wood, vibrating—*translating*—in the wind.

Notes

1. Germaine de Staël, *Corinne, or Italy*, ed. and trans. Avriel Goldberger (New Brunswick: Rutgers University Press, 1987), 152. For a recent explication of the important parallels between landscape ruins and figures of female ruin in Romantic-era narratives and aesthetics, see Suzie Asha Park, "Picturesque Interiority: Eliza Fenwick's *Secresy* and the Novel of Information," *Literature Compass* 7/8 (2010): 659–73.

2. Staël, *Corinne, or Italy*, 152.

3. For a longer discussion of the title's "indeterminacy" in the novel's critical legacy, see Robert Casillo's *The Empire of Stereotypes: Germaine de Staël and the Idea of Italy* (New York: Palgrave Macmillan, 2006), 2, 235, n6 and n7.

4. Staël, *Corinne, or Italy*, 152.

5. For an analysis of Corinne as the "embodiment of enthusiasm" and sustained discussion of enthusiasm in Staël's work, see Kari Lokke, "Staël's Enthusiasm, Eternity, and 'les armes du temps,'" *Prism(s): Essays in Romanticism* 15 (2007): 34, 45.

6. It would be hard to overestimate the significance of Ossian, the (supposed) Scottish poet whose work was "translated" by James Macpherson in the 1760s, in Staël's thought. She begins the section "On Northern Literature" of *On Literature* as follows: "There are two completely different kinds of literature, it seems to me, Southern and Northern: the literature that comes from Homer and the literature that starts with Ossian," in *Major Writings of Germaine de Staël*, ed. and trans. Vivien Folkenflik (New York: Columbia University Press, 1992), 174.

7. Staël, *Corinne, or Italy*, 157.

8. As Geoffrey Grigson notes, James Macpherson, translator of Ossian, managed, anachronistically, to include many Aeolian moments into his works by "incautiously allow[ing] an Aeolian Harp, not very well disguised as a harp hanging and sounding in a tree before the musician takes hold of it, into *Berrathon*, and *Temora*, and *Dar Thula*," in *The Harp of Aeolus and Other Essays on Art, Literature & Nature* (London: Routledge, 1947), 31.

9. Staël, *Corinne, or Italy*, 157.

10. Felicia Hemans and Dorothea Browne, *Selected Poems, Prose, and Letters*, ed. Gary Kelley (Peterborough, Ontario: Broadview, 2002), 356.

11. Staël, *Corinne, or Italy*, 44–45. "[C]'est à mes amis que je dois surtout en *ce genre* la plus grande partie de mon talent," in Germaine de Staël, *Corinne ou l'Italie*, ed. Simone Balayé, *Œuvres complètes; Œuvres littéraires* (Paris: Champion, 2000), series 2, 3:46.

12. See also Angela Esterhammer, "The Cosmopolitan *Improvvisatore*: Spontaneity and Performance in Romantic Poetics," *European Romantic Review* 16, no. 2 (April 2005): 153–65; and her *Romanticism and Improvisation, 1750–1850* (Cambridge: Cambridge University Press, 2009); Kari Lokke, *Tracing Women's Romanticism: Gender, History and Transcendence* (New York: Routledge, 2004), 40; and Paola Giuli, "Poetry and National Identity: *Corinne*, Corilla, and the Idea of Italy," in *Germaine de Staël: Forging a Politics of Mediation*, ed. Karyna Szmurlo (Oxford: Voltaire Foundation, 2011), 213–32.

13. M. H. Abrams, "The Correspondent Breeze: A Romantic Metaphor," *The Kenyon Review* 19, no. 1 (1957): 115.

14. Andrew Brown, *Aeolian Harp, The Aeolian Harp in European Literature, 1591–1892* (Cambridge: Bois de Boulogne, 1970), 3:73–90.

15. Thomas L. Hankins and Robert J. Silverman, *Instruments and the Imagination* (Princeton, NJ: Princeton University Press, 1995), 90.

16. Cited in Hankins and Silverman, *Instruments*, 89.

17. Timothy Morton, *Ecology without Nature: Rethinking Environmental Aesthetics* (Cambridge, MA: Harvard University Press, 2007), 41.

18. Morton, *Ecology*, 43.

19. Hankins and Silverman, *Instruments*, 91–92.

20. Stephen Bonner, *Aeolian Harp, The History and Organology of the Aeolian Harp* (Cambridge: Bois de Boulogne, 1970), 2:18; Grigson, *Harp*, 26.

21. William Jones, "On the Aeolian Harp," *Physiological Disquisitions, or, Discourses on the Natural Philosophy of the Elements* (London: Rivington, 1781), 338–45; Hankins and Silverman, *Instruments*, 93.

22. Staël, *On Germany*, in *Major Writings*, 294.

23. Staël, *De l'Allemagne*, 4:247. For a description of Chladni's work as a "marriage of aesthetics and science" and a longer discussion of Romantic-era instruments through the work of E. T. A. Hoffmann, see Emily Dolan, "E. T. A. Hoffmann and the Ethereal Technologies of 'Nature Music,'" *Eighteenth-Century Music* 5, no. 1 (2008): 16–19.

24. The canonical examples of Wordsworth, Shelley, Hemans, and Byron are augmented by earlier writers such as William Collins, Thomas Gray, Amelia Opie, Mary Darby Robinson, and Erasmus Darwin, and dozens upon dozens of lesser known poets and novelists.

25. Jerome McGann cites S. T. Coleridge's "The Eolian Harp" as a privileged topos of "eroticized sensations and . . . philosophical speculations," for simultaneously experiencing and critiquing sensibility, in *The Poetics of Sensibility: A Revolution in Literary Style* (Oxford: Clarendon Press, 1996), 19.

26. My translations are based on *De l'esprit des traductions* as it appears in *Œuvres complètes de Madame la Baronne de Staël-Holstein*, 2 vols. (Paris: Firmin Didot Frères, 1844): 2:294–97. *De l'esprit* appears in *Translating Slavery: Gender and Race in French Women's Writing, 1783–1823*, eds. Doris Y. Kadish and Françoise Massardier-Kenney (Kent: Kent State University Press, 1994), 287–92. Doris Y. Kadish translates the article as "The Spirit of Translations" in this same collection (162–67). Joseph Luzzi translates Staël's article as "The Spirit of Translation" in *Romantic Review* 97, nos. 3–4 (2006): 275–84.

27. Grazia Avitabile, *The Controversy in Romanticism in Italy: First Phase 1816–1823* (New York: S. F. Vanni, 1959), 13; I. L. McClellend, *The Origins of the Romantic Movement in Spain* (Liverpool: Liverpool University Press, 1975), 171; and Douglas Radcliff-Umstead, *Ugo Foscolo* (New York: Twayne Publishers, 1970), 131. Grazia Avitabile called it "the spark that touched off the romantic

controversy in Italy," (*Controversy*, 13). Almost every prolegomena to a discussion of the Italian Romantic begins with reference to Staël's article. See Gianni Spera, *Significati e Poetiche della Narrativa Italiana: Fra Romanticismo e Idealismo* (Firenze: Casa Editrice le Lettere, 1989), 11; Kurt Mueller-Vollmer, "On Germany: Germaine de Staël and the Internationalization of Romanticism," in *The Spirit of Poetry*, eds. Richard Block and Peter Ferves (Evanston: Northwestern University Press, 2000), 151; Giuseppe Zamboni, *Die italienische Romantik: Ihre Ausenandersetzung mit der Tradition* (Krefeld: Scherpe-Verlag, 1953), 7.

28. Jacques Derrida, "The Law of Genre," trans. Avital Ronell, *Critical Inquiry* 7, no. 1 (Autumn 1980), 57.

29. Ibid., 59.

30. Ibid., 63. The concern with genre resonates with the general study of the Romantic since the term "Romanticism" uniquely defines an historical literary period through reference to a genre—specifically, the medieval genres of *romanz, roman, romanzo*, works produced through composition or translation into the vernacular, "romance" languages. To speak of the "Romantic era," then, is to already speak of genre, and of translation. See C. C. Wharram, "Translation as Symptom: The 'Sickness' of the Romantic," in *Translation of Romantic Texts: Proceedings of the Association of Slovene Literary Translators*, ed. Martina Ozbot (Ljubljana, Slovenia: University of Ljubljana, 2004), 28:184–203.

31. Novalis points towards a similar consideration of the potentiality of translation in his 1797 letter to A.W. Schlegel on his earliest published translations of Shakespeare. Antoine Berman reads Novalis's claim, that "the German Shakespeare is now better than the English," as indicative of the Jena Romantic "drive to translate": "The German Shakespeare is better *precisely because it is a translation*" (Antoine Berman, *The Experience of the Foreign: Culture and Translation in Romantic Germany*, trans. S. Heyvaert [Albany: State University of New York Press, 1992], 106).

32. Recent critics have had a variety of responses to Staël's "Italianism." Jane Elisabeth Wilhelm reads "On the Spirit of Translation" as articulating Staël's "political liberalism" in a deliberate attempt to encourage political progress through the "intercultural connections" of literature in translation. Staël is therefore less concerned in her treatise with the details of her presentation of Italian culture as she is with the demonstration of a method for the "perfectibility of the human species," in "La Traduction, principe de perfectibilité, chez Mme de Staël," *Meta* 29, no. 3 (2004): 693. Robert Casillo demonstrates in detail that many of the traits Staël ascribed to Italian culture (undisciplined behavior, cowardice, social and political degradation, hypocrisy) in *Corinne* and elsewhere are grounded in a historical (mis)understanding of the influence of climate on social and political formation, coupled with her sympathetic desire to present Italian sensibility as a "counterweight" to Northern European civilization (Casillo, *Empire of Stereotypes*, 25–33, 44, 46–82). Joseph Luzzi notes "the perennially divided opinions as to her legacy in Italian literary history" stem specifically from Staël's criticisms of Italian culture and her recommendation that Italians should embark on a project of cultural renewal through translation (Luzzi, "The Spirit of Translation," 278). Elsewhere, Luzzi diagnoses Italy's tragic shortcomings as caused by the "lack of civil society in Italy." Both Staël (in *Corinne*) and Vittorio Alfieri recognized that this absence doomed Italian tragedy without an influx of popular engagement in aesthetic and economic life. Joseph Luzzi, "Tragedy without Society: Alfieri's Italian Theater and the Discourse of Value," *European Romantic Review* 20, no. 5 [2009]: 583–84, 588).

33. Staël, *Œuvres complètes*, 2:294.

34. Ibid., 2:294.

35. Ibid., 2:296.

36. Chamberlain proposes that this gendering captured "a cultural complicity between the issues of fidelity in translation and in marriage. . . . Fidelity is defined by an implicit contract between translation (as woman) and original (as husband, father, or author). However, the infamous "double standard" operates here as it might have in traditional marriages: the "unfaithful" wife/ translation is publicly tried for crimes the husband/original is by law incapable of committing" (Lori Chamberlain, "Gender and the Metaphorics of Translation," *Signs: Journal of Women in Culture and Society* 13, no. 3 [1988], 456).

37. Staël, *Œuvres complètes*, 2:296.

38. "It would be possible to obtain a result of the same *genre* in Italy" (my emphasis; ibid., 2:296).

39. Staël, *Corinne, or Italy*, 121.

40. In that work, Staël considered the literary genres of a nation as reflective of their social surroundings: a nation's literary genres will develop or stagnate, embrace or shun generic complexity, according to the willingness of the nation to alter its social institutions. Great cultural and literary shifts in history take place, according to Staël's model, as a result of the blending of cultural forces, the most profound example of which was the merging of northern with southern European cultural sensibilities at the beginning of the Middle Ages: this "blending of the spirit of the North with the customs of the South" was "absolutely indispensable to the process of civilizations"; "the mingling of Northern and southern peoples . . . resulted in very great progress for learning and civilization." See Germaine de Staël, *Madame De Staël on Politics, Literature, and National Character*, ed. and trans. Morroe Berger (New Brunswick, NJ: Transaction Publishers, 2000), 181, 225.

41. Staël, *Corinne, or Italy*, 126. The incorporation of the translated text into the body of *Corinne, or Italy* recalls Goethe's strategy of grafting translations from Ossian and Shakespeare into *The Sorrows of Young Werther* and *Wilhelm Meister's Apprenticeship*, respectively. Just as Corinne and Oswald are better able to come to grips with their own passions through Shakespeare's transmission into Italian, both Werther and Wilhelm find their sentiments more forcefully articulated when they are translated into German from a foreign source.

42. Yota Batsaki, "Exile as the Inaudible Accent in Germaine de Staël's *Corinne, or Italy*," *Comparative Literature* 61, no. 1 (2009): 37.

43. Sherry Simon, "Germaine de Staël and Gayatri Spivak: Culture Brokers," in *Translation and Power*, eds. Maria Tymoczko and Edwin Gentzler (Amherst: University of Massachusetts Press, 2002), 122–40.

44. Staël, *Corinne, or Italy*, 130.

45. One can read this conception informing Staël's *Corinne, or Italy*. Deirdre Lynch notes "the crossbreeding of national literary traditions that structures *Corinne*" in the relationship between the Italian woman Corinne and the Scottish man Oswald. Lynch cites hostile critics of the novel: "Staël's presentation of the contrasting situation of genetic hybridity of a heroine who unites 'Italian and French voluptuousness with English virtue' represents 'a physical impossibility,'" (Deirdre Shauna Lynch, "The (Dis)locations of Romantic Nationalism: Shelley, Staël, and the

Home-Schooling of Monsters," in *The Literary Channel: The Inter-National Invention of the Novel*, edited by Margaret Cohen and Carolyn Dever [Princeton, NJ: Princeton University Press, 2002], 202). Perhaps her most agile exercise in genre-crossing, Staël's vast tome, *On Germany* (1813), exemplifies the formal principles of political manifesto, cultural study, sociological treatise, literary criticism, and "propaganda," while including long translations of important German writers.

46. Theresa Kelley, "Romantic Exemplarity: Botany and 'Material' Culture," in *Romantic Science: The Literary Forms of Natural History*, ed. Noah Heringman (Albany: State University of New York Press, 2003), 226.

47. Alan Bewell, "'Jacobin Plants': Botany as Social Theory in the 1790s," *The Wordsworth Circle* 20, no. 3 (1989): 134.

48. "[L]es variétés . . . sont plus nombreuses, plus multipliées dans les oiseaux que dans les quadru- pèdes" (Georges-Louis Leclerc, comte de Buffon, *Histoire naturelle des oiseaux* [Paris: L'Imprimerie Royale, 1770–1783], 1:xxi).

49. Georges-Louis Leclerc Buffon, "Plan de l'ouvrage," *Histoire naturelle des oiseaux* (Paris: L'imprimeur Royal, 1770) 1:xxxii; slightly revised, as cited in Alan Bewell, "Romanticism and Colonial Natural History," *Studies in Romanticism* 43 (Spring 2004), 30.

50. Buffon, *Histoire*, 1: xxxiii, as cited in Bewell, "Romanticism," 31.

51. In her comparison of Staël with Gayatri Spivak, Simon similarly notes that "as a process of hybrid- ization, . . . translation constantly plays with borders, threatening or confirming them" (Simon, "Culture Brokers," 139).

52. Germaine de Staël, *Germany, Translated from the French in Three Volumes* (London: John Murray, 1813), 3:150–51; "c'est la même pensée du créateur qui se traduit dans les deux langages dif- férents, et l'un peut servir d'interprète à l'autre" (*De l'Allemagne*, 4:245–46).

53. William Reddy, *The Navigation of Feeling: A Framework for the History of Emotions* (Cambridge: Cambridge University Press, 2001), 207–08.

54. Ibid., 64.

55. Ibid., 87, 64.

56. "Emotives are translations into words about, into 'descriptions' of, the ongoing translation tasks that currently occupy attention as well as the other tasks that remain in the queue, overflowing its current capacities" (ibid., 128).

57. Ibid., 111.

58. Ibid., 94.

59. Ibid., 95.

60. Douglas Robinson, *Performative Linguistics: Speaking and Translating as Doing Things with Words* (New York: Routledge, 2003), 71.

61. Ibid., 73.

62. Staël, *Germany*, 3:94. Ellen Dissanayake, for example, whose *Homo Aestheticus* and *Art and Inti- macy* paved the way for larger discussions of "evolutionary aesthetics" in the twenty-first century, recalls Staël's "reciprocal interpretation" when defining the "aesthetic": "What we call 'aesthetic' are those perceptions that have more than usual emotional and cognitive interconnections and

resonances, often felt to be 'undescribable' or 'ineffable'" (Ellen Dissanayake, *Homo Aestheticus: Where Art Comes From and Why* [Seattle: University of Washington Press, 1995], 153).

63. Ernst Cassirer, *Language and Myth*, trans. Susanne K. Langer (New York: Dover Publications, 1953), 35.

64. Ibid., 36.

65. Alan Richardson, *The Neural Sublime: Cognitive Theories and Romantic Texts* (Baltimore: Johns Hopkins University Press, 2010), 120.

66. Ibid., 122.

67. *Inception*, film, directed by Christopher Nolan (Burbank, CA: Warner Bros. Pictures, 2010).

68. It is a telling coincidence that the vexed relationship between the corporate heir and his recently deceased father in *Inception* aptly updates Oswald's problematic and unresolved grief over the death of his father in *Corinne*.

69. Batsaki, "Inaudible," 40. Similarly, Tili Boon Cuillé has remarked that Corinne's staged tableaux "translate" musical performance into narrative. Cuillé traces the term "tableau," a particularly vivid depiction of high affect, in its migration from painting, through theater, and into narration, honing in on the particulars of the musical tableau. The encounter between Corinne and Oswald at the conclusion of their gallery tour offers a model example of the musical tableau, especially since, as Cuillé observes, the painting of Ossian, the "literal tableau," cannot by itself produce "the requisite cathartic effect": only Corinne's Aeolian translation of the Scottish atmosphere can bring about the desired emotional transformation of Oswald (Tili Boon Cuillé, *Narrative Interludes: Musical Tableaux in Eighteenth-Century French Texts* [Toronto: University of Toronto Press, 2006], 193).

70. In arguing that Staël tried to revive sentimentalist ideals in *On Germany*, Reddy claims that she attempted "to fit German metaphysical idealism into a sentimentalist straightjacket," an entertaining, if somewhat hasty, assertion, bearing in mind that Kant's third critique pivoted on the feelings [Gefühle] of pleasure and displeasure serving as mediators between the faculties of the understanding and reason (cf. Kant's second "Introduction," section 9, "How Judgment Connects the Legislations of the Understanding and Reason"; Reddy, *Navigation of Feeling*, 207–08 and Immanuel Kant, *Critique of Judgment*, trans. Werner S. Pluhar [Indianapolis: Hackett, 1987], 35–38).

9

BRITISH LEGACIES OF *CORINNE* AND THE COMMERCIALIZATION OF ENTHUSIASM

Kari Lokke

M ARIA JANE JEWSBURY opens her 1831 *Athenæum* review of Joanna Baillie's *The Nature and Dignity of Christ* by observing "the striking difference in the mind and writings of the literary women of thirty and forty years ago, and the literary women of the present time."[1] In her contemporaries, Jewsbury finds talent but not the genius of a Mary Wollstonecraft, Elizabeth Inchbald, Ann Radcliffe or, above all, a Joanna Baillie. The "nerve, simplicity, vigour" and "power of mind" that characterized the previous generation of women writers have disappeared from the writings of literary women who are now women of fashion and "elegant accomplishments." In the "female poetry" of her own day, Jewsbury finds that "fascinating tenderness, brilliancy of fancy, and beauty of feeling stand in place of sustained loftiness of imagination, and compact, artist-like diction."[2] Though Jewsbury restricts her comments in this article to British women writers, she might very well have included Germaine de Staël among the earlier generation of writers whose strength of mind she sees as dwarfing the accomplishments of her contemporaries—for, in a previous essay entitled "Woman's Love," she pairs Staël with Shakespeare as examples of the heights of female and male genius respectively.[3]

Given her high estimation of Staël's literary worth, Jewsbury's critical and sometimes parodic portrait of Staël's heroine Corinne in *The History of an Enthusiast* (1830) seems an act of singular boldness and "nerve" on her part. Jewsbury's *History* furthermore offers an intriguing measure of the distance poetic enthusiasm had traveled in European cultural consciousness between its embodiment in Staël's *improvisatrice* in 1807 and her reincarnation in the British Julia of 1830. In this chapter, I will examine ways in which nineteenth-century British women writers' understandings of enthusiasm were conditioned by and conceived in dialogue with Staël's own definitions of the term, as exemplified in her novel *Corinne, or Italy* and her non-fiction works *On Literature* and *On Germany*. I will further argue that the professionalization and commodification of female authorship in Regency Britain shaped women writers' responses to Staël's continental and idealist conception of enthusiasm, tainting it with associations of excessive self-promotion and commercialization. In addition to discussing Jewsbury's novella, my focus will also be Letitia Landon's poem "Erinna" (1826) in order to suggest the ubiquity and complexity of Staël's impact on British women writers of both prose and poetry.

Staël's elaboration of the significance of enthusiasm constitutes the heart of her oeuvre, figuring prominently in her thought from her earliest published work *Letters on Rousseau*, praising Rousseau for insisting on persuasion through enthusiasm, to the final chapters of *On Germany*, celebrating the emancipatory influence of enthusiasm in all cultural realms, from aesthetics, politics, and ethics to philosophy and religion. Furthermore, Staël's contributions to the Enlightenment and Romantic discourse of enthusiasm are unique in their freedom from ambiguity and their unequivocal praise of the beneficent and ameliorative effects of enthusiastic inspiration. Suspicion of the power of enthusiastic possession was not limited to eighteenth-century Enlightenment thinkers and did not, as one might think, readily disappear into a Romantic glorification of poetic inspiration. As Jon Mee has convincingly shown, British "literature in the Romantic period continued to define itself against the dangers of enthusiasm."[4] The term never completely overcame its association with the popular foment of seventeenth-century Protestant uprisings and with religious and political fanaticism. Similarly, in Germany, Luther coined the derogatory term *Schwärmerei* to discredit rival Protestant sects such as the Anabaptists who were allied to peasant unrest. Kant's repeated attacks on *Schwärmerei* suggest the vehemence with which Romantic-era German philosophers continued to reject its purportedly delusive influence.[5]

Staël steps boldly into this debate in the concluding chapters of *On Germany*, which stand in direct opposition to the prevailing discourse on enthusiasm as dangerous, delusive exaltation. In direct and explicit contrast to this long-standing international tradition, Staël asserts that enthusiasm controverts monomania and obsession: "Enthusiasm has nothing to do with fanaticism, and cannot lead people astray. Enthusiasm is tolerant—not out of indifference, but because it makes us feel the interest and beauty of everything."[6] A daughter of Rousseau writing in the wake of the French Revolution, Staël shares the ardent spiritual thirst that Michel Brix identifies in post-Revolutionary France as rejecting institutionalized religion in favor of a spirituality derived from Platonic and Neo-Platonic doctrines that emphasize *enthousiasmos*, the presence of a god within.[7]

For Staël, locked in a battle with Napoleonic tyranny and imperialism, religious delusion is the least of her concerns. A passionate believer in republican forms of government, Staël sought to combat the association of enthusiasm, which had become a code word for Revolutionary sympathy, with the violence and fanaticism of the Terror. Staël's goal was to reclaim—and, in a sense, to reinvent—an enthusiasm for nineteenth-century political and aesthetic theory that was freed from its associations with Revolutionary bloodshed in the name of Reason. The primary enemy of political progress and artistic freedom was Napoleonic will to power and opportunism, which she saw as the ultimate outgrowth of eighteenth-century materialism and utilitarianism and summarized with the terms self-interest and "calcul." Instead of associating Revolutionary violence with enthusiasm, then, Staël links the Terror, in *Considerations on the Principal Events of the French Revolution*, to conflicts rooted in deeply ingrained power inequities:

> A sort of fury took hold of the poor in the presence of the rich; as the jealousy inspired by property was reinforced by aristocratic distinctions, the people grew proud of their own numbers. Everything constituting the power and brilliance of the minority seemed to them simple usurpation.[8]

For Staël, only the liberty and detachment offered by a representative government can quell the violence of political and religious fanaticism: "The abstract power of representative government does not irritate men's pride; it is therefore through this institution that the torches of the furies can be extinguished."[9] Staël identifies representative government with the rule of law, which enables concern for the greater good of the many to prevail over both the *amour propre* of the few and the unruly passions of the crowd. In *Mania and Literary Style*, Clement Hawes has suggested that enthusiasm, in the English seventeenth- and eighteenth-century context, is "the profoundly ambivalent signifier of two revolutions: the bourgeois revolution that did occur and the far more democratic and egalitarian revolution whose possibility was tantalizingly glimpsed and then suppressed."[10] If, for the most part, enthusiasm was denigrated as the marker of plebian struggle in Britain, Staël, at the beginning of the nineteenth century, seeks in her discourse on enthusiasm to create a bridge between bourgeois and egalitarian revolutions through her advocacy of representative government. At the same time, in a radically new move, she imagines an abyss between destructive fanaticism, associated with myopic individual interest, and emancipatory enthusiasm identified with visionary collective good.

If, for Staël, fanaticism can "be calmed only by liberty,"[11] it is her heroine Corinne who embodies this liberty, both artistic and political, just as it is Corinne who is Staël's ultimate incarnation of enthusiasm.[12] Every one of her words is inspired by "enthusiasm, that inexhaustible well of feelings and ideas," explains her friend and confidant Prince Castel-Forte.[13] And it is the scenes from the chapter "Corinne at the Capitol" where Corinne is crowned with laurels in a ceremony consecrated by the names of Petrarch and Tasso that caught hold of the imaginations and fed the aspirations of countless nineteenth-century women writers for generations to come. Dressed as Domenichino's Sybil, Corinne is a kind of inspired prophetess who unites, in a transcendent present, Rome's glorious past with visions of a utopian future. "Favorite of the gods and adored by the multitudes" [*favorite des dieux et adorée des foules*], as Brix writes of her, Corinne thus poses a potential threat to guardians of rational order and social hierarchy.[14] She fits perfectly David Hume's ambivalent definition of the enthusiast as one who believes herself "a distinguished favorite of the Divinity" and, in so doing, possesses the strength and boldness to challenge tyranny and promote civil liberty.[15] Corinne's public performance also reflects Staël's reliance on sentiment or passion as opposed to reason as the key to harmonious sociability—a reliance central to Hume's early work on sympathy, the *Treatise on Human Nature*.[16] Yet, in contrast to the sceptical secularist Hume, Staël's understanding of sentiment is above all else spiritual. Rather than inducing frenzy or lack of control, her inspiration generates in Corinne and in the Roman populace a kind of fervor that is "the source of ideal beauty in the arts, religion in solitary souls, generosity in heroes, disinterestedness in men."[17] Enthusiasm, then, for Staël, and for her *improvisatrice*, is above all else a form of mystical self-possession and detachment, a genuine attunement to the infinite and the divine, that she repeatedly terms elevation of soul.

This elevation of soul—this enthusiasm that lifts one beyond one's own powers—makes possible a detachment from the self and the present that Staël represents as historical perspective, as the capacity to see one's place in historical process and progress in a panorama of collective and anonymous effort she terms in her discourse on the passions "the vast tableau of destinies."[18] "Physical nature," Staël writes in *On Germany*, "follows its unvarying course through the destruction of individuals; man's thought becomes sublime when he succeeds in thinking of himself from a universal point of view. He then quietly contributes to the triumph of truth."[19] The vanity associated with personal fame has no place in her ideal of enthusiasm. Corinne thus emphasizes that her improvisational powers have their source in her interaction with her audience:

> At times the interest lifts me beyond my own powers, brings me to discover in nature and in my own heart bold truths and language full of life that solitary thought would not have brought into being. At such times, it seems to me that I am experiencing a supernatural enthusiasm, and I sense full well that what is speaking within me has a value beyond myself . . . I am a poet when I admire, when I scorn, when I hate—not out of personal feelings, not for my own cause, but for the dignity of the human race and the glory of the world.[20]

Like Staël, both Letitia Landon and Maria Jane Jewsbury possessed a strong historical consciousness and an equally strong desire to understand the relation of their literary era to previous cultural epochs. Yet neither British writer can assert the firm faith in art's contributions to perfectibility and progress so prominent in Staël as a writer with deep personal roots in the Enlightenment. And each is haunted by a sense of the futility of fighting the commercial spirit of her age. In the opening essay of Jewsbury's *Phantasmagoria* (1825) entitled "The Age of Books," Jewsbury comments on the tendency of her age to divide the past up into periods characterized by epithets such as the Middle Ages or the Elizabethan Age. Imagining herself a character born in the eleventh century and still alive in 1825 (who could easily have served as a model for Virginia Woolf's *Orlando*), Jewsbury has no doubts as to how historical perspective would allow one to characterize her current era: "Surely no one will deny the propriety of distinguishing the present as an age of books! of book making! book reading! book reviewing! And book forgetting!"[21] The repetitiveness of her prose drives home the reality of mass production and consumption of culture in her age. Now, Jewsbury laments, anyone can and does write, so that publication confers no distinction: "Authors, some fifty years ago, were perhaps, with reference to the rest of the population, in the proportion of one in twenty thousand; but since then they have so multiplied and increased, that were they all suddenly swept away, the kingdom would be as much depopulated, (I do not say impoverished) as though it had been the seat of a five years' war."[22] The consequence of this proliferation of books and authors is a mass culture that Jewsbury sardonically characterizes as trash: "In point of feeding, the public rather resembles a spoiled child, that is crammed with trash from morning till night, and then upbraided with its unhealthy appetite."[23]

Seven years later, in her essay "On the Ancient and Modern Influence of Poetry," Letitia Landon articulates her equally acute sense of the gap that separates her literary era from the preceding one.

> We ourselves are standing on the threshold of a new era. . . . In religion,
> in philosophy, in politics, in manners, there has passed a great change;
> but in none has been worked a greater change than in poetry, whether as
> it regards the art itself, or the general feeling towards it.[24]

And like Jewsbury, Landon assesses this sea change in literary taste in negative terms, eloquently lamenting the excessive commercialization of poetry in her day: "There is a base macadamizing spirit in literature; we seek to level all the high places of old."[25]

It is to enthusiasm that Landon looks to counteract this degradation of contemporary art. Here, following Staël, Landon flies in the face of a prestigious literary tradition, dating back to Jonathan Swift's *A Tale of a Tub*, that associates the enthusiastic mode with "popular or 'hack' writing": Swift's satire of religious zealotry and sectarianism was, in fact, also clearly intended as a "patrician critique of commercial modernity."[26] In her defense of enthusiasm, Landon explicitly echoes and reworks Staël's conceptualization of this emotion as the antidote to the self-interest, opportunism, and "calcul" of the Napoleonic era. In what amounts to a summary of Staël's argument in the concluding chapters of *On Germany*, Landon writes:

> Again we repeat, that though the taste be not, the spirit of the day is, ad-
> verse to the production of poetry. Selfishness is its principle, indifference
> its affectation, and ridicule its commonplace. We allow no appeals save
> to our reason, or to our fear of laughter. We must either be convinced
> or sneered into things. Neither calculation nor sarcasm are the elements
> of poetry.[27]

But whereas the axis of Staël's argument is national—she holds up the German "philosophy of belief, of enthusiasm—a philosophy which confirms through reason, the revelations of feeling" as a model to be emulated by the cynical French—Landon's is historical. The mindset of the present, Landon fears, precludes the possibility of the production of great poetry or relegates it to the past.[28]

Despite the aura of despair that shadows Landon's portrait of Regency society, she refuses to relinquish her conviction that the urgent task of contemporary poetry is "to prevent . . . civilization from growing too cold and too selfish" and that whereas poetry's "first effort was against barbarism, its last is against selfishness."[29] And once again, as with Staël, enthusiasm is the key to this effort. Poetry, for Landon, is "the fountain whence youth draws enthusiasm for its hopes"—the product, like Milton's *Paradise Lost*, of "that indefinable spirit, whose enthusiasm is nature's own gift to the poet."[30] And, finally, she concludes the essay with a panegyric to enthusiasm that emphasizes its link to the far away, in both space and time: "Enthusiasm is no passion of the drawing-room, or of the pence-table; its home is the heart, and its hope is afar. This is too little the creed of our generation: yet without such creed, poetry has neither present life nor future immortality."[31] Here we find a translation into affective terms of Staël's activist, political credo: "One must fight for the cause of eternity, but with the arms of the times."[32]

Much as Landon and Jewsbury's invocations of enthusiasm echo those of Staël, their difference in tone, as I have suggested, is striking. This difference is not only linked to the relative absence in their writings of the strong sense of political activism ever present in the works of the enormously influential daughter of Jacques Necker.[33] As Landon asserts, prefiguring Percy Shelley's "Defence of Poetry," posthumously published in 1840, "We have graceful singing in the bower, but no voice that startles us into wonder, and hurries us forth to see whose trumpet is awakening the land."[34] Perhaps even more crucial to note is that—whereas Staël represents herself in clear opposition to the opportunism and self-promotion of her day—both Landon and Jewsbury cannot escape the sense that they, themselves, are complicit with and contaminated by it. Like Jewsbury, Landon views the poetry of her day, unlike that of Wordsworth, Byron, Scott and Shelley, as undistinguished and indistinguishable, the result not of craft, but of a kind of mass production: "The writers of today do not set their mark on their property; one might have put forth the work of the other."[35] Furthermore, the aura originally associated with the work of literature has been transferred to the author herself, to the detriment of art: "The personal is the destroyer of the spiritual; and to the former everything is now referred. We talk of the author's self more than his works, and we know his name rather than his writings."[36] Staël's emphasis on the impersonal and collective nature of artistic production has been turned inside out—ironically, of course—in part by her own self-dramatization and international renown. And who would understand the detrimental effects of this cult of personality, this commodification of the author better than the enormously popular L. E. L., icon of the poetess, and, as Anne Mellor has put it, an early and infamous example of the media "star"?[37]

Landon's fame soared with the publication of her interpretation of the Corinne motif in 1824. Advertised by extravagant reviews in the *Literary Gazette* written by her editor William Jerdan, *The Improvisatrice* was hugely successful, going through six editions in its first year.[38] The poem capitalizes on the myth of Corinne (rewritten hundreds of times by nineteenth-century women poets and novelists worldwide) as the female artist who—torn between her love and her art, between domestic and public roles—is ultimately destroyed by this conflict after being abandoned by her beloved.[39] Significantly, by 1826, when "Erinna," Landon's new version of Corinne, appeared in the collection *The Golden Violet*, the Grecian poet Erinna takes the place of Sappho rejected by Phaon, or Ariadne abandoned by Theseus.[40] The single male lover has vanished from the poem to be replaced by a love affair between the poet and her audience.[41] And betrayal by the beloved has been transformed into self-betrayal through profanation of her poetic vocation, as she has become "the low slave of vanity":

> To what use have I turn'd
> The golden gifts in which I pride myself?
> They are profaned; with their pure ore I made
> A temple resting only on the breath
> Of heedless worshippers.[42]

Such metaphors of gilding and idolatry abound in "Erinna" and suggest Landon's awareness that the profession of women's poetry—the "golden violet" of the volume's title—cannot, in her day, be separated from the religion of the marketplace. We recognize here the L. E. L. who contributed hundreds of love lyrics and orientalized, imperial fantasies to the ornate giftbooks and annuals of her day.[43] Thus Erinna's relation to her lyre becomes "sweet commerce," and communion with her audience is figured in terms of economic exchange. When, like Corinne, she stands alone "'mid thousands" and her performance is honored with a laurel crown, she depicts her rewards in terms of a rich inheritance: "For I was like some young and sudden heir / Of a rich palace heap'd with gems and gold."[44] Ultimately this ecstatic exchange is doomed to failure as the fountain of enthusiasm that Landon glorifies in "On the Ancient and Modern Influence of Poetry" is contaminated, in "Erinna," by celebrity and vanity: "I drank the maddening cup of praise, which grew / Henceforth the fountain of my life."[45] "[E]xchange of flattery," "cautious coldness" and "mockery" overpower that sympathy she has sought with her audience. "Alas! The idols which our hopes set up, / They are Chaldean ones, half gold, half clay."[46]

Yet "Erinna" concludes on a note of fragile promise rather than with a sense of disillusionment and despair. Evoking her "early feelings" in the poem's last lines, Landon compels us to return to the meditation on enthusiasm at the heart of her poem. In her youth, before her corruption by fame, Erinna is

> . . . fill'd
> With rich enthusiasm, which once flung
> Its purple colouring o'er all things of earth,
> And without which our utmost power of thought
> But sharpens arrows that will drink our blood.[47]

In a modification of the Wordsworthian paradigm—a modification that accords with Staël's privileging of feeling over reason—the power of sensuous, emotional inspiration trumps the power of thought. And in the lush beauty of the Mediterranean landscape, Erinna finds a source of enthusiasm distinct from the more humanistic visions of Staël.

> How have I loved, when the red evening fill'd
> Our temple with its glory, first, to gaze
> On the strange contrast of the crimson air,
> Lighted as if with passion, and flung back,
> From silver vase and tripod rich with gems,
> To pale statues round, where human life
> Was not, but beauty was, which seemed to have
> Apart existence from humanity.[48]

Furthermore, in contradistinction to the prevailing denigration of enthusiasm as a feminized and sexualized response, Erinna proudly claims this enthusiasm as an explicitly female/feminine poetic power:[49]

> Like woman's soothing influence o'er man
> Enthusiasm is upon the mind;
> Softening and beautifying that which is
> Too harsh and sullen in itself.[50]

Like Staël's Corinne, Landon's Erinna, in claiming it as her own, depicts enthusiasm as heightened, sublimated feeling inducing emotional calm, rather than the fury or madness with which the masculine philosophical tradition—be it Hume, Voltaire or Wieland—invariably associates it.

Indeed, in this crucial disquisition on enthusiasm, Landon takes up the question, central to Enlightenment religious and philosophical debate surrounding the term, that of the (im)possibility of direct divine inspiration of the individual, and seems to answer it in the affirmative, as had Staël: "I gave my soul entire unto the gift / I deem'd mine own, direct from heaven."[51] And the music, the immaterial art produced by her lyre, confirms Erinna in the conviction that it is no delusion to believe the divine can speak directly, if enigmatically, through human art. Comparing music to painting, she exclaims:

> But music is a mystery, and viewless
> Even when present, and is less man's act,
> And less within his order; . . .
> And then, as if it were an unreal thing,
> The wind will sweep from the neglected strings
> As rich a swell as ever minstrel drew.[52]

Once created, music escapes the artist to lead a mysterious life of its own, analogous to the impersonal strains of the Aeolian harp. Indeed the elusive, indefinable emotional impact of poetry's music seems to confirm its otherworldly (Platonic) origin:

> Is it the language of some other state,
> Born of its memory? For what can wake
> The soul's strong instinct of another world,
> Like music?[53]

The immateriality of music allows a transmutation of what Landon represents as the commercial and degrading nature of personal fame into an impersonal—and perhaps anonymous—emotional and spiritual bond with future readers and singers of poetry, whom she identifies as youthful poets, maidens and lovers. Significantly, Erinna/Landon finds the truth and immortality of her poetry not in the written words, but in the ethereal, elusive and sympathetic responses of what she terms "the spirit's gentlest chords."[54] Thus, in the poem's conclusion, Landon's Erinna relinquishes "stern ambition" and "petty vanities," holding true to the belief that enthusiasm possesses a kind of purifying power akin to sympathy that transcends the commercial and the commodified.[55]

Five years later, in an anonymous contribution to the *Athenæum* entitled "Nobody's Happy Now: Verses by a Proser," Maria Jane Jewsbury seems to respond directly to the "truth and tenderness" of Landon's lyre, to Landon's sensational display of sentimentality, when she writes:

> Nobody's happy now—what shall I do?
> I want to write verses all tender and true;
> But I'm come to buy goods a day after the fair,
> I can't find an ounce of death or despair! . . .
> Then, all of my forerunners have torn up the passions,
> Nor left me a shred wherewith to show fashions.
> The heart is dissected till, sick of itself,
> It longs to be quietly laid on the shelf;
> How shall I be wretched in very good verse?
> Make eloquent grief, put coins in my purse?
> Sweet souls of the lyre, if ye've charity, show it,
> And sell me some sorrow, and make me a poet.[56]

In this hilarious send-up of the Romantic poetess marketing her sorrows, Jewsbury reveals the essence of her satiric genius. Jewsbury's *The History of an Enthusiast*, published a year earlier, combines autobiographical elements and attributes famously associated with Staël's Corinne in a narrative trajectory that mimics L. E. L.'s meteoric rise to fame and subsequent disenchantment. In accord with the tendencies of the "proser" as opposed to the poet/ess, this novella is much harsher in its treatment of enthusiasm than is Landon's "Erinna." Jewsbury seems to understand perfectly that, as Patrick Vincent writes, "In the new market economy, the poetess's tears are no longer so much a sign of sympathy, as they are a form of currency; when capitalism co-opts sentiment, it is not virtue, but value that accrues through loss."[57]

Jewsbury's heroine, Julia Osborne, is clearly intended as an avatar of Staël's prototypical and, by 1830, legendary female artist Corinne. As Nanora Sweet has noted, Julia's name alludes to the possibilities of female subjectivity entailed in Rousseau's Julie, Shakespeare's Juliet as she is performed by Corinne, and Juliette, daughter of Oswald and Lucile and Corinne's artistic legatee.[58] Furthermore, the opposition between Corinne and Lucile is repeated in *The History*'s two central female characters, the childhood friends Julia and Annette. When Annette's father, Mr. Mortimer, asks his "golden-haired sylph" what she wishes to be when she grows up, she replies that she wants "to make a charming wife, to some very, very charming man, just like yourself."[59] The brunette Julia, on the other hand, chooses

"Fame" and the laurel crown, asserting that "a poet is far nobler than a king" and that she will "make amends for being a woman" by gaining immortality through her writing.[60]

Thus Jewsbury represents the desire for fame as inextricable from the character—indeed, as the *essence* of the character of the enthusiast—and the stage is set for the novella's central conflict, replicating that in *Corinne*: between North and South, domesticity and public accomplishment, happiness and ambition, innocence and knowledge, common sense and enthusiasm.[61] The wise and worldly Mr. Mortimer recognizes in Julia "a child of grace and genius," who "with her soft, dark, earnest, spiritual eyes," "seems . . . to think, speak and feel full of the spirit of the south, full of ardor and intelligence."[62] Enthusiasm, in the social world of Jewsbury's novella, is distinctly at odds with Britishness. When, for example, Julia makes her stunning debut in London, after leaving her country village at twenty-one, gossips describe her as a British Corinne:

> Miss Osborne is . . . full of brilliant energy in conversation, and so un-mannered, that [people] lift up their hands, call her an enthusiast, and hope she will come to no harm. I should think from what I hear, that she is a compound of Italian passion, English thought and French vivacity.[63]

Here we witness precisely the kind of attribution of national characteristics typical of Staël's *Corinne*, with enthusiasm depicted as a distinct threat to British reasonableness and well-being.

Like her creator, Julia was consumed by a passion for books and for learning as a child—a passion that is partially fulfilled when the local parson, Mr. Percy, agrees to give her lessons in the classics, at age sixteen, along with his son Cecil during his vacations from Oxford.[64] During these lessons, Julia falls in love with Cecil, unbeknownst to him, and without being fully aware of it herself. In the end, her enthusiastic spirit leaves him far behind; Jewsbury is quick to point out that he is devoid of imagination or poetry. Cecil sees, in the literature of his day, a blending of emotion and intellect—but, instead of celebrating that union that Staël had termed "enthusiasm," he fears and condemns it in a starkly economic calculus: "I remain of the same opinion still, that your having wholly, and all at once, plunged your spirit into an intellectual fountain of emotion, of which Goëthe and Schiller, Petrarch and de Staël, and Shelly [*sic*], and a dozen others, are the presiding spirits, will be productive of more loss than gain."[65]

Julia's passion is indeed an intellectual one, as she herself acknowledges in her diary entries recorded before her spectacular appearance on the London literary scene. She dedicates herself to her craft in "the burning hope of self-emancipation" from the confines of her stultifying country life: "I pine for living intercourse with the great, the gay, and the gifted, for access at will to what is various and splendid. Oh, this dull, dreary, and most virtuous domestic life!"[66] Yet, just as eighteenth-century philosophers had argued that fanaticism or monomania in the name of reason could be as dangerous as religious enthusiasm, so Jewsbury warns against the exclusive worship of intellectual beauty in her description of Julia's life as a celebrated London artist and salonnière:[67]

> [I]s it strange that Julia was the enthusiast in society no less than she had once been in solitude? Energy was her leading characteristic, and whatsoever employed it, yielded a delight that she never deemed less valuable . . . because it involved ambition . . . she threw the radiance of fancy even around the conventional habits of fashion . . . —but emparadised in dreams of intellectual beauty,—religious responsibility and moral utility had "no form or comeliness."[68]

Through its association with fame and public renown, enthusiasm comes to stand for values such as self-promotion and personal ambition that are in exact opposition to the divine inspiration Staël associates with it.

For Jewsbury, the amorality of Julia's poetic vocation is inseparable from her relation to the literary marketplace: a realm of ephemeral, trivialized fashion. Tellingly, her wealthy patron and lionizer, Mrs. Lawrence Hervey—ruler of this feminized realm and emblem of the fickle nature of public favor—is compared to the fairy tale figure of Bluebeard, the fabulously wealthy aristocrat whose cruel and insatiable appetite leaves a series of young brides interred in his cellar. As does Landon with Erinna, Jewsbury makes clear the inevitability of Julia's corruption by the crass, commercial nature of literary trade, despite the fact that she is independently wealthy and does not need to write to support herself. Jewsbury terms Julia's life in London a "gilded state of existence," and Julia herself comes to view fashionable society as a "Moloch with diamond eyes," and her situation that of a "jeweled captive" of her public.[69] Similarly, Erinna brands her audience as tainting the beauty they cannot feel with "foul plague spots" and calls out "O dream of fame, what hast thou been to me / But the destroyer of life's calm content!"[70] Here Landon echoes Staël's epigram from *On Germany* that was quoted *ad infinitum* by women writers throughout the nineteenth century: "Fame itself is only a brilliant way to bury the happiness of a woman."[71] Not to be outdone, Jewsbury's Julia laments to her diary, "Ah, what is genius to woman, but a splendid misfortune!

What is fame to woman, but a dazzling degradation!"[72] Jewsbury's ironic wit cannot resist pushing Staël's epigram over the edge into melodrama and the "failed seriousness" of camp.[73] In so doing, she exposes the potential for disingenuousness and self-aggrandizement in the theatricality common to many Regency poetesses.

In the end, Jewsbury depicts Julia as utterly jaded, so caught up in the masquerade of high society and literary fame that she becomes incapable of both personal devotion and meaningful artistic accomplishment. In the wake of her climactic encounter with Cecil, she discovers that her secret passion for him is not returned. He announces that he is leaving with his new bride for missionary work in India, and Julia comes face-to-face with the emptiness of her life. Julia is overcome with the "degrading sense of [her] thralldom to artificial tastes and habits" coupled with a "cold abandonment to desolate loneliness." Her "fiery dream of enthusiastic, yet faithful passion" shared with Cecil proves illusory, her artistic career, a charade. After decking herself out with jewels and festal attire for her soirée, she returns to her lonely solitude, unmasks, and reveals herself "haggard and disrobed—a Pythoness after the moment of inspiration—cold, collapsed, and still."[74] Here Jewsbury takes up the age-old sexualized rendering of the enthusiastic, frenzied prophetess and reinforces its misogynist undertones.[75]

Jewsbury, then—like Landon—grafts Staël's conception of enthusiasm onto a Wordsworthian model of development, with an all-important difference: the redemptive reclaiming of youthful enthusiasm that fuels the emotive and sympathetic power of Erinna's poetry is an impossibility for the disenchanted Julia. She represents herself as one who has cast "the first born" of her soul—simplicity—into the fiery furnace of fame.[76] And unlike Landon's Erinna, who finds solace in a conscious return to Nature, Jewsbury represents Nature as an unforgiving Deity that rebuffs prodigals who seek to return. Julia is equally incapable of the kind of moral, socio-political effort that Staël sees as key to the ameliorative historical influence of enthusiasm. Claiming that such humanitarian effort is unfit—indeed, impossible for a woman—she explicitly rejects Cecil's exhortation that she employ her genius for the ennoblement of humankind, "to strengthen weakness, console sorrow, and invigorate character."[77] Here Jewsbury seems to endorse a model of "silent fame": the study, at home, of the great [male] writers of one's time put forth by Parson Percy, Cecil's father.

In some of the most powerful writing of her career, Jewsbury, portraying Julia's early poetic reveries, evokes her conviction that youthful enthusiasm will inevitably be corrupted by disillusionment, disenchantment, and despair:

And night—what enthusiast loves not the night when the day has died
in oriental pomp, and entire blackness, or a "grave splendour" succeeds
on the face of heaven? . . . Dreams are the mythology of poetry—admired, not believed; and night is the soul's canopy of state; then we
feel; . . . the world passes in review before us, and the high heavens
themselves seem less unattainable. . . . But this can only be in buoyant,
gifted, enthusiastic youth. When passion and sorrow have traced their
fiery writing on the soul, we love the stars no longer. They are like the
eyes of a lovely stranger, beauteous but cold; mute mockers of our spirits
and their woes.[78]

Here Jewsbury echoes the meditations of Landon's Erinna, who calls dreams "re-
vealings of another world, / More pure, more perfect than our weary one, / Where
day is darkness to the starry soul."[79] But again, whereas Erinna suggests poetry's
sublime potential to evoke better worlds, Jewsbury's narrator denies the utopian
potential of dreams, transforming the starry sky into an emblem of a cold, unre-
ceptive, and cynical audience.

In conclusion, then, the writings of Landon and Jewsbury attest to the success
of Staël's efforts to reclaim and redefine enthusiasm for the nineteenth century. The
powerful legacy of Staël's meditations on enthusiasm takes very different forms in the
writings of Landon and Jewsbury, however. If Landon's poetry and critical writings
give form to Staël's belief in the power of enthusiasm to transcend vanity, egotism
and self-interest in the name of beauty, Jewsbury calls this idealism and aestheticism
into question, suggesting that her female enthusiast is doomed, by the nature of the
literary marketplace, to disillusionment and disenchantment. In her work, enthusiasm comes to mean precisely the opposite of Staël's definition: self-aggrandizement
and assertion of ego. Through her satiric inclinations, Jewsbury furthermore aligns
herself with the Swiftian tradition that identifies enthusiasm with the commercial
degradation of art. And yet Jewsbury, clearly reluctant to relinquish the "mythology
of poetry" completely, refuses to conclude her *History* on this note of despair and de-
feat. Instead, her enthusiast pens a couple of outrageous poems that flout propriety
and public opinion, defiantly quotes Shelley's "Ode to the West Wind" and heads
off to the continent and perhaps ultimately to Italy, land of Corinne! Julia's parting
poems assert a refreshing rejection of sentimentality as they toy with an unabashed
materialism. Claiming her right to "manufacture puns," paradoxes, and *bons-mots*,[80]
Julia refuses to mourn her loss of love, which she portrays as mere economic transaction. Her unabashedly materialist perspective furthermore banishes the ghosts of
retrospection and regret from her future: "And memory is mental indigestion; / You

are not healthy if it much afflicts you; / Hope, which is hunger, without any question, / By no means in your health so much restricts you."[81] Thus Jewsbury cleverly gives her readers the conventional warning and condemnation of the dangers of female literary acclaim, all the while opening up the possibility of a new and exciting life for her headstrong artist heroine.[82]

Ironically, it was not youthful enthusiasm or literary acclaim, but pragmatism and marriage that brought untimely deaths to both Jewsbury and Landon. Unlike her character Julia, Maria Jane did marry her "Cecil." She died after a few months in India, having accompanied the Reverend Fletcher there for his chaplaincy in the East India Company. She had made it clear prior to her marriage in a letter to Dora Wordsworth that this was a marriage based on reason, not on love.[83] Similarly, Landon—in an attempt to salvage her scandal-plagued reputation—made a questionable marriage to George Maclean, governor of Cape Coast Africa, formerly the major British slave trading post in West Africa. Within two months of her arrival there, she was dead. Both poets produced some of their finest poetry on their sea voyages to these distant colonial realms—Jewsbury's *Oceanides* and Landon's "Night at Sea," poems that continued their conflict-ridden dialogues with their metropolitan, British audiences. In her posthumous recognition of Jewsbury, Landon praises her "generous enthusiasm,"[84] just as Wordsworth had acknowledged, in his praise of Jewsbury, that "her enthusiasm was ardent."[85] One hopes that Jewsbury would have been pleased by these tributes.

Notes

1. Maria Jane Jewsbury, review of *The Nature and Dignity of Christ* by Joanna Baillie, *The Athenæum* 187 (May 28, 1831), 337. Kari Lokke wishes to thank Brynne Gray for her invaluable help with the research for this essay.

2. Ibid., 337.

3. Maria Jane Jewsbury, "Woman's Love," in *Phantasmagoria* (London: Hurst, Robinson, & Co., 1825), 1:113.

4. Jon Mee, *Romanticism, Enthusiasm, and Regulation: Poetics and the Policing of Culture in the Romantic Period* (Oxford: Oxford University Press, 2003), 11.

5. For Immanuel Kant on *Schwärmerei*, see *Raising the Tone of Philosophy: Late Essays by Immanuel Kant, Transformative Critique by Jacques Derrida*, ed. and trans. Peter Fenves (Baltimore: Johns Hopkins University Press, 1993), 101–13.

6. Germaine de Staël, *On Germany*, in *Major Writings of Germaine de Staël*, ed. and trans. Vivian Folkenflik (New York: Columbia University Press, 1992), 322. Unless otherwise indicated, all subsequent English translations of Staël's works will be from this anthology.

7. Michel Brix, "Les sources mystiques de *Corinne*: la femme, l'amour et le sacré" in *Mme de Staël: Actes du colloque de la Sorbonne du 20 novembre 1999*, ed. Michel Delon and Françoise Mélonio (Paris: Presses de l'Université de Paris-Sorbonne, 2000), 85–97.

8. Germaine de Staël, *Considerations on the Main Events of the French Revolution* in *Major Writings*, 363.

9. Ibid., 364.

10. Clement Hawes, *Mania and Literary Style: The Rhetoric of Enthusiasm from the Ranters to Christopher Smart* (Cambridge: Cambridge University Press, 1996), 2.

11. Staël, *Considerations*, in *Major Writings*, 364.

12. Ibid.

13. Germaine de Staël, *Corinne, or Italy*, ed. and trans. Avriel Goldberger (New Brunswick, NJ: Rutgers University Press, 1987), 24.

14. Brix, "Les sources mystiques de *Corinne*," 85; translation mine.

15. David Hume, "Of Superstition and Enthusiasm," in *Essays: Moral, Political, and Literary*, ed. Eugene F. Miller (Indianapolis: Liberty Classics, 1985), 74.

16. For Hume's early theories of the relation of reason and passion, see John Mullan, *Sentiment and Sociability: The Language of Feeling in the Eighteenth Century* (Oxford: Oxford University Press, 1988), 18–56.

17. Staël, *Corinne, or Italy*, 45.

18. Staël, *The Influence of the Passions on the Happiness of Individuals and Nations*, in *Major Writings*, 170. Staël is perhaps here indebted to Adam Smith's conception of the capacity for impartial spectatorship of one's own feelings as central to social morality. See Mullan, *Sentiment and Sociability*, 43–56.

19. Staël, *On Germany*, in *Major Writings*, 321–22.

20. Staël, *Corinne, or Italy*, 45.

21. Jewsbury, "Woman's Love," 3.

22. Ibid.

23. Ibid., 4.

24. Letitia Elizabeth Landon, "On the Ancient and Modern Influence of Poetry," in *Letitia Elizabeth Landon: Selected Writings*, ed. Jerome McGann and Daniel Riess (Peterborough, Ontario: Broadview, 1997), 160.

25. Ibid., 168.

26. See Hawes, *Mania and Literary Style*, 102–3.

27. Landon, *Selected Writings*, 167.

28. Staël, *On Germany*, in *Major Writings*, 312.

29. Landon, *Selected Writings*, 165, 168.

30. Ibid., 164, 166.

31. Ibid., 168.

32. Germaine de Staël, *De l'Allemagne*, ed. Jean de Pange and Simone Balayé (Paris: Librairie Hachette, 1959), 4:281; my translation.

33. Her friend Mme de Chastenay wrote that Napoleon felt so compelled to persecute her that people said "in Europe one had to count three Great Powers: England, Russia, and Mme de Staël" (John Isbell, *The Birth of European Romanticism: Truth and Propaganda in Staël's* De l'Allemagne, *1810–1813* [Cambridge: Cambridge University Press, 1994], 6).

34. Landon, *Selected Writings*, 167.

35. Ibid., 167.

36. Ibid., 167–68.

37. Anne K. Mellor and Richard E. Matlak, eds., *British Literature 1780–1830* (Fort Worth, TX: Harcourt Brace & Co., 1996), 1377.

38. See "Introduction" in Landon, *Selected Writings*, 12. According to Cynthia Lawford, Landon carried on a long-term affair with Jerden and bore him three children. This secret relation with a married man who marketed her poetry would certainly have added to Landon's sense that she was "selling herself." See Cynthia Lawford, "Diary," *London Review of Books* (September 21, 2000): 36–37.

39. For the legacy of Staël's *Corinne* in the European poetess tradition, see Patrick Vincent, *The Romantic Poetess: European Culture, Politics and Gender, 1820–1840* (Hanover: University Press of New England, 2004). For her influence on the novel, see Kari Lokke, *Tracing Women's Romanticism: Gender, History and Transcendence* (London: Routledge, 2004) and Judith E. Martin, *Germaine de Staël in Germany: Gender and Literary Authority (1800–1850)* (Madison and Teaneck, NJ: Fairleigh Dickinson University Press, 2011).

40. *The Oxford Classical Dictionary* calls Erinna a "poetess, of the Dorian island of Telos . . . who probably lived at the end of the fourth century BC. . . . She was famous for her *Distaff*, a poem in 300 hexameters in memory of her friend Baucis. . . . She herself died at the age of nineteen" (N. G. L. Hammond and H. H. Scullard, eds., *The Oxford Classical Dictionary*, 2nd ed. [Oxford: Oxford University Press, 1970], 406).

41. Indeed Landon's "On the Character of Mrs. Hemans's Writings" is an extended meditation on the erotic relationship between poetess and public. See Landon, *Selected Writings*, 173–86. Significantly, Landon appends a tribute to Jewsbury to the end of her eulogy for Hemans.

42. "Erinna," ll. 231–35 in Landon, *Selected Writings*, 95.

43. For the economic significance of annuals as venues for Regency women's poetry, see Paula Feldman, "The Poet and the Profits: Felicia Hemans and the Literary Marketplace," *Keats-Shelley Journal* 46 (1997): 148–76 and William St. Clair, *The Reading Nation in the Romantic Period* (Cambridge: Cambridge University Press, 2004), 229–34.

44. "Erinna," l. 24 and ll. 36–39 in Landon, *Selected Writings*, 89–90.

45. ll. 197–200 in ibid., 94.

46. ll. 205–07 and ll. 261–62 in ibid., 94 and 96.

47. ll. 109–12 in ibid., 92.

48. ll. 157–64 in ibid., 93.

49. For the sexual threat posed by female enthusiasm, see Hawes, *Mania and Literary Style*, 11–12 and 50–76; Mee, *Romanticism, Enthusiasm, and Regulation*, 49–58; Mary D. Sheriff, "Passionate Spectators: On Enthusiasm, Nymphomania, and the Imagined Tableau," in *Enthusiasm and Enlightenment in Europe, 1650–1850*, ed. Lawrence Klein and Anthony J. La Vopa (San Marino, CA: Huntington Library, 1998), 51–83.

50. "Erinna," ll. 113–16 in Landon, *Selected Writings*, 92.

51. ll. 81–83 in ibid., 91.

52. ll. 133–35 and 139–41 in ibid., 92.

53. ll. 147–52 in ibid., 93.

54. l. 351 in ibid., 98. Compare the conclusion to Landon's elegy "Felicia Hemans": "Fame's troubled hour has cleared, and now replying, / A thousand hearts their music ask of thine" ("Felicia Hemans," ll. 77–78 in ibid., 252).

55. l. 361 and l. 362 in ibid., 99. For the crucial cultural and socio-political role of sympathy in Romantic women poets, see Vincent, *The Romantic Poetess*, 5–9 and 18–25.

56. Maria Jane Jewsbury, "Nobody's Happy Now: Verses by a Proser," *The Athenæum* 167 (January 8, 1831): 25.

57. Vincent, *The Romantic Poetess*, 25.

58. Ellen Peel and Nanora Sweet, "*Corinne* and the Woman as Poet in England: Hemans, Jewsbury, and Barrett Browning," in *The Novel's Seductions: Staël's* Corinne *in Critical Inquiry*, ed. Karyna Szmurlo (Lewisburg, PA: Bucknell University Press, 1999), 213.

59. Jewsbury, *The History of an Enthusiast*, in *The Three Histories* (Boston: Perkins and Marvin, 1831), 23.

60. Ibid., 24–25.

61. For discussion of this conflict within Jewsbury herself, see Norma Clarke, *Ambitious Heights: Writing, Friendship, Love—The Jewsbury Sisters, Felicia Hemans and Jane Welsh Carlyle* (London: Routledge, 1990) and Susan Wolfson, *Borderlines: The Shiftings of Gender in British Romanticism* (Stanford: Stanford University Press, 2006), 92–131.

62. Jewsbury, *The History of an Enthusiast*, 22.

63. Ibid., 78–79.

64. See Eric Gillett, *Maria Jane Jewsbury: Occasional Papers, Selected, with a Memoir* (London: Oxford University Press, 1932), xlvi–xlviii, for a letter that offers an intriguing glimpse into the economic realities of authorship in Regency England and for the autobiographical origins of the character of Julia (xiv).

65. Jewsbury, *The History of an Enthusiast*, 59.

66. Ibid., 69.

67. See, for example, Johann Gottfried Herder, "Philosophei und Schwärmerei, zwo Schwestern," *Sämtliche Werke*, ed. Bernhard Supha (Berlin: Weidmannsche Buchhandlung, 1893), 498. See also J. G. A. Pocock, "Enthusiasm: The Antiself of the Enlightenment," Fenves, "The Scale of Enthusiasm," and La Vopa, "The Philosopher and the Schwärmer: On the Career of a German Epithet

from Luther to Kant," in *Enthusiasm and Enlightenment*, ed. Lawrence Klein and Anthony J. La Vopa, 7–28, 85–115, and 117–52.

68. Jewsbury, *The History of an Enthusiast*, 103.

69. Ibid., 104, 112–13.

70. "Erinna," ll. 215–16 in Landon, *Selected Writings*, 94–95.

71. Staël, *On Germany*, in *Major Writings*, 318.

72. Jewsbury, *The History of an Enthusiast*, 112.

73. I'm using Susan Sontag's definition of camp here from "Notes on Camp," *A Susan Sontag Reader*, ed. Elizabeth Hardwick (New York: Farrar, Strauss, and Giroux, 1982). Sontag defines camp as "the sensibility of failed seriousness, of the theatricalization of experience" (115). She allies it with a "flamboyant femaleness" (109) and a "sweet cynicism" (119) and suggests it can be either conscious or unconscious on the part of the author.

74. Jewsbury, *The History of an Enthusiast*, 126.

75. Voltaire's *Dictionnaire Philosophique* entry "Enthousiasme" is typical. While defining enthusiasm as equivalent to a series of extreme emotional states, Voltaire offers up a vision of the Delphic oracle that represents a particularly crass version of the more subtle misogyny that underlies most eighteenth-century commentary on enthusiastic possession: "Or, was the term enthusiasm first used for the contortions of the Pythia who, after the troubles in her bowels, on the tripod of Delphi, received Apollo's spirit in a place that seems better suited to receive bodies?" [Ou bien donna-t-on d'abord le nom d'*enthousiasme*, de trouble des entrailles, aux contorsions de cette Pythie qui, sur le trépied de Delphes, recevait l'esprit d'Apollon par un endroit qui ne semble fait que pour recevoir des corps?] Voltaire, *Dictionnaire Philosophique*, ed. Béatrice Didier (Paris: Imprimerie Nationale, 1994), 256; translation mine.

76. Jewsbury, *The History of an Enthusiast*, 112.

77. Ibid., 138.

78. Ibid., 45.

79. "Erinna," ll. 302–04 in Landon, *Selected Writings*, 97.

80. Jewsbury, *The History of an Enthusiast*, 145.

81. Ibid., 150.

82. See Clarke's insightful reading of the novella's conclusion in *Ambitious Heights*, 86.

83. See ibid., 155–61.

84. Landon, *Selected Writings*, 184.

85. See Gillett, *Maria Jane Jewsbury*, lxvii.

PHILOSOPHY AND THE ARTS

THE POWER TO CORRUPT: A STAËLIAN
PERSPECTIVE ON THE FINE ARTS

Susan Tenenbaum

G ERMAINE DE STAËL made no claims for the intrinsic value of the arts. For Staël, the arts operated as one of the many social forces that defined a nation's character and shaped the behavior of its citizens and, as such, must be viewed as a matter of moral consequence. Among the determinants of a nation's culture, however, the fine arts stood out as an anomaly. Whereas Staël regarded the literary arts to be open to development and growth, she held that the fine arts had attained their highest expression in classical antiquity. Staël's moral appraisal of the fine arts may thus be seen as closely related to her reception of the classical aesthetic model. This linkage yields a curious paradox: while Staël associates the ideal of classical perfection with the apprehension of "perfect virtue," she nonetheless cautions that the fine arts instill "a sensuous outlook, a deliberate indifference, a passion for the present and neglect of the future." The present chapter takes as its subject the roots of this paradox.

Staël's novel *Corinne, or Italy* depicts the paradox of the fine arts in narrative terms. Serving as Oswald's guide to Rome's statues and paintings in Book VII, Corinne describes the classical statuary displayed in the Vatican Museum as the symbolic embodiment of a spiritual order which extols the dignity of humankind:

> There the most perfect beauty, eternally at rest, seems to delight in itself. Contemplation of those admirable lines and shapes reveals an indefinable divine plan for humanity expressed in the noble face that has been granted to man . . . These faces are sheer poetry, the most sublime expression is set there forever, and the greatest thoughts are clothed in an image worthy of them.[1]

The ennobling qualities of this art—alluded to in her many invocations of Italy's glorious past—could, Corinne insisted, not simply becalm the troubled soul of her lover, but conduce to the moral regeneration of her country. Yet the moral pleasures that attended the perfection of the fine arts were inextricably tied to a sensuality which, finding pleasure in the allure of external beauty, was regarded by Staël as morally suspect. The arts' powers of seduction, their ability "to charm the senses," could lure men away from practical civic concerns and reconcile them to servitude.[2] Oswald gives voice to this fear: "the arts are magnificent here; the imagination shows genius; but what about human dignity, how is that protected? . . . What institutions, what weakness in most Italian governments!"[3] While Corinne continued to defend the arts' emancipatory potential, she did so against the backdrop of a politically quiescent Italian people for whom "all the art of classical antiquity . . . [is] a national preoccupation."[4] Only in the person of Corinne, the *improvisatrice*, did the arts' elevated and sensual qualities seamlessly merge. Corinne was "one of the most beautiful women in Rome."[5] She "seemed at once a priestess of Apollo making her way towards the Temple of the Sun, and a woman perfectly simple in the ordinary relations of life."[6] Captivated by Corinne's charms yet inspired by her genius, Oswald marveled at how "so many contradictory qualities" could be united in one person.[7] The tension inhering in the fine arts, as portrayed in Staël's novel, resolved itself in the unique being of Corinne.

With the example of Corinne by way of introduction, I now turn to *On Literature,* an earlier work that offers a fuller account of Staël's views on the fine arts. In that treatise, the relation between the fine arts and classical antiquity is explained, and Staël's moral ambivalence towards the arts is given more concrete expression. I shall argue that the roots of her ambivalence are to be found in the dual nature of the classical aesthetic as ideal referent and sensuous representation.[8] This double identity, I suggest, opens up an important distinction between Staël's treatment of "political" and "aesthetic" classicism. Whereas she condemned the participatory liberty of the ancients as historically vitiated and oppressive in a modern context, Staël's critique of the arts remains largely a-historical, tied to the tensions inherent in the arts' paradigmatic classical aesthetic. The identification of these two strands of criticism, I shall further argue, reveals Staël's celebrated ancient/modern dichotomy to harbor an unacknowledged complexity.

In *On Literature* the fine arts stand out as the singular exception to Staël's broadly conceived trajectory of historical progress:

> It is possible to set a limit to the progress of the arts, but not to the dis-
> coveries of the intellect . . . the fine arts are not infinitely perfectible, so

the very first creations of the imagination, which gave birth to the fine arts, are far more brilliant than their happiest successors.[9]

Staël's demarcation of a separate historical track for the fine arts—their perfection being contained within a privileged historical moment—was a function of their defining principle (the imitation of nature) and their association with a non-rational faculty of the mind (the imagination). The ancients, by virtue of their position at the "beginnings of civilization," were afforded an unreflective experience of nature that could not be recaptured and that endowed the imagination with heightened powers of receptivity.[10] Embracing an empiricist conception of nature, Staël ascribed the achievement of the ancients to their immediate immersion in the physical world. The perfection of the arts, she held, consisted in the "vivid depiction of external things."[11] The greatness of ancient poetry lay in its capacity "to paint in words everything that strikes the eye."[12] The ancients' closeness to nature accounted for their unparalleled powers of imagination; as the faculty most dependant on the vivacity of sensation, the imagination "is keener as its exercise is fresher."[13]

This understanding did not, however, lead Staël to a disembodied primitivism, but to a Montesquieuian focus on the causes shaping the distinct character of the arts of the North and South. Staël's claims regarding the ancients' closeness to nature merged seamlessly with Montesquieu's theory of the predominance of physical causes in archaic societies.[14] Placing the arts in geographic and climatic perspective, Staël opposed the poetry of Homer to that of Ossian in terms echoing Montesquieu's observation that "in cold countries men have very little sensibility for the pleasures of life; in temperate countries they have more; in warm countries, their sensibility is exquisite."[15] Correspondingly, Staël identified Homer and Ossian as ancient models for two aesthetic cultures: the South, rooted in pleasure; the North, in melancholy and suffering. Staël's typology cast the physical factors of climate and terrain in a central role. The poetry of the South summoned up "the coolness of dense woods and limpid streams . . . the benevolent shade that . . . protects from the burning heat of the sun,"[16] while that of the North evoked "the harshness of the soil and the gloom of the sky."[17] Staël's discussion of the moral causes shaping the arts of classical Greece follows Montesquieu in her emphasis on the importance of religion and custom. Both, she suggested, reinforced the Greeks' sensitivity to their natural surroundings. Paganism "sanctified elegance and beauty of form,"[18] while the "simplicity" of ancient customs allowed for unmediated responses to the sensuous presence of their world.[19]

The historical distance separating modern aesthetic practice from the conditions that nurtured its perfection presented Staël with a dilemma. Were ancient models of perfection available to be reconstituted and sustained by the moderns, or were their forms alien to the modern world and the arts forever locked in a pattern of decline? Staël's writings provide no unambiguous answer here. She can be found to slide from a belief in the aesthetic perfection of a privileged past, to a relativist perspective allowing for multiple aesthetic cultures to be judged by internal norms, as well as to a position which appears to mediate between the two approaches: "The arts have a limit, I believe, beyond which they do not rise, but they can maintain the eminence they have reached."[20] Staël's consistent linkage of the fine arts with "pleasure," however, would appear to locate their exemplary expression in the classical aesthetic of the South. Whereas the "melancholy" model of the North was associated by Staël with progress and the evolution of modern institutions,[21] the classical aesthetic remained the product of a singular historical moment in which ideal and empirical nature occupied the same conceptual space. The ancients' privileged circumstances, their unique configuration of social and moral determinants, afforded them access to an order of nature that rose above the contingencies of time and place and conferred upon their arts an "elegance and beauty of form" that harbored the possibility of uplifting or corrupting the soul. The inherent tension between the elevated style and beautiful form of the classical model provides, I suggest, a basis for the opposing images of the fine arts presented in *On Literature*.

The two contrasting images appear in separate passages in *On Literature*. The first is found in a prefatory section of the work. The passage alludes to a classical ideal of perfection in which the fine arts harmoniously unite reason and moral values, while carrying a rhetorical charge that inspires love of virtue. I shall quote the passage in full:

> Perfect virtue is, in the intellectual realm, perfect beauty. There are connections between the impression that perfect virtue makes upon us and the feeling that is aroused by all that is sublime, whether in the fine arts or in physical nature. The regular proportions of ancient statues, the calm and pure expressions of certain paintings, the harmony of music, the appearance of a beautiful vista in fertile open country carry us away with an enthusiasm not unlike the admiration of the sight of honorable behavior inspires. Oddities, produced by man or nature, may momentarily stun the imagination, but the intellect requires peace based on order.[22]

A strikingly dichotomous image of the fine arts is presented some pages later, where the arts are identified with sensual, shallow pleasures. Staël associated this aspect of the classical ideal with a propensity toward servility, a point she drew upon later in the text to explain the ease with which the Greeks submitted to foreign domination:

> The arts can, by the amusements of each day, divert the mind from any grand and commanding conception; they lead men back to their feelings, and they instill in the mind a sensuous outlook, a deliberate indifference, a passion for the present and neglect of the future, all highly favorable to tyranny. In a curious contrast, the arts, which enable us to enjoy life, make us rather indifferent to death. Only deep emotions, creating a passionate will to reach their objective, bind us firmly to life; but a life devoted to pleasures amuses without persuading; it prepares us for intoxication, sleep and death.[23]

In what follows, I examine Staël's double reading of the Greek ideal as a legacy of the neoclassical understanding that the true function of art is to represent not the "accidental" appearances of objects, but their ideal substantial forms. This framework pivoted on distinctions between the "servile" copying of "common" nature and mimetic activity directed toward the representation of an "ideal" nature: the latter, engaging the higher faculties; the former, more narrowly associated with the senses and the appetites. Winckelmann had bequeathed to Staël's generation a classical model, at once elevated in style and beautiful in form, that embraced both dimensions: the representation of the ideal (*le beau idéal* later evoked by Staël) and, as the product of a privileged historical moment, a representation of physical reality, the living sensuous presence of the Greek world. Out of this unified vision of aesthetic perfection, I suggest, Staël constructed two opposing conceptions of the fine arts: the first, operating within the idealist tradition of French aesthetics, referenced a higher immaterial order; the second, reflecting an idealist antipathy to sensual experience, referenced material reality and associated the arts with purely sensual beauty.

To uncover the roots of this dual portrait I begin with Plato, for whom artistic practice was a form of mimetic activity directed toward the simulation of appearances. The eternal, incorporeal realm of the forms was, for Plato, intractable to the representational field of mimesis. Appearance-making, dependent on the realm of sense perception, held out a false pretense of knowledge and, with its powers of sensual gratification, strengthened the lower appetitive parts of the soul, substituting for the rational pursuit of the good a devotion to the merely pleasing.[24] Aristotle's more generous conception of mimesis laid the foundation for a rehabilitation of aesthetic practice, as did the writings of neo-Platonists like Ficino, whose theory of the "double Venus" allowed for an ascent from the love of physical beauty to love of the immaterial beauty of the divine.[25] A door had opened for art to operate as a mode of apprehending the ideal, representing not the accidental and particular realm of appearances, but a higher universal order that could not be commandeered by the lower appetites. This set of understandings came to inform a distinction between the "mechanical" and the "liberal" arts, and nourished the founding debates of the French Royal Academy.

In the official doctrine of the Royal Academy, the priority of design over color was asserted to secure the status of painting as a liberal art against the rival institution of the guilds. Line was associated with "invention," the power of abstracting the substantial form of things from the material realm of concrete particulars; based on the intellect, it privileged the mind over the hand. By contrast, color was depicted as narrowly sensory in character; it took its bearings from the material world, and its sole object was to "satisfy the eye." The representation of color was a matter of servile copying from actual nature—a mechanical task mastered by the pigment grinders of the guild—whereas line "pertained to intellect alone" and "established the merit of painting" as a liberal art. Those aspects of art that appealed to our sensual nature (color) were to be admitted in a subordinate role. When this proper ordering was preserved, art fulfilled its ultimate purpose, which, for Charles Le Brun, was "to please the senses and the intellect."[26]

The dualities that framed Le Brun's argument—between mind and body, between representation of the ideal and the "servile" copying of the real, between narrowly appetitive and higher forms of pleasure—found echoes in Charles Batteux's efforts the following century to establish within the category of liberal arts a distinctive grouping of "fine arts." In his seminal treatise *Les Beaux-arts réduits à un même principe* (*The Fine Arts Reduced to a Single Principle*, 1747), Batteux identified the fine arts with a core set of practices, attributing to them a single unifying principle: the imitation of beautiful nature [*la belle nature*].[27] Imitation referred not to "servile" copying, but to the translation of a higher, more perfect order into the material world; its vehicle was "genius," that quality of mind which, akin to Le Brun's "invention," perceived the general behind the particular. If the representation of the ideal took on a range of qualities and dispositions that distanced it from the austere vision of Le Brun, the locus of the arts continued to be poised between the real and the ideal, elevated above the ordinary but given sensuous expression in the material world. Reflecting a traditional emphasis of French aesthetic theory, Batteux identified the purpose of the fine arts as pleasure, distinguishing them from the mechanical arts, which, rooted in "common" nature, were directed toward the lower appetitive needs of utility. Pleasure, on this understanding, incorporated yet transcended sensual satisfaction to describe the elevated mode of response that attended representation of ideal beauty: *la belle nature.*

Against this background, the dualities of neoclassical aesthetics may be seen as providing a scaffold for Staël's dual portrait of classical perfection in the arts: The first, *le beau idéal*, attaching to "ideal" nature; the second, *la belle nature*, to the living sensuous beauty of the Greek world. To each image of perfection, Staël assigned a distinct mode of reception: the *beau idéal* was identified with the experience of the *sublime*; while *pleasure*, the elevated mode of response attributed to the fine arts by Batteux, was stripped by Staël of its ideal referent, to denote pure sensual gratification.

The *beau idéal* carried forward the tradition of an ideal aesthetic, and was associated with the model of classical perfection bequeathed by Winckelmann. In its appeal to a perfect order of beauty, *le beau idéal* bore affinities to *la belle nature*, yet its foregrounding of the moral dimension of beauty set it apart from Batteux's concept and heightened its level of signification. The elevated nature of *le beau idéal* may be seen in Winckelmann's description of the Apollo Belvedere in which the statue itself appears to dematerialize and become synonymous with its invisible referent:

> Let thy spirit penetrate into the kingdom of incorporeal beauties, and strive to become a creator of a heavenly nature, in order that thy mind may be filled with beauties that are elevated above nature; for there is nothing mortal here. . . . Neither blood vessels nor sinews heat and stir this body, but a heavenly essence . . . seems to fill the whole contour of the figure.[28]

It is useful to compare Winckelmann's comments with Staël's *beau idéal* passage, which I again excerpt here:

> Perfect virtue is in the intellectual realm, perfect beauty. There are connections between the impression that perfect virtue makes upon us and the feeling that is aroused by all that is sublime . . . the regular proportions of ancient statues, the calm and pure expressions of certain paintings, the harmony of music . . . carry us away with an enthusiasm not unlike the admiration the sight of honorable behavior inspires.

Staël portrays the fine arts as bearers of meaning whose perfection lie in their embodiment of abstract truth. The arts' presence in the material world—statues, paintings, music—dissolve into their formal values—proportion, purity, and harmony—and dissolve again into the intellectual realm in which perfect virtue equals perfect beauty. The nature of this aesthetic encounter is, for Staël, the "sublime," a sudden overwhelming experience that "carries us away with enthusiasm" and affirms our moral nature. Left behind is the refined pleasure of *la belle nature*. The "masculine" force of the Burkean sublime, now sited within the confines of classical regularities, overwhelms the means of representation, allowing no time for sensual enjoyment of the arts, but instantly "carr[ies] us away" to a higher immaterial realm.

As Staël turned to depict the classical perfection of the arts in the context of her historical narrative, however, she lowered her gaze from the immanence of the ideal to the materiality of the real. If antiquity had afforded a privileged moment of synthesis between the ideal and its sensual embodiment, its existence in history brought to the fore its grounding in sensuous nature and the relative beauties of Greek culture. Staël now entered the realm that, for her intellectual forebears, was "common" or "accidental" nature. In this context Staël no longer spoke of classical perfection offering an experience of the sublime, but instead offering one of sensuous pleasure. The *beau idéal* had, in effect, been transformed by Staël into the Burkean beautiful: the easy, gratifying object of desire that delighted our senses and made us at home in the world. For Staël, the Greeks' unmediated closeness to a benign nature sharpened their imagination, that faculty of mind most closely related to the senses. The perfection of the arts consisted in the "vivid description of external things" and was, for the Greeks, a matter of "merely" copying the living, sensuous, readily appropriated beauty that surrounded them. Staël's previously cited description of the Homeric model of poetry is particularly telling in this regard: "The poets of the South continually mingle the representation of coolness, dense woods and limpid streams with all their impressions of life. They cannot even describe the pleasures of the heart without combining them with the idea of the benevolent shade that protects them from the burning heat of the sun." The image of serene beauty evoked by a beneficent nature did not, however, serve as conduit to an elevated ideal but as a vehicle of seduction that bound the Greeks to the gratification of the senses and disengaged them from the moral exertions required to preserve their freedom.

Whereas Winckelmann had claimed a connection between the Greek ideal of freedom and the classical beauty of their art, Staël suggested a less ennobling parallel. Pleasure, the hallmark of Greek art and culture, made love of liberty "a habit, a way of life and not a controlling passion."[29] Bound to their pleasures, "the Athenians were deprived of those very pleasures that they preferred to the defense of their liberty."[30] This image of the Greeks contradicts and complicates the image found in Staël and Constant's more famous ancient/modern political dichotomy which portrayed the Greeks, à la Winckelmann, as absorbed by their roles as citizens. The ancients' rudimental private life, on Staël's political model, accounted for their eager "sacrifice of personal interests to the common good" and to their understanding of liberty as participation "in the exercise of political power."[31] The pleasures of the private sphere, by contrast, attached to the life of the moderns and constituted the conceptual space of modern liberty, which Staël defined as "everything that protects the citizen's independence of the government."[32] In *On Literature*, however, the delights of the private sphere were associated with the ancients; they issued not from the material and social pleasures enjoyed by the moderns, but from their senses being seduced and captivated by the "accidental" beauties of their perfect world.

As distilled in the classical aesthetic, the power of the fine arts pulled in two directions: the first, depicted by Staël as the arts' corrupting force, isolates man from society through their ability to "divert the mind" and "intoxicate the imagination"; the second, portrayed by Staël as the arts' beneficent force, turned man towards society, inspiring its betterment by modeling feelings of admiration for good order and virtuous conduct. This latter conception was found in *Corinne*, who, in her person, embodied the emancipatory potential of the fine arts and in the previously cited passage from *On Literature*. The themes encountered in this passage are enlarged upon in the Preface to Staël's earlier novel *Delphine*, where she associates "ideal beauty" ("harmony with accepted proportions") with the imagination "tightly bound to reason" and suggests that it inspires "the need to rise above the limits of reality but allows no world contrary to that reality."[33] Thus conceived, such aestheticism is outwardly directed, imbuing the beholder with the attitudes and feelings to morally engage with social life and to applaud social practices that are themselves proportionate and regular. The essential moderation of this reformist vision is noteworthy. It is underscored by the assertion in *Delphine* that ideal beauty "allows no word contrary" to reality. If aesthetic beauty represented, for Staël, a supreme manifestation of humanity and referenced a higher immaterial order, it was nonetheless anchored in the world and defined by boundaries and limitations. This aesthetic orientation to social life, I would suggest, found parallels in Staël's more explicitly political efforts to define a centrist path in a revolutionary era. Despite its more immediate ties to the comforts of material well-being, Staël's conception of public opinion reflected this aesthetic disposition in its alliance with reason, its love of order and—when not corrupted—its acclaim of the virtuous statesman. The capacity to hold moderate opinions in immoderate times shared with the elevated aesthetic response "courage of soul and breath of mind" together with the ability to "distinguish what is momentary from what is enduring."[34] Fanaticism and extremism, by their very nature betraying the regularities implicit in good order and ideal beauty, stood condemned on both political and aesthetic grounds. Whereas the Jacobins had seized the classical ideal to deny the realities of historical change, Staël would re-appropriate it to impart lessons in moderation and to inspire its pursuit.

Staël's opposing portrait of the fine arts as a corrupting force depicts the appreciation of beauty as an inward turning response: a detachment from the world which absorbs the beholder to the exclusion of all else. Indeed, much of Staël's discomfort with modern imitators of the ancients inhered in the detachment of its formal achievements from the lived social world. The perfection of the arts defined itself against Staël's historical trajectory. Yet the arts' threat of absorption was one to which the Greeks themselves had succumbed. The arts' sensual hold, their essential separateness from other social practices, their appetitive attitude towards nature had sapped the Greeks of the will to maintain their freedom. For Staël, the true danger of the arts lay outside of history, and attached instead to the human craving for sensual pleasure.

This quality led Staël to distrust the fine arts as handmaidens of tyranny by encouraging the desertion of public affairs for the sating of private appetites. Such a perspective would appear to have much in common with the position of Rousseau, for whom the arts "spread garlands of flowers over the iron chains with which men are burdened."[35] Yet, unlike Staël, Rousseau defined the arts against nature as a product of civilized refinement. The classical perfection of the Greeks did not, on Rousseau's account, arise from their closeness to nature, but from the artifice of developed society, "the vices which accompany the fine arts entered Athens with them . . . Athens became the abode of civility and good taste."[36] For Rousseau, the fine arts impoverished the personality by valuing formal perfection over moral purpose, by dividing man against his fellows and against himself. Not only did the fine arts nourish social division by making culture a "competitive asset," but, as they were judged by form and style alone, they repressed all that was natural to man.[37] By contrast, Staël regarded art's corrupting power as lying within its very humanity—its appeal to our sensuous nature, its seductive force arousing our most elemental desires. For Staël, art was defined not against nature, but as an imitation of it. Her more generous reading of the neoclassical tradition took its bearings from the duality between the real and the ideal, a duality that was, in fact, a unity. Classical beauty, the perfection of the fine arts, represented a "Staëlian" double Venus, whose beauty can either elevate our soul or so captivate our senses that we cannot free our eyes from the subject of our desire.

Notes

1. All English quotations will be taken from Germaine de Staël, *Corinne, or Italy*, ed. and trans. Avriel Goldberger (New Brunswick, NJ: Rutgers University Press, 1991), 142.

2. Ibid., 43.

3. Ibid., 59.

4. Ibid., 19.

5. Ibid.

6. Ibid., 21.

7. Ibid., 38.

8. On this point, I am indebted to Alex Potts, *Flesh and the Ideal: Winckelmann and the Origins of Art History* (New Haven, CT: Yale University Press, 1994).

9. All English quotations from *Literature Considered in Its Relation to Social Institutions* will be taken from Germaine de Staël, *Politics, Literature and National Character*, ed. and trans. Morroe Berger (New York: Doubleday, 1964), 154.

10. Ibid., 156.

11. Ibid., 154.

12. Ibid.

13. Ibid., 155.

14. On this point, see Raymond Aron, *Main Currents in Sociological Thought* (Garden City, NY: Anchor Books, 1968), 1:45.

15. Melvin Richter, *The Political Theory of Montesquieu* (Cambridge: Cambridge University Press, 1977), 259.

16. Staël, *Literature*, 193.

17. Ibid., 194.

18. Ibid., 157.

19. Ibid., 156.

20. Ibid. 177.

21. On Staël's treatment of melancholy, see Eric Gidal, "Civic Melancholy: English Gloom and French Enlightenment," *Eighteenth Century Studies* 37, no. 1 (2003): 23–45.

22. Staël, *Literature*, 142.

23. Ibid., 149–50.

24. An excellent work on this topic is Christopher Janaway's *Images of Excellence: Plato's Critique of the Arts* (Oxford: Oxford University Press, 1995).

25. See Anthony Levi, *French Moralists* (Oxford: Clarendon Press, 1964), 46–49.

26. Charles Le Brun, "Thoughts on M. Blanchard's Discourse on the Merits of Colour," in *Art in Theory 1648–1815*, eds. Charles Harrison, Paul Wood, and Jason Gaiger (Oxford: Blackwell Publishers, 2000), 182–85.

27. Charles Batteux, *Les Beaux-arts réduits à un même principe* (Geneva: Slatkine Reprints, 1969). On Batteux's role in the development of the conceptualization of the fine arts, see Larry Shiner, *The Invention of Art: A Cultural History* (Chicago: University of Chicago Press, 2001).

28. Quoted in Elizabeth Prettejohn, *Beauty and Art* (Oxford: Oxford University Press, 2005), 28–29.

29. Staël, *Madame de Staël on Politics*, 162.

30. Ibid., 165.

31. Ibid., 129. All English quotations from *Des circonstances actuelles qui peuvent terminer la Révolution* will be taken from Staël, *Madame de Staël on Politics*.

32. Staël, *Madame de Staël on Politics*, 129.

33. Germaine de Staël, *Delphine*, ed. and trans. Avriel H. Goldberger (DeKalb: Northern Illinois University Press, 1995), 7–87. All English quotations from *Delphine* are from this edition.

34. Staël, "How Can We Determine What Is the Opinion of the Majority of the Nation?" in *Madame de Staël on Politics*, 131–32.

35. Jean-Jacques Rousseau, *The First and Second Discourses*, ed. and trans. Roger D. Masters and Judith R. Masters (New York: St. Martin's Press, 1964), 36.

36. Rousseau, *Discourses*, 43.

37. Marshall Berman, *The Politics of Authenticity: Radical Individualism and the Emergence of Modern Society* (New York: Atheneum, 1972), 139.

11

THE MANY FACES OF GERMAINE DE STAËL

Mary D. Sheriff

For Madelyn Gutwirth with admiration and affection

LYON, 2009. IT WAS THERE, at the Musée des Beaux Arts, that four portraits of Germaine de Staël came together to celebrate the life of her intimate friend Juliette Récamier.[1] Few knew better than Madame Récamier the faces of Germaine de Staël: daughter of the finance minister Jacques Necker (figure 11.1); mother of Albertine, duchesse de Broglie (figure 11.2); beloved friend taken before her time (figure 11.3); and powerful genius, creator of Corinne (figure 11.4).

Although an exhibition dedicated to "Juliette Récamier, Muse et mécène" provided the occasion for this gathering, when seen together, the four portraits exceed their assigned task of representing the *amitié* between Staël and Récamier. They invite us to interrogate Staël's relation to her images, to ask what choices were made by whom and to what end. How do the portraits ask us to remember Germaine de Staël? These questions become especially pointed in relation to one of those works: Elisabeth Vigée-Lebrun's monumental image of Madame de Staël as Corinne, an allegorical portrait that challenged the expectations not only of Staël's circle, but of Staël herself.

Of Family, Fashion, and Femininity

Of the four portraits exhibited in Lyon, none showed Staël through the established conventions for depicting "the author." Nowhere was she seen seated at her desk before a manuscript, pen in hand; nowhere did she appear holding one of her

Figure 11.1.   Firmin Massot, portrait of Germaine as Necker's daughter. Courtesy of the Château de Coppet, Switzerland.

Figure 11.2.   Attributed to Marguerite Gérard, Elisabeth Vigée-Lebrun, and Firmin Massot, portrait of Staël as Albertine's mother. Courtesy of the Château de Coppet, Switzerland.

Figure 11.3.   Marie Godefroid, replica of François Gérard's portrait of Staël, Châteaux de Versailles et de Trianon, France. Réunion des Musées Nationaux / Art Resource, NY.

Figure 11.4.   Elisabeth Vigée-Lebrun, *Portrait of Madame de Staël as Corinne*, 1807, Musée d'Art et d'Histoire, Geneva, Switzerland. Source: bpk, Berlin / Art Resource, NY.

many publications. While other women writers, such as Françoise Graffigny and Olympe de Gouges, were portrayed through these conventions, Staël was not.[2] Rather than associating Staël with her literary achievements, two of the paintings in Lyon represented the author in her familial relations. In their own way, these works are outside pictorial norms for representing writers. We can hardly imagine a portrait of Jean-Jacques Rousseau and his family; François-René de

Chateaubriand is never shown in any sort of sentimental relation, nor are Isabelle de Charrière and Françoise Graffigny. Yet an undated portrait of Staël attributed to Firmin Massot (figure 11.1) memorializes Staël's relation with her beloved father, Jacques Necker. Standing before an open loggia that gives onto a landscape view, Staël poses near a plinth that supports a portrait bust of her father. Although it does not represent an actual sculpture, the bust is a remake of Joseph Siffred Duplessis's painted portrait (1793), a version of which hung in the family chateau at Coppet. In picturing Duplessis's portrait as a sculpted bust, the artist lent the father figure more physicality, more presence, so to speak. And if Staël is represented as a real body and Necker as a sculpted one, each presented the illusion of three-dimensionality, which rendered them easier to associate one with the other. Massot adjusted the expression and features of the original painted portrait so that Necker appears to gaze at his daughter, thus linking the two through imagined sight lines. Staël's pose furthers the tie as she drapes her right arm over the plinth so as to touch the base of the sculpture. And if Massot took advantage of sculpture's physicality to help forge the association, he also availed himself of painting's coloristic effects to achieve the same end. A red curtain that seems to come from somewhere behind the bust flows over the plinth in such a way that it appears to merge with the sculpted drapery cast over Necker's shoulder. Staël too is draped in red, in a fashionable cashmere shawl.

Rather than enlivening Staël's image by suggesting movement through elaborate knots and curves, the shawl falls downward in heavy folds, and this fall continues the tug of her hand gestures. The sitter's left arm hangs limply at her side, and the fingers of her right hand droop over the pedestal's edge. Between the index and middle finger of her right hand, we see a sprig of foliage like those that Staël was known to move to and fro as she conversed or entered a room. Here she does not even give the sprig a little shake, and it hangs from her fingers as if sapped of life. With her eyes cast to the side, slightly downturned, and seemingly unfocused, Staël has the look of sweet, melancholic reverie. This mood is underscored by the landscape with its darkening clouds, and by the shadows that lightly veil the portrait bust. Despite the fluttering drapery, which is a throwback to an earlier portrait tradition, the image conforms to the latest pictorial fashion in its moody, outdoor setting. The relation between human sentiment and the natural landscape was, moreover, a key element in Staël's writings.

Rendered in the shadows, the father as portrait bust hovers behind Staël as a guardian angel might, his presence felt but not necessarily seen by the daughter who remembers him. That reminiscence in her activity is suggested not only by her expression, but also by the lassitude of her limbs and relatively immobile pose. What alone brings movement and animation to the figure is her curling hair, which here is not held in check by a turban, as it will be in so many other portraits. The agitated curls suggest that the action of the scene is all in her head, in her mental activity. I imagine what made this portrait meaningful for Staël was its representation of the sentimental and intellectual bond between father and daughter. But today the work appears as both an image of sentiment and one of the connections—dynastic and emotional—between father and daughter. Germaine de Staël was Jacques Necker's literal heir as well as heir to his political life, which brings me back to portrait conventions. Although writers were not shown in relation to family, other sitters were. This group was mainly comprised of those who wished to picture and preserve dynastic ties: royals and rulers, aristocrats and the upper social ranks. Massot's portrait differs from those traditions, however, in associating father to daughter instead of to son. But in taking the place of a male heir, this daughter is also a fashionable woman.

In Massot's portrayal, Staël wears the latest empire dress, and it is noteworthy here that she wears similar garb in all of her portraits—except for those that portray her as Corinne. The cashmere shawl introduced in the 1780s reached its height of popularity during the empire when modish women wore low-cut sleeveless dresses made out of the finest and thinnest cotton called *mousseline*. Staël's red wrap might have been a favorite garment—a signature piece, for some version of it appears in nearly all her portrayals. Here she wears it over a low-cut square-necked empire gown embroidered in gold. Such gowns were displayed in fashion books such as the *Journal des Dames*, and Staël's characteristic dress accords with images of the latest Parisian designs. Even her short, curly, black hair seems done up in the modish *coiffure à la titus*. In this costume she joins the icons of fashion who appeared in the Lyon exhibition, including Désirée Clary, Madame Tallien, Caroline Murat, and, of course, Madame Récamier.[3] While both men and women desired to be à la mode, a concern with fashion had long been gendered as a "feminine" trait related to women's supposed taste for luxury. Shown in fashionable dress, Staël appears to perform as a feminine woman. And for a woman who demonstrated qualities gendered as masculine, such as reason, intellect, and involvement in political life, appearing as a feminine woman in both her actual and represented dress may have served purposes other than deflecting attention from her assumption of roles traditionally reserved for men. Fashionability might display a proper (if problematic) femininity, but the particular dress she chose also identified her with a bevy of beauties whose lives, interests, and physical endowments may have been quite different from her own. In addition, her costume marks her as cosmopolitan, as a "Parisian," even during those times that she lived in provincial Coppet.

Similar concerns for family and fashion emerge in a second portrait of Staël shown in Lyon, and attributed alternately to Marguerite Gérard, Elisabeth Vigée-Lebrun, and Firmin Massot (figure 11.2). In this work we see Staël with her daughter Albertine, born in 1797. No matter who made the work, it was a private commission never exhibited in public, a painting likely made for a familial space.[4] Like the portrait of Staël with the bust of her father, this image depicts the sitters in an outdoor setting, but one that seems even more natural for there is no plinth, sculpture, loggia, or fluttering drapery in sight. Staël and Albertine are posed in front of a massive tree that provides a darkened ground against which to play the white and light blue of their costumes. This background might seem somber, were it not for the patches of sky visible through the foliage that echo the blue of Albertine's dress, and the dappled sunlight on the tree trunk that illuminates both sitters. Mother and daughter appear to be caught in an intimate moment as they enjoy the pleasure of a shady nook on a sunny day. Their placement within nature is secured with details, such as the tufts of grass growing up against the bottoms of their skirts, and the sprig of foliage Staël holds. This sprig has a freshly picked look, and as well as being emblematic of Staël, it suggests that mother and daughter had been botanizing together. In this constructed setting, Staël appears to sit on some natural formation—perhaps a hillock?—although it is difficult to tell which; her support is hidden on one side by the figure of Albertine and on the other by her red shawl. Within this setting no furnishings or artisanal products interfere with the natural background, nothing save the fashionable empire dresses mother and daughter wear. Fashion, of course, was anything but natural; the sitters, moreover, are posed to look directly out at the viewer, belying the notion that we have caught them in a "natural" state.

To depict women and children in a natural setting might be seen to reflect on the naturalness of motherhood or to suggest that motherhood was woman's natural state. Such ideals had been updated and made attractive in the writings of Rousseau. Most often, however, those whom artists represented in this way were aristocratic mothers who lived their lives in society—or in the case of women like Staël, in the public sphere—free from the tasks childrearing required of less-privileged folk. To have oneself portrayed in a way that invoked the ideals of a naturalized motherhood did not necessarily denote agreement with those ideals. It was certainly, however, to follow fashion. To be depicted in this way was to be shown in a type of romantic portraiture in vogue at the time. Such representations, such images of natural maternal tenderness were always fabrications of art, whether or not mother and child felt any real affection for one another. At the same time, when affection was, in fact, genuinely felt, such images would commemorate and idealize a moment of mutual pleasure in one another's company. The sense of a close mother-daughter relation is well constructed in the portrait through gesture, proximity, costume, and resemblance. Albertine is shown leaning up against her mother so that the two form a single unit: Staël embraces her daughter, and Albertine touches her mother's arm with her right hand while resting her left arm against her mother's body. Although not garbed in identical robes, there is clearly an affinity in their costume: their dresses of a lightweight fabric share a wide neckline with capped sleeves, and we can see that each wears the same style of slipper, as their pointed toes extend from beneath their skirts. Although the young girl has blond locks, her hair, like that of her mother's, is partially covered by a scarf that matches her dress, and in each case the curls escape to frame an oval face. Indeed, the features of mother and daughter—the cupid's bow mouth and the penetrating dark eyes—resemble one another. I wonder, however, if we would even recognize Staël in this portrait were it not for recurrent aspects of her images: the white empire gown, the red cashmere shawl, the headdress wrapped as a turban, the large black eyes, curly black hair, and the twig of linden.

What neither the image of Staël with Albertine nor that of the writer with her father suggests is the turmoil of Staël's personal life. In each the emotional range is limited; in one we sense a peaceful tenderness, in the other a wistful reverie. Neither suggests the range of passions that her life might have aroused. Missing are emotional highs and lows, the fidelity and the faithlessness that might be said to characterize Staël's amorous relations. All this emotional life is masked in these images of familial piety and affection directed to her father and daughter. Over the last few decades, many theorists (Barthes, Derrida) have associated representations, including portraits, with absence and death. Yet from the Renaissance through the nineteenth century, portrait theory put the emphasis on presence, or at least seeming presence: portraits were touted as what could make the absent loved one still present to sensation, what could keep the dead loved one alive, at least in memory. The fictional origin of portraiture lay in sentiment, in the story of Dibutadis who invented portraiture by tracing on the wall the silhouette of her lover about to leave for a distant shore. In a sense it was emotion itself that the portrait kept alive, and many images in the eighteenth and nineteenth century show the emotional impact of portraits, whether they be in the form of miniatures, portrait busts, or even grave markers. They are clutched, kissed and regarded with loving gaze.[5] Within the portrait, moreover, it was the representation of emotion on the part of the sitter that created a sense of liveliness—of livingness—and enabled the viewer to engage, albeit vicariously, with that emotion. It is the total absence of expression that I believe accounts for what I see as the failure of the third, and perhaps most famous portrayal of Staël, the one represented in Lyon through a later copy.

A Killer Portrait?

The third portrait shown in Lyon copied a posthumous portrait of Staël that Albertine had commissioned from François Gérard in 1817. It was Juliette Récamier who ordered a replica of the work from Gérard's student Marie Godefroid (figure 11.3). The replica appeared in Lyon because of its connection with Récamier, who displayed it in her apartment at the Abbaye-aux-Bois.[6] At the time of the original commission, Albertine sent Gérard the miniature portrait of her mother that Pierre Louis Bouvier executed (figure 11.5). A bust-length portrait, it shows Staël as a mature woman, neither old nor young, wearing a low-cut white empire dress embroidered with a gold pattern. She wears a matching turban with three feathery plumes that lighten the visual weight of the turban and curl toward her face to bring our attention there. The dark background allows the white of her turban and dress to shine, and the contrasting red cashmere shawl draped over her left shoulder punctuates and enlivens the contrast of light and dark. In this engaging work, the sitter looks out at us with a glance that is just enough sideways to add a sense of liveliness and mobility to her features. Her mouth is slightly turned up with the hint of a smile, and the face is idealized in the sense that the features have been regularized and softened through delicate shading.

Gérard's painting (figure 11.6), as a whole, bears little resemblance to the miniature; changes in purpose, format, size, and medium account for some of the differences, but not all of them. Albertine presumably lent Bouvier's miniature because she found it a good likeness of her mother—or at least a likeness she wanted reproduced. But a miniature is among the most private, and often most sentimental, of portraits. It was traditionally given as a token of love or friendship, often worn or carried rather than displayed, and sometimes kept in a special case in a boudoir or bedroom. To transform the miniature into a large-scale portrait was no easy matter. It is no wonder, then, that Gérard's portrait lacks the intimacy, delicacy, lightness and grace of Bouvier's work. While it is true that Gérard also

Figure 11.5.   Pierre Louis Bouvier, miniature portrait of Staël, 1816. Courtesy of the Château de Coppet, Switzerland.

shows Staël as a mature woman, he has curiously exaggerated the length of the face in contrast to the miniature. Not only is the face elongated, but also the turban sits awkwardly and heavily on the sitter's head with no plumes to lighten the effect. The expression, too, is altered: Gérard's Staël looks away from the sitter, turning her head to the left and slightly raising her eyes. The features are less delicately drawn, and they seem fixed and immobile.

Although both Gérard's portrait and Godefroid's copy are unlike Bouvier's miniature, they are nearly identical to one another. The major difference between

Figure 11.6.   François Gérard, posthumous portrait of Staël, 1817, Château de Coppet, Switzerland. Source: Erich Lessing / Art Resource, NY.

the works comes in the color tonalities. Gérard changed the habitual color of Staël's dress from white to red, and of her shawl from red to black. These changes provide a dramatic coloristic contrast and, indeed, the entire image is rendered in black and red, relieved here and there by touches of white and green. But whether the black was chosen for its associations with death remains an open question. The overall tonality could just as easily have been selected to harmonize with the other family portraits at Coppet, such as the portrait of her father, Jacques Necker, by Duplessis, which shows him in a dark suit, seated on a red chair in front of a green background, or that which Gérard painted of her son, Auguste de Staël, standing in front of Coppet in a black coat dramatically lined in red. I imagine that in commissioning a copy of the portrait Récamier preferred a return to the familiar Staël, although it is possible that the changes Godefroid made were meant to harmonize with her décor. It is notable, however, that in Godefroid's copy Staël is dressed as she was in other portrayals, wearing a white empire dress with a red cashmere shawl. Godefroid has also softened the flesh tones and hair color, made the face less ruddy, and lightened up the background and setting. Aside from these differences, both Gérard's image and Godefroid's copy show Staël in three-quarter-length pose in an ambiguous space. If we concentrate on the lower part of the canvas, Staël seems to stand at a plinth situated within an interior setting with no perceptible spatial logic. If we concentrate on the larger, upper portion of the canvas against which her head is silhouetted, Staël appears to be pictured against a flat, virtually unrelieved black background. No real architectural interior could show this impossible combination, and this no-where place might have been thought appropriate for a work made after the sitter's death.

Within this setting, Staël's right arm rests on the plinth while her left stretches across her body to support the weight of an elaborately draped shawl. In her left hand she grasps between thumb and forefinger a sprig of linden leaf. Here, however, it is not depicted as something that Staël happens to be holding: it becomes a prominently displayed iconographic element, one that seems to enter into the picture only so it can be shown to the viewer. The rigid sprig, moreover, hardly appears as if it could flutter in her hands, even if those hands could move. The facial expression is equally immobile: the eyes are slightly raised and glance off to the left in an open-eyed stare and the lips are slightly parted, although it does not appear that she is about to speak. Even the famous black curls seem glued into place. The whole bespeaks a sort of stasis, which we might find appropriate for a posthumous portrait if we had never seen how Antoine Gros handled the genre in his poetic posthumous portrait of Christine Boyer, which her husband commissioned, or how Adelaide Labille-Guiard gave life to Louise Elisabeth of France in her stunning portrayal in the collection at Versailles. Gérard's portrait—like that of Labille-Guiard—was likely meant to be more than a private commemorative piece: at least, its iconic nature suggests as much, and it was circulated as an engraving immediately after its completion. But to my eye Gérard has made a most unflattering image, one that both represents a deceased woman and simultaneously kills her again. Certainly the features are idealized—the long nose is straight, the eyebrows perfectly arched, the complexion clear of all faults. But the portrait hardens her features and freezes them into a mask, with cheeks obviously rouged and lips overly reddened. Yet both Albertine and Récamier appear to have been satisfied, each with her commissioned work, and Récamier kept the replica on display in her private quarters where it could function both as an icon of her intimate friend and a counterpoint to Gérard's image of *Corinne at Cape Miseno*, a work whose history is entwined with that of the fourth portrait of Staël shown in Lyon: Elisabeth Vigée-Lebrun's portrayal of Madame de Staël as Corinne, the eponymous heroine of Staël's 1807, *Corinne, or Italy* (figure 11.4).

Corinne Comes to Life[7]

Although words were the stock in trade of both Germaine de Staël and the improvisational poet Corinne, Vigée-Lebrun's portrait impresses by its visual impact, by the illusion of physicality. The sitter is presented as a monumental figure with sculptural limbs and expressive features. The artist makes her statement on an epic scale in this oversized portrait, which strives for grand—even sublime—effects.[8] Seated amidst towering cliffs and rolling hills, Staël-Corinne is dressed *à l'antique* in a white tunic trimmed in gold at the neck, which is partially covered with a large red shawl that is draped over her left shoulder and circles around her body. Although her garb recalls empire costume, the dress has been returned to its source in the tunic, and the shawl is draped not in the style of fashionable ladies, but in the way Greek poets such as Homer threw cloth around their nude bodies—or, at least, in the way that French artists portrayed such cultural icons. Balancing a lyre on her left thigh, Staël-Corinne has paused for a moment to seek inspiration, and Vigée-Lebrun has arranged her in the conventional pose to suggest that state: head turned away from the body and slightly raised, eyes rolled upwards. Her black, curly hair appears to be blown by the winds of genius, further dramatizing the effects of poetic enthusiasm. With her left hand Staël-Corinne reaches toward her lyre to pluck it again, and together with her parted lips, the gesture suggests that inspiration has come, and she is about to continue her poetic declamation.

It is often assumed that the learned Madame de Staël wanted to have herself painted as Corinne, and it is commonly believed that, in general, sitters dictated the terms of the portrait commission. The artist's claim in her *Souvenirs* that it was she who conceived the idea after reading the novel is easily discounted as a bit of self-aggrandizement. Yet in this case, Vigée-Lebrun, whose *Souvenirs* so often reworked incidents to her advantage, may indeed be the source of the conceit. Reading Staël's letter to Henri Meister of August 7, 1807, might clarify the issue: "Why could you not come, with Madame Meister, to Coppet. I would like it very much if Madame Vigée-Lebrun came to Coppet. I do not know if I would dare have myself painted as Corinne by her, but Madame Récamier would be a charming model. In any case, the company of Madame Vigée-Lebrun is as pleasant as her talent and we would be enchanted to see her."[9] In commenting that she would not "dare" to have herself painted as Corinne and in her proposing Récamier as a model, Staël's letter suggests that she has not herself proposed an allegorical portrait. That Vigée-Lebrun would be welcome at Coppet for her company as well as her talent perhaps also suggests it was the painter who made the suggestion to Staël. It is, of course, possible that Madame de Staël is totally disingenuous about not daring to have herself painted "en Corinne," but adding weight to the artist's claim was her history of commandeering models that were of use to her. Seeing the work also reminds us that Vigée-Lebrun regenerated the allegorical portrait, and continued to work in that genre even after she developed portrait manners in both the neo-classical mode (which opted for a more direct portrayal with fewer artistic flourishes) and the newer romantic one that placed sitters in natural surroundings. Although throughout the eighteenth century men and women both sat in allegorical disguise, the subgenre had long been connected with circles of famous women. It was first popularized by the *précieuses* in the late sixteenth century, and women continued to show themselves in allegorical disguise long after male sitters had forsaken the genre around the middle of the eighteenth century. Allegorical portraits engaged a play of resemblance and difference in which the sitter was and was not merged with the fictive identity. Here the similarity of Staël to Corinne is primarily based on shared talent. Madelyn Gutwirth, who has written so insightfully on Staël, views Corinne's talent as a projection of the author's famed skill at conversation.[10] Vigée-Lebrun perceived a more literal resemblance, as her description of the author at Coppet suggests: "We saw her then walking into her salon, holding in her hand a small branch of green; when she spoke, she agitated this branch, and her words had a warmth that belonged only to her alone; it was impossible to interrupt her; in this moment she seemed to me an *improvisatrice*."[11]

But what of Staël's suggestion that Récamier would make a more charming model for Corinne? Staël claimed that she had based aspects of Corinne—such as her elegant dancing—on qualities of Récamier, and Corinne was gifted with exceptional beauty, as was "*la belle des belles*." In the context of an exhibit that insistently displayed the renowned allure of Juliette Récamier—representing it in paintings and sculptures, recalling it in her clothing and furnishings, mirroring it in a bevy of other lovelies—Staël's portraits, as a group, could not help but raise the specter of "beauty" and her reputed lack thereof. During Staël's lifetime, her detractors found her plain at best, manlike at worst. To her enemies she was the monstrous modern hermaphrodite: an unattractive woman who usurped the intellectual privilege of man. Napoleon, for example, remarked that Staël was not even a woman in her genitals.[12] Her supporters, in contrast, searched for attributes, such as her expressive physiognomy, to compensate for her lack of beauty.[13] In her *Souvenirs*, Vigée-Lebrun summarized many similar descriptions when she wrote: "Madame de Staël was not pretty, but the animation of her face could take the place of beauty."[14] If Staël was as concerned with her own physical appearance as contemporary observers claimed her to be, then perhaps the fashionability in her portraits also functioned to supplement her physical body with the beauty of its assumed envelope.[15] Moreover, the repeated appearance of a pictured Staël in the same sort of fashionable dress and turban creates the sense that these clothes are not a cover for but an extension of her body.

No portrait of Staël raises the question of beauty as pointedly as that of Vigée-Lebrun, which neither idealizes the sitter, nor shows her fashionable dress. And no portrait of Staël has left as much commentary. On September 18, 1807, Staël wrote to Henri Meister: "Madame LeBrun has made a portrait of me that every one finds very remarkable. She has brought it to Paris. It captures me as a sibyl or as Corinne, if you like that better."[16] But the evidence that she approved of it is primarily contained in letters to Vigée-Lebrun or to the artist's daughter, Madame Nigris. For example, on July 14, 1809, the novelist wrote to the painter: "I finally received your magnificent painting, Madame, and without thinking about the fact that it is my portrait, I admired your work. All your talent is there and I very much wish that mine could be encouraged by your example. But I fear that my talent could not be greater than the talent one can read in the eyes you have given me."[17] Yet Vigée-Lebrun's portrait of Staël as Corinne has never been well loved, and it, too, has been criticized for its lack of beauty. For some observers, its expressive portrayal of Staël did not, like the expressiveness of Staël herself, substitute for beauty. Quite the contrary: the portrait drew criticism precisely because of its expressiveness, which some found wanting in beauty and grace.

The baron de Voght wrote to Juliette Récamier from Coppet on November 12, 1810: "I went with Corinne to Massot's studio. To relieve the boredom of the

Figure 11.7.   Firmin Massot, replica of Elisabeth Vigée-Lebrun's *Portrait of Madame de Staël as Corinne*, 1808/1809, Chateau de Coppet, Switzerland. Source: Erich Lessing / Art Resource, NY.

sitting we had arranged some nice music; a miss Romilly plucked the harp quite pleasantly, the studio was the temple of the muses. The portrait will be resembling without that exaggeration of inspiration which, among other things, mars the portrait by Madame Le Brun."[18] The image that she sits for, one supposes, is Massot's remake of Vigée-Lebrun's portrait, which is now at Coppet (figure 11.7).

The expression, which the baron singled out as the most problematic aspect of Vigée-Lebrun's image, is clearly changed in Massot's reimagined portrait. Where the original portrait insists that we see Staël-Corinne in an inspired state, the copy has toned down the expression and made it seem so tentative that the figure does not appear to be deeply moved. But this is not the only change that Massot has made. Staël-Corinne still wears the same shawl draped *à l'antique*, but now it is worn over a fashionable empire gown. This change may refer more directly to Staël, but at the same time the face is made more to resemble Staël's description of Corinne: it is idealized and prettified so that the appearance of traditional beauty is greatly enhanced. And Staël-Corinne here looks younger than she does in Vigée-Lebrun's image: the flesh tones are lighter, the complexion less ruddy; the skin is smoother, the hair neater, the features more generalized. The lips are only slightly parted, and the eyes notably less emphatic. Gone are the powerful, muscular arms, so conspicuous in Vigée-Lebrun's portrait, the shoulders now hidden by small capped sleeves. Perhaps just as significant is that the size of the painting itself has been reduced, which greatly changes its overall impact. In other words, Massot has erased the elements that made Vigée-Lebrun's Staël-Corinne a sublime figure. Several other aspects of Vigée-Lebrun's portrayal have been altered in the same vein, presumably to ease the abrupt transitions in her painting. For example, Massot has added a triangular bush that eases the transition between the figure and the cliff soaring beside her. Other elements are missing or diminished: gone are the flowers that mark the foreground of Vigée-Lebrun's painting and the hillock that adds a bit of visual distance between the figure and the viewer. Diminished is the temple of the Sibyl. These changes were presumably introduced to improve the gracefulness of the setting, yet they eliminate elements critical to a complex reading of Vigée-Lebrun's challenging painting.

Two Women of Genius

Despite what some in Staël's circle saw as the weakness of Vigée-Lebrun's portrayal, the work had its supporters. After seeing the work in Paris, the prolific *littératrice* Madame Beaufort d'Hautpoul created a poem in praise of the painting, which begins by lauding the expression and animation of the work and ends by forging a perfect alliance between two women of genius:

I see her, I hear her
Your creative brushes
Give soul and life and spirit to paint.
Here are her eyes glowing with fiery sparks
Those melodious sounds, those immortal chords
Which accompany the verses of her divine songs.
And the animated painting scents the air with them.
I don't know which of the two is victorious
The one guiding the hand, the other creating the glory.
And the same crown entwines in this painting
The inspiring mind and the immortal brush.
Staël offers to Lebrun a talent worthy of her
Lebrun alone deserves so perfect a model.
The Universe astonished by this happy twosome
Without choosing falls in silence at their feet.[19]

The poem posits an exclusive relation between Staël and Vigée-Lebrun, crowning them with a single crown, separating them from everyone else, and rendering them only interchangeable with one another. Staël alone is worthy of being painted by Vigée-Lebrun and only Vigée-Lebrun merits so perfect a model. What the poem makes clear is the artist's determination to paint Staël as a creative genius and, at the same time, to show her own genius by representing her as Corinne. And it is equally clear why Vigée-Lebrun did not seek out Récamier as a model: she had already painted her share of beauty queens, now it was the singular Germaine de Staël that Vigée-Lebrun was determined to portray.

For Madame Beaufort d'Hautpoul, the genius of Vigée-Lebrun's image lay in its animated representation of Germaine de Staël, but for me its interest lies in the complex way it engages with Staël's *Corinne*. Some of this complication the artist likely intended from the start; some was likely the unplanned consequence of Staël's intervention in the work. In signifying as both Staël and Corinne, the portrait is certainly the most complicated and challenging of all Staël's portrayals, the only one that represents her as a creative genius. If we only consider the painting superficially, our response may be somewhat like that of the Comtesse de Boigne who on first sight found the novelist "ugly and ridiculous." Her description of Staël in many ways recalls the sitter's look in Vigée-Lebrun's portrait: "A

[223]

large red face, without freshness, coifed with hair that she called picturesquely arranged, that is to say badly pinned; no head scarf, a tunic of white muslin cut very low, bare arms and shoulders, no shawl, no wrap, no veil of any kind."[20] After an hour's conversation, however, the Comtesse was under the writer's spell. Vigée-Lebrun's portrait also rewards conversation as it opens itself up to deeper levels of interpretation.

If the portrait impresses with its sublime effects, it can be read more subtly through attention to its details, such as the temple of the Sibyl at Tivoli represented in the background.[21] The inclusion of this element was a point of discussion between artist and sitter. Vigée-Lebrun wanted to place the Bay of Naples in the distance. This feature would have situated the painting in the countryside surrounding Naples, and the landscape would include a view of the city's most famous monument: Vesuvius. Staël's friends, however, apparently convinced her that the temple and waterfall at Tivoli would be more appropriate. Not only were these also recognizable monuments, but also in her story the temple sits above Corinne's villa near Tivoli. The novel claims the temple as Corinne's most appropriate symbol. Writing to Madame de Staël, Vigée-Lebrun seems to acquiesce: "If the temple can be arranged with the composition and the lines that form the pose, I will choose that which you desire."[22] It seems to be a question of the painting's formal dynamics, and indeed, in other portraits, Vigée-Lebrun carefully planned the relation of sitter to landscape. The artist did acquiesce to the sitter's desire, and although the waterfall is skillfully blended into the landscape at the right side of the canvas, the temple stuck high atop the cliff is not particularly well harmonized with the composition. In terms of formal structure, little would be lost if this detail were effaced. In terms of iconography, however, the temple at Tivoli and the inclusion of the waterfall are significant details. Had Vigée-Lebrun included only the Bay of Naples, the landscape might have restricted our reading to a specific moment in the story when Corinne performs an improvisation in the Neapolitan countryside near Cape Miseno, only this improvisation is sung in a landscape setting. In bowing to Staël's wishes, the artist, perhaps inadvertently, enhanced the painting with references to the location that Staël preferred: Tivoli. Yet something of Cape Miseno remains in the final work: the trees dotting hills in the background and the flowers in the foreground recall the novel's description of the area around Naples where trees—often missing in the Italian countryside—are plentiful, and the "earth is covered with so many flowers that here one can most easily get along without the forests."[23] The flowers attract attention in the painted image as its most visibly touched, most sensuously brushed elements. These small specks of color hold their own against the more dramatic features of this landscape: the detail balances the sublime. Moreover, the very obviously worked flowers in the foreground suggest the comparison of Corinne to flowers that enriches the imagery surrounding the second improvisation: "This lovely Corinne whose lively features and animated expression were meant to convey happiness, this daughter of the sun stricken with hidden sorrows, was like those flowers still fresh and sparkling, but threatened with an untimely end by the black dot of a fatal sting."[24] Indeed Corinne, "daughter of the sun," who in Vigée-Lebrun's painting holds a lyre bedecked with the head of the Sun god, Apollo, is poised in a landscape with steep and craggy rocks and gathering dark clouds. Her setting is at once verdant and ominous, flowering and threatening.

The subject of the improvisation at Cape Miseno also enters the painting. At that moment in the story, Corinne's specific anguish of losing her talent through her ill-omened love for Oswald and her longing to have Oswald experience her genius one last time are imaged in painting and text as the melancholy of sunset. In her work, Vigée-Lebrun renders the setting sun, and deepening shadows are apparent both in the background and around the lyre balanced on Corinne's left thigh. The surrounding landscape, with its great contrasts, sets a heightened emotional tone appropriate to the feelings Staël describes:

> Still, Corinne longed to have Oswald hear her once more as she had been that day at the Capitol, with all the talent she had received from heaven. If that talent were to be lost forever, she wanted its last rays to shine for the one she loved before they went out. Through that desire she found the inspiration she needed, in the very ferment of her soul.[25]

In this improvisation, the association of the landscape with human memories, feelings, and passions is all bound up with the reminiscences conjured by the area around Naples. The improvisation begins: "Nature, poetry, and history challenge each other for grandeur in this place where a single glance embraces all times, all marvels."[26] Vallois has observed that Corinne establishes at Miseno—in a sequence situated at the heart of the novel—the general equivalence that supports the novel's structure: nature as a reflection of the human soul.[27] It is here that we might see a correspondence with those other less complicated images of Staël in which emotional states seem mirrored in landscape settings.

The theme of Corinne's improvisation at Cape Miseno also reaches beyond her impending personal tragedy, and the whole is inspired by images of death and loss. Corinne sings of Roman women—Cornelia, Agrippina, Portia—abandoned by the death of their husbands. She continues, in obvious reference to her own fate:

> Love! the heart's supreme power, mysterious enthusiasm embracing poetry, heroism, and religion. What happens when destiny separates us from the one who held the secret to our soul, the one who had given us the life of the heart, the heavenly life? What happens when absence or death leaves a woman alone on earth? She languishes, she falls.[28]

At the end of her improvisation, fearing the loss of both her talent and Oswald's love, Corinne grows mortally pale and nearly falls to the ground. The Italians gathered before her are surprised by the dark strain in Corinne's poetry; the English are delighted to see her express melancholy feelings with an Italian imagination. It is the English response to Corinne and the specifically Nordic melancholy they admire in her art that ties this improvisation at Miseno back to an earlier scene at Tivoli, and allows a further interpretation of Vigée-Lebrun's doubled siting.

It is here that Staël's suggestion of including the temple from Tivoli expands the range of available references. Corinne performs no improvisation at Tivoli, but she moves Oswald to tears with a Scottish ballad sung in front of a painting. The song concludes a segment of the novel set in the picture gallery of Corinne's villa, and it is performed before an image in which, Corinne opines, history and poetry are successfully combined with landscape. The combination of history, poetry, and landscape anticipates in painting the history, poetry, and nature that Corinne will entwine in her second improvisation. In the picture gallery, nature represented as landscape provokes thoughts similar to those that "real" nature will elicit at Cape Miseno. The scene that inspires Corinne is set in a stormy northern clime and depicts Calibar's son asleep on his father's grave. He has waited for three days and nights for the arrival of the bard Ossian, who comes to sing the honors in memory of the dead—which is, of course, what Corinne will do later in her improvisation at Miseno. In the distance of the painting, Ossian comes down from the mountains, and Calibar's ghost hovers on the clouds above. The image conjures for Oswald thoughts of Scotland and of his father's grave, and his response to the painted landscape establishes what will be the theme of Corinne's second improvisation: memories recalled by particular places.

In its emphasis on memory, death, and mourning, and with its response to landscape elements, the scene in Corinne's gallery is remembered in her improvisation at Cape Miseno. Taken together, the improvisation at Naples and the painting at Tivoli assemble the forces and tensions that structure the novel—the contraries of North and South, Romantic and Classic, Ossian and Virgil, duty and love. Corinne herself, of an Italian mother and an English father, embodies these polarities, just as she embodies those perceived between the proper womanly woman and the genius. With its references to these contrasting forces, the painting transcribes not just a single scene in the novel, but something of the entire novel itself. It also invites us to understand the artist as an analytical reader of the novel, whose painting gets to the heart of the very paradoxes that structure the novel by using the aesthetic strategies suggested in it. For if at times the character Corinne touts the virtues of the Classic, the novel partakes of the emotional Romanticism exemplified in works by writers such as Chateaubriand. The portrait's evocation of two distinct sites and moments forecloses any attempt to read the image literally as a scene from *Corinne*. François Gérard, however, was later to represent precisely the scene at Cape Miseno in another posthumous tribute to Staël. His *Corinne at Cape Miseno* also appeared in the exhibition, and it depicts the episode from the story quite literally: Corinne is presented under Oswald's gaze as he stands amidst the crowd. Her lyre has fallen, and she is searching for inspiration (figure 11.8).

Gérard at Cape Miseno

In 1818 Juliette Récamier, together with Prince Auguste of Prussia, conceived the idea of commissioning a painting that would render homage to their mutual friend who died the previous year. They decided its subject should illustrate an episode from *Corinne*, and the result was Gérard's *Corinne at Cape Miseno*. Auguste provided the financial support, but he gave the painting to Récamier, who in 1821 installed it in her salon at the Abbaye-au-Bois where it could communicate with Godefroid's copy of Gérard's posthumous portrait. As to the subject matter, Prince Auguste made these suggestions in a letter to Gérard: "I will defer to your judgment if it would not be advantageous to represent Corinne under the idealized features of Madame de Staël, and in choosing the moment of her triumph at the Capitol or that when she finds herself on Cape Misene." The letter suggests that what the patrons wanted from Gérard was a sort of remake of Vigée-Lebrun's painting. But for them, it would not be an allegorical portrait of Staël as Corinne, but rather a scene from the novel in which Corinne would wear the features of Staël. This idea shifts the emphasis from portrait to narrative painting, and from Staël to Corinne.

Figure 11.8.   François Gérard, *Corinne at Cape Miseno*, 1819. Courtesy of the Musée des Beaux-Arts de Lyon, France. © Lyon MBA/Photo Alain Basset.

Gérard chose as the basis for his work the episode at Cape Miseno: precisely the episode that would have been the sole reference in Vigée-Lebrun's painting, had the sitter not intervened. But he did not want to transcribe the idealized features of the writer onto those of Corinne. It is likely that he knew about Vigée-Lebrun's image and its lack of success, and wrote to Auguste in November 1819: "I rejected from the first the idea of recalling some resemblance to Madame de Staël in the features of Corinne . . . I would not have enough resources of artistry to render Corinne as beautiful and as interesting as the eloquent pen of Madame de Staël had represented her to us." But despite the evidence of this letter, we must ask ourselves if his figure of Corinne does not at least hint at an idealized Staël—a Staël who would be all but unrecognizable were it not for the curly black hair, large dark eyes, white and gold tunic and red shawl, which bring us back to Vigée-Lebrun's allegorical image.

Allegory and Identity: How Staël Is Not Corinne

I doubt it was easy to depict a woman as an inspired poetic genius in 1807: history had already begun to construct a pantheon populated by blind male bards originating with Homer in the South and Ossian in the North. Yet Vigée-Lebrun attempts to create a female equivalent of the Homers and Ossians. There were, of course, models for inspired women who were saints and sibyls, and the sibyl would seem a likely choice for Vigée-Lebrun since in Staël's novel Corinne is described specifically as Domenichino's sibyl, a painting well known to the artist and on which she based an earlier portrait of Lady Hamilton.[29] But the costume of Domenichino's figure is better recalled in Gérard's posthumous portrait, which copies the form, if not the details, of the sibyl's turban. In Vigée-Lebrun's portrait Staël wears no turban, but she does hold a lyre. Together, these suggest that if Staël chose to portray Corinne as a sibyl, the artist took a different tack.

In Vigée-Lebrun's depiction of Staël as Corinne, her costume and lyre bring her closer to images of another inspired female figure represented in French art since the seventeenth century: the poet Sappho. In pose and attribute, the figure of Staël-Corinne resembles the Sappho of Michel Corneille the Elder's *Sappho Singing Her Verses and Playing Her Lyre in the Presence of the Muses,* which he completed for the Salon des Nobles de la Reine at Versailles. That work could be seen not only at the palace, but also—and more easily—in the engraved 1730 volume, *Versailles Immortalized* by Jean-Baptiste Monicart. In Corneille's composition we see Sappho seated in a panoramic landscape directly on the ground. Holding her lyre to her left side and grasping it at the top with her left hand, with her right arm she reaches across her body to pluck it. Her head is turned away from her body, and she gazes up for inspiration. While the pose of the two figures is not identical, Vigée-Lebrun's Staël-Corinne, lyre in hand, echoes this Sappho more pointedly than she does any representation of the sibyl. Based on a model for the lyric poet Sappho, rather than on a sibyl or saint, Staël-Corinne could more easily be slipped into the pantheon of original genius.

It was fairly common in the late eighteenth century for women to have themselves portrayed either as Sappho or as holding a lyre in imitation of her.[30] Angelica Kauffman, whom Vigée-Lebrun knew in Rome, never appeared as the poet, but in 1775 she made a seductive image of Sappho inspired by love. Many of these works relied on Sappho's reputation as the greatest and most inspired of love poets, which is also how she appears in Corneille's painting designed for a room decorated with scenes from the lives of heroic or famous women. In early nineteenth-century France, however, Sappho began to be shown as a woman killed by love—in fact, who committed suicide by throwing herself off a cliff. That is how she appears in Antoine Gros's beautiful image of 1801, as well as in Joseph Taillasson's late eighteenth-century version. My point here is that the visual image of Sappho had changed over time: if at first she was primarily represented as a great poet and model of inspiration, later she would be shown as a suicide driven to desperation by love. If, in the first instance, Sappho could provide an appropriate guise for Germaine de Staël, in the second she could be a model for Corinne, who does not commit suicide, but who loses her talent and her life after her lover abandons her.

It is in the context of another art exhibition that we find the most provocative discussion of the pantheon of original male genius. In 1990, Jacques Derrida engaged with this pantheon in an exhibit at the Louvre that was distant in time and conception from the show of beauties in Lyon. In the catalog of that exhibition, *Memoires of the Blind: The Self-Portrait and Other Ruins*, Derrida wrote himself into the history of illustrious blind men, joining, "A singular genealogy, a singular illustration, an illustration of oneself among all these illustrious blind men who keep each other in memory, who greet and recognize one another in the night."[31] That tradition, of course, began with the beginning of Western literature, in the figure of the original genius: the blind bard Homer. What does it mean that Vigée-Lebrun inserts into this history of great writers posed as blind men a woman in full possession of her sight, whose eyes are her most expressive characteristic? And that she does so at a time when women are represented alongside the gifted blind either as allegorical figures, as in Ingres's *Apotheosis of Homer* (1827), or as desirable attendants bearing tokens of homage, as in Girodet's *Ossian Receiving the French Generals into Valhalla* (1802, Malmaison)? At a time when artists like François Gérard showed the inspired bard Ossian—who has such an important role in *Corinne*—strumming his lyre in an ecstatic state of enthusiasm (1801, Malmaison)?

Surely there is a simple answer to why Vigée-Lebrun paints Staël-Corinne as a sighted bard: Staël does not represent Corinne as blind, and even if she did, in a portrait an artist cannot extinguish a sighted sitter's eyes. At the same time that Vigée-Lebrun emphasizes the expressive eyes of the woman bard, however, their upward cast substitutes for blindness, and like it indicates that the figure peers into her imagination rather than focusing on the sights of this world. This code for inward vision had several variants and was commonly used to represent artists of all sorts. The convention of the upturned eyes hinders the possibility of seeing the eye as seeing, because it allows viewers to look at the eye (as organ) instead of imagining that their glance either meets that of the sitter, or charts its look on some exterior object. Those representations that show the artist's eye staring ahead, blindly, function more emphatically in the same way, and that convention, too, helped form the artist's image in later Romantic portrayals.

Even if, as Derrida disingenuously claimed, Oedipus had become tiresome, we should not close our eyes to the long-standing cultural association between blinding and castration, particularly in this context. The tiresome Oedipus is writ large throughout Derrida's text, and he surfaces, for example, in the description of a more recent author, Jorge Luis Borges, who writes himself into the pantheon of male genius: "Borges begins with Homer; he then ends with Joyce—and, still just as modestly, with the self-portrait of the author as a blind man, as a man of memory, and this, just after an allusion to castration."[32] If the illustrious blind male author is the castrated father of art, it is not simply by being blind, but through the privilege of *choosing* blindness/castration—as Borges claims Milton did and as Derrida does in his *Memoirs of the Blind*—that male geniuses identify with one another. The artist who accepts castration abdicates his fantasy of control, but he takes a privileged place on the side of the feminine as an outsider, a transgressor, a disrupter—a modern notion of the artist already prepared in the Romantic period. Where, then, does that leave the *woman* bard Corinne-Staël, not only sighted but also blinded—that is, castrated—as all women are in the psychoanalytic model that Derrida invokes? Does her sightedness signal her refusal to accept her castration? Is she then Freud's phallic woman, the "exceptional" woman achiever who still clings to her infantile fantasies and imagines she has a penis? In other words, is she still—as she was to Napoleon—the modern monstrous hermaphrodite, the *femme-homme*? Or is she the exception that disproves the rule, the one who bursts the fantasy of some natural connection between having a penis to lose and gaining cultural achievement? If, as some critics have claimed, "Who is Corinne?" is the central question of Staël's novel, then "What is Staël?" remains a central question posed by Vigée-Lebrun's painting.[33]

Barbara Stafford has articulated, in terms of landscape painting, the rise of singularity as an "aesthetic category."[34] Although Stafford explicitly detaches the lone, natural object from any interpretation as a "human surrogate," the notion of natural singularity is useful in articulating the relationships in Vigée-Lebrun's portrait. The artist shows not the natural object as human surrogate, but the figure of a woman, Germaine de Staël, as a singular, natural formation. Bareheaded, hair tousled by the winds (of genius), and seated directly on a grassy hillock, she is presented as growing out of a particular landscape as much as the great rock formation that rises alongside her as a parallel form. This association accords well with a novel that poses human passions and landscape as reflections of one another. Showing Staël as a singular natural phenomenon does not designate her as passive feminine object; rather, viewing her as one of nature's sublime and singular creations transgresses the acceptable manifestations of woman as Nature, which are suggested in the portrait of Staël with her daughter. Staël does not blend into the landscape. She stands out from it, massive and sublime. *Madame de Staël as Corinne* is one of the few portraits in which Vigée-Lebrun attempts a sublime mode that eschews those characteristics most associated with woman's work: prettiness, fussy detail, soft handling, and a superficial and light exploration of surfaces. Taking his cue from reading Burke's treatise, W. J. T. Mitchell has pointed out that in Romantic aesthetics, sublimity signified in a masculine mode because it is founded on ideas of pain, terror, vigorous exertion, and power. Beauty, by contrast, Burke located in qualities that mechanically induced a sense of pleasure, such as littleness, smoothness, delicacy, and weakness—all feminine.[35] Similarly, in relation to Burke's concept of the sublime as the monumental and the expansive, Naomi Schor has argued persuasively that, in the eighteenth century, the sublime was a category set at odds with the detail, which was gendered as feminine.[36] Vigée-Lebrun's portrait of Staël, however, deploys details such as the touched flowers, the braid around her costume, and the Apollo's head on the lyre to set off the grander gestures of the image—its monumental scale, vertical elevation, craggy cliff, darkening sky, and powerful, vigorously expressive figure—all of which reach toward the sublime. By including details that disrupt an otherwise sublime image, Vigée-Lebrun's work muddies the clear distinction between the sublime and beautiful.

Not easily grasped or understood, the sublime spoke of obscurity, and this obscurity linked it to poetry. In the painting of Madame de Staël as Corinne, a painting Staël called "more poetic than my work," boundaries (between the categories) are sublimely and poetically obscured. Neither smooth, nor little, nor delicate, nor weak, Madame de Staël is not beautiful, so she cannot be "Woman." She is a woman, so she cannot be sublime. She is not sublime, yet she is powerful, vigorous, and compared visually to the irregular cliff that rises steeply beside her. Moreover, it is precisely her naturalness, her position as a singular natural wonder that is stressed in this portrait. Because women were disassociated from the power of the sublime, the portrait seems doubly perverse—a sublime woman represented in a sublime mode by another woman.

Looking at Vigée-Lebrun's portrait today, the picture doubly thwarts our expectations, for it is not a showcase for beautifully painted feminine beauty. It might provoke the sort of response that Christine Battersby claims Staël's novel elicits: the tensions in the image, like those in the prose, may seem to us "simple pretentiousness."[37] Indeed, the portrait might seem as bizarre as when Madame de Staël first appeared to the Comtesse de Boigne. Today Vigée-Lebrun's portrait still calls for conversation, especially to viewers for whom this sort of allegorical masquerade seems particularly alien when seen outside a postmodern context. Merely looking at this work may give little pleasure, just as merely looking at Madame de Staël gave the Comtesse little appreciation for her charisma. Yet it is one of the most challenging of all Vigée-Lebrun's paintings and the most challenging of all Staël's portraits. That challenge comes not only from replacing a blind male bard with a sighted female poet, but also—and perhaps more forcefully—from offering viewers a flawed and expressive Madame de Staël where they expect a perfect and idealized woman. With individualization, the portrait of Madame de Staël as Corinne keeps the distance of the "as," allowing Madame de Staël to distinguish herself from Corinne.

I have argued that this allegorical portrait transcribes not just a single scene in the novel but something of the entire novel itself. Yet the painting is also not a condensation of the novel, but a portrait of the novelist, Germaine de Staël, whose distance from Corinne can be measured by the artist's refusal to idealize the sitter. Moreover, even as the painting refers to the scene of Corinne's waning powers, the monumentality, strength, and impressive force of the figure belies that Corinne whose tragic love for Oswald brings on the loss of her genius. If this scene evokes in the setting sun the last summoning of Corinne's creative powers, it represents an author capable of writing such a tragedy, but not necessarily susceptible to living it. In Vigée-Lebrun's painting, Corinne might well be imagined as singing of her sorrows, her passionate suffering, and the failure of love. It is certainly possible that Staël may have felt some of those same emotions and disappointments in her own life. Yet Corinne is both moved and undone by love, and in the end she dies for want of it. Although in her novel Staël describes the fate awaiting the deviant woman artist, this fate was not one the novelist herself ever met. And this is another critical point, another point at which Staël is not Corinne. What Vigée-Lebrun has painted is less Madame de Staël as Corinne, and more Madame de Staël declaiming *Corinne*. Or better still, Madame de Staël imagining, imagining a scene in which Corinne gives an inspired performance. So strong are Staël's imaginative powers, so intense is the passion that moves her to create, that we see her becoming Corinne. The ability to lose oneself in a character or fictive scene marked both great artists and ideal spectators. Yet neither lost themselves entirely, for to do so would be to fall into a delirium or a madness, and that too was not Staël's fate.

In Vigée-Lebrun's monumental representation, the expressive Staël embodies what much late eighteenth-century thinking conceptualized as a natural, sublime force: a singular genius. As the artist wrote to her sitter, "To tell you the truth, one cannot paint you as one paints everyone else."[38] But perhaps what the writer expected of Vigée-Lebrun was something closer to her ordinary idealization of sitters. Vigée-Lebrun's monumental portrait reveals the effect of situating a woman in the pantheon of "genius." To represent the women genius seriously, as I believe the artist hoped to do, is not only to confuse the assumptions that structure the categories. It is also to unmask, without perhaps realizing it, those grand illusions that have seemed natural idealizations when donned by men and ridiculous vanities when worn by women. Could Staël, in the end, not accept her imaginary projection, Corinne, projected back onto herself? Or did she still expect that painting should harmonize all the fissures and contradictions into a beautified aesthetic whole? What did she make of Massot's copy, which, although superficially more pleasing, shows nothing of her power? In its generalized facial features, the copy of Vigée-Lebrun's portrait now at Coppet undercuts Staël's individuality, and in the change of scale all grandeur and sublimity is lost. At Coppet, Madame de Staël looks just like everybody else. Elisabeth Vigée-Lebrun may have left us the least pleasing image of Germaine de Staël, but from her we also inherit the most powerful one. It is a work that comes from the brush of a woman who continually placed herself in a lineage of great artists, and who likewise positions Staël in the pantheon of genius.

The four portraits of Staël that gathered in Lyon for the 2009 celebration of Juliette Récamier together pose the question of how best to remember her intimate friend Germaine de Staël. It is a question, of course, that every reader, interpreter, and admirer of Staël must answer for herself. Récamier hung images of the writer made by or copied after the well-regarded Francois Gérard in her public salon. But is this necessarily to say that these were the ones she loved best, the ones that she treasured in private? For my part, I cannot imagine embracing either Gérard's posthumous portrait or Godefroid's replica of it: in those works the "beauty" of

Staël—her expressive face, her creative energy, her passionate temperament, her intellectual power—all these are replaced by an iconic image of stasis and death. No matter what their perceived quality or value as works of art, it is those other portraits also shown in Lyon that bring Staël back to life, reminding us of how she adored her father, imagined Albertine in her own image, and challenged all the restrictions on woman's intelligence, creativity, and power.

Notes

1. Stéphane Paccoud and Léna Widerkehr, eds., *Juliette Récamier. Muse et mécene* (Paris: Editions Hazan and Lyon: Musée des Beaux-Arts, 2009).

2. See, for example, Louis Jacques Cathelin's 1763 engraved portrait of Mme de Graffigny (Versailles), or the anonymous drawing of Olympe de Gouges (Louvre).

3. These fashions are shown and discussed in Paccoud and Widerkehr, *Juliette Récamier*, 149–71.

4. Récamier's will indicates that Staël gave her a portrait of herself with Albertine, and in her will Récamier provided that the painting eventually be returned to the family (ibid., 125).

5. See, for example, Jean-Baptiste Greuze, *The Inconsolable Widow*, c. 1762 (London: Wallace Collection).

6. Paccoud and Widerkehr, *Juliette Récamier*, 220.

7. My analysis was first developed in *The Exceptional Woman: Elisabeth Vigée-Lebrun and the Cultural Politics of Art* (Chicago: University of Chicago Press, 1996), 239–61.

8. Vigée-Lebrun had the canvas enlarged.

9. Germaine de Staël, *Lettres inédites de Mme de Staël à Henri Meister*, eds. Paul Ustéri and Eugène Ritter (Paris: Hachette, 1903), 193.

10. Madelyn Gutwirth, *Madame de Staël, Novelist: The Emergence of the Artist as Woman* (Urbana: University of Illinois Press, 1978), 173.

11. Elisabeth Vigée-Lebrun, *Souvenirs*, 2 vols., ed. Claudine Herrmann (Paris: Edition des femmes, 1986), 2:184.

12. Gutwirth, *Madame de Staël*, 287.

13. Comtesse de Boigne, *Récits d'une tante: Mémoires de la Comtesse de Boigne* (Paris: Emile-Paul Frères, 1921), 223.

14. Vigée-Lebrun, *Souvenirs*, 2:181.

15. As reported in *Mémoires de Madame la vicomtesse de Fars Fausselandry, ou Souvenirs d'une octogénaire*, 3 vols. (Paris: Ledoyen libraire, 1830), 2:6.

16. Staël, *Lettres inédites*, 195–96.

17. Vigée-Lebrun, *Souvenirs*, 2:182.

18. As quoted in Paccoud and Widerkehr, *Juliette Récamier*, 124.

19. Vigée-Lebrun, *Souvenirs*, 3:183–84.

20. Comtesse de Boigne, *Récits,* 223.

21. What eighteenth-century writers and artists called the Temple of the Sibyl we now know was misnamed; the temple the ancients dedicated to the Sibyl is a rectangular structure behind the more famous temple.

22. Comtesse de Boigne, *Récits,* 17.

23. Germaine de Staël, *Corinne, or Italy,* ed. and trans. Avriel H. Goldberger (New Brunswick, NJ: Rutgers University Press, 1987), 239.

24. Ibid., 246.

25. Ibid., 240–41.

26. Ibid., 241.

27. Marie-Claire Vallois, *Fictions féminines. Mme de Staël et les voix de la sibylle* (Saratoga, CA: Anma Libri & Co., 1987), 151.

28. Staël, *Corinne, or Italy,* 244.

29. For an extended analysis see Sheriff, *Exceptional Woman,* 239–47.

30. For a discussion of Sappho as a model for enthusiasm, see my *Moved by Love: Inspired Artists and Deviant Women in Eighteenth-Century France* (Chicago: University of Chicago Press, 2004), chapter 2. This work is also indebted to Joan DeJean's *Fictions of Sappho, 1546–1937* (Chicago: University of Chicago Press, 1989).

31. Jacques Derrida, *Memoirs of the Blind: The Self-Portrait and Other Ruins,* trans. Pascale-Anne Braule and Michael Naas (Chicago: Chicago University Press, 1993), 34.

32. Derrida, *Memoirs,* 34–35.

33. Vallois, *Fictions féminines,* 129.

34. Barbara Stafford, "Toward Romantic Landscape Perception: Illustrated Travels and the Rise of 'Singularity' as an Aesthetic Category," *Studies in Eighteenth-Century Culture* 10 (1981): 17.

35. W. J. T. Mitchell, *Iconology. Image, Text, Ideology* (Chicago: University of Chicago Press, 1986), 129–31.

36. Naomi Schor, *Reading in Detail: Aesthetics and the Feminine* (New York and London: Routledge, 1989), 11–22.

37. Christine Battersby, *Gender and Genius: Towards a Feminist Aesthetics* (Bloomington, IN: Indiana University Press, 1989), 99.

38. Yvonne Bezard, *Madame de Staël d'après ses portraits* (Paris: Editions Victor Attinger, 1938), 17.

12

STAËL, CORINNE, AND THE WOMEN
COLLECTORS OF NAPOLEONIC EUROPE

Heather Belnap Jensen

I N 1808, STÉPHANIE-FÉLICITÉ de Genlis published a book composed of two novellas, *Sainclair, ou la victime des sciences et des arts* and *Hortense, ou la victime des romans et des voyages* (*Sainclair, or the Victim of the Arts and Sciences* and *Hortense, or the Victim of Novels and Travels*).[1] The main objective of these novels appears to be the complete denigration of women who dare to cultivate the arts. Of particular interest for my purposes in this chapter is how *Hortense* parodies Staël's recently published *Corinne, or Italy* and the claims Staël had made for women's participation in the art world.[2] Among the roles that Genlis caricatures is that of the woman as art collector. Taking up residency in a Roman tavern, Hortense determines to fill her room with artistic treasures. Yet, while she "would have liked to make of it a museum, a temple, to adorn it with statues, and to receive much of the world," she finds that this all requires too much time, as she is intent upon finding her lover.[3] And when Hortense settles into a permanent home and begins her collecting efforts in earnest, she decorates her abode with copies and fakes. Genlis confides:

> Antiques, dispatched from the cabinet and from under the chisels of some young starving artists, were placed in profusion at each flight of stairs and in every corner. They purchased, from [a man named] Cadez, the paintings of Guido and Correggio, which it was much more certain he had made himself.[4]

Thus, with the character Hortense, Genlis creates the anti-Corinne: her knowledge of art is faulty, her engagement with art is superficial, and her collecting practices are deplorable.

The novels of both Staël and Genlis, with their emphasis on women's positions in the art world, presented imaginary solutions (or consequences) to lived experiences, for in post-Revolutionary France, women were engaging in the arts as never before.[5] In this chapter, I will consider the collecting patterns of Staël and her protagonist and how they intersected with those of the most visible women in Napoleonic Europe—including Joséphine Bonaparte and her sisters-in-law, Caroline Murat and Pauline Borghese—in order to create viable alternatives to the androcentrism of the official French art world. Indeed, it was precisely because women were making such strides in the arts that Genlis felt compelled to write her searing critique of this *femme nouvelle*.

All of these women collectors demonstrated a reluctance to embrace the kind of Neoclassicism valorized by the Napoleonic regime. The art commissioned and collected by the French government was frequently dedicated to the sacralization of the state, the advocation of abstract public virtues over individual, private virtues, and the celebration of a distinctly patriarchal order. Staël and the Bonaparte women found Napoleon's appropriation of the ancient Roman republic as a model for contemporary French art and society to be wanting. Instead, they preferred new aesthetic modes that valorized women as subjects and makers, centered on themes of empathy and social connectivity, lauded historical periods in which women exercised a modicum of power, and legitimized their ambitions. Frequently, the art they acquired embraced some form of classicism, but always in a form that repudiated the "male, severe, and terrifying" elements of the Napoleonic regime's version of this aesthetic.[6] Theirs was a romantic Classicism consonant with the emerging definitions rendered by German philosophers like the Schlegels and Friedrich Schiller. The Christian subjects, medieval and Renaissance epochs, and female-centered *topos* that stood at the heart of this developing Romanticism appealed to the post-Revolutionary women art collectors precisely because they enabled the exploration and expression of difference. Furthermore, the highly public collecting activities of Staël's protagonist and contemporaries were caught up in their bids for cultural and political legitimacy. The world of art was a context in which they could articulate their shared desire for empowerment and could model women's emancipation from restrictive modes to those that facilitated participation in the public sphere.

Corinne's Gallery at Tivoli

In *Corinne, or Italy*, Staël's heroine composes a gallery of paintings that functions as an antidote to what she sees as the stultified nature of the contemporary art scene. With art ranging from Italian Renaissance religious works to British and German Romantic landscapes and contemporary French history painting, Corinne's collection emblematizes Staël's desire to witness the development of a more holistic European culture in which differences are recognized, celebrated, and then integrated so as to promote individual potential. Her advocacy of a pan-European perspective and aesthetic expansiveness stand in contradistinction to the imperial Napoleonic cultural paradigm, and she became one of its most outspoken critics.

This desire for change informs the construction of Corinne's gallery at Tivoli, which functions as a key example of how women were constructing spaces that countered Napoleon's hegemonic practices.[7] Speaking through the voice of Corinne, Staël fashions the gallery as a means to promote her aesthetic, and indeed ethical, values. The site of Corinne's domicile and art collection is significant, for it housed two ancient temples: that of Vesta and that of the Sibyl. With the creation of a museum (or temple of the muses) within these sacred environs, Corinne's spiritual powers resemble those of a priestess of art.[8] Filled with both original works of art and copies of modern masters, this collection is crafted not only to further Staël's narrative goals within the novel, but also to contribute to the most critical debates of the post-Revolutionary art world: the role of art in modern society, Napoleon's transportation of European art objects to Paris, the status of contemporary French painting, and women's roles in the public sphere all enter into the framing of this fictional collection.[9] Corinne's gallery argues against the androcentric confines of Napoleonic art and culture, and in turn, heralds those spaces (geographical, historical, psychological) outside modern France that promote female presence within the public sphere of art. Staël repeatedly expresses a strong preference for works that are religious in nature and that give primacy to empathy and individual autonomy. She finds works from Italy, and particularly the Renaissance, to be most consonant with her aesthetics, though she also speaks favorably of the arts of Germany and Great Britain.

A visit to this picture gallery is the culminating activity in Corinne and Oswald's tour of key art sites in Rome (figure 12.1).[10] This venture serves to underscore the superiority of the artworks of earlier ages. One of the highlights of this tour is the Vatican, where they view its superb collection of ancient sculpture and where Corinne lauds the inapproachable perfection of the ancients. Her collection, which functions as a kind of laboratory for determining the most efficacious art for social progress, is composed of works from myriad periods, genres, and subjects. Interestingly, although she spurns this aesthetic mode that was so heavily promoted by the Napoleonic regime and finds such art inimical to de-sirable aesthetic developments, Corinne owns copies of three examples of such works: Jean-Germain Drouais's *Marius at Minturnae* (1786), Jacques-Louis Da-vid's *The Lictors Returning to Brutus the Bodies of his Sons* (1789), and François Gérard's *Belisarius* (1795).[11] All three of these paintings address the subject of civic virtue and highlight individuals who have been victimized by the state. As Simone Balayé has noted, Staël's exile and that of her father, Jacques Necker, are suggestive of why she selected these works for her gallery.[12] In this novel and elsewhere, Staël casts aspersion on forms of cultural discourse—literature, theater, music, and so on—that were merely formulaic and detached from worthy aims and that were considered, along with Neoclassicism, to engender a kind of despotism.[13]

A key aspect of Staël's philosophy involves her vision of a pan-European community in which diverse cultural expressions are recognized as necessary and invigorating. In what could be construed as an anti-Napoleonic gesture, Staël promotes this ideal in Corinne's Tivoli gallery by foregrounding works produced outside of Italy and France, the bastions of art. For example, Corinne displays an "English" painting of Shakespeare's *Macbeth* (which cannot be definitively attrib-uted),[14] paintings by contemporary German artist Friedrich Rehberg, including *Aeneas Encountering Dido in the Underworld*,[15] and two literary paintings by the Scotsman Georg Wallis (a historical landscape known as *Cincinnatus* and a rep-resentation of the Ossianic tale of Caïrbar sleeping on the tomb of his father).[16] Staël's advocacy of paintings that drew inspiration from alternative mythologies and cultural heritages points to her commitment to a European Romanticism that would transcend national interests and boundaries.[17]

The composition and arrangement of this fictional collection were similarly progressive. It must be noted that many of the key works discussed in this section were among the spoils of Napoleon's Italian conquest that were on display in the Musée Napoléon when the novel was published.[18] That Staël composed a gallery full of works accessible to her reading public is in keeping with her commitment to social instruction.[19] The arrangement of these works is significant as well. If we assume that the discussion between Corinne and Oswald follows the placement of these paintings in the gallery, Staël has adopted the latest exhibitionary practices. Here, not only does she organize her collection into national schools—a develop-ment that was just beginning to gain traction in the early nineteenth century—but she also groups them within these schools according to thematic interest and to the end of promoting her own politics. The gallery's conception was inevitably informed by the discursive and working practices related to this era's modes of collection and display.[20]

Figure 12.1. H. S. Grieg, Corinne Showing Oswald Her Pictures, from *Corinne, or Italy*, by Mme. de Staël. London: J. M. Dent and Co., 1894. Published as part of the Gutenberg Project.

In addition, Corinne's collection offers an alternative vision for post-Revolutionary France, which features the intersections between women, religion, and art. While Corinne embraces art from diverse cultures and varying genres, she privileges religious paintings above all other pictorial representations because of their timelessness, their ability to evoke powerful emotions, and their emphasis on the role of women. This embrace of the spiritual in art challenged the state-sponsored cultural production in Napoleonic France.[21] Indeed, Corinne extols "a simple virgin holding her child in her arms . . . [and] Saint Cecilia," referring to works by Raphael that are part of this fictive painting gallery.[22] Perhaps her most prized possession is a representation of Christ carrying the cross, as witnessed by his mother, the Virgin Mary. This painting—then attributed to Titian but now known to be Bartolomé Esteban Murillo's *Christ Carrying the Cross* of c. 1665–1675 (figure 12.2)—exemplifies Staël's ideal of virtue. Commenting on Mary's reaction to her son's suffering, as represented in this painting, Corinne exclaims: "How splendid a mother's respect for her son's misfortunes and heavenly virtues! . . . Of all my paintings, this is surely the most beautiful. It is the one my eyes always go back to, and yet the emotion it brings is never exhausted."[23] Staël's valorization of this maternal image is consonant with contemporary developments in the early nineteenth-century art world, where portraits and genre scenes that foregrounded motherhood were highly fashionable.[24]

Although Staël lauds the accomplishments of Italian Renaissance painters in her novel, the aesthetic that she champions is essentially romantic, as defined by

Figure 12.2.   Bartolome Esteban Murillo, *Christ Carrying the Cross*, c. 1665–1675. Courtesy of the Philadelphia Museum of Art.

her German colleagues.[25] By privileging feeling and enthusiasm above all else, as she does in her discussion of religious painters, she expresses the primacy of emotion in this nascent aesthetic. Staël also embraces the notion of art as a vehicle for personal expression, which countered the classical privileging of imitation:

> [I]t is impossible for us to create the way [the ancients] did, to invent ideas in what might be called their territory. They can be imitated by dint of study, but how could genius soar where memory and erudition are so vital! The situation is different for subjects belonging to our own history or to our own religions: painters can tap into their own personal inspiration, feeling what they paint, painting what they have seen.[26]

While Staël found art throughout the ages that exemplified her guiding aesthetic principle—that art should encourage the realization and liberation of the individual—she found something most appealing in those Italian Renaissance artists who attempted "to fuse the Romantic spirit and classical form in most beautiful harmony."[27] Staël's aesthetic discourse in *Corinne* advocates the genuine classical ideals adopted by Italian Renaissance artists and then transformed under the lens of Catholicism. In the end, it becomes impossible—and ultimately meaningless—to declare Staël's aesthetics as categorically "Classical" or "Romantic," or to assign individual characters in *Corinne* to concrete positions within these camps. That Staël herself embraced plurality is indicated in her statement: "Art should not regress but combine, if possible, the diverse qualities which the human mind has developed in different periods."[28] Corinne's gallery at Tivoli, which has been variously categorized as eclectic, unfocused, and impure, is reflective of the complexities of Staël's aesthetic vision.[29] The author's protagonist should be credited for creating a thoughtfully composed collection that engaged with salient, even crucial issues—aesthetic, political, and otherwise—of the day.

Staël's Art at Coppet

Staël's personal art collection at the château de Coppet was predicated upon the same precepts that informed Corinne's collecting practices: a commitment to art that promoted values of familial piety, sociability, and freedom of the individual. Following the death of her father Jacques Necker in 1804, Staël inherited Coppet and its contents. These holdings were primarily *objets d'art* and portraits, including Aubusson tapestries, a copy of Antoine-François Callet's portrait of Louis XVI, and paintings executed by the likes of Joseph-Siffred Duplessis, Jean-Etienne

Liotard, and Adolf Ulrik Wertmüller.[30] Given that Coppet was considered the "salon of Europe" and was highly trafficked by the period's arbiters of taste, Staël's art collection was ideally positioned to both reflect and contribute to the developments of early nineteenth-century aesthetics and material culture. The additions Staël made to the existing collection at Coppet were primarily paintings and sculptures of family members and close friends. In this respect, her taste was akin to other bourgeois collectors of the period, who similarly favored portraiture.[31] Featuring some of the finest artists of the era, including François Gérard, Friedrich Tieck, and Elisabeth Vigée-Lebrun, her collection displays aesthetic proclivities that connect her to Corinne and other women art collectors.

The decor of the Grand Salon can be seen as a demonstration of general artistic trends of the age, as well as a declaration of Staël's personal values. The three large Aubusson tapestries—which take as their subject the pastoral landscape—attest to the cult of nature that was ubiquitous in the late eighteenth century. Portraits of two of the leading philosophers of the natural world, Jean-Jacques Rousseau and Georges-Louis Leclerc, Comte de Buffon, were included in this room. The painting of Rousseau has been attributed to Sir Allan Ramsay, and there are two portrait busts of Buffon, one attributed to Augustin Pajou and the other to Jean-Antoine Houdon.[32] Portraits of two of her children, Albertine and August, complete this space. We can surmise that this is the room in which Staël hosted the hundreds of European luminaries that flocked to Coppet during her exile, and that the theme of nature was orchestrated to emphasize the beauty of the surrounding environs of the château as well as to remind visitors of her valuation of the natural in its myriad manifestations.

The family portraits that are gathered into one room at Coppet constitute the core of Staël's collection and display the importance she placed on her relationships (figure 12.3). Staël particularly cherished Duplessis's grand double portrait of her parents, Jacques and Suzanne Necker.[33] One of the most important works Staël ordered was a double portrait of Staël and her father, which was executed soon after Necker's death, emphasizing her position as a torchbearer for Necker's Enlightenment ideals.[34] Staël also commissioned Friedrich Tieck, a sculptor who had trained with Antonio Canova and brother to poet Ludwig Tieck, to immortalize her parents after their death. His representation of Staël's father as a Roman senator (1816–1818) attests to Staël's desire to commemorate her father as a pre-eminent political figure.[35] His high-relief sculpture of her mother's ascent into heaven, which was placed in the family tomb, has been described thus: "The artist represented Madame Necker as ascending to heaven with her husband in her

Figure 12.3.   The Portrait Room, Château de Coppet. Courtesy of the Château de Coppet, Switzerland.

wake, holding him by the hand. The latter glances back, as though in a gesture of regret to look at his daughter, kneeling down, her head covered with a veil."[36] The commission is an important indicator not only of Staël's filial piety, but also her recognition of her mother's deep-seated fear of separation from her husband.[37] Other portraits of family members that figured in Staël's collection include Carmontelle's red chalk drawing of Staël at the age of fourteen, Wertmüller's portrait of her husband, Eric-Magnus Baron de Staël-Holstein, and the portrait of her son, Auguste, by François Gérard.[38] In Pierre-Louis Bouvier's full-length portrait of the last great love of Staël's life, John Rocca, the sitter is shown leaning up against a black horse and surrounded by a suitably Romantic landscape.

Central to this collection are the portraits of Staël that were executed by women artists. This includes the portrait of Staël and Albertine, variously attributed to Marguerite Gérard and Elisabeth Vigée-Lebrun, in which maternal love and filial piety, two leitmotifs in the period art collections of women, are lyrically expressed. A copy of Eulalie Morin's *Portrait of Madame Récamier* can be found in Staël's bedroom in Coppet.[39] This portrait serves as a reminder of the great value the author placed on her friendship with Récamier, who was a collector in her own right.[40] Another critical component to her collection is Massot's copy of Vigée-Lebrun's extraordinary *Portrait of Madame de Staël as Corinne* (1807). In this painting, we see the various roles of women in art mapped: woman as artist (Vigée-Lebrun), sitter and collector (Staël), and subject (Corinne as artist).[41] This portrait, which Mary D. Sheriff discusses in the previous chapter, serves as a powerful summation of the artistic communities of women that existed in post-Revolutionary Europe and the various ways in which women were weaving themselves into its rich cultural fabric.

The Bonaparte Women

While Staël's *Corinne* presents a fictive gallery that proffered another possible direction for cultural development, the Bonaparte women fashioned important art collections that also suggested an alternative visual culture to that adopted by the Napoleonic state. Soon after her husband's rise to power, Joséphine Bonaparte began amassing a formidable art collection with a particular emphasis on the modern French school.[42] In addition to purchasing neoclassical works of a non-didactic nature (and thus counter to the kind of neoclassicism supported by the state), she showed an early and sustained interest in historical genre paintings, with a predilection for subjects culled from French history or focused on women of virtue, and then crafted in the *style troubadour*.[43] These preferences can be construed as a means of emphasizing Joséphine's family's distinctly French and aristocratic connections, which were of no little importance to Napoleon's agenda of cultivating a sense of grandeur and history for his empire. Joséphine's sisters-in-law, Caroline Murat and Pauline Borghese, were also significant art patrons with collecting practices indicative of both their personal agendas, as well as of broader cultural concerns. Napoleon's sisters chose to capitalize on their Corsican roots and to patronize artists working in an Italianate vein, perhaps to validate their positions as rulers of Italian principalities and kingdoms. And finally, the collections of the Bonaparte women emphasized maternity, that most pervasive of discourses shaping women's identity and place within Napoleonic France.[44]

Women as subjects and artists figured frequently in the patronage of the Bonaparte women, who privileged art with themes drawn from classical mythology and medieval history. Furthermore, they capitalized upon—and perhaps even led—the movement of the return to the primacy of the female nude in art,[45] commissioning and collecting paintings and sculptures that manifested a decided turn towards what Robert Rosenblum has termed "the neoclassic erotic," or a focus on sensual mythological themes, graceful and voluptuous contours, and a sense of preciosity.[46] It seems that Joséphine Bonaparte, Caroline Murat, and Pauline Borghese were intent upon using art to define ideals of womanhood that served personal aims of assuring ascendancy or security in the political, social, and cultural spheres. They also did much to further the careers of artists Elisabeth Vigée-Lebrun, Henriette Lorimier, and Marguerite Gérard by commissioning and purchasing their works.

Joséphine's importance as a patron of the art scene in early nineteenth-century Europe was second only to that of her illustrious husband. She was a regular visitor to art sites such as the Musée des Monuments Français and to the biannual salons at the Louvre, as well as to the studios of various artists. Her home, Malmaison, housed the largest collection of contemporary art in France.[47] Key artists of the period—painters François Gérard, Anne-Louis Girodet, Jean-Antoine Gros, Jean-Baptiste Isabey, Pierre-Paul Prud'hon, and Elisabeth Vigée-Lebrun, along with sculptors François Joseph Bosio, Pierre Cartellier, and Joseph Chinard, among others—were part of Joséphine's coterie. Upon the pronouncement that Napoleon would divorce her, Joséphine proclaimed that she could now retire to Malmaison and focus on her two great passions: botany and art.[48] She displayed great generosity with her unrivalled collections in both arenas, as visitors could traverse her gardens and request a visit to her gallery. August Garneray's 1812 watercolor of her music salon shows the disposition of Joséphine's famous art collection of contemporary paintings (figure 12.4).[49] In 1811, a catalog of her painting collection was published to assist the visitors who flocked to Malmaison.[50]

Arguably, Joséphine's primary social purpose was to embody beauty and refinement and to thus define ideals of womanhood deemed appropriate by Napoleon, an objective that is also manifest in her art collecting.[51] There were numerous paintings and sculptures of the female nude into Joséphine's gallery at Malmaison, thus begging the question of the potential motivations at play. Many of the classically inspired works found in her collection were sculptural and of a decidedly different ilk than those promoted and purchased by the state. Indeed, they were of the type that thematized sentimental love and that privileged Joséphine's means to power (beauty, charm, grace), particularly during her early years with Napoleon. She gave value to a Classicism that did not advocate civic duty or moral virtue, but rather, stood on the cusp of what is now defined as Romantic. One of her most well-known commissions was the sensational *Three Graces* (1810–1814) by Italian sculptor Antonio Canova, an ensemble that celebrates attributes associated

Figure 12.4.   Auguste Garneray, *Le Salon de musique* (Music Room at the Château de Malmaison, France, in 1812). Photo Credit: Gianni Dagli Orti / The Art Archive at Art Resource.

with the empress.[52] This sculpture may have been envisioned as an evocation of a time in which Joséphine, Mme Tallien, and Mme Hamelin—the three leading socialites of the Directory, known as the Three Graces—were at the heyday of their power. One wonders whether Joséphine could have commissioned this sculpture to invoke that epoch in which she ruled over the heart of Napoleon and to remind her former husband of his reliance upon her in the first years of their marriage.

One of the most significant aspects of Joséphine's art patronage was the way in which she used the visual arts to emphasize her place in the Bonaparte dynasty.[53] The more precarious her position as empress of France, the more intent she became upon stressing her aristocratic lineage. Joséphine achieved this aim in part through the cultivation of art connected to the golden age of France and in *le style troubadour*, a practice she commenced around 1800, when she first became aware of the tenuous nature of her claim to the throne.[54] The empress was perhaps the first, and certainly the leading, patron of *troubadour* paintings done prior to the Restoration.[55] Several of the women artists who worked in this genre, including

Elisabeth-Jeanne Chaudet, Henriette Lorimier, and Marguerite Gérard, figured prominently in her collection.[56] This mode valorized French medieval historical subjects in a way that had distinct nationalist overtones. *Troubadour* paintings appealed to the former members of the ancien régime, with their preference for monarchical historical subjects and celebration of Gothic aesthetics, and thereby offered a counterculture art that could be read as a subversion of the official neoclassical style of the state. While Staël's Corinne proffered a rather strong critique of Napoleonic aesthetics, Joséphine preferred a subtler means of suggesting alternative modes in art. Although *le style troubadour* would come to represent conservative and monarchical values after 1815, Joséphine's cultivation of this new artistic approach had a rather progressive motive, which was to emphasize the important roles women had played in the history of France.

The themes of such paintings resonated with Josephine's personal and political experiences. Jean-Antoine Laurent's *Héloise Embracing the Monastic Life* (1812), which Joséphine purchased just before her death in 1814, had relevance to her own situation. Her sequestering at Malmaison and subsequent embrace of a quiet, private existence, following her divorce from Napoleon in 1809 (widely seen as a sacrifice the couple made for the expansion and consolidation of the empire), was reminiscent of Héloïse's experience. Viewers of François-Fleury Richard's *Valentine of Milan Mourning the Death of Her Husband, the Duc d'Orléans* (1802) or Jean-Baptiste Vermay's *Mary Queen of Scots Hearing Her Death Sentence* (1814), both of which were in Joséphine's collection, would readily understand the implicit comparison between Joséphine's hearing the divorce decree and the plight of these women of yesteryear. After Joséphine's deposition, such works would serve as a visual rebuke to her former husband—who visited her frequently at Malmaison—and a reminder to the gallery's visitors that her story of love beset by tragedy and by political machinations, and yet endured with humble piety in the face of grief. This secured her place in the line of powerful women who were wronged, calling to mind Corinne's improvisation on the subject at Cape Miseno in view of Mount Vesuvius.[57] Joséphine's sponsorship of this style did more than underscore her personal narrative, however. It emphasized French history in its formative stages and at the apex of Catholicism's return to power. Joséphine was thus instrumental in developing an aristocratic mode of nationalistic art during the Napoleonic era that would flower during the Bourbon Restoration.

Joséphine's sisters-in-law, Pauline Borghese and Caroline Murat, also showed interest in collecting art as a means of asserting their public positions. While the reconstruction of the collecting and exhibitionary practices of these two sisters is more difficult than that of Joséphine—given that they were rather itiner-ant and that their collections were dispersed after Napoleon's fall from power—a recent spate of publications on Caroline Murat and her involvement in the arts enables us to draw some conclusions regarding their contributions.[58] Both women, whose husbands ruled over Italian principalities, elected to align themselves with indigenous traditions. Their ulterior aims differed, however. Whereas Pauline emphasized female beauty and seduction, Caroline proved more interested in promoting the maternal ideal and the political capabilities of women.

In comparison to her other siblings, Pauline Borghese merely dabbled in art patronage. However, the paintings, sculptures, and *objets d'art* that she acquired intimate her recognition of the propagandistic possibilities of art. To validate her reign over the principalities and kingdoms gifted to her by her brother, Pauline chose to patronize artists working in an Italianate vein. She also commissioned art that would secure her position as the most beautiful woman in Europe. While it is reported that Pauline's husband commissioned Antonio Canova's *Pauline Borghese as Venus Victrix* (1804) (figure 12.5), there is little doubt that she exerted a measur-able influence in its conception. This work garnered enormous popular interest and the Villa Borghese became a tourist destination, much like the studio of Canova visited by Staël's Corinne and Oswald. Apparently, the hordes of visitors coming to see the sculpture made it necessary to build an enclosure for the portrait sculpture in order to protect it.[59] Thus one could argue that the sculpture promoted Pauline's place within Italian culture. While Pauline's well-known narcissism surely played into this work's conception and display, political ends may also have inspired this commission. Her portrait of the pagan goddess of love and beauty, so reminiscent of Etruscan imagery of reclining figures, was a blatant attempt to link her rule to that of the ancients.[60] In another such bid, Pauline had cups cast from a mold of her breast, a practice of ancient Roman times that had been revived by Marie Antoinette. With the handle in the form of a butterfly—a symbol of the goddess Psyche—Pauline further underscored her connection to the classical world. With their frivolity and sensuality, the forms of Classicism embraced by Pauline were a far cry from the moralistic ones adopted by the Napoleonic state.

Caroline Murat also used art patronage for personal and political empow-erment, favoring painting genres and motifs that valorized women's roles and that were connected specifically to Italianate traditions. Key pieces that she com-missioned served to legitimize her position as Queen of Naples, which she held from 1808–1815. Jean-Dominique Ingres's *Grande Odalisque* (1814) was com-missioned as a pendant piece for an earlier Ingres painting that her husband had

Figure 12.5.   Antonio Canova, Pauline Borghese as *Venus Victrix*, 1805–1808, Galleria Borghese, Rome, Italy. Photo credit: Scala / Art Resource, NY.

purchased. What has not been noted is that Joachim Murat purchased Ingres's painting *Sleeper of Naples* in 1809, the year following his coronation as king of Naples. This work (now lost) was clearly connected to the classical, and especially the Italianate, tradition of the recumbent female nude.[61] Its pendant piece, the *Grande Odalisque*, continues this theme; although the subject is a Turkish concubine, its formalistic qualities allude to sixteenth-century Florentine mannerism. And interestingly, while Caroline Murat did traffic as a patron of some *style troubadour* works, they were almost exclusively related to Italian themes. These include Ingres's first version of *Paolo and Francesca* (1814) and the now-lost *Betrothal of Raphael* (1813–1814) and François-Marius Granet's *The Choir of the Capuchin Church in Rome* (1814–1815).

Moreover, in 1814 Caroline Murat commissioned Ingres to paint her portrait, which is a striking tour de force in the advocacy of a woman's ability to rule ably (figure 12.6). In the year of its execution, Caroline was actually functioning as the regent, and this portrait foregrounds her considerable leadership abilities. Carefully situated in a rather sedate setting, Caroline stands with an alert posture and attentive disposition. Although the interior is somewhat spartan, the few objects included suggest the sitter's piety: her finger marks her place in what appears to be a small prayer book, the small footstool that peeks out from under her gown may be a kneeler, a component of the *prie-dieu*, and the small bell at the desk is suggestive of the church bells that call worshippers to prayer. It is almost as if the viewer has interrupted Caroline's private devotions. Her deep purple and black velvet dress, which is excessively conservative in its cut and deemphasizes her body, underscores her religiosity. The contrast is especially striking when placed against the vast majority of representations of Caroline and the Bonaparte women that favored the display of large areas of smooth, alabaster skin. Given the precarious state of the Napoleonic empire at the time of the portrait's execution, these allusions to Caroline's piety may have been a way to curry the favor of the powerful (and anti-Napoleonic) papal court.

Another element of the painting that can be read as a means of shoring up her political position is the formal parallelism between Caroline's hat and the eruption of Vesuvius, shown in the distance. The somber and modest clothing has the effect of drawing the eye upward to the implacable visage of Caroline, which rests under a plumed hat visually echoed in the tufts of smoke that Vesuvius emits in the carefully framed window behind her. The motif connects the regent of Naples with its most preeminent symbol and serves to strengthen ideals of rightful rule. Moreover, Ingres's portrait—with its insistent linear purity and imperturbable compositional structure—evinces stability. The institution of the Napoleonic Code and other social reforms, along with the cultivation of the arts and sciences, meant that many viewed this as a rather positive period in Neapolitan history.[62] Thus, it would appear that Ingres's portrait adroitly advocated for Caroline's political prowess and the legitimacy of the Napoleonic reign in Naples.

Another period painting that connects powerful women and the expressive possibilities of the Neapolitan landscape is François Gérard's *Corinne at Cape Miseno* (1819), which was the centerpiece of the collection of another woman art collector, Juliette Récamier.[63] Both of these portraits position their subjects as women of action and presence (Corinne was viewed by many as bearing a great likeness to Staël).[64] Whereas Caroline Murat stands regally and with an air of self-assurance as she makes eye contact with the viewer, Corinne asserts her power otherwise. Perched on a stone and with body twisted at an oblique angle, she turns her face away from her pictured audience and toward the implied viewer,

Figure 12.6. Jean Auguste Dominique Ingres, portrait of Caroline Murat, Queen of Naples, 1814, oil on canvas, Private collection. Photo credit: The Bridgeman Art Library.

raising her eyes to the heavens. Like Ingres's portrait of Murat, Gérard's painting finds recourse in the Christian iconographic tradition and thus aligns women and the power of religion. Indeed, with her animated body lit from above and eyes upturned, Corinne invokes associations of woman as sibyl and as martyr.[65] In both paintings, the women are represented as "the producing *subject* of a gaze," to use Nancy Miller's description, rather than its object.[66]

Furthermore, while both paintings use Mt. Vesuvius to evoke a sense of place, the representations of this landmark are handled in a markedly differing fashion. In the portrait of Murat, it is a carefully controlled element, and the crystalline blue skies and billowing white tufts of smoke read like clouds, thereby rendering the volcanic mountain benign. The handling of this motif works to suggest Murat's ability to keep order in the political domain. In *Corinne at Cape Miseno*, Vesuvius is the centerpiece of a sublime landscape, and its dark emissions blend into ominous clouds that threaten the figures below. The charged atmosphere of the natural world mirrors the narrative tensions imbued in this scene from Staël's novel, wherein the inspired protagonist invokes the lineage of wronged women to which she belongs. In both of these portraits, we find representations of women desirous of power. While Murat's portrait suggests she seeks power in the political realm, the image based upon Staël's novel intimates Corinne's wish for a more expansive definition of women's empire.[67]

Several works in Caroline's collection highlight other aspects of women's roles, especially their maternal ones. For example, Caroline purchased *A Young Woman (The Nursing Goat*, 1804), a painting in which a young mother who, unable to breastfeed her infant, watches the child suckling from a goat. This work was critically hailed and featured in Landon's influential *Annales du musée et de L'Ecole moderne des beaux-arts* of 1806. Three years later, she purchased François Gérard's *Three Ages* (1808), an allegorical painting situated within an Arcadian landscape and one where woman serves as a link between the generations of man. Indeed, in the salon *livret*, the following maxim was included in the entry on this painting: "In life's travels, woman is the guide, the charm, and the support of man."[68] The central figure of the nurturing mother whose child lies sleepily at her breast intimates the importance placed on the maternal in post-Revolutionary France. That Caroline wanted to be viewed as a good mother is suggested by the numerous portraits in which she is presented with her children. These include François Gérard's *Caroline Murat with Achille and Letizia* (c. 1804), as well as *Caroline and Her Children* (1808), in which she is portrayed as a modern-day Madonna, with her four children artfully placed around her. Moreover, there are an abundance of maternal images in her collection that were produced by women artists, including Marguerite Gérard's *Maternal Lesson* (c. 1805) and Vigée-Lebrun's 1807 portrait of Caroline and her daughter. This focus on the maternal resonates with that of Staël's Corinne, who held up the canvas of the Virgin Mother with Christ as her favorite piece in her painting gallery.

The art collecting practices of the Bonaparte women could thus be characterized as gynocentric: women were frequently the subjects of the art they patronized, they cultivated relationships with women artists, and they were also bent on emphasizing their own roles as cultural agents and as political entities. While rooted in the personal, their patronage had implications for artistic trends in early nineteenth-century Europe. Like Staël's Corinne, the collecting practices of the Bonaparte women raise important questions regarding the politics of gender and image-making in Europe, c. 1800–1815. Goethe's much-rehearsed assessment that Staël cared little for the visual arts has had the unfortunate effect of obscuring the author's interest and engagement with painting, sculpture, and other visual media.[69] But examination of both Staël's *Corinne* and of her collection at Coppet illustrates how much art mattered to her. Placed within the context of broader art collecting activities, it is evident that Staël was also responding to and shaping broader aesthetic discourses and practices. The fictional and real instances of women collecting art constitute a significant cultural phenomenon. Corinne's gallery at Tivoli was plausible because it corresponded to the art collecting approaches of actual women in early nineteenth-century Europe. Genlis's parody of Corinne as collector was enabled by the ideals of patronage and collecting in circulation at that time—and indeed, one wonders if some of Genlis's acerbic criticism regarding women in the arts was not fostered by the extravagance of Joséphine's expenditures, the impropriety of Pauline's modeling *au naturel* for the great Canova, or the enviable sophistication of Staël's collections, fictive and actual. What must be acknowledged, however, is that the art activities of highly visible figures in life—such as the Bonaparte women—and in art—like Corinne or even Hortense—were mutually formative, and that these figures contributed to the development of nascent art institutions and to the fashioning of aesthetic sensibilities in post-Revolutionary Europe. In that respect, theirs was a collective, even collaborative, enterprise as sisters in the arts.

Notes

I am most grateful to Tili Boon Cuillé and Karyna Szmurlo, along with the anonymous reviewers, whose comments have done much to help me refine this essay. It seems fitting that I dedicate this to my oldest daughter, Anna Corinne Jensen, whose pitter-patter filled the halls of her namesake's château at age two. All translations are mine, unless otherwise noted.

1. Stéphanie-Félicité de Genlis, *Hortense, or Victim of Novels and Travels*, trans. Archibald Haralson (Georgetown, DC: Richards and Mallory, 1813). The original French text was published in 1808.

2. An adequate gloss of Genlis's satirical novella is beyond the scope of this essay; suffice it to say, it offers a patent denigration of women's artistic aspirations, whether as artists, critics, or connoisseurs. Briefly, Hortense is a wealthy spinster who spends her days devouring second-rate novels and fantasizing about their sensational heroines. After reading an unnamed novel (the reader recognizes the allusion to *Corinne*, of course), Hortense decides to fashion herself as the protagonist and travel to Italy, where she is determined to find love, fame, and life as a woman of art.

3. Genlis, *Hortense*, 125.

4. Ibid., 128.

5. For an excellent overview, see Gen Doy, *Women and Visual Culture in 19th-Century France, 1800–1852* (New York: Leicester University Press, 1998).

6. These adjectives were used to describe Jacques-Louis David's *Brutus* of 1789. See R. L. Herbert, *David, Voltaire, Brutus, and the French Revolution: An Essay in Art and Politics* (New York: Viking, 1973), 123–24.

7. See my "Diversionary Tactics: Art Criticism as Political Weapon in Staël's *Corinne, or Italy* (1807)," in *Women Against Napoleon: Historical and Fictional Responses*, eds. Waltraud Maierhofer and Gertrud Roesch with Caroline Bland (Frankfurt: Campus, 2007): 161–85.

8. See Marie-Claire Vallois, *Fictions féminines: Mme de Staël et les voix de la sibylle* (Saratoga, CA: Anma Libri, 1987).

9. For a discussion of the relationship between the art works selected and their narrative function, see Simone Balayé, "Du sens romanesque de quelques Œuvres d'art dans *Corinne*," in *Madame de Staël: Écrire, luttre, vivre* (Paris: Droz, 1994), 345–64. My reading extends Balayé's argument by attending to the historical and political implications of her aesthetic choices.

10. Other treatments of Staël's analysis of Book VII, "Statues and Paintings" in *Corinne* include Jean Ménard, "Mme de Staël et la peinture," in *Madame de Staël et l'Europe*, ed. Simone Balayé (Paris: Klincksieck, 1970), 253–64; Laura Lepschy, "Madame de Staël's Views on Art in *Corinne*," *Studi francesi* 14 (1970): 481–89; Balayé, "Du sens romanesque," 345–64; Marie-Hélène Girard, "Corinne collectionneur, ou le musée imaginaire de Madame de Staël," *Art et littérature* (Aix-en-Provence: Université de Provence, 1988), 241–61; and Enrico Bruschini and Alba Amoia, "Rome's Monuments and Artistic Treasures in Mme de Staël's *Corinne* (1807): Then and Now," *Nineteenth-Century French Studies* 22, nos. 3/4 (Spring–Summer 1994): 311–47.

11. For scholarship detailing the androcentric nature of late eighteenth- and early nineteenth-century art, see Thomas Crow, *Emulation: Making Artists for Revolutionary France* (New Haven, CT: Yale University Press, 1995); Alex Potts, "Beautiful Bodies and Dying Heroes: Images of Ideal Manhood in the French Revolution," *History Workshop Journal* 30 (Autumn 1990): 1–21; Joan B. Landes, *Visualizing the Nation: Gender, Representation, and Revolution in Eighteenth-Century France*

(Ithaca, NY: Cornell University Press, 2001); and Abigail Solomon-Godeau, *Male Trouble: A Crisis in Representation* (New York: Thames and Hudson, 1997).

12. Balayé, "Du sens romanesque," 126.

13. Susan Tenenbaum, "The Coppet Circle: Literary Criticism as Political Discourse," *History of Political Thought* 1, no. 3 (December 1980): 453–73.

14. This work is variously attributed to Henry Fuseli or Joshua Reynolds; I believe that Staël may have had in mind the *Macbeth and the Witches* painting (1765) by Francesco Zuccarelli, R.A., a wildly popular artist in late eighteenth-century England.

15. This painting has never been located. Staël became acquainted with Rehberg (1758–1835) in Frankfurt in 1803, where she discussed painting with the artist, who would also paint her portrait.

16. Both of these works are known today only through contemporary travelogues.

17. See John Clairborne Isbell, *The Birth of European Romanticism: Truth and Propaganda in Staël's* De l'Allemagne, *1810–1813* (Cambridge: Cambridge University Press, 1994).

18. Napoleon's armies had stripped Italy of its art treasures by 1807 and placed them in the Musée Napoléon in the year of *Corinne's* publication. For discussions of this phenomenon, see especially C. Gould, *Trophy of Conquest: The Musée Napoléon and the Creation of the Louvre* (London: Faber and Faber, 1965).

19. Given that Staël lived in Paris when the art booty from Napoleon's conquests was entering the city (this commenced in 1798)—and that she was considered one of the premiere cultural luminaries of the era—there is little doubt that this writer spent time in the halls of the Louvre viewing these works.

20. See Andrew McClellan, *Inventing the Louvre: Art, Politics, and the Origins of the Modern Museum* (Los Angeles: University of California Press, 1999); and Theodore Ziolkowski, "The Museum: Temple of Art," *German Romanticism and Its Institutions* (Princeton, NJ: Princeton University Press, 1990), 309–77. Interestingly, the makeup of Corinne's collection bears a striking resemblance to the appearance of the editions of the *Almanach des dames* published around the time of the novel's execution. This almanac featured engravings after several of the artworks "held" in Corinne's gallery, including Pierre-Narcisse Guérin's *Phaedra* (1802), Dominichino's *Communion of St. Jerome* (1614), and Raphael's *St. Cecilia* (1514). Such publications constitute a form of art collecting, albeit fictive, that may have been suggestive for the formation of women's actual collections. While not necessarily a source for Staël's collection, the blending of old and new art in these almanacs was consonant with Staël's own conciliatory approach to aesthetics and culture.

21. Although religion experienced a rebirth of sorts in France during the early years of Napoleon's reign, this did not carry over into art. Religious painting had been largely replaced by secular art in the salons of late eighteenth-century France, and by the mid-1790s (the time frame for the novels under discussion), there was a noticeable decline in the production of sacred art. See Philip Conisbee, *Painting in Eighteenth-Century France* (Ithaca, NY: Cornell University Press, 1981), 108.

22. Germaine de Staël, *Corinne, or Italy*, ed. and trans. Avriel H. Goldberger (New Brunswick: Rutgers University Press, 1987), 147. Admittedly, the works Staël characterizes as "early" for Raphael are now deemed part of his late period.

23. Ibid., 154–55. See also the interpretation of the sculptures of Laocoön and Niobe; "pour tous deux, la vie est interrompue dans la chair de leur chair; les parents voient la mort de leurs enfants, thème de prédilection dans la galerie de Corinne" (Simone Balayé, "Du sens romanesque," 121).

24. For a discussion of the fashionability of maternal imagery at this time, see my "Modern Motherhood and Female Sociability in the Art of Marguerite Gérard," in *Reconciling Art and Mothering*, ed. Rachel Epp Buller (Burlington, VT: Ashgate, 2012): 15–29.

25. Romanticism proper did not develop in France until some years after the publication of Staël's *Corinne*. *Préromantisme* is the rather unhelpful descriptor that is sometimes used to denote art, literature and philosophy of late-eighteenth- and early-nineteenth-century France that manifests romantic impulses. See Paul Van Tieghem, *Le Préromantisme français*, 2 vols. (Paris: Félix Alcan, 1924).

26. Staël, *Corinne*, 147.

27. Friedrich Schlegel gave this characterization in his discussion of Italian Renaissance writers, as found in *Dialogue on Poetry and Literary Aphorisms*, trans. Ernst Behler and Roman Struc (University Park, PA: Penn State University Press, 1968), 101.

28. "Il ne s'agit pas de faire reculer l'art, mais de réunir autant qu'on le peut les qualités diverses développées dans l'esprit humain à différentes époques" (Germaine de Staël, *Œuvres complètes* [Paris: Firmin Didot, 1836], 2:100).

29. In her discussion of the function of art in Staël's *Corinne*, Marie-Hélène Girard writes: "Le goût de Corinne, on le voit, est impur. Ce mélange d'archéologie néo-classique, de parti pris maniériste et de préromantisme avoué a de quoi dérouter le lecteur du 20ème siècle, même s'il est prêt à admettre que cette suite de sujets historiques, de compositions religieuses, de 'tableaux dramatiques' et de paysages est disposée avant tout de manière à nous présenter le miroir d'une personnalité" (Girard, "Corinne collectionneur," 248–49).

30. For a general survey of Staël's collection of paintings and drawings, see Yvonne Bézard, *Madame de Staël d'après ses portraits* (Paris: Victor Attinger, 1938).

31. See Sébastien Allard et al., *Citizens and Kings: Portraits in the Age of Revolution, 1760–1830*, exhibition catalogue (London: Royal Academy of the Arts, 2007).

32. Buffon had been a regular guest at Suzanne Necker's salon during Staël's youth.

33. Purportedly, when Staël found that her ill health would prevent her from assisting in the birth of her granddaughter, Pauline, she sent this portrait of Necker to her daughter, Albertine, to protect her from the dangers of childbirth (Georges Solovieff, *Madame de Staël*, trans. B. d'Andlau and O. d'Haussonville [Coppet, Switzerland: Château de Coppet, 1975], 87). The Duplessis portraits were later placed above Staël's coffin in the room where her funeral services were conducted (Pierre Picot quoted in Solovieff, *Madame de Staël*, 89).

34. I believe this double portrait has its antecedent in Anne-Louis Girodet's highly unusual *Portrait of Jean-Baptiste Belley* of 1797, where the representative of Saint Domingue is placed adjacent to the bust of noted abolitionist, Abbé Raynal. If this connection were indeed cultivated by the artist and/or his sitter, Massot's portrait gives visual indication of Staël's commitment to the abolitionist movement and to the virtue of individual liberty. For an extended analysis of the subject see Doris

Kadish, "Patriarchy and Abolition: Staël and the Fathers," in *Germaine de Staël: Forging a Politics of Mediation*, ed. Karyna Szmurlo (Oxford: Voltaire Foundation, 2011), 63–78.

35. On the subject of Staël's filial piety, see Jean-Claude Bonnet, "Le Musée staëlien," *Littérature* 42 (May 1981): 4–19, and also Margaret Cohen, "Melancholia, Mania, and the Reproduction of the Dead Father," in *The Novel's Seductions: Staël's* Corinne *in Critical Inquiry*, ed. Karyna Szmurlo (Lewisburg: Bucknell University Press, 1999), 95–113.

36. Solvieff, *Madame de Staël*, 52; translation modified. The family tomb is not available to the public.

37. On this subject, see Sonja Boon, "Last Rites, Last Rights: Corporeal Abjection as Autobiographical Performance in Suzanne Curchod Necker's *Des inhumations précipitées* (1790)," *Eighteenth-Century Fiction* 21, no. 1 (2008): 89–107.

38. Additional portraits were added to the Coppet collection after Staël's death, including a portrait of Albertine done by Ary Scheffer, and François Gérard's 1818 portrait of Staël.

39. For discussion of Morin's portrait, see Jordana Pomeroy, ed., *Royalists to Romantics: Women Artists from the Louvre, Versailles, and Other French National Collections*, exhibition catalogue (New York: Scala, 2012), 104–05.

40. See Stéphane Paccoud and Léna Widerkehr, *Juliette Récamier. Muse et mécène*, exhibition catalogue (Paris: Editions Hazan and Lyon: Musée des Beaux-Arts, 2009).

41. See Mary D. Sheriff, "Germaine, or Corinne," in *The Exceptional Woman: Elisabeth Vigée-Lebrun and the Cultural Politics of Art* (Chicago: University of Chicago Press, 1996), 243–61.

42. The significance of Joséphine to the development of the visual arts under Napoleon is only now coming to the fore. Major works contributing to this renaissance include Eleanor P. DeLorme, ed., *Joséphine and the Arts of the Empire* (Los Angeles: J. Paul Getty Museum, 2005); DeLorme, *Joséphine: Napoléon's Incomparable Empress* (New York: Harry N. Abrams, 2002); Martine Denoyelle and Sophie Descamps-Lequime, *The Eye of Josephine: The Antiquities Collection of the Empress in the Musée de Louvre*, exhibition catalogue (Atlanta: High Museum, 2007); Carol Solomon Kiefer, *The Empress Josephine: Art & Royal Identity*, exhibition catalogue (Amherst: Mead Art Museum, 2005); and *France in Russia: Empress Josephine's Malmaison Collection*, exhibition catalogue, eds. Frank Althaus and Mark Sutcliffe (London: Fontanka, 2007).

43. Connections between *le style troubadour* and the restoration of the Bourbon are made in publications such as Nadia Tscherny and Guy Stair Sainty, *Romance and Chivalry: History and Literature Reflected in Early Nineteenth-Century French Painting*, exhibition catalogue (London and New York: The Matthiesen Gallery and Stair Sainty Matthiesen Inc., 1996); François Pupil, *Le Style troubadour, ou la nostalgie du bon vieux temps* (Nancy: Presses Universitaires de Nancy, 1985); and Henri Jacoubet, *Le Genre troubadour et les origines françaises du romanticisme* (Paris: Société d'Édition "Les Belles Lettres," 1929).

44. The literature on this subject is vast. Two recent contributions to this discussion are June K. Burton, *Napoleon and the Woman Question: Discourses of the Other Sex in French Education, Medicine, and Medical Law 1799–1815* (Lubbock: Texas Tech University Press, 2007) and Lesley H. Walker, *A Mother's Love: Crafting Feminine Virtue in Enlightenment France* (Lewisburg: Bucknell University Press, 2008).

45. There is surprisingly little theorization as to why there was a return to the female body as a primary subject and site of production in Western art in the early nineteenth century. For some discussion of the artist Ingres's focus on the female body in art and possible connections to female patronage, see Carol Ockman, *Ingres's Eroticized Bodies: Retracing the Serpentine Line* (New Haven, CT: Yale University Press, 1995). Ingres's focus on the female subject is treated at length in Susan L. Siegfried, *Ingres: Painting Reimagined* (New Haven, CT: Yale University Press, 2009).

46. Robert Rosenblum, *Transformations in Late Eighteenth-Century Art* (Princeton, NJ: Princeton University Press, 1967), 22.

47. See Alain Pougetoux, *La Collection de peintures de l'Impératrice Joséphine* (Paris: Éditions de la Réunion des Musées Nationaux, 2003).

48. Bernard Chevallier and Christophe Pincemaille, *L'Impératrice Joséphine* (Paris: Presses de la Renaissance, 1998), 242.

49. For additional information on this site, see Bernard Chevallier, "Le Salon de la musique de Malmaison," *La Revue du Louvre et des musées de France* 48, no. 4 (October 1998): 59–63. In fact, the art gallery at Malmaison seems to have been the room most identified with Joséphine. When her grandson, Napoléon III, purchased Malmaison in 1861, he had it restored to its former majesty, and even, we are told, "shut himself for several hours in the gallery, and with his own hands hung up the principal pictures in the places where he remembered having seen them when he was a child" (Imbert de Saint-Amand, *The Wife of the First Consul,* trans. Thomas Sergeant Perry [New York: Charles Scribner and Sons, 1890], 12).

50. The *grande galerie* that housed the premier works in her collection (excepting contemporary painting) has since been destroyed. For additional information on this collection, see Alexandra Gerstein, "Josephine at Malmaison," in *France in Russia*, 11–24; and Alain Pougetoux, *La Collection de peinture de l'impératrice Joséphine. Notes et documents des musées de France* (Paris: Réunion des Musées Nationaux, 2003).

51. A particularly helpful gloss on Napoleon's position on women can be found in Burton, *Napoleon and the Woman Question*, chapter 1.

52. Joséphine's collection of this sculptor's work was unrivaled, and Malmaison became a pilgrimage site for devotées of Canova. For additional information on Joséphine's patronage of Canova, see Christopher M. S. Johns, *Antonio Canova and the Politics of Patronage in Revolutionary and Napoleonic Europe* (Berkeley: University of California, 1998).

53. From the outset of her relationship with Napoleon, Joséphine recognized one of her principal values was her connection to the aristocracy, by birth, by her first marriage to Alexandre de Beauharnais, and by her experiences of imprisonment and near execution during the Revolution. As an untitled soldier from Corsica, Napoleon's legitimacy as a ruler of the French had to have been thought of as bit suspect, and even with his grand military successes and political acumen, Napoleon needed the validation proffered by an alliance with Joséphine, who served as the embodiment of the aristocracy in Napoleonic France. Her noble heritage, knowledge of court etiquette (she had spent some time in Fontainebleau as part of the entourage of Louis XVI and Marie-Antoinette) and close connections to the royalist faction and émigrés of the Revolution positioned Joséphine as an indispensable tool for her husband's ascension to the throne as emperor. This point is em-

phasized in Carolly Erickson's biography, *Josephine: A Life of the Empress* (New York: St. Martin's, 1999).

54. Joséphine also had an ancestor who was a Crusader, so the themes of medieval chivalry and honor may have been viewed as rightful subjects to promote in art.

55. Guy and Denise Ledoux-Lebard, "L'Impératrice Joséphine et le retour au gothique sous l'Empire," *Revue de l'Institut Napoléon* 92 (July 1964): 117–24.

56. Other women artists that figured into Joséphine's collection include Anne Vallayer-Coster, one of the premiere flower painters of the eighteenth century, and Marie-Victoire Jaquotot, whose miniatures and art reproductions could be found in royal collections throughout Europe.

57. An anecdote is told relating to Napoleon's visit to Malmaison following the death of his former wife, in which he is said to gone into her picture gallery in a daze, where he studied every one of her pictures before leaving. One wonders if he was sufficiently chastised by the subjects of Joséphine's paintings (Saint-Amand, *The Wife of the First Consul*, 5–6). For Corinne's improvisation see Staël, *Corinne, or Italy*, 236–38.

58. See Nicoletta D'Arbitrio and Luigi Ziviello, *Carolina Murat: La Regina Francese del Regno delle Due Sicilie. Le Architetture, La Moda, L'Office de la Bouche* (Naples: Savarese, 2003) and Ornella Scognamiglio, *I dipinti di Gioacchino e Carolina Murat* (Naples: Edizioni Scientifiche Italiane, 2008).

59. See Carol Ockman, "A Woman's Pleasure: Ingres's *Grande Odalisque*," in *Ingres's Eroticized Bodies*, 32–65. Corinne also shows Oswald the statue of the Medici Venus "une seule statue (représentante) la vie dans sa fleur; c'est Corinne, pleine de jeunesse et de vie, comme à sa première apparition aux yeux d'Oswald" (Simone Balayé, "Du sens romanesque," 120).

60. Originally, this sculpture was placed on a wooden mechanism that rotated the work around whilst the spectator stood still and admired the work from all angles—a staging that could have furthered Pauline's purposes of establishing cultural legitimacy by conjuring up associations with the movement associated with Etruscan funerary processions.

61. In fact, this painting shows striking similarities to Titian's *Danäe* in the Museo di Capodimonte in Naples.

62. See John A. Davis, *Naples and Napoleon: Southern Italy and the European Revolutions, 1780–1860* (Oxford: Oxford University Press, 2006).

63. For consideration of her importance as a collector, see Stéphane Paccoud, "Juliette Récamier et les arts: construire une image et conserver un souvenir," in *Juliette Récamier*, 25–34. Additional information on Gérard's painting can be found in Stéphane Paccoud's catalogue entry, *Juliette Récamier*, 232–36. See also Mary D. Sheriff, *The Exceptional Woman*, 243–61.

64. Although Gérard was resistant to the idea of painting Corinne as Staël, his patrons wanted viewers to see the similarities, and contemporaries commented upon the resemblance between Gérard's Corinne and Staël herself. See Daniel Harkett, "Mediating Private and Public: Representing Juliette Récamier and her L'Abbaye-aux-Bois Salon," in *Women, Public Space in European Visual Culture, 1789–1914*, eds. Temma Balducci and Heather Belnap Jensen, work in progress.

65. For discussion of Corinne's sybilline associations, see Vallois, *Fictions féminines* and Simone Balayé and Esther Renfrew, "Madame de Staël et la Sibylle du Dominiquin," *Cahiers staëliens* 2 (1964): 34–36.

66. Nancy K. Miller, "Emphasis Added: Plots and Plausibilities in Women's Fiction," in *Subject to Change: Reading Feminist Writing* (New York: Columbia University Press, 1988), 25–46.

67. The subject of women's desires in the life and art of Staël is assiduously pursued in Madelyn Gutwirth, *Madame de Staël, Novelist: The Emergence of the Artist as Woman* (Urbana: University of Illinois Press, 1978).

68. "Dans le voyage de la vie, la femme est le guide, le charme et le soutien de l'homme" (*Maximes des Orientaux*). *Explications des ouvrages de peinture, sculpture, architecture et gravure des artistes vivans, exposés au Musée Napoléon. . . .* (Paris: Dubray, Imprimeur du Musée Napoléon, 1808), 37.

69. For sustained analysis of Staël's engagement with the visual arts, see my chapter on Germaine de Staël in my unpublished dissertation, "Portraitistes à la plume: Women Art Critics in Revolutionary and Napoleonic France," (PhD diss., University of Kansas, 2007).

13

GERMAINE DE STAËL DEFINES ROMANTICISM, OR
THE ANALOGY OF THE GLASS HARMONICA

Fabienne Moore

ACCORDING TO William Zeitler, world-class glass harmonica player and composer: "There is a story printed in an early Irish musical dictionary of how, upon his return to America, while his wife was asleep, Benjamin Franklin went up to the attic of his Philadelphia home and set up his Glass Armonica which she had not yet heard. Upon completing this, he started to draw forth its 'angelick strains.' Floating down from above, these sounds were apparently so heavenly, that 'his wife awakened with the conviction that she had died and gone to heaven and was listening to the music of the angels.'"[1] What kind of instrument is the glass harmonica, to produce such angelic music that Mrs. Franklin imagined herself dead and in heaven? Rubbing a wet finger around the rim of a drinking glass creates a very pure musical note whose pitch varies according to the amount of water in the glass. In the second half of the eighteenth century, a more elaborate version of this party trick involving sets of singing glasses became a musical pastime during social gatherings. The *Encyclopedia* defined the sounds emitted as *musique des verres*, favorably describing its harmony while attributing its origin to Germany and drawing a comparison with an ancient Persian practice:

> GLASSES, Music of, (Arts) A few years ago we invented with the help of glasses a new kind of harmony very flattering to the ear. . . .
>
> The instrument used for this effect is an oblong box, in which are aligned and attached several round glasses of different diameters, in which one pours water in various quantities. By rubbing a wetted finger on the rims of these glasses, which are slightly curved in, one draws very sweet, very melodious and long lasting sounds; and in this manner one is able to play very pleasant tunes.[2]

After listening to a performance by a virtuoso player, Edward Hussey Delaval (1729–1814), Benjamin Franklin was so fascinated by this new sound that he set his inventive mind to work improving upon the possibilities of musical glasses. He had glasses of different diameters blown, each corresponding to a note, instead of filling glasses with water. He removed the stems and bottoms from the glasses, inserted corks in the holes in the bottoms and mounted them one after the other on a horizontal spindle. The spindle was rotated rapidly by means of a foot pedal (like an old fashioned sewing machine), and the player sat in front of the machine and touched moistened fingers to the edges of the rotating glasses. The first model was completed in 1761 and—in honor of the musical Italian language—he baptized it the "armonica," borrowing the Italian word for "harmony." In a 1762 letter, he enthusiastically shared his invention with his friend and supporter, the Italian scientist Giambatista Beccaria, whom he thought would appreciate this new instrument "as it is an instrument that seems peculiarly adapted to Italian music, especially that of the soft and plaintive kind."[3] Franklin proceeded with a lengthy and exact description of how to cut and tune the glasses, how to fix them to a spindle, and how to draw a tone with one finger as they turn around. He then explained in a passage evocative of Père Castel's 1740 description of his "harpsicord for the eyes" [*clavecin occulaire*]:

> My largest glass is G, a little below reach of a common voice, and my highest G, including three complete octaves. To distinguish the glasses the more readily to the eye, I have painted the apparent parts of the glasses within side, every semitone white, and the other notes of the octave with the seven prismatic colours, viz. C, red; D, orange; E, yellow; F, green; G, blue; A, indigo; B, purple; and C, red again; so that glasses of the same colour (the white excepted) are always octaves to each other.[4]

Franklin ends the letter with advice on how to perform:

> This instrument is played upon, by sitting before the middle of the set of glasses as before the keys of a harpsichord, turning them with the foot, and wetting them now and then with a sponge and clean water. The fingers should be first a little soaked in water, and quite free from all greasiness; a little fine chalk upon them is sometimes useful, to make them catch the glass and bring out the tone more readily. Both hands are used, by which means different parts are played together. Observe, that the tones are best drawn out when the glasses turn from the ends of the fingers, not when they turn to them.

The advantages of this instrument are, that its tones are incomparably sweet beyond those of any other; that they may be swelled and softened at pleasure by stronger or weaker pressures of the finger, and continued to any length; and that the instrument, being once well tuned, never again wants tuning.

In honour of your musical language, I have borrowed from it the name of the instrument, calling it the Armonica.[5]

The new instrument unexpectedly surfaces in Germaine de Staël's *On Literature*, the first instance of an association between the Romantic movement not yet constituted and an instrument which, together with the Aeolian harp, gradually became emblematic of heightened sensitivity, rêverie and transcendence. My purpose in this chapter is to sketch the unusual history of this rare instrument, then to analyze how and why it could provide Staël with a fertile analogy to describe English and German romantic poetry and the ambivalence at its core. Franklin's description of his invention already alerts us to the kinship between the exceedingly "sweet" sounds of the armonica and Italian music—in particular, its "soft and plaintive kind." If Enlightenment debates on music constituted the common backdrop to Franklin's comments and Staël's references to the armonica, by the end of the eighteenth century Staël's contribution significantly surmounted a whole set of binary oppositions stalling such debates (including nature vs. artifice, physical vs. metaphysical, voice vs. instrument, melody vs. harmony, masculine vs. feminine). Moreover, the pressing need to characterize and define romantic poetry ten years later in her work *On Germany* led Staël back to an instrument that effectively tested its listeners' sensibility by introducing a measure of pain in pleasure, akin to Staël's own reception of overly vague and abstract romantic poetry. From sounds full of sweetness praised in Franklin's correspondence to the dangerous lure of (romantic) musical and poetical abstractions analyzed in *On Germany*, perceptions of the glass harmonica allow us to approach the evolution of sensibility and its expressions, both from the original perspective of a forgotten instrument and from the perspective of Staël, who invokes it in order to expose the limitations of both the Enlightenment *and* Romanticism.

Musicologist Heather Hadlock and Thomas Bloch, one of the most prominent musicians currently performing and recording with the glass harmonica, have studied this curious instrument from a socio-cultural, literary, and musical perspective.[6] While Bloch researched the musical properties of the glass harmonica and pondered its decline, Hadlock investigated the symbolic conjunctions between women and an instrument that—like the harp—embodied femininity.[7]

The following characteristic verses from 1785, by British poet William Hayley, underscore both the gendering of the glass harmonica and the metaphorical instrumentalization of the female body:

> Woman, I say, or dame or lass,
> Is an *Harmonica of glass*,
> Celestial and complete:
> If new, or by some trials known,
> It matters not
> A single jot;
> When rightly touch'd, its every tone
> Is ravishingly sweet.[8]

François-René de Chateaubriand would also later gender the instrument as feminine in the 1826 prose epic *Les Natchez* when evoking the fields of paradise, where "a mortal would think that his ear perceived the plaintive accents of a divine armonica,"[9] an interesting revision of a fragment originally describing Christian paradise, and at first intended for the *Génie du christianisme* (*Genius of Christianity*, 1802):

> A ravishing music rises endlessly from everything. Sometimes, there are uninterrupted shivers, similar to the rare vibrations of an Aeolian harp if touched by the soft breath of the wind during a silent summer night; sometimes a mortal would think that he heard the plaintive accents of a divine armonica, these whispers of glass, which do not seem to belong to anything earthly.[10]

Chateaubriand's initial analogy and its rephrasing appropriate the instrument for strictly poetic and suggestive effects, such as the striking metonymic metaphor "sighs of glass" [*soupirs de verre*] born of the imaginative search for transcribing the divine. Staël's own genius consists in a *critical* appropriation—namely, evoking the instrument to debunk a series of aesthetic and cultural dichotomies. Neither Bloch nor Hadlock mention Staël, yet her original perspective adds a new and more critical dimension to the instrument's close association with the feminine. Unpacking the history of this instrument with its heavenly notes and bizarre fate allows for a better understanding of the aesthetic pertinence of Staël's definition and the implications of her musical revisionism.

The quotation at the origin of my inquiry occurs in chapter xii of *On Literature*, titled "De la littérature du Nord" [Of Northern Literature]:

Melancholy poetry is not capable of infinite variety. The shudder we feel at certain natural beauties is always the same feeling; the emotion that the poetry retracing this feeling inspires in us is *very close to the effect of the armonica*. The soul, gently shaken, takes pleasure in prolonging this condition as long as it can bear it. What makes us feel tired after a while is not the poetry's fault, but the weakness of our own organs; what we feel is not bored, but exhausted, as if by *aerial music which we have been enjoying a little too long*.[11]

Just before this passage Staël gives the names of three representative, early romantic poets: Edward Young, famous for his *Night Thoughts* (1742), James Thomson, who celebrated the poetry of nature in *The Seasons* (1730), and the German Friedrich Gottlieb Klopstock, who revived sacred poetry. The three poets have in common a melancholy perspective. Shuddering and shaking [*frémissement* and *ébranlement*] are physical as well as emotional and mental reactions: body and soul shiver as they contemplate nature's sublime spectacle, a shiver prolonged by the poetic experience of reading poems that capture this awe. Though a direct influence is unlikely, Staël's analogy echoes Friedrich Schlegel's portrayal of the philosopher Jacobi's "sensitive character . . . resonating everywhere like a far away harmonica of the world of the mind."[12]

Staël analyzed readers' response to romantic poetry based on two co-determinants: first, the weakness of our organs limits our sensorial perception, therefore melancholy poetry—while emotionally powerful—generates fatigue; secondly, weariness also arises if a perfect aesthetic experience lasts too long. Clearly, for Staël, duration attenuates aesthetic pleasure, leading her to argue that discontinuity, not continuity, should be sought; otherwise the absence of variation creates "a kind of uniformity," which turns pleasure into discomfort and pain. In her novel *Corinne, or Italy*, moments when the soul vibrates in unison with a duet of voices, while delicious and tender, would become excruciating if they lasted too long: too perfect a harmony sustained for too long would "break the accord."[13] One experiences this paradox while listening to even just a few minutes of music performed on the glass harmonica, which is delightful at first, but whose high pitch is difficult to sustain acoustically after a while.[14]

A Mixed Reception

Franklin's popularity and connections throughout Europe helped spread his invention in courts and salons: "Some 400 works were composed for it, some unfortunately lost, and probably about 4,000 instruments were built over the course of some seventy years."[15] The notoriety of gifted performers contributed to the instrument's popularity. Franklin himself, true to his idiosyncratic tastes, liked to play Scottish ballads.[16] The future queen Marie-Antoinette was taught at the Viennese court by Marianne Davies (1740–1792), the eighteenth-century's best player, who spent the end of her life in a mental hospital. The notorious Viennese doctor and hypnotist, Franz Anton Mesmer, used the glass harmonica to relax his patients as part of his treatment and to convey and reinforce magnetism. Furthermore, as per Leopold Mozart's correspondence, we know that father and son admired Mesmer's performance in Vienna in 1773, and that seventeen-year-old Mozart had the opportunity to play Mesmer's armonica himself. Later, in spring 1791, Mozart wrote two pieces for the blind armonica player Marianne Kirchgaessner (1769–1808).[17] On December 10, 1803, during her first journey to Germany, Staël wrote a letter to her father from Gotha, in which she tells of having taken two armonica lessons: if she succeeds in playing it, she plans to buy one in Paris. Tellingly, just before this reference, Staël informs Necker that she has sent him an Aeolian harp—affordable and easy to transport in contrast to the expensive and fragile glass harmonica:

> I'm sending you what is called here an Aeolian harp. You'll only receive it in about two months. I'll explain to you in my first letter how it needs to be exposed to a draft wind to emit sounds that you'll hear in another room. It also produces them in the middle of the garden when it is well set between leaves, and it's a rather soft effect for whoever loves to dream. Besides, it is an inexpensive amusement and if it works in your home, we can order some: it costs eighteen francs, including packing. I have taken two armonica lessons; if I manage to play, I'll buy one in Paris, but not here. It's expensive and fragile.[18]

Responses to the glass harmonica grew passionate and ranged from initial praise to gradual distrust and dismissal. Among its enthusiasts were Johann Sebastian Bach, Niccoló Paganini, Thomas Jefferson, Johann Wolfgang von Goethe, Théophile Gautier, and George Sand. In her 1848 novel *La Comtesse de Rudolstadt* (*The Countess of Rudolstadt*), Sand encapsulated this musical devotion, speaking of "the magical voice of the armonica, that recently invented instrument, whose vibrant, penetrating quality was a wonder unknown to Consuelo's ears, was borne on the air, and seemed to descend from the dome that lay open to the moonlight and the refreshing breezes of the night."[19] According to its detractors however, the instrument drove performers and listeners to mental disturbance and insanity. A negative press account from 1798 underlined how "it excessively stimulates the nerves, plunges the player into a nagging depression and hence into a dark and melancholy mood, that it is an apt method for slow self-annihilation."[20] A *Traité des effets de la musique sur le corps humain* (*Treatise on the Effects of Music on the Human Body*) by Joseph Louis Roger in 1803 warned that "its melancholy tone plunges you into dejection . . . to a point the strongest man could not hear it for an hour without fainting."[21] As I mentioned, some interpreters went mad—among them, one of the best, Marianne Davies—and "the Armonica was accused of causing evils such as nervous problems, domestic squabbles, premature deliveries, fatal disorders, animal convulsions. The instrument was even banned from one German town by the police for ruining the health of people and disturbing public order (a child died during a concert)."[22] Eventually the glass harmonica became a prop in theatrical parodies of Mesmerism.[23]

We know today that the 30 percent lead content of the blown glasses might have been responsible for the mental illnesses that befell its performers. But this modern, prosaic hypothesis does not suppress the instrument's association with physical and moral danger, very much in the background of Staël's analogy. There seems to be a strange curse on the glass harmonica. The one man responsible for its revival in the twentieth century, the only person able to recreate the instrument in the 1980s, Gerhard Finkenbeiner, disappeared with his plane in 1999 off the Massachusetts coast.[24]

The Instrumental Imaginary

The glass harmonica's haunting past, which I have just evoked, is part of what one might call "the instrumental imaginary" [*l'imaginaire de l'instrument*], namely a world of connotations brought about by its distinctive sound, at once captivating and dangerous, treacherous in its very sweetness akin to the fascination of a siren's song. Epithets used to describe its sound (angelic, heavenly, celestial, ethereal) often referred to the otherworldly due to the instrument's unique physical properties. This is its great paradox: the evocation of the metaphysical, superhuman realm can be attributed to the instrument's distinctive physical attributes and human acoustic limitations. First, its very pure sound—almost exclusively high-pitched—rapidly approaches ultrasounds, not perceptible to a human ear but affecting babies and pets such as dogs. Ultrasounds were discovered later, but popular intuition had already grasped the phenomenon at the time. Secondly, variations are impossible, unlike the ability to modulate breath when playing the flute, for instance, or when the wind blows through an Aeolian harp. The sound is actually mechanical and cannot be fully expressive. Staël's warning against the fatigue born of a lack of variation therefore captured the armonica's unusual, monotone vibrations, and she transferred the instrument's musical uniformity to melancholy poetry.

Add to these elements the fact that the instrument is extremely difficult to build and exceedingly fragile, as Staël wrote to her father, which is why so few survived from its heyday. It also remains somewhat of a scientific enigma: "The actual vibrational modes which produce the sound are not at all well understood . . . the underlying physics of the . . . 'Glass Harmonica' remains as mysterious as its sound."[25] In its delicacy and mystery, Franklin's invention escapes reality and rationality. The instrument was a marvel of engineering progress and precision that emitted an indefinable music: on the one hand, a modern invention in the spirit of the Enlightenment and, on the other, a sensual and quasi-mystical experience in the spirit of Romanticism. The paradoxical combination of these two aspects mirror the Enlightenment's intrinsic contradictions, the fascination for all things mechanical—witness the craze for mechanical dolls and the invention of the metronome, clashing with the perpetuation of sensibility as well as the irrational, the spiritual, or the sacred. The glass harmonica was not merely metaphorical, it literally embodied this dualism. According to Hadlock:

> The immediacy of its effect on the listener—its ability to produce a spontaneous, sensuous response—made it the perfect instrument for the "age of sensibility." Yet that same immediacy raised doubts about the intellectual and aesthetic status of the armonica's music, for its "automatic" effect on listeners could be discounted as a mere mechanical response to a physical stimulus.[26]

The novel instrument echoed a split aesthetic, with a fault line that also ran beneath the eighteenth-century debate about music pitting defenders of French music, most notably Jean-Philippe Rameau and Jacques Cazotte, against partisans of Italian music including Jean-Jacques Rousseau and Denis Diderot.[27]

Enlightenment Music

A reminder of the aesthetic and musical dichotomies of the quarrel on "Enlightenment music," as Béatrice Didier strikingly put it in the synesthetic title of her book *La Musique des Lumières*, helps to situate the glass harmonica and to give the context of Staël's analogy at the turn of the nineteenth century. I will leave aside the political undertones of this musical division along national boundaries to concentrate on its aesthetics: the case of Italian vs. French music was the case of voice vs. instrument. On one side, Italy, the feminine and the voice. On the other, France, the masculine and the instrument. On the Italian side stood melody; on the French side harmony. Expression belonged to the Italian, the feminine, the natural, the vocal, and the melodic, whereas imitation was associated with the French, the masculine, the artificial, the instrumental, and the harmonic. This overly schematic picture aligns a rich set of oppositions that characterize comparisons between French and Italian music, which Rousseau recapitulated in part I, letter XLVIII of his epistolary novel, *Julie, or the New Heloise*.[28] When Saint-Preux writes to Julie of "his conversion from French to Italian music,"[29] he criticizes the former as consisting in "a mannered poetry unakin to nature . . . shouts that make the sounds not more melodious but more noisy."[30] He denounces "the forced style and all the French frills . . . that boring and lamentable French song that is more like the cries of colic than the transports of passion."[31] On the contrary, when listening to Italian music, Saint-Preux's imagination takes flight and his emotions flow:

> At each phrase some image entered my brain or some sentiment my heart; the pleasure did not stop at the ear, but entered the soul; . . . I thought I was hearing the voice of grief, rage, despair; in my mind's eye, I saw mothers in tears, lovers betrayed, furious Tyrants.[32]

Saint-Preux's aesthetic epiphany, that pleasure derived from music could be experienced at far deeper mental, emotional, and spiritual levels, engaging not only the ear, but "the brain," "the heart" and "the soul," is couched in terms of a newly discovered *jouissance* (as opposed to "coliques" à la française) that Saint-Preux is eager to share with his beloved, and Rousseau with his readers. In addition, as Rousseau argued in his *Lettre sur la musique française* (*Letter on French Music*, 1753) and later, his *Essay on the Origin of Languages*, "parole" as conveyed in songs is essential, which is why "Like Rousseau, Diderot does not much appreciate purely instrumental music. It strays from the essence, the origin of music, which is founded upon language."[33] Instruments were suspicious, more a luxury item than a genuine musical source.[34] At the same time, in the wake of Rousseau and influential treatises on language theory, writers dissatisfied with versification as ornamental rather than melodic generated poetic experiments in prose that introduced orality and musicality to escape from the neo-classical confines of eighteenth-century poetry. The opera quarrel is mirrored by a second quarrel around the liberties taken by experimental prose poems in seeking a rejuvenated "parole," and expressive rhythms by shunning the "instrument" of verse.[35] While the philosophes could not accept a strict imitative view of instrumental music, namely the mimetic understanding of music dominating the century, desiring freer expression, a similar resistance occurred in literature.[36] Such was the aesthetic environment from which Staël's new approach to reading literature and listening to music emerged.

The glass harmonica overturned staid oppositions: here was an instrument, named for the harmony of its music, which turned out to be intensely expressive. In other words harmony and instrumentality did not have to be incompatible with expressivity. Indeed, the glass harmonica conjured up a *super*natural, a numinous musical sphere: music played on the glass harmonica escaped the confines of imitation (of sounds in nature) by lifting listeners into the imaginary realm of the otherworldly. Describing a concert with flute, harpsichord, violin and voice, Louis-Sébastien Mercier distinguished the celestial music of the glass harmonica with superlatives:

> In the next room, one could hear a concert. There were soft flutes accompanying the sound of voice. The high-pitched harpsichord and the monotonous violin yielded to the enchanting organ of a beautiful woman. Which instrument has more power over the heart! And yet the perfected armonica seemed to challenge it. It produced the fullest, the purest, the most melodious sounds that could flatter one's ear. It was a ravishing and celestial music that resembled in no way the racket of our operas, where men of taste, sensitive men, look for consonance and unity but never find them.[37]

For Mercier "the perfected armonica" rivaled with the human voice—a provocative claim that effectively transcended the by now sterile dichotomy between French instrumentalist music and Italian vocal melodies. Moreover, this exceedingly complex, rare, and fragile instrument, though epitomizing the kind of material luxury that one would expect Rousseauian adepts to criticize, produced music so "celestial" as to lift the listener into a higher *immaterial* realm. However, as I mentioned, the expressivity praised by Mercier was but short-lived, as mechanical uniformity could soon take over. Hadlock justly writes of the armonica as a "poetic sign of liminality."[38] That the glass harmonica was Mesmer's indispensable instrument to achieve therapeutic magnetism confirms the instrument's perceived association with superior forces, the connection of its music with the occult and the uncanny (to use an ancient and a modern term).[39]

The glass harmonica offered evidence that Enlightenment dichotomies could be overcome, an objective at the heart of Staël's aesthetic analyses. Indeed, Staël's merit as a "revisionist" of musical aesthetics and a precursor of Romantic sensibility was to legitimize the autonomy of music by insisting on its spiritual and metaphysical properties—leaving aside, though not discounting, its imitative aspect.[40] Though absent from James Johnson's rich cultural history, *Listening in Paris*, hers is an important contribution in the gradual evolution of musical experience from the Enlightenment to the 1830s. As early as 1800, she had conjoined a new mode of listening (away from imitation toward affect) documented by Johnson, with literary models (Young, Thompson and Klopstock) that provided in turn the vocabulary to express this new aesthetic understanding of music as expressive rather than strictly referential. A new type of "listener" in the realm of music *and* poetry, Staël searched for an adequate language to express the emotions aroused by melancholy poetry as well as to describe the ineffable music of the glass harmonica.

Germaine de Staël's *On Germany*

The second occurrence of the glass harmonica in Staël's writing appears when she refers to the instrument in *On Germany* to explain Jean-Paul Richter's poetic style, emphasizing yet again the ambivalent *pleasure in pain* aroused by the armonica:

> J[ean] Paul [Richter]'s sensitivity touches the soul but does not strengthen it enough. The poetry of his style resembles the sound of the armonica, which delights at first then hurts after a few moments, because *the exaltation it arouses does not have a fixed object.*[41]

Staël adds here another reason—besides our sensorial limitations and the monotony of uniform sound—why rapture turns into pain when listening to the armonica or reading Jean Paul Richter's verse. The absence of a determined object, the want of spiritual direction that would match spiritual elevation, the lack of a referent behind and beyond the sound means the listener loses herself in vagueness, in abstract and sterile phantasms.[42] Staël's measured criticism reminds us that, while she advanced the cause of music's autonomy, it would still take some years before music could be appreciated abstractly, for its own sake, without a referential anchor.⁴³ Similarly, her critical distance vis-à-vis Richter's romantic poetic exaltation reflects a sensibility that still retains Enlightenment boundaries.⁴⁴

In a graceful and symbolic aesthetic move, Staël displaced the classic string instrument of the lyre with the recent invention of the glass harmonica. The analogy between the harmonica's crystalline vibrations and the shivers of "the soul, gently shaken" [*l'âme, doucement ébranlée*] is emblematic of the displacement of the Greco-Latin tradition in favor of new inspiration coming from England and Germany. The musical sensibility at the core of Staël's understanding of Romanticism succeeds (at least in her theoretical writings) in overcoming the pictorial mimesis central to the neoclassical aesthetic that still dominated the Enlightenment.⁴⁵ A similar revision is at work during the Enlightenment and accelerates towards the end of the century from treatises such as Charles Batteux, *The Fine Arts Reduced to a Single Principle*, François-Jean de Chastellux, *Essai sur l'union de la poésie et de la musique* (*Essay on the Union of Poetry and Music*, 1765), Michel Paul Guy de Chabanon, *De la Musique considérée en elle-même et dans ses rapports avec la parole, les langues, la poésie et le théâtre* (*Of Music Considered Independently and in Its Relations with Speech, Languages, Poetry, and Theater*, 1785), and Bernard-Germain-Étienne de Lacépède's *Poëtique de la musique* (*Poetics of Music*, 1785).⁴⁶ This revision, in which painting still serves as a systematic analogy to describe music (the musician "paints"), culminates in Mercier who, in contrast, reverses the customary superiority of painting over music: "We do not talk about Paradise's paintings, but about the music that one will hear there; it's because a melodious tune is more touching than a gallery of paintings."⁴⁷ And indeed, as we saw earlier, Chateaubriand twice describes the music heard in paradise by referring to the glass harmonica. One finds two more revealing analogies in his later writing: in the 1844 *Vie de Rancé* (*Life of Rancé*), the melancholy penitence of the Christian hermit Rancé is compared to "a voice at the bottom of the sea, like the sounds of the armonica, born of water and crystal, and that hurt,"⁴⁸ and in the *Mémoires d'outre-tombe* (*Memoirs beyond the Grave*, 1848), his adolescent self conjures up his imaginary lover [*la sylphide*] from the "liquid sounds" of the glass harmonica.⁴⁹ Writing on Chateaubriand, whose metaphors become musical when exploring melancholy, Yves Hersant interrogates this change: "Why this slide toward music whereas the theme of melancholy was for a long time the prerogative of painters? Why, in the representation of the darkest of temperament, this passage from the pictorial to the musical?" Hersant sees the source of this change in the shifting *medical* conception of melancholy during the Enlightenment—a melancholy no longer generated by a brooding mind or black bile but located in overly sensitive hearts. Now associated with sensibility, it turned to music as an artistic expression more congenial than painting. Musical theories, too, reinforced the change: "During the XVIIIth century a 'melancolisation' of music responds to the musicalisation of melancholy."[50]

The principles of representation, figuration, and imitation defined visual arts, and by extension neoclassical poetics based on the *ut pictura poesis* precept that prevailed throughout the eighteenth century. By contrast, music was gradually understood less as a representational mode than an expressive mode, signaling a shift from an aesthetic of mimesis to one of sensibility—as Johnson has documented—thereby opening the door to idealism, mysticism, and enthusiasm, which for Staël dominated German genius but was sorely lacking in the French, Cartesian analytical mind and tradition. Following Rousseau, Staël suggested the incompatibility between musical sensibility and a purely sensualist appreciation (similar to tasting fruit or seeing colors) that would disunite physical and spiritual, the senses and the soul:[51]

> Is there music for those incapable of enthusiasm? A certain habit makes harmonious sounds necessary to them, they enjoy them like tasteful fruit or colorful decorations. But did their entire being resonate like a lyre when, in the dead of night, silence was suddenly broken by songs or by those instruments resembling a human voice? Did they feel then the mystery of existence in the tenderness that reunites our two natures and collides, in a single *jouissance*, sensations and the soul? Have their heart's palpitations followed music's rhythm? Did an emotion full of charm teach them those cries that have nothing personal, those cries that do not ask for pity but deliver us from an anxious pain pricked by the need to admire and to love?[52]

Staël's interrogative style and her evocation of a dual *jouissance*, sensual and spiritual, echo here Saint-Preux's exaltation at discovering music's full potential. Staël's comparison of the romantic or enthusiastic person to a resonating Orphic lyre perfectly translates the new way of hearing and listening that Johnson demonstrates is taking place in theaters and concert halls at the beginning of the nineteenth century.[53] However, the critical analogy of the glass harmonica shows that while Staël identified the spiritual longings of Romanticism, she also made visible a glass ceiling, so to speak: Romantic poetry, like chords from the glass harmonica, could only reach a certain height before reaching the limits of expression and communication.

Notes

1. Cited in *The Glass Armonica: Benjamin Franklin's Magical Musical Invention*, http://www.glassar-monica.com/armonica/franklin_armonica2.php#tthFtNtAAI. Franklin named the instrument "armonica" without an "h" and I will follow his usage. While subsequent spellings in French vary, English spelling is generally "glass harmonica." The glass instrument should not be confused with its wind namesake, the mouth harmonica, invented in 1821 (Thomas Bloch, *L'Armonica de verre ou Glassharmonica: données et synthèse historique, organologique, acoustique et bibliographique sur l'instrument de Benjamin Franklin et sur les instruments dérivés* [Paris: Conservatoire National Supérieur de Musique, 1989], 18 and 36).

2. "Verres, musique des" in *Encyclopédie, ou dictionnaire raisonné des sciences, des arts et des métiers,* eds. Denis Diderot and Jean le Rond D'Alembert. University of Chicago: ARTFL Encyclopédie Project (Spring 2011 Edition), ed. Robert Morrissey, http://encyclopedie.uchicago.edu/. All translations are mine unless otherwise noted.

3. Letter from Benjamin Franklin to Giambastita Beccaria, July 13, 1762, in *The Papers of Benjamin Franklin*, http://www.yale.edu/franklinpapers/, cited in *The Glass Armonica*, http://www.glassar-monica.com/armonica/franklin_correspondence/1.html.

4. Ibid., 10:126.

5. Ibid., 10:126. For Franklin's complete correspondence relating to the glass harmonica, see *The Glass Armonica*, http://www.glassarmonica.com/armonica/franklin_correspondence/index.php.

6. Heather Hadlock, "Sonorous Bodies: Women and the Glass Harmonica." *Journal of the American Musicological Society* 53 (2000): 506–42.

7. "*The harp.* An instrument renewed from the Ancients, our masters in every genre; a harmonious instrument with cords that unite naturally with the sweet accents of voice. The posture that it requires casts a favorable light on the development of all graces. Then, a beautiful woman's head conveys enthusiasm and ravishment; her delicate, docile fingers fly about the strings; sounds seem to descend from the heavens; a rounded arm unfolds, a pretty foot moves forward and seems to attract all eyes. This instrument, a rival to the harpsichord, is in fashion, and the queen's predilection for it further contributed to its preference by the Court and the city" (Louis Sébastien Mercier, *Tableau de Paris*, ed. Jean-Claude Bonnet [Paris: Mercure de France, 1994], 2:1290).

8. William Hayley, "Epigram on this Question: "Which Is the more Eligible for a Wife, a Widow or an Old Maid?" Essay on Old Maids, in *A Philosophical, Historical, and Moral Essay on Old Maids. By a Friend to the Sisterhood.* 3 vols. (London: 1785), 3:173–74.

9. François-René de Chateaubriand, *Les Natchez,* ed. Gilbert Chinard (Baltimore: John Hopkins University Press, 1932), 4, 174.

10. Chateaubriand, "Fragments du Génie" in *Essai sur les Révolutions. Génie du Christianisme*, ed. Maurice Regard (Paris: Gallimard, 1978), 1337. When reworking this passage more than twenty years later to insert it in his prose epic on the Indians, *Les Natchez*, Chateaubriand adopted neo-classical tropes to ennoble his prose (feminine gendering of the harmonica, "ouïr" instead of "entendre"), thereby taming his more poetic and original first draft. The glass harmonica and the Aeolian harp are often contrasted, as we will see subsequently.

11. My emphasis; Germaine de Staël, *On Literature,* in *Major Writings of Germaine de Staël,* ed. and trans. Vivian Folkenflik (New York: Columbia University Press, 1992), 178.

12. August Wilhelm and Friedrich Schlegel, Fragment 449, *Athenaeum,* in *Kritische Ausgabe,* 3 vols., quoted by Tzvetan Todorov, *Théories du symbole* (Paris: Seuil, 1977), 197. Founded by August Wilhelm and Friedrich Schlegel, the literary journal *Anatheum* was published from 1798 to 1800. However, it seems Staël became acquainted with the Schlegel brothers' works only after the publication of *On Literature* and during her first trip to Germany (1803–1804) when she convinced August-Wilhelm Schlegel to return with her to Coppet to be her children's preceptor. Whereas the chapter on German literature in *On Literature* does not refer to the Schlegels, by the time she published *On Germany,* Staël was thoroughly familiar with the writings of both brothers, which she analyzes and compares. See Germaine de Staël, *De l'Allemagne,* ed. Simone Balayé (Paris: Garnier-Flammarion, 1968), 2:69–75 and 152–54.

13. "The wonderful correctness of two voices in perfect harmony, in the duets of the great Italian masters, produces a delightfully touching emotion, one which, however, cannot be prolonged without a kind of pain . . . the soul then vibrates like an instrument in an accord with others which would be broken by too perfect a harmony" (Staël, *Corinne, or Italy,* ed. and trans. Avriel Goldberger [New Brunswick, NJ: Rutgers University Press, 1987], 162). For an analysis of music in Staël's *Corinne,* see Tili Boon Cuillé, "Staël's Sweet Revenge," in *Narrative Interludes: Musical Tableaux in Eighteenth-Century French Texts* (Toronto: University of Toronto Press, 2006), 173–203; and Anne Deneys-Tunney, "*Corinne* by Madame de Staël: The Utopia of Feminine Voice as Music within the Novel." *Dalhousie French Studies* 28 (Fall 1994): 55–63.

14. See recordings by Thomas Bloch, *Glass Harmonica: Mozart, Beethoven, Donizetti, Schulz, Roellig, Naumann, Reichardt, von Holt Sombach, von Apell, Bloch* (Naxos, 2001) and Bruno Hoffman, *Music for Glass Harmonica* (Vox Unique, 1990).

15. Bloch, *Glass Harmonica,* in-leaf 4.

16. "I play some of the softest Tunes on my Armonica, with which Entertainment our People here are quite charmed, and conceive the Scottish Tunes to be the finest in the World. And indeed, there is so much simple Beauty in many of them, that it is my Opinion they will never die, but in all Ages find a Number of Admirers among those whose Taste is not debauch'd by Art" (Letter from Benjamin Franklin to Sir Alexander Dick, December 11, 1763, in *The Papers of Benjamin Franklin,* 19:384, cited in *The Glass Armonica,* http://www.glassarmonica.com/armonica/franklin_correspondence/8.html).

17. Adagio in C and Adagio and Rondo for Armonica, Flute, Oboe, Viola, and Cello. See *The Glass Armonica,* http://www.glassarmonica.com/armonica/mozart.php.

18. Germaine de Staël, *Correspondance générale de Madame de Staël,* ed. Béatrice Jasinski and Othenin d'Haussonville (Paris: Hachette, 1982–1985), 5:139–40. See also Simone Balayé ed., *Les Carnets de voyage de Madame de Staël* (Genève: Droz, 1971), 61–62.

19. George Sand, *Consuelo,* in *Consuelo. La Comtesse de Rudolstadt,* 2 vols., ed. Léon Cellier and Léon Guichard (Paris: Gallimard, 2004), 2:478–79.

20. In 1798 Friedrich Rochlitz wrote in the *Allgemeine Musikalische Zeitung:* "'There may be various reasons for the scarcity of armonica players, principally the almost universally shared opinion that playing it is damaging to the health, that it excessively stimulates the nerves, plunges the player

into a nagging depression and hence into a dark and melancholy mood, that it is an apt method for slow self-annihilation. . . . Many (physicians with whom I have discussed this matter) say the sharp penetrating tone runs like a spark through the entire nervous system, forcibly shaking it up and causing nervous disorders.' He went on to give some warnings: 'If you are suffering from any nervous disorder you should not play it, / If you are not yet ill you should not play it excessively, / If you are feeling melancholy you should not play it or else play uplifting pieces, / If tired, avoid playing it late at night.'" Cited in *Yatri's Glass Armonica*, http://www.crystalmusic. com/glassarmonica.html.

21. In his *Method to Teach Yourself Armonica* (1788), J. C. Miller answered objections: "It is true that the Armonica has strange effects on people. If you are irritated or disturbed by bad news, by friends or even by a disappointing lady, abstain from playing, it would only increase your disturbance." Cited in *Yatri's Glass Armonica*, http://www.crystalmusic.com/glassarmonica.html.

22. Bloch, *Glass Harmonica*, in-leaf 4.

23. Pierre Guigoud-Pigale, *Le Banquet magnétique* (Londres [i.e., Lyons], 1784); Louis-Nicolas Mareschal, *Le Magnétisme animal, Mesmer ou les sots* (London: James Flesher, 1786).

24. Michael Pollack, "Glass, Wet Fingers and a Mysterious Disappearance," *New York Times* (December 12, 2001).

25. Nigel Bunce and Jim Hunt, "The Glass Harmonica," *The Science Corner* (College of Physical Science, University of Guelph, March 29, 1989).

26. Hadlock, "Sonorous Bodies," 509.

27. See Part I of Cuillé, *Narrative Interludes*.

28. For a more thorough contextualization, see Cuillé, "Introduction: Tableau Theory," in *Narrative Interludes*, 1–21.

29. Ibid., 4.

30. Rousseau, *Julie, or the New Heloise*, in *The Collected Writings of Rousseau*, eds. Roger D. Masters and Christopher Kelly, trans. Philip Stewart and Jean Vaché (Hanover, NH: University Press of New England, 1997), 6:108.

31. Ibid., 110. See also Julie's reply, letter LII in ibid., 117.

32. Ibid., 109.

33. Marie Naudin, "Madame de Staël, précurseur de l'esthétique musicale romantique," *Revue des sciences humaines* 139 (Juillet–Septembre 1970), 394.

34. For her part, Staël suggests a musical (and pictorial) appreciation preceding the origin of language: "If we were able to imagine the impressions to which our soul was susceptible before coming to language, we would better understand the effect of painting and music" ("Des beaux-arts en Allemagne," in *De l'Allemagne*, 83–85).

35. For more on this subject, see my *Prose Poems of the French Enlightenment: Delimiting Genre* (Aldershot: Ashgate, 2009).

36. Cuillé makes important distinctions between Rousseau's vehement criticism of French music and language, and Diderot's more nuanced and open-minded musical appreciation based in part on his belief that French language could improve (Cuillé, "Diderot and Musical Mimesis," in *Narrative*

Interludes, 25–55). See also James H. Johnson, *Listening in Paris: A Cultural History* (Berkeley and Los Angeles: University of California Press, 1995), in particular, "Expression as Imitation," 35–50.

37. Louis Sébastien Mercier, *L'An deux mille quatre cent quarante. Rêve s'il en fut jamais* (London: Gale ECCO print editions, 2010), 428.

38. Hadlock, "Sonorous Bodies," 509.

39. "Music in mesmerist practice became an intangible correlative of the magic/magnetic objects that increased the body's receptiveness and charged the atmosphere, causing magnetism to flow more freely and inducing trance or collapse ('crisis')" (Heather Hadlock, *Mad Loves: Women and Music in Offenbach's* Les Contes d'Hoffmann [Princeton, NJ: Princeton University Press, 2000], 52). For a more detailed discussion on "the mesmerist paradigm" and how its discourse anticipated Freudian psychoanalysis, see Hadlock's "Mesmerizing Voices: Music, Medicine and the Invention of Dr. Miracle," in *Mad Loves,* chapter 2, 42–66.

40. "Merit is due to Madame de Staël for legitimizing the autonomy of music by neglecting its imitative aspect on the one hand, and on the other by insisting on its spiritualist and metaphysical properties" (Naudin, "Madame de Staël," 394).

41. My emphasis; Staël, "Des romans," in *De l'Allemagne,* 2:52.

42. See the sentence preceding the insertion of René's story in Chateaubriand's *Génie du Christianisme*: "We witnessed the birth of this guilty melancholy which rises in the midst of passions, when these passions without object consume themselves in a solitary heart" (716). Unlike Staël, Chateaubriand emphasized here "guilty" melancholy.

43. On this transitional period, see Johnson, "In Search of Harmony's Sentiments," in *Listening in Paris,* 206–27.

44. "Romantic effects are the *accents of a primitive language* that all men do not know and that becomes foreign to several countries. We soon cease to hear them if we do not live with them; and yet this *romantic harmony* is the only one that preserves in our hearts the colors of youth and the joy of life. . . . *Nature placed the strongest expression of the romantic character in sounds and it is especially to the sense of hearing that we can impress in a few strokes and in an energetic manner extraordinary places and things.* Smells give rise to quick and great perceptions, albeit vague; perceptions by sight seems to interest the mind more than the heart; *we admire what we see, but we feel what we hear*" (my emphasis; Etienne-Pivert de Senancour, *Obermann* [Paris: Garnier, 2003], lettre 38, *De l'expression romantique et du "ranz des vaches,"* 183–85. Also cited in Gérard Gengembre, *Le Romantisme en France et en Europe* (Paris: Pocket, 2003), 19 and in Fernand Baldensperger, *Sensibilité musicale et romantisme* (Paris: Presses Universitaires de France, 1925), 34.

45. "As long as there is no opposition between the poem and music, we give way to the art that must always win over all the others. For the delicious reverie into which it projects us destroys the thoughts that words can express, and as music awakens in us the feeling of the infinite, everything that tends to particularize the object of the melody must diminish its effect" (Staël, "Des beaux-arts en Allemagne," in *De l'Allemagne,* chapter 32, 83–84).

46. See also Guillaume André Villoteau, *Recherches sur l'analogie de la musique avec les arts qui ont pour objet l'imitation du langage, pour servir d'introduction à l'étude des principes naturels de cet art,* 2 vols. (Paris: L'Imprimerie Impériale, 1807).

47. Mercier, *Tableau de Paris*, 1290.

48. Chateaubriand, *Vie de Rancé*, ed. George Condominas (Paris: Flammarion, 1991), 194.

49. Chateaubriand, *Mémoires d'outre-tombe*, eds. Maurice Levaillant and Georges Moulinier (Paris: Gallimard, 1951), 1, 3:95.

50. Yves Hersant, "Une lyre où il manque des cordes," in *Chateaubriand: Le Tremblement du Temps*, ed. Jean-Claude Berchet (Toulouse: Presses universitaires du Mirail, 1994), 279–88. On the medicalization of sensibility during the Enlightenment, see Anne C. Vila, *Enlightenment and Pathology: Sensibility in the Literature and Medicine of Eighteenth-Century France* (Baltimore: Johns Hopkins University Press, 1998).

51. For an analysis of Staël's knowledge of Rousseau's writings on music, and her strategic incorporation of/distancing from Rousseau's views on music in her novel *Corinne*, see Cuillé, "Revoicing Rousseau: Staël's *Corinne* and the Song of the South" in *Phrase and Subject: Studies in Literature and Music*, ed. Delia Da Sousa Correa (Oxford: Legenda, 2006), 100–11.

52. Staël, "Influence de l'enthousiasme sur le bonheur," in *De l'Allemagne*, 313.

53. Johnson, *Listening in Paris*, 270.

14

BETWEEN IDEAL AND PERFORMANCE:
CORINNE IN FEMALE-AUTHORED SINGER
NARRATIVES OF THE 1830S

Julia Effertz

T HIS CHAPTER EXAMINES the legacy of Germaine de Staël's *Corinne* in three musical narratives of the 1830s, which dramatise the woman singer as heroine: George Sand's *La Prima donna* (*The Prima Donna*, 1831), Sophie Ulliac-Trémadeure's *Emmeline, ou la jeune musicienne* (*Emmeline, or the Young Musician*, 1836), and Mme de Thellusson's *Lucile, ou la cantatrice* (*Lucile, or the Singer*, 1833). Establishing Staël's *Corinne* as an archetypal female singer who sets up key issues with regard to the problematic link between women and music in late eighteenth- and early nineteenth-century musical-literary discourse, I shall demonstrate how subsequent authors of the French canon rewrote the Staëlian musician and further elaborated on the contradictory views on women singers—which Staël poignantly addressed as early as 1807, and which became increasingly pronounced throughout the first half of the nineteenth century. Between traditionally restrictive views of the singer as an idealised, aestheticised symbol of sublime vocal music, and the reality of the woman as a performer in the flesh—who, displaying her talent and body on stage, was viewed as a sexualised object of desire—the woman singer in the wake of Corinne continues to strive to create art and to express herself as an autonomous artist, as these three narratives show.

The ambiguity, if not suspicion, with which women musicians,[1] and in particular singers,[2] have been treated has been well-documented. Furthermore, scholarship in the area of "music and literature" has shown the intensity of the musical-literary discourse towards the end of the eighteenth and throughout the nineteenth century in France and beyond,[3] as well as the close bond between music, literature and culture,[4] and their encoding in feminised terminology and imagery.[5]

Underpinned by eighteenth-century theories on gender and by the Rousseauean ideal of the musical origin of language and humankind, the aesthetics of song and music throughout the late eighteenth and early nineteenth century were encoded in feminised imagery, while the imagery and fantasy of musical practice was linked with idealised concepts of women as demure, emotional and naturally musical creatures.[6] Diametrically opposed to the rational, male realm of language, music was perceived as emotional, irrational, sublime, and thus ideally symbolised in the feminine principle—with the German Romantics, in particular, formulating strong views on musical aesthetics firmly tied to the feminine imagery of the sublime, the irrational-emotional and the uncanny.[7] Unsurprisingly, the perceived natural link between music and femininity—paired with the de facto rise of professional singers performing on stage during the late eighteenth and the nineteenth century—led to a surge in musical narratives depicting scenes of women making music: juxtaposing these two stereotypical sides of musical women and often blurring the boundaries between the musical ideal embodied in woman, and the woman musician herself as an (autonomous) artist character in her own right. E. T. A. Hoffmann's iconic singers must be mentioned here, although Hoffmann's ironic stance towards Romantic aesthetics makes for rather complex singer characters in his writings, and his take on the woman singer as a seemingly passive, doomed muse that is sacrificed for the sake of male artistic procreation, must be taken with a grain of salt.[8]

In contrast to the rapidly developing musical scene and the increased professionalism of women performers, the Romantic view of women singers—fueled by the long-standing perception of music and women as potentially threatening—implied a carefully circumscribed and sanctioned space, confining women musicians to the realm of abstract poetic ideals on the one hand, and to their naturally predetermined roles of wife and mother at home on the other.[9]

In this aesthetic context of the woman singer as a creature at the crossroads between (disembodied) poetic ideals and musical reality, Staël's early treatment of the subject matter is significant, as—through her musician Corinne—she challenges such diverging views on women and music, questioning the legitimacy of musical embodiment through her performer as well as the legitimacy of Corinne's performance spaces, between the privacy of her salon and the publicity of the Roman stage or the Venetian opera house. A poetess, an *improvisatrice*, a *déclamatrice*, an actress and a singer who does not need to earn a living from her art, Corinne is not the professional *cantatrice* who explicitly addresses the ambivalence with which female singers are perceived in Parisian music culture during the 1830s and 1840s. Yet she is a singer archetype who sets up key issues associated with the female singing voice: namely, the discrepancy between the feminised musical ideal and its bodily performance, and, as a consequence, the legitimacy of the woman performer proper, which becomes a more pressing topic for women novelists of the 1830s and 1840s.

Starting with her first improvisation, Corinne is introduced as an ideal vocalist, through whom Staël links the Greco-Roman heritage of original, lyrical genius in the image of Orpheus, Sappho or Corinna, to the ineffable, sublime union between music and words which was favoured by the Romantics and with which eighteenth- and nineteenth-century authors were so fascinated.[10] Staël took a strong liking to the archetypal German singer of the time—Goethe's child-singer Mignon—who, like no other character in the German canon, fuelled the rewriting of the female singer myth.[11] Like Mignon, Corinne may be read as an idealised, unrealistic vocalist whose musical gifts remain in the symbolic realm—even more so, as she is not a professional artist who needs to earn a living, but enjoys the luxury of choosing her performances. Yet Corinne is also surprisingly present in her physicality and performances, an embodied ideal which serves to negotiate the question of what is acceptable art practice for a woman. Much as Corinne is admired as a vocal artist, it is precisely her lyrical genius that excludes her from society and makes her happiness as a woman impossible. Corinne's ideal voice is contrasted with—if not undermined by—the physical displays of her talent in public that meet with her lover Oswald's irritation, if not criticism. In one of the novel's key moments, Corinne's triumph as an opera performer on stage in Venice is juxtaposed with her utter failure as a woman, and with the onset of her mental and physical demise. As the "ideal" voice of Italy, Corinne was able to draw Oswald into her realm—yet, as a woman performing on stage, she eventually loses him to a more suitable woman: her docile, taciturn, non-performative half-sister Lucile.[12]

As early as 1807, Staël thus dramatises the ambiguous nature of female song and its performer within a contradictory socio-cultural context which either confines woman to the realm of "safe music"—i.e., to the role of the domestic mother-musician or to a disembodied musical ideal—or vilifies the actual performer as an immoral, sexualised femme fatale of the stage. If we want to understand the fascination surrounding the woman singer throughout the nineteenth century, it is crucial to look at an early archetype such as Corinne, who bridges the gap between eighteenth-century visions of idealised female song and later literary treatments of the professional singer, and who strikingly opposes a vision of female musical genius to the heroine's performance and struggle as a woman.

Throughout the first half of the nineteenth century, French music culture develops rapidly, with more and more women pursuing the route of professional musician: as singers (or instrumentalists, most notably pianists), actresses, and music teachers. Views on women and music shifted away from the German Romantic ideal of the disembodied female voice, and towards a more pragmatic image of the woman performer. Yet, in the process, singers also acquired a more carnal, sexualised image, with Parisian music culture catering towards male entertainment and pleasure, and the woman of the stage becoming a sexualised object of male desire.[13] Compared to the turn of the century, the woman singer of the 1830s and 1840s is a more visible and acclaimed creature, a fact reflected in the multitude and variety of literary treatments of this character; yet, as a professional performer, she is also more prone to the contradictory receptions by the public. While critics, authors and composers hail the genius of Maria Malibran, or her sister Pauline Viardot, for example, the majority of contemporary reviews—toying with the connection between performance and prostitution—emphasize a singer's femininity and sexual attractiveness rather than her actual musical talent.[14]

Still, the *cantatrice* takes center-stage during the 1830s and 1840s as a popular literary character who sings with a claim to publicity, critical acclaim and artistic genius and, as such, renews the long-standing debate surrounding women performers. An iconic specimen of her time, in whom the public expressed an almost frenzied interest, the singer represents a new breed of performing artist in the public realm, subject to admiration and acclaim and who serves as a canvas for the socio-cultural discourse on the arts, and on artistic genius. Viewed as both an ideal and a realistic performer on stage, she continues to face the problems encountered already by earlier, more idealised singers such as Corinne, in that she is viewed as a transgressive woman in breach of her naturally prescribed role as wife and mother, as a performer who seeks agency beyond the confines of domestic music practice, a struggle which sees her at odds with aesthetic preconceptions of the abstract, musical ideal and with societal preconceptions of the singer as a carnal, sexual creature. Though presented with more professional opportunities than her predecessors, the singer of the 1830s remains a transgressive character who defies the patriarchal order and the ideals attached to women and music through her voice: a sign of agency which, through her profession, she expresses as life-fulfilling.

The *cantatrice* is a popular character in several narratives written by male authors, including Stendhal, Balzac, Gautier and Berlioz who traditionally, though not exclusively, followed the more stereotypical depictions of women singers at the time.[15] Yet interestingly, a considerable number of female *musicien-littérateurs* also developed singer narratives, centering on the prima donna as heroine and as the focus of a literary discussion of female artistry and music practice in the 1830s. It would be exaggerated to claim that all women writers of this era drew explicitly on Staël's novel in order to develop their own singing heroines—even more so as performance culture and pragmatics had significantly changed towards a more professional context for women singers. Yet, the influence of Corinne as an archetypal figure of female song (and Staël's role as a model for subsequent French female novelists) cannot be discarded. Some narratives offer striking developments of the key paradigms that Staël set up with her woman performer: most notably, the issue of reconciling both idealised and sexualised imagery tied to the woman singer with the reality of a professional woman musician. The following case studies of George Sand, Sophie Ulliac and Mme de Thellusson show the singer as a vehicle for a renewed questioning of woman and artist, while re-thinking the reality, the ideal, and the validity of Corinne's voice.

In her musical novella *The Prima Donna*, George Sand develops the opera singer as the quintessential Romantic artist facing an existentialist struggle. Although hailed as the foremost soprano of Verona and a performer of absolute genius, Gina marries an older aristocrat for the sake of social acceptance and convenience. Having to end her career on stage as a respectable wife, Gina falls ill and gradually declines into madness. Many years later, the prima donna decides to return to the stage, performing in Zingarelli's *Giulietta e Romeo*, and, with the renewal of her genius, she experiences artistic sublimation on stage. However, experiencing her own musical transcendence while performing, Gina dies on stage: "So many feelings, long since forgotten yet desired for a long time, then found again and experienced so powerfully, had broken this body, exhausted from illness. Gina had died to the smooth, religious sounds of Zingarelli, right in the middle of her last and most beautiful triumph."[16]

Sand juxtaposes the two extremes of the woman singer's existence: drawing on the Romantic imagery of the sublime artist, who possesses an unearthly voice, as well as formulating a strong view on the performer's obligation to remain faithful towards her nature, which marks her as different from the rest of society. Like Corinne, Gina is different from other women because of her extraordinary vocal gifts—yet Sand goes further than Staël, whose Corinne faced an ambivalent reception by society and by her lover. Gina is both a musical-feminine ideal and a fully-fledged performer, unanimously accepted and acclaimed and thus not in the least concerned with the implication of female musical ambivalence. Sand casts her as a legitimate musician of genius, acclaimed by all, and preaching the religion of music to her audience:

> Voice of heaven; voice of hell, stirring the hearts and vibrating within the souls, refreshing them with smooth melodies, torturing them mercilessly with cruel and strident sounds. The crowd was powerless, voiceless, not daring to breathe. Her appearance infused the heart with the memory of heavenly melodies. Throughout the piece, fuelled by frenetic applause, she rose above everything that had ever come out of Italy in terms of genius and melody.[17]

Unlike Oswald, who disapproves of Corinne's public performances, Gina's male admirer, the German Valterna, worships the singer without reserve, commenting on her performances that "it was like a religion that I carried in my heart, a religion to which I devoted the life she had given me."[18] Not societal expectations, but the singer's own bad choices cause her decline into physical and mental ill health, and ultimately her death. Trying to integrate herself into upper-class society as the wife of a count and conform to what she believes to be the "norm," Gina violates the foremost rule of artistic genius. Contrary to other singers who face the insoluble conflict between artistic self-expression and the desire to love, Gina consciously betrays herself and the sacredness of her art for her own illusions about the existence of a respectable woman of society. Like Staël, Sand was well aware of the socio-cultural attitudes towards women singers, yet—writing during a time where professional artists, including women artists, were more "established" and accepted, and when the question of the artist's exceptional nature takes center-stage—Sand's preoccupation lies with the artist's struggle with herself, and with her beliefs, more so than with what society may or may not expect of her. Gina's existential purgatory sets in as a direct response to her dishonouring her gift and compromising the realism of her existence as a singer on stage. There can be no compromise for her through seemingly more appropriate forms of female music practice, such as singing in the salons, or teaching music. On the contrary, Sand develops such confined musical spaces as the singer's purgatory, with Gina literally singing herself to madness. Tracing Gina's physical and mental decline, Sand picks up on the reflexive structure that is already present in Staël's text and which further emphasises the woman artist's negotiating of her identity as a performer and of the possible forms of self-expression. In a key scene of foreboding, Gina re-enacts the role of Desdemona in her garden: singing in a natural setting which appears as a nightmarish distortion of Italian poetic utopia, Gina no longer differentiates between herself and the role, nor does her voice follow regular patterns of vocal harmony but rather seems to echo Corinne's "cry of pain, which in the end becomes monotonous, like the cry of night birds."[19] In a clear nod to Romantic transcendence, Gina becomes one with her role, yet by singing without a purpose, she derides the ideal of the naturally musical woman, whose song constitutes a harmonious extension of her inner self that serves no genuine artistic purpose:

> The grass bent, screaming; the touch of a dress moved the leaves and through the lemon trees and the myrtle I saw Gina, with a plaintive, sad voice she sang the willow song: it was Shakespeare's Desdemona; melancholic like the night that moaned with her, prefiguring her terrible fate in each sound, each look. I listened to her in silent ecstasy; all of a sudden, she screamed deliriously, and I shivered. Poor Venetian, you must die.—Die! and she fled, pale, wide-eyed, sublime in her fear, and just as her love for life expressed itself most vividly and her voice stabbed the heart with the most heartbreaking harmony, she stopped, as if hit by an electric shock, her gaze fixed, her neck rigid, a motionless, cold statue.[20]

The narration sharply contrasts the singer's extraordinary constitution with the harmful environment of society, in which—nourished by the wrong type of (literally constrictive) air—her surreal voice turns into mere screams. Neither singing in the salon nor singing in nature alleviates the mental distress of a singer who appears larger than the life to which she has confined herself:

> Her large lungs required both a harsher and more liberal kind of air. She tried in vain to master the bitter reverie that consumed her, to sing lively, happy songs; whenever her hands wandered over the piano and she forced her voice into lively, rushed beats, she would soon come back to the dark thoughts besieging her incessantly and, alone in the middle of an astonished crowd, her hands slowly erred over plaintive keys, her voice grew feeble, heartbreaking harmonies would dully leave her chest and songs that had started joyfully would end in pain.[21]

Through the exclusiveness of her vocality as well as the importance of the right performance context, and her physical and mental suffering, Gina displays interesting similarities to Corinne, who compromises her genius from her first improvisation onwards, adapting it to her feelings for Oswald, and hastening her demise through her "substitute" artistic existence in writing (first in her written "Histoire de Corinne," but most prominently in her "Fragments"). However—in contrast to Corinne, who carefully chooses her performances, and who loses her gift as a result of her failed love affair with Oswald—Gina is an autonomous singer whose demise is a result of her own choice to compromise her artistic nature and to forcefully integrate herself into society by marriage.

In the conclusion of her *conte*, Sand celebrates the apotheosis of the singer and her voice through Gina's triumphal re-integration into her original, musical sphere. A parallel may be drawn between Gina's performance as Juliet in Zingarelli's *Romeo e Giulietta*, and Corinne's performance of the Italian version of Shakespeare's *Romeo and Juliet*: in both cases, Gina and Corinne, through their performances, reveal their innermost feelings. Yet, whereas Corinne uses the play to express her feelings towards Oswald, Gina's operatic performance constitutes her ultimate dissociation from society, and her reunion with her true self, culminating in her "love death" on stage. Her quest for freedom and for authentic, sublime self-expression—as well as her death in the happiest moment of her performance—is preceded by an almost erotic vocal and artistic transcendence. She experiences her own genius as a voice that is not her own but seems to animate her from the outside, an image that draws on the Romantic notion of genius as well as on the paradigmatic dissociation of singer and voice, which is a frequent trait of Romantic narratives. This dissociation of performing body and voice was already thematised in Corinne's *Swan Song* (*Dernier chant*) but is also heavily indebted to *Wilhelm Meister*'s Mignon, whose last song prefigures her death and ultimate disembodied state, and to Hoffmann's singer Antonie in *Rat Krespel*, whose impossibly sublime voice ultimately causes her death. Gina possesses a utopian, androgynous voice that not only renders her performance sublime but unmistakably marks her body as redundant and incapable of being sustained any longer: "Surprised herself by the power of her skills, she said to Rosetta during the last interval that it seemed to her that a voice other than her own, a magical voice was breathing out from her enlarged lungs."[22] This constitutes an irreconcilable conflict between the ideal sound and its physical, mechanical execution through the *mise-en-corps* in a female singer, which is bound to fail and thus results in the destruction of the singing body. Gina experiences the transcendence of her physical being through art, and ultimately, this transcendence into genius can only be achieved through physical death, and through the impossible mixture of masculine and feminine traits—a paradigm already implied by Corinne's multi-faceted, transgressive nature. Where Corinne passes on her art to her niece Juliette, Gina creates an artistic bond with the contralto Rosetta whom she carefully groomed to succeed her and who, in the role of Romeo, buries the prima donna in her coffin on stage.[23] Despite its tragic outcome, this climactic scene also contains the positive message, already voiced in *Corinne*, of a symbolic artistic motherhood and female lineage that undermines the dichotomy of nature and art and, to some extent, of (biological) femaleness and (aesthetic) femininity. While this abrupt, dramatic end may be viewed as a continuation of the *topos* of the dying singer often found in German Romanticism, the conclusive scene equally constitutes a glorification of the absolute artist Gina—for whom there can be no distinction between the stage and the "real world"—creating an equivalence between herself as a performer of music and the divine ideal of music that is generated through her yet in turn generates her. Sand's prima donna demands respect for the singer and her art, but, more importantly, Sand demands respect from the artist for herself and her profession without apologizing for, or compromising, her status as a fully-fledged artist. The author's great merit is her affirmative establishment of the singer as a legitimate performer of both music incarnate and artistic genius. Thus, taking a strong position on the prima donna's agency, George Sand's *conte* must be considered a landmark in the writing about the woman singer during the 1830s, revisiting the important key issue of musical genius set up by Madame de Staël, while further developing it in light of female artistic agency.

Sophie Ulliac-Trémadeure, author of a series of educational novellas geared towards young people and their career choices,[24] chooses to treat the subject of the singer in a manner that radically departs from both Sand's and Staël's vision of the woman performer. Her novella *Emmeline, or the Young Musician* dramatises the coming-of-age of Emmeline Adelmond—a musically gifted, yet spoiled young girl who, because of her family's financial ruin, is forced to earn a living and who, through a rigorous musical apprenticeship, finds a place in society as a music teacher. The links between *Emmeline* and *Corinne* may at first glance seem less pronounced; yet, upon closer inspection, the development of Emmeline as a woman musician is significant and—in the context of the increased professionalization of women singers in 1830s—offers an interesting take on the problem of musical ambivalence raised by Staël. Indeed, it is through music that Emmeline reaches not only artistic, but more importantly, personal maturity, transforming herself into a conscientious and "good" woman and daughter, who puts her voice and musical skills to good use.

The narrative focuses in great detail on Emmeline's musical apprenticeship as a rigorously structured, cathartic experience for the former salon girl who is gradually transformed from a muse (who performs for pleasure and her male admirers) into a hard-working professional. Where Staël only touched upon the taboo associated with female music teaching, and Romantic discourse confined female musical apprenticeship to carefully sanctioned areas and instruments,[25] Ulliac breaks new ground with her music novella in which the relationship between woman and music radically turns away from Romantic stereotypes in the image of the muse or the femme fatale, using the musical apprenticeship as a measured documentary of professionalization and acquiring respectability as a female artist. Interestingly, it is the music teacher who takes center stage in Ulliac's novella, not the stage perfomer as in the majority of musical narratives. With this choice, Ulliac sets herself apart from other *musicien-littérateurs*, while still reflecting on contemporary music culture and on the importance of this profession, as well as the hardship of music teachers, whose income was nowhere near that of established, acclaimed women singers and who lived rather obscure lives away from the flamboyance and sexual ambivalence which the stage performers inhabited.

Furthermore, Ulliac goes down the interesting route of establishing female music practice in positive terms, rewriting the *topos* of "forbidden music" that is omnipresent in Staël's novel, in which Corinne is explicitly forbidden to teach her half-sister Lucile music. By moving away from the imagery of music as a threat, Ulliac strives to create a morally irreproachable female musician, which—in the context of the frivolous Parisian music culture—was not an obvious task. Music does not entirely lose its poetic qualities for Ulliac's Emmeline, yet the emotional gratification that she experiences when performing is inseparably linked with the realistic purpose her studies need to fulfil. A serious music student, Emmeline has neither the time nor the social or financial status to allow herself to get lost in the pose of the singing muse or dwell on romances written in her honour. Rather, the emotional catharsis triggered by music serves to strengthen her in her pursuits—as well as in her allegiance to her mother— which defines her explicitly altruistic identity as an artist. Echoing the *topos* of female music practice as moral threat, Ulliac crafts a very careful image of music teaching as a road to female morality, allowing Emmeline to reintegrate the society from which she was expelled after her family's financial ruin. However, during her quasi-religious exercise in musical self-discipline, Emmeline has to navigate the dangers that a specific type of singing career pose for her. In contrast to Corinne's limitless vocality and Gina's status as an acclaimed stage singer, Emmeline's song requires careful guidance and restraint. Although her exceptional voice is an indispensable prerequisite allowing her to study music, she is constantly tempted by the danger of the opera singer's career, which initially appears as a logical continuation of her studies:

Emmeline knew which decision to make; but that day she found the simple music teacher's renown to be too obscure, and despite her better judgment, she sighed everytime she witnessed the admiration, the enthusiasm caused by a beautiful voice in concert, the hommages given to famous singers; and she imagined the pleasures of travelling with a beautiful name, welcomed everywhere with exhilaration, celebrated, sought after, venerated. Finally understanding the extent of her duty, she resigned herself to completing her musical education that same year in order to be free to pursue the less glamourous career of music teacher. In that obscure career path, she could finally distinguish herself, train students who would do her proud and ensure her mother's happiness in old age.[26]

Resisting the temptation to become a *cantatrice* turns out to be the true moral test for Emmeline, who has to choose the right type of female musicianship. Like Staël, Ulliac is clearly aware of the musical culture of her time and of the erotic underpinnings of the *cantatrice*, who was both venerated and disdained because of her perceived immorality. If the hard-earned, quiet existence of the music teacher is portrayed as being decent and realistic, the illustrious life of the *actrice*— i.e., of the singer who performs on stage, in front of a paying audience—is the epitome of falsity, obscenity and decadence, appearing as a nightmarish distortion of the attention Emmeline received as a salon dilettante.

In this respect, Ulliac shows much more clearly than both Staël and Sand that she is conscious of the socio-cultural polemics and fantasies surrounding the public singer, and makes a point of crafting her musician as a counter-figure to the perceived immorality of the *cantatrice*, which Emmeline must repudiate. In that decision, she must furthermore comply with her mother's wishes—an interesting echo of the parental taboo already thematized in *Corinne*:

Madame Adelmond nurtured prejudices against theatre life which originated in feelings of modesty and reason that are too well-founded for them to be dismissed entirely. As for Emmeline, passing the majority of her days at the Conservatoire, she now saw with her own eyes the proof that the life of artists is a bizarre mixture where falsehood triumphs over truthfulness; moreover it pained her that perhaps public opinion put her in the same category as some of the immoral women whose idea of virtue is subordinate to a multitude of other things, so that this idea vanishes quickly, sometimes irrevocably. One thing shocked her, namely the high-handed manner of the men, musical connoisseurs who fluttered around these young girls, most of whom were destined for a career in the theatres. Emmeline was too pretty to not attract attention; her reserve made her even more striking; but it was soon realised that the *prudish one*, as colleagues and fellow students called her, was not *approachable*.[27]

In a clear departure from Staël and Sand, who build their heroines around their sublime vocal gifts, Ulliac de-emphasises the female singing voice in view of the musician's more important duties as a good woman and conscientious artist—in that Ulliac reconnects with the paradigm of the ambivalence, and latent threat, of female song that needs to be contained, as female musical practice needs to be monitored. Thus, female song and its expression through the profession of singer takes the form of a potentially dangerous, morally corrupting force that needs to be controlled and channelled into the right type of art practice. In Ulliac's novella, the notion of *cantatrice* possesses neither artistic merit nor aesthetic value, but is presented as a seemingly easy shortcut to financial security and a glamorous life-style, without the hardship and daily hassle of teaching: a moral threat exemplified by Emmeline's fellow student Armande who deserts her ailing mother in order to take up an engagement as a court singer in Russia, leaving Emmeline to care for her as well, thus doubly proving her worth as a dutiful daughter.

Although Emmeline possesses the necessary talent and education to succeed as a *cantatrice*, this specific type of female musicianship is, due to its social and moral implications, inappropriate and unacceptable. Ulliac exposes the dangers of the singer's public life under the scrutiny of a volatile audience and subject to the games of male courting and patronage in a merciless music business ruled by envy and intrigues:

> Only a man can aspire to all types of glory with impunity; a woman who respects herself and wants to be respected must fear them. Emmeline had just learned the value of the obscurity she had so dismissed; she only showed herself at her students' and her friends, and distanced herself with fear from anything remotely linked to her triumphs, which had so cruelly and promptly been poisoned.[28]

No matter how modest and morally irreproachable a woman artist may be, Emmeline has to learn that there is no guarantee that she will remain unscathed in the public eye. This is not so much a disappointing dénouement on the part of the author as it is factual: underneath the *conte*'s conservative morality lies a carefully constructed realistic scenario of the situation that a female musician might have found herself in during Ulliac's time, when public opinion was volatile and gossip frequent, and when the singer's public image was impossible to control—a fact which, paradoxically, added to the prima donna myth.

If Emmeline seems removed from Staël's poetic utopia of the female singing voice which tries to articulate and develop female genius against a constrictive society, and from Sand's acclaimed prima donna Gina and her flamboyant vocality, Ulliac's heroine is nevertheless a pertinent example of the further development of the woman musician: in particular, the realistic implications of possible female musicianship in the form of the music teacher, who was just as much a reality of Parisian music culture as the prima donna. A chronicler of her time, Ulliac meticulously details the realistic implications of a profession defined by a long apprenticeship, hard work and financial hardship to which female music teachers were especially vulnerable.

As such, Emmeline is, on the one hand, a female musician who, through hard work, dedication and loyalty to her mother, rises above the stereotype of the domestic, well-bred woman who sings and plays the piano, as well as the stereotypes of the female voice as muse and the fantasy of the woman singer and operatic diva portrayed by many texts of the 1830s and 1840s. On the other hand, Ulliac fails to address the potential and the positive sides of the stage singer as a legitimate musical genius, as portrayed by both Staël and Sand. There is little mystery, little poetry left in the music teacher Emmeline; yet, she is an important type of singer, too as, through her, the author shows a legitimate, feasible way for women to pursue music professionally and establish themselves as respectable working women in society: a facet that, if not untreated, was nevertheless left underdeveloped in texts of the late eighteenth and early nineteenth century, in which the myth of female song, and its perceived threat, outweighed (and perhaps avoided) the question of the woman singer's validity in real life.

Although Staël—certainly ahead of her time—already addressed such issues in *Corinne*, it is during the 1830s that authors start fully developing these notions. Despite her shortcomings and her overall conservative, moralistic tone, Ulliac stands out from the crowd of authors who choose to focus more on the woman singer on stage—the prima donna who was the primary female musician of the time—by focusing on a less flamboyant, but nevertheless vital, character in Parisian music culture. Ulliac shows an unorthodox position through her demystification of poetry and female song ideals, as well as the realism of a musical career for a middle-class woman whose concern is far less with the poetic fantasy of song than with moving up the social ladder, and who wishes to build on her musical gift and educate herself professionally as a musician yet still claim her place as a member of the *juste-milieu*. Unlike so many women singers in literature, Emmeline does not die an untimely death caused by an unforgiving society or by her own sublime, unsustainable singing voice, but goes on to live an unspectacular, yet realistic life.

Another female author of the 1830s chooses to let her singer heroine survive, and I shall briefly discuss her contribution to the popular *roman-feuilleton* vogue of the July Monarchy, which appears rather trivial in retrospect, but illustrates quite well the popular appeal of a public figure such as the woman singer and the strong repercussions that an archetype such as Corinne had on subsequent emulations.[29] The music novel *Lucile, or the Singer*, authored by the anonymous Mme de Thellusson, constitutes an interesting echo of *Corinne*: not only through its title, which invites comparisons with Staël's choice of title and name for Corinne's half-sister, but also through what appears to be the author's attempt to revisit Corinne's written confession in order to achieve reconciliation for her singer Lucile. Interestingly, Mme de Thellusson chooses a first-person point of view, giving her singer ample narrative space to confess and—not unlike Corinne—to reflect on her life and on her art, to reveal her side of the story to the reader. It is easy to dismiss *Lucile* as yet another of the countless texts produced for the fast-paced musical-literary market of the 1830s. The plot line appears simplistic, featuring tried and tested clichés, such as the singer as a public figure and coveted object for an admiring male audience, the impossible love affair and the parental taboo, the singer's atonement and eventual happy ending—all narrated in a sentimental, confessional style. Lucile displays the archetypal ambivalence of the woman artist on the margins of society, through her mixed Franco-German heritage and her ambiguous place within society. Entrusting her written life story to a French doctor, Saindal, whom she meets while living in seclusion in Greece, Lucile recounts her rise as a woman musician of extraordinary talent. Both fêted and shunned for her art, Lucile develops a strong, confident artistic identity. Her assertiveness, however, turns into an existential problem when she falls in love with the aristocrat Charles, which relegates her to the position of a social pariah and in turn compromises her existence as an artist:

> I had hated my profession, feared the glitter, success, the praises; I would have wanted, at whatever cost, to be the unknown, modest young girl who alone had the right to claim Charles' love; and all of a sudden, a few words, spoken as a joke change my desire, my resolution. Thrown back into my realm from which I know I could never escape, all the pride

about myself and my talent seizes me; the desire for prominence takes hold of me again and, if I am not the woman one respects silently, I want to be the woman whom one admires and envies noisily; but still, I have but one goal: to be the object of envy of Charles' happiness.[30]

As this quotation shows, the question of morality and decency is once more an area of contention for this woman singer, as it was in *Corinne* and *Emmeline* and, to a lesser extent, in *The Prima donna*, and—by extension—the question about her place in society, the validity of her art practice, and finally, her possibility to find happiness in love with a man from which her very nature and profession as singer would normally preclude her. Similarly to Staël, Sand and Ulliac, Thellusson depicts musical apprenticeship as a positive type of female legacy which Lucile is openly proud of. As her father fell in love with and married her mother (who was a professional singer herself at the time), Lucile's profession is from the very beginning legitimised within a bourgeois context. The legitimate female lineage from mother to daughter certainly invites comparison with Gina's artistic sisterhood as well as Corinne's legacy, preserved through her niece Juliette and her sister Lucile. Like Ulliac, Thellusson further legitimises her singer and emphasizes her moral purity through the fact that Lucile becomes a professional singer because of her mother's financial ruin and the need to secure an income. However, even Lucile does not entirely escape the problematic status of the woman performer. In the part of her written confession dedicated to her upbringing, she makes a point of describing herself not merely as a singer, but also as an accomplished, morally conscious and idealised multi-talented artist who lives for and through her art, and who does not succumb to emotions or to a volatile life style:

> Music studies had taken up the majority of my time; but loving all art forms, loving education, literature, . . . I had used those moments snatched away from sleep and other distractions to paint, to learn, to study several languages which I knew well. I had the exaltation, dreamy disposition and vibrant sensitivity that give rise to passion, but not to light-hearted feelings.[31]

It is interesting to note the diversity of talents and artistic skills for all of the women musicians discussed so far: an artistic diversity that—by combining female song with the more idealised concept of music itself, as well as with other art forms and with the claim for the "extra" that artistic genius implies—seems to try and attenuate the provocation and the sexualised fantasy which the woman singer alone embodies. From the thorough musical tuition in Germany to Lucile's triumphs in

Italy, the author crafts an entirely positive image of the singer who is both proud of her artistic portfolio and experiences the best aspects of her profession through the public's unanimous, untarnished acclaim and admiration. However, the author characterizes Lucile's singing as a "musical art form," rather than a performative profession: in other words, Lucile is a *musicienne,* not an *actrice.* She exclusively sings in concerts, salons or in upper-class contexts, avoiding being associated with the image of the singer as *actrice* who exposes herself on stage, and as such is perceived as frivolous and immoral.[32]

> Several directors of big theatres in Germany and Italy lobbied my mother so that I would give my debut as an actress; but my mother constantly refused, and, after hearing her motives, on which she insisted, I was entirely of her opinion. She certainly wished for me to sing in public; but she would never give her consent for me to play a role: she gave her consent and desired that I accept an engagement to sing in Italy.[33]

Only when she falls in love, and aspires to a place in society as a wife and mother, does Lucile become aware of the moral ambiguity which surrounds her status as a singer outside respectable society. Madame de Thellusson depicts French society as discriminatory, repressive and wrongly conservative in contrast to the liberal, art-loving Italy where the singer found personal and professional happiness. A stereotypical nod to Italy as the country of poetic utopia and female artistic liberation, the *locus amoenus* of female artistic self-expression, further invites comparison with forerunners such as Goethe's Mignon and Staël's Corinne.

As a singer and as Charles's mistress, Lucile is doubly disqualified from any hypothetical marriage prospects: reminiscent of the parental taboo dramatised in *Corinne*—Charles's mother, her sympathy for the singer notwithstanding—makes it very clear that her son is to marry into a well-situated and decent family. Urged into exile, Lucile falls silent, filling the void of her singing voice with the written account of her life, a preparation for the happy end to come. Inviting further comparison with *Corinne*, the narrator stages Lucile's written confession almost as an echo of Corinne's letter to Oswald, entitled "Histoire de Corinne"—in both cases, the singer's silence and failure to communicate face-to-face filled with a written account acting as a piece of justification and atonement for the female artist. However, in Corinne's case, her written confession is an important key moment in the degradation of her relationship with Oswald, which only serves to accentuate the gradual loss of her vocality and her transformation from a predominantly oral artist of genius to a "fragmented" artist-in-writing when she loses her gift to improvise and unsuccessfully jots down isolated thoughts in her "Fragments et pensées de Corinne." In Lucile's case, the singer's artistic compromise eventually pays off: by substituting her artistic silence with her written life story, and thus by "confessing" herself, Lucile is able to reconnect with Charles, and eventually marry him, albeit at the price of her voice.

Unlike Corinne, Lucile loses neither talent nor voice, but simply makes the conscious choice to cease her performance, symbolically sacrificing her status as a professional singer. The novel's final scene illustrates the symbolic death of the singer rather clearly. When, a few years later, Saindal pays a visit to the couple to witness their marital bliss, he finally hears Lucile sing for the first and last time:

> Inspired by heaven and by love, she sang a song. It was neither a grand aria nor sophisticated music, but an angelic harmony which I cannot put into words. Charles possessed forever that which he loved, Charles had all his wishes fulfilled; and suddenly he burst into tears, like he'd doubtless never before, he became agitated and seemed close to fainting. "I shall not sing it to you again," said Lucile, who came running to him. To my scolding him about the state to which he exposed himself he replied: "Saindal, music is an ineffable language! There are certain sounds, certain harmonies which, for me, constitute the voice that retells me my entire life: pain, happiness, pleasure, chagrin, that which I lost and which I possess, in one single instant everything is present in my mind."[34]

In a foreboding scene earlier on in the novel, Charles had already called Lucile his "muse." Now, as a wife and mother, and through her conscious retreat from singing, Lucile acquires this longed-for status of muse to her husband, and is henceforth described as the incarnation of music as Charles experiences it. A far cry from her former performances, Lucile's song appears as a sublime harmony that can no longer be described in regular terms. Charles experiences his own transcendence in his wife's song: the ineffable quality of music which, despite its elusive and metaphysical quality, expresses the entirety of his existence. As a wife and mother, Lucile acts as a mouthpiece for her husband, not as a singer in the proper sense who creates and owns her song—let alone performs it publicly. Rather, referring to her written "confession," Lucile affirms that "henceforth my talent is the emptiest page of my story."[35]

Although it certainly leaves much to desire in terms of literary merit, *Lucile, ou la cantatrice* constitutes at least an interesting rewrite of Corinne's dilemma as a performing artist, and, one may speculate, Mme de Thellusson's desire to rewrite Corinne's confession with the aim of reconciling the woman singer with love, and giving her the possibility of domestic happiness. However, as these three case studies from the 1830s clearly show, the sharpness of the conflict which Corinne experiences between, on the one hand, her vocal genius and exceptional status as a woman musician and, on the other, society's norms and expectations does not fade with later texts. In the 1830s, the woman singer still needs to make a choice between two opposing principles, and she needs to make it well. Still, neither choice guarantees her a liveable as well as a satisfying existence that does justice to the exceptional nature of the woman singer.

Notes

1. Key works include Jane Bowers and Judith Tick, eds. *Women Making Music: The Western Art Tradition, 1150–1950* (Urbana/Chicago: University of Illinois Press, 1986); Kimberly Marshall, *Rediscovering the Muses: Women's Musical Traditions* (Boston: Northeastern University Press, 1993); Carol Neuls-Bates, *Women in Music: An Anthology of Source Readings from the Middle Ages to the Present* (Boston: Northeastern University Press, 1996); Karin Pendle, *Women and Music: A History* (Bloomington: Indiana University Press, 2001); Eva Rieger, *Frau und Musik* (Frankfurt: Fischer, 1980); Rieger, *Frau, Musik und Männerherrschaft* (Kassel: Furore-Verlag, 1988); Ruth Solie, ed., *Musicology and Difference: Gender and Sexuality in Music Scholarship* (Berkeley: University of California Press, 1993).

2. See, for instance, Rupert Christiansen, *Prima Donna: A History* (London: Bodley Head, 1984); Isabelle Putnam Emerson, *Five Centuries of Women Singers* (Westport, CT: Greenwood Publishing Group, 2005); Susan Rutherford, *The Prima Donna and Opera, 1815–1930* (Cambridge: Cambridge University Press, 2006).

3. Key works include Béatrice Didier, *La Musique des Lumières* (Paris: Presses Universitaires de France, 1985); Didier, "Le Mythe musical dans le texte littéraire des Lumières au Romantisme: du mythe de la musique au mythe du musicien," in *Le Mythe en littérature: Essais offerts à Pierre Brunel à l'occasion de son soixantième anniversaire* (Paris: Presses Universitaires de France, 2000), 81–94; Francis Claudon, *La Musique des romantiques* (Paris: Presses Universitaires de France, 1992); Jean-Louis Backès, *Musique et littérature. Essai de poétique comparée* (Paris: Presses Universitaires de France, 1994); Michel Delon, "La Musique dans le roman, de *La Nouvelle Héloïse* à *Corinne*," in *L'Art du roman. L'Art dans le roman*, eds. Thomas Hunkeler, Sylvie Jeanneret, and Martin Rizek (Bern: Lang, 2000), 23–36; Christine Lubkoll, *Mythos Musik. Poetische Entwürfe des Musikalischen in der Literatur um 1800* (Freiburg im Breisgau: Rombach, 1995); Corinna Caduff, *Die Literarisierung von Musik und bildender Kunst um 1800* (München: Fink, 2003); Steven Paul Scher, *Literatur und Musik* (Berlin: Erich Schmidt, 1984).

4. Joseph-Marc Bailbé, *Le Roman et la musique en France sous la monarchie de juillet* (Paris: Minard, 1969); Jacques Barzun and Peter Bloom, *Music in Paris in the Eighteen-Thirties: La Musique à Paris dans les années mil huit cent trente* (Stuyvesant, NY: Pendragon Press, 1987); Jean Mongrédien, *La Musique en France, des Lumières au Romantisme, 1789–1830* (Paris: Flammarion, 1986); David Tunley, *Music in the 19th-Century Parisian Salon* (Armidale, N.S.W.: University of New England, Armidale, 1997); Tunley, *Salons, Singers and Songs: A Background to Romantic French Song 1830–1870* (Aldershot: Ashgate, 2002); William Weber, *Music and the Middle Class: The Social Structure of Concert Life in London, Paris and Vienna* (Aldershot: Ashgate, 2004).

5. Christine Battersby, *Gender and Genius: Towards a Feminist Aesthetics* (London: Women's Press, 1989); Corinna Caduff and Siegrid Weigel, *Das Geschlecht der Künste* (Köln: Böhlau, 1996); Freia Hoffmann, *Instrument und Körper. Die musizierende Frau in der bürgerlichen Kultur* (Frankfurt: Insel, 1992); Nancy Reich, "Women as Musicians: A Question of Class," in *Musicology and Difference*, 125–46; Julie Anne Sadie, "*Musiciennes* of the Ancien Régime," in *Women Making Music*, 191–223.

6. See Matthew Head, "Birdsong and the Origins of Music," *Journal of the Royal Musical Association* 122, no. 1 (1997): 1–23; Didier, *La Musique des Lumières*, 111–27; Downing Thomas, *Music and the Origins of Language: Theories from the French Enlightenment* (Cambridge: Cambridge University Press, 1995), 34–56. Rousseau's *Essay on the Origin of Languages* was published posthumously in 1781, but had been conceptualized in different variations from the 1750s onwards, starting with his *Letter on French Music* and his attack on Rameau and French singing. See Jean Starobinski's introduction in Rousseau, *Œuvres complètes*, eds. B. Gagnebin and M. Raymond (Paris: Gallimard, 1969), 5:clxv–cciv. Pre-Rousseauian thought understood music in mathematical, rational terms, less as an expression of the human heart and soul than a "géométrie musicale" (Claude Jamain, *L'Imaginaire de la musique au siècle des Lumières* [Paris: Honoré Champion, 2003], 67–69). Rousseau's musical imagery must obviously also be seen in the light of the eighteenth-century musical disputes and the author's preference of Italian over French music (see Henri Coulet, ed. *Julie ou la nouvelle Héloïse* [Paris: Gallimard, 1993], 185).

7. Amongst the many German authors describing music as a feminine principle and music as an art form belonging to woman, Hegel's *Ästhetik*, Jean Paul's *Levana*, Humboldt's *Geschlechtscharakter*, Caroline de la Motte Fouqué's *Die Frauen in der großen Welt* as well as Novalis's *Schriften* must be mentioned here.

8. See Harmut Steinecke, "Die Liebe des Künstlers. Männer-Phantasien und Frauen-Bilder bei E. T. A. Hoffmann," in *Codierungen der Liebe in der Kunstperiode*, ed. Walter Hinderer (Würzburg: Königshausen & Neumann, 1997), 303–08.

9. See David Gramit, *Cultivating Music: The Aspirations, Interests and Limits of German Musical Culture, 1770–1848* (Berkeley: University of California Press, 2002), 113ff; Bonnie Anderson and Judith Zinsser, *A History of Their Own: Women in Europe from Prehistory to the Present* (London: Penguin, 1990). Abraham Mendelssohn's advice to his daughter Fanny is well known: "You must train more ambitiously and more thoroughly for your true profession, the only profession that exists for a girl: that of housewife" (Sebastian Hensel, *Die Familie Mendelssohn, 1729–1847: Nach Briefen und Tagebüchern* [Leipzig: Insel, 1924], 115–16); my translation.

10. In addition, Corinne is likened to the Cumaean Sybil, which implies her potential as a prophetess and oracle.

11. For a discussion of the similarities between Corinne and Mignon as singer archetypes, see my thesis "The Woman Singer and Her Song in French and German Prose Fiction, 1780–1848" (PhD diss., Oxford, 2009).

12. As Tili Boon Cuillé pertinently points out, the precariousness of Corinne's public opera performance, in the socio-cultural and aesthetic context of the time, cannot be ignored as the woman musician remained a controversial figure during Staël's time: "Women Performing Music: Staging a Social Protest," *Women in French Studies* 8 (2000): 40–54. On Corinne as a musical character, see also Cuillé, *Narrative Interludes: Musical Tableaux in Eighteenth-Century French Texts* (Toronto: University of Toronto Press, 2006), 184–203.

13. For an excellent study of the public perception of female stage performers, see Lenard Berlanstein, *Daughters of Eve: A Cultural History of French Theater Women from the Old Regime to the Fin-de-siècle* (Cambridge, MA: Harvard University Press, 2001).

14. See Paul Scudo, *Critique et littérature musicales: Première et deuxième séries*. Preface by François Lesure (Genève: Minkoff, 1986).

15. Balzac's singer Clara Tinti in *Massimilla Doni* (1839) must be mentioned, yet Berlioz crafts a rather intriguing, strong singer, Mina, who defies the patriarchal order in his futuristic novella *Euphonia, ou la ville musicale* (1844).

16. George [Jules] Sand, *La Prima Donna*, Revue de Paris 25 (April 1831), 248 (in the absence of official English editions of the texts discussed, all translations are my own). This music novella, though among the lesser-known works of Sand, is an interesting precursor to her *opus summum* of the woman singer, *Consuelo/La Comtesse de Rudolstadt* (1842/43).

17. Sand, *Prima Donna*, 237, 247. Sand frequently uses religious imagery to refer to the sacredness of the art form and its performers, calling Pauline Viardot "the priestess of the ideal in music" who must preach true music to the world (George Sand, *Correspondance*, ed. Georges Lubin [Paris: Garnier, 1964–1995], 5:705).

18. Sand, *Prima Donna*, 238.

19. Staël, *Corinne, or Italy*, ed. and trans. Avriel Goldberger (New Brunswick, NJ: Rutgers University Press, 1987), 356; *Corinne, ou l'Italie*, ed. Simone Balayé (Paris: Gallimard Folio, 1985), 473.

20. Sand, *Prima Donna*, 242–43.

21. Ibid., 239–40.

22. Ibid., 248.

23. As a contralto, Rosetta unites both male and female vocal traits, and forebodes Sand's other great singer to come, Consuelo.

24. Sophie Ulliac-Trémadeure, *Emmeline, ou la jeune musicienne* forms part of her *Contes aux jeunes artistes* (Paris: Didier, 1836).

25. For excellent studies on the limitations and difficulties of female music teaching, see Freia Hoffmann, "Institutionelle Ausbildungsmöglichkeiten für Musikerinnen in der ersten Hälfte des 19. Jahrhunderts," in *Von der Spielfrau zur Performance-Künstlerin. Auf der Suche nach einer Musikgeschichte der Frauen*, eds. Freia Hoffmann and Eva Rieger (Kassel: Furore, 1993), 77–91; Hoffmann

and Rieger, *Instrument und Körper*; and Nancy Reich, "Women as Musicians: A Question of Class," in *Musicology and Difference*, 125–46.

26. Ulliac-Trémadeure, *Emmeline*, 370.

27. Ibid., 148. By depicting Emmeline's mother as so blatantly opposed to a career on stage and horrified at the prospect of male admirers and their obvious sexual interest in Emmeline, Ulliac furthermore comments on another stereotypical figure of her time, namely pushy mothers wanting their daughters to succeed on stage and acquire a wealthy lover for financial security. See for example L. Couailhac, "La Mère d'actrice," in *Les Français peints par eux-mêmes. Encyclopédie morale du dix-neuvième siècle* (Paris: L. Curmer, 1841), 1:75–89.

28. Ulliac-Trémadeure, *Emmeline*, 378–79.

29. For further reading on this subject, see Lise Queffélec, *Le Roman-feuilleton français au XIXe siècle* (Paris: Presses Universitaires de France, 1989); Patrick Berthier, *La Presse littéraire et dramatique au début de la Monarchie de Juillet (1830–1836)* (Villeneuve d'Ascq: Presses Universitaires du Septentrion, 1997). Théophile Gautier took a notably critical stance towards the bourgeois obsession with all things artistic during his time "where literature and society are topsy-turvy and where the life of the artist and of the man of the world seem perpetually interchangeable" [où la littérature et la société sont dans un tel pêle-mêle, et où la vie d'artiste et celle de l'homme du monde semblent perpétuellement s'échanger] (*Revue des deux mondes*, 15.09.1840; cited in Anne Martin-Fugier, *Les Romantiques: figures de l'artiste, 1820–1848* [Paris: Hachette, 1998], 229). He similarly expressed in his "Excès d'artiste": "The green-grocer no longer exists. The artist killed him! . . . What a surfeit of arts, of artists, and of artistic things!" [L'épicier n'existe plus. C'est l'artiste qui l'a tué. . . . Quel déluge d'arts, d'artistes et de choses artistiques!] (*Le Figaro* 25, no. 4, 1837).

30. Madame de Thellusson, *Lucile, ou la cantatrice* (Paris: Fournier jeune, 1833), 1:98.

31. Ibid., 1:25–26.

32. With regards to terminology for women performers, see Ingrid Arthur, "Le Mot cantatrice dans la langue française," *Studia Neophilologica: A Journal of Germanic and Romance Languages and Literature* 38 (1966), 65–75; Marian Smith, "Poésie lyrique" and "Chorégraphie' at the Opéra in the July Monarchy," *Cambridge Opera Journal*, 4, no. 1 (March 1992), 1–19; Cuillé, "Women Performing Music," 42, 51.

33. Thellusson, *Lucile*, 1:23–24.

34. Ibid., 2:143–45.

35. Ibid., 1:148.

Abrams, M. H. "The Correspondent Breeze: A Romantic Metaphor." *The Kenyon Review* 19, no. 1 (1957): 113–30.

Allard, Sebastien, et al. *Citizens and Kings: Portraits in the Age of Revolution, 1760–1830*. London: Royal Academy of the Arts, 2007. An exhibition catalog.

Alliston, April. "Transnational Sympathies, Imaginary Communities." In *The Literary Channel: The Inter-National Invention of the Novel*, edited by Margaret Cohen and Carolyn Dever, 133–48. Princeton, NJ: Princeton University Press, 2002.

Althaus, Frank, and Mark Sutcliffe. *France in Russia: Empress Josephine's Malmaison Collection*. London: Fontanka, 2007. An exhibition catalog.

Amend-Söchting, Anne. "La Mélancolie dans *Corinne*." In *Madame de Staël, Corinne ou l'Italie, "l'âme se mêle à tout,"* edited by José-Luis Diaz, 101–10. Paris: SEDES, 1999.

Anderson, Bonnie and Judith Zinsser. *A History of Their Own: Women in Europe from Prehistory to the Present*. London: Penguin, 1990.

Andlau, Béatrix D'. *La Jeunesse de Madame de Staël, de 1766 à 1786, avec des documents inédits*. Geneva: Droz, 1970.

Arendt, Hannah. *On Revolution*. New York: Viking Press, 1963.

Aron, Raymond. *Main Currents in Sociological Thought*. 2 vols. Garden City, NY: Anchor Books, 1968.

Arthur, Ingrid. "Le Mot cantatrice dans la langue française." *Studia Neophilologica: A Journal of Germanic and Romance Languages and Literature* 38 (1966): 65–75.

Atkinson, Paul. *Understanding Ethnographic Texts*. Newbury Park, CA: Sage Publications, 1992.

Auricchio, Laura. *Adélaïde Labille–Guiard: Artist in the Age of Revolution*. Los Angeles: J. P. Getty Museum, 2009.

Avitabile, Grazia. *The Controversy in Romanticism in Italy: First Phase 1816–1823*. New York: S. F. Vanni, 1959.

Backès, Jean-Louis. *Musique et littérature. Essai de poétique comparée*. Paris: Presses Universitaires de France, 1994.

Bailbé, Joseph-Marc. *Le Roman et la musique en France sous la Monarchie de Juillet*. Paris: Minard, 1969.

Balayé, Simone. "Fonction romanesque de la musique et des sons dans *Corinne*." *Romantisme* 3 (1972): 17–32.

——. *Madame de Staël: Écrire, lutter, vivre*. Paris: Droz, 1994.

——. "Madame de Staël et Sismondi ou un dialogue critique." *Cahiers staëliens* 8 (1969): 33–43.

——. *Madame de Staël: Lumières et liberté*. Paris: Éditions Klincksieck, 1979.

Balayé, Simone and Esther Renfrew. "Madame de Staël et la Sibylle du Dominiquin." *Cahiers staëliens* 2 (1964): 34–36.

Baldensperger, Fernand. *Sensibilité musicale et romantisme*. Paris: Presses Universitaires de France, 1925.

Barthes, Roland. "Écoute." *L'Obvie et l'obtus: essais critiques III*. Paris: Seuil, 1982.

——. *Fragments d'un discours amoureux*. In *Œuvres complètes*. Edited by Éric Marty. Vol. 3. Paris: Seuil, 1995.

——. "The Grain of the Voice." In *Image, Music, Text*. Translated by Stephen Heath. New York: Hill-Farrar, 1977.

Barzun, Jacques and Peter Bloom. *Music in Paris in the Eighteen-Thirties: la musique à Paris dans les années mil huit cent trente*. Stuyvesant, NY: Pendragon Press, 1987.

Batsaki, Yota. "Exile as the Inaudible Accent in Germaine de Staël's *Corinne, or Italy*." *Comparative Literature* 61, no. 1 (2009): 26–42.

Battersby, Christine. *Gender and Genius: Towards a Feminist Aesthetics*. Bloomington, IN: Indiana University Press, 1989.

——. *The Sublime, Terror and Human Difference*. New York: Routledge, 2007.

Batteux, Charles. *Les Beaux-Arts réduits à un même principe*. Geneva: Slatkine Reprints, 1969.

Baudelaire, Charles. *Œuvres complètes*. Edited by Claude Pichois. 2 vols. Paris: Gallimard, 1975.

Berger, Morroe, ed. "Introduction." In *Politics, Literature, and National Character*, by Germaine de Staël. Edited and translated by Morroe Berger. New Brunswick, NJ: Transaction Publishers, 2000.

Berlanstein, Lenard. *Daughters of Eve. A Cultural History of French Theater Women from the Old Regime to the Fin-de-siècle*. Cambridge, MA: Harvard University Press, 2001.

Berman, Antoine. *The Experience of the Foreign: Culture and Translation in Romantic Germany*. Translated by S. Heyvaert. Albany: State University of New York Press, 1992.

Berman, Marshall. *The Politics of Authenticity: Radical Individualism and the Emergence of Modern Society*. New York: Atheneum, 1972.

Berthier, Patrick. *La Presse littéraire et dramatique au début de la Monarchie de Juillet (1830–1836)*. Villeneuve d'Ascq: Presses Universitaires du Septentrion, 1997.

Bewell, Alan. "'Jacobin Plants': Botany as Social Theory in the 1790s." *The Wordsworth Circle* 20, no. 3 (1989): 132–39.

——. "Romanticism and Colonial Natural History." *Studies in Romanticism* 43 (Spring 2004): 5–34.

Bézard, Yvonne, *Madame de Staël d'après ses portraits*. Paris: Editions Victor Attinger, 1938.

Birkett, Jennifer. "Speech in Action: Language, Society, and Subject in Germaine de Staël's *Corinne*." *Eighteenth-Century Fiction* 7, no. 4 (July 1995): 393–408.

Black, Jeremy. *The British Abroad: The Grand Tour in the Eighteenth Century*. New York: St. Martin's, 1992.

Blennerhassett, Charlotte Lady. *Madame de Staël: Her Friends and her Influence in Politics and Literature*. 3 vols. London: Chapman and Hall, Ltd., 1889.

Bloch, Thomas. *L'Armonica de verre ou Glassharmonica: données et synthèse historique, organologique, acoustique et bibliographique sur l'instrument de Benjamin Franklin et sur les instruments dérivés*. Paris: Conservatoire National Supérieur de Musique, 1989.

——. *Glass Harmonica*: Mozart, Beethoven, Donizetti, Schulz, Roellig, Naumann, Reichardt, von Holt Sombach, von Apell, Bloch. Naxos, 2001.

Boigne, Éléonore-Adèle d'Osmond Comtesse de. *Récits d'une tante: Mémoires de la Comtesse de Boigne*. Paris: Emile-Paul Frères, 1921.

Bonner, Stephen. *Aeolian Harp. The History and Organology of the Aeolian Harp*. Vol. 2. Cambridge: Bois de Boulogne, 1970.

Bonnet, Jean-Claude. "Le Culte des grands hommes en France au XVIIIe siècle ou la défaite de la monarchie." *Modern Language Notes* 116 (2001): 689–704.

——. "Le Musée staëlien." *Littérature* 42 (May 1981): 4–19.

Boon, Sonja. "Does a Dutiful Wife Write; or, Should Suzanne Get Divorced? Reflections on Suzanne Curchod Necker, Divorce, and the Construction of the Biographical Subject." *Lumen* 27 (2008): 59–73.

——. "Last Rites, Last Rights: Corporeal Abjection as Autobiographical Performance in Suzanne Curchod Necker's *Des inhumations précipitées* (1790)." *Eighteenth-Century Fiction* 21, no. 1 (2008): 89–107.

——. *The Life of Madame Necker: Sin, Redemption and the Parisian Salon*. London: Pickering & Chatto, 2011.

Bouhouch, Souad. "*Corinne ou l'Italie*: Une esthétique d'un savoir tragique." *Cahiers staëliens* 61 (2011): 165–95.

Bowers, Jane, and Judith Tick, eds. *Women Making Music: The Western Art Tradition, 1150–1950*. Urbana/Chicago: University of Illinois Press, 1986.

Bowman, Frank Paul. "Communication and Power in Germaine de Staël: Transparency and Obstacle." In *Germaine de Staël: Crossing the Borders*, edited by Madelyn Gutwirth, Avriel H. Goldberger, and Karyna Szmurlo, 55–68. New Brunswick, NJ: Rutgers University Press, 1991.

——. "*Corinne* et la religion." In *L'Éclat et le silence:* Corinne ou l'Italie *de Madame de Staël*, edited by Simone Balayé, 145–60. Paris: Honoré Champion, 1999.

Bredin, Jean-Denis. *Une singulière famille: Jacques Necker, Suzanne Necker et Germaine de Staël*. Paris: Fayard, 1999.

Britton, Jeanne. "Translating Sympathy by the Letter: Henry Mackenzie, Sophie de Condorcet, and Adam Smith." *Eighteenth-Century Fiction* 22, no. 1 (2009): 71–98.

Brix, Michel. "Les Sources mystiques de *Corinne*: la femme, l'amour et le sacré." In *Mme de Staël: Actes du colloque de la Sorbonne du 20 novembre 1999*, edited by Michel Delon and Françoise Mélonio, 85–97. Paris: Presses de l'Université de Paris-Sorbonne, 2000.

Brooks, Peter. *The Melodramatic Imagination: Balzac, Henry James, Melodrama, and the Mode of Excess*. New Haven, CT: Yale University Press, 1995.

Brousteau, Anne. "L'Éloge de *La Nouvelle Héloïse* de Madame de Staël: Un 'essai sur le roman, considéré du côté moral.'" *Cahiers staëliens* 52 (2001): 95–109.

Brown, Andrew. *Aeolian Harp. The Aeolian Harp in European Literature, 1591–1892*. Vol. 3. Cambridge: Bois de Boulogne, 1970.

Bruin, Karen de. "The Helm and the Compass: The Great Man and the Superior Woman in Germaine de Staël's Republic." In *Héroïsme et Lumières*, edited by Sylvain Menant and Robert Morrissey, 235–50. Paris: Honoré Champion, 2010.

———. "'La Femme supérieure': L'individu, le roman et la république de Germaine de Staël." PhD diss., University of Chicago, 2007.

Bruschini, Enrico, and Alba Amoia. "Rome's Monuments and Artistic Treasures in Mme de Staël's *Corinne* (1807): Then and Now." *Nineteenth-Century French Studies* 22, nos. 3/4 (Spring–Summer 1994): 311–47.

Buffon, Georges-Louis Leclerc Comte de. *Histoire naturelle des oiseaux.* 9 vols. Paris: L'Imprimerie Royale, 1770–1783.

———. "Plan de l'ouvrage," *Histoire naturelle des oiseaux.* 3 vols. Paris: L'Imprimeur Royal, 1770.

Bunce, Nigel, and Jim Hunt. "The Glass Harmonica." *The Science Corner.* College of Physical Science, University of Guelph, March 29, 1989.

Burton, June K. *Napoleon and the Woman Question: Discourses of the Other Sex in French Education, Medicine, and Medical Law 1799–1815.* Lubbock: Texas Tech University Press, 2007.

Caduff, Corinna. *Die Literarisierung von Musik und bildender Kunst um 1800.* München: Fink, 2003.

Caduff, Corinna, and Siegrid Weigel. *Das Geschlecht der Künste.* Köln: Böhlau, 1996.

Candaux, Jean-Daniel, and Norman King. "La Correspondance de Benjamin Constant et de Sismondi, 1801–1830," *Annales Benjamin Constant* 1 (1980): 82–171.

———. "Théâtre et société, la correspondance des Staël et des Odier, 1806–1817." *Cahiers staëliens* 38 (1987): 1–111.

Caplan, Jay. *Framed Narratives: Diderot's Genealogy of the Beholder.* Minneapolis: University of Minnesota Press, 1985.

Casillo, Robert. *The Empire of Stereotypes: Germaine de Staël and the Idea of Italy.* New York: Palgrave Macmillan, 2006.

Cassirer, Ernst. *Language and Myth.* Translated by Susanne K. Langer. New York: Dover Publications, 1953.

Chabanon, Michel-Paul-Guy de. *De la musique considérée en elle-même et dans ses rapports avec la parole, les langues, la poésie et le théâtre.* Paris: Chez Pissot, 1785.

Chalier, Catherine. *Traité des larmes: Fragilité de Dieu, fragilité de l'âme.* Paris: Albin Michel, 2003.

Chamberlain, Lori. "Gender and the Metaphorics of Translation." *Signs: Journal of Women in Culture and Society* 13, no. 3 (1988): 454–72.

Chastellux, François-Jean de. *Essai sur l'union de la poésie et de la musique* (1765). Genève: Slatkine Reprints, 1970.

Chateaubriand, François René, vicomte de. *Essai sur les Révolutions. Génie du Christianisme.* Edited by Maurice Regard. Paris: Gallimard, 1978.

———. *Mémoires d'outre-tombe.* Edited by Maurice Levaillant and Georges Moulinier. 2 vols. Paris: Gallimard, 1951.

———. *Les Natchez.* Edited by Gilbert Chinard. Baltimore: The John Hopkins University Press, 1932.

———. *Vie de Rancé.* Edited by George Condominas. Paris: Flammarion, 1991.

Chevallier, Bernard. "Le Salon de la musique de Malmaison." *La Revue du Louvre et des musées de France* 48, no. 4 (October 1998): 59–63.

Chevallier, Bernard, and Christophe Pincemaille. *L'Impératrice Joséphine.* Paris: Presses de la Renaissance, 1998.

Christiansen, Rupert. *Prima Donna: A History.* London: Bodley Head, 1984.

Clarke, Norma. *Ambitious Heights: Writing, Friendship, Love—The Jewsbury Sisters, Felicia Hemans and Jane Welsh Carlyle*. London: Routledge, 1990.

Claudon, Francis. *La Musique des romantiques*. Paris: Presses Universitaires de France, 1992.

——. "Women Performing Music: Staging a Social Protest," *Women in French Studies* 8 (2000): 40–54.

Clifford, James and George E. Marcus, eds. *Writing Culture: The Poetics and Politics of Ethnography*. Berkeley: University of California Press, 1986.

Cohen, Margaret. "Melancholia, Mania, and the Reproduction of the Dead Father." In *The Novel's Seductions: Staël's* Corinne *in Critical Inquiry*, edited by Karyna Szmurlo, 95–113. Lewisburg, PA: Bucknell University Press, 1999.

——. "Sentimental Communities." In *The Literary Channel: The Inter-National Invention of the Novel*, edited by Margaret Cohen and Carolyn Dever, 106–32. Princeton, NJ: Princeton University Press, 2002.

Conisbee, Philip. *Painting in Eighteenth-Century France*. Ithaca, NY: Cornell University Press, 1981.

Connolly, Claire. "'I Accuse Miss Owenson': *The Wild Irish Girl* as Media Event." *Colby Quarterly* 36, no. 2 (2000): 98–115.

——. "Introduction: The Politics of Love in *The Wild Irish Girl*." In *The Wild Irish Girl*, by Sydney Owenson, xxv–lxvi. London: Pickering and Chatto, 2000.

Craiutu, Aurelian. *A Virtue for Courageous Minds: Moderation in French Political Thought, 1748–1830*. Princeton, NJ: Princeton University Press, 2012.

——. "Moderation and the Groupe de Coppet." In *Germaine de Staël: Forging a Politics of Mediation*, edited by Karyna Szmurlo, 109–24. Oxford: Voltaire Foundation, 2011.

Crow, Thomas. *Emulation: Making Artists for Revolutionary France*. New Haven, CT: Yale University Press, 1995.

Crummy, M. Ione. "Le Barde féminin comme génie national: *The Wild Irish Girl* de Sydney Owenson, un modèle de *Corinne ou l'Italie* de Mme de Staël." *Cahiers staëliens* 59 (2008): 79–95.

Cuillé, Tili Boon. *Narrative Interludes: Musical Tableaux in Eighteenth-Century French Texts*. Toronto: Toronto University Press, 2006.

——. "Revoicing Rousseau: Staël's *Corinne* and the Song of the South." In *Phrase and Subject: Studies in Literature and Music*, edited by Delia Da Sousa Correa, 100–111. Oxford: Legenda, 2006.

——. "Women Performing Music: Staging a Social Protest," *Women in French Studies* 8 (2000): 40–54.

D'Arbitrio, Nicoletta and Luigi Ziviello. *Carolina Murat: La Regina Francese del Regno delle Due Sicilie. Le Architetture, La Moda, L'Office de la Bouche*. Naples: Savarese, 2003.

Davis, John A. *Naples and Napoleon. Southern Italy and the European Revolutions, 1780–1860*. Oxford: Oxford University Press, 2006.

DeJean, Joan. *Ancients Against Moderns: Culture Wars and the Making of a Fin de Siècle*. Chicago: University of Chicago Press, 1997.

——. *Fictions of Sappho, 1546–1937*. Chicago: University of Chicago Press, 1989.

——. "Portrait of the Artist as Sappho." In *Germaine de Staël: Crossing the Borders*, edited by Madelyn Gutwirth, Avriel Goldberger, and Karyna Szmurlo, 122–37. New Brunswick, NJ: Rutgers University Press, 1991.

——. "Staël's *Corinne*: The Novel's Other Dilemma." In *The Novel's Seductions: Staël's Corinne in Critical Inquiry*, edited by Karyna Szmurlo, 117–26. Lewisburg, PA: Bucknell University Press, 1999.

Delon, Michel. "Du vague staëlien des passions." In *Mme de Staël: Actes du colloque de la Sorbonne du 20 novembre 1999*, edited by Michel Delon and François Mélonio, 75–83. Paris: Presses de l'Université de Paris–Sorbonne, 2000.

——. "La Musique dans le roman, de *La Nouvelle Héloïse* à *Corinne*." In *L'Art du roman. L'Art dans le roman*, edited by Thomas Hunkeler, Sylvie Jeanneret, and Martin Rizek, 23–36. Bern: Lang, 2000.

DeLorme, Eleanor P., ed. *Joséphine and the Arts of the Empire*. Los Angeles: J. Paul Getty Museum, 2005.

——. *Joséphine: Napoléon's Incomparable Empress*. New York: Harry N. Abrams, 2002.

Denby, David. *Sentimental Narrative and the Social Order in France, 1760–1820*. Cambridge: Cambridge University Press, 1994.

Deneys-Tunney, Anne. "*Corinne* by Madame de Staël: The Utopia of Feminine Voice as Music within the Novel," *Dalhousie French Studies* 28 (Fall 1994): 55–63.

Denoyelle, Martine and Sophie Descamps-Lequime. *The Eye of Josephine: The Antiquities Collection of the Empress in the Musée de Louvre*. Atlanta: High Museum, 2007. An exhibition catalog.

Derrida, Jacques. "The Law of Genre." Translated by Avital Ronell. *Critical Inquiry* 7, no. 1 (Autumn 1980): 55–81.

——. *Memoirs of the Blind: The Self-Portrait and Other Ruins*. Translated by Pascale-Anne Braule and Michael Naas. Chicago: Chicago University Press, 1993.

Diderot, Denis. *Éloge de Richardson*. In *Œuvres*, edited by André Billy. Paris: Gallimard, Bibliothèque de la Pléiade, 1946.

——. *Éloge de Richardson*. In *Œuvres*, edited by Laurent Versini. Vol. 4. Paris: Robert Laffont, 1996.

——. *Entretiens sur le fils naturel*. In *Œuvres*, edited by André Billy. Paris: Gallimard, Bibliothèque de la Pléiade, 1946.

——. *Ruines et paysages: Salons de 1767*. Edited by Else Marie Bukdahl, Michel Delon, and Annette Lorenceau. Paris: Hermann, 1995.

——. *Selected Writings on Art and Literature*. Translated by Geoffrey Bremner. London: Penguin, 1994.

Didier, Béatrice. *La Musique des Lumières. Diderot. L'Encyclopédie. Rousseau*. Paris: Presses Universitaires de France, 1985.

——. "Le Mythe musical dans le texte littéraire des Lumières au Romantisme: du mythe de la musique au mythe du musicien." In *Le Mythe en littérature: essais offerts à Pierre Brunel à l'occasion de son soixantième anniversaire*, edited by Yves Chevrel and Camille Dumoulié, 81–94. Paris: Presses Universitaires de France, 2000.

Dissanayake, Ellen. *Homo Aestheticus: Where Art Comes From and Why*. Seattle: University of Washington Press, 1995.

Dixon, W. Hepworth, ed. *Lady Morgan's Memoirs: Autobiography, Diaries and Correspondence*. 2 vols. London: William H. Allen & Co., 1862.

Dolan, Emily I. "E. T. A. Hoffmann and the Ethereal Technologies of 'Nature Music.'" *Eighteenth-Century Music* 5, no. 1 (2008): 7–26.

Doy, Gen. *Women and Visual Culture in 19th–Century France, 1800–1852*. New York: Leicester University Press, 1998.

Dubeau, Catherine. "L'Homme féroce: passions, violence et limites de l'invention littéraire dans *De la littérature* de Germaine de Staël." In *Littérature et invention chez Madame de Staël*, edited by Marc André Bernier, 107–30. Québec: PUL, 2011.

———. "La Lettre et la mère: Roman familial et écriture de la passion chez Suzanne Necker (1737–1794) et Germaine de Staël (1766–1817)." PhD diss., Université Laval, 2007.

———. "Des livres et des hommes: Suzanne Necker lectrice." *Cahiers staëliens* 58 (2007): 13–24.

———. "L'Épreuve du salon ou le monde comme performance dans les *Mélanges* et les *Nouveaux mélanges* de Suzanne Necker." *Cahiers staëliens* 57 (2006): 201–25.

———. "Mrs Spectator: Journal, comptes moraux et tyrannie de l'introspection dans les *Mélanges* et les *Nouveaux mélanges* de Suzanne Necker." In *Influences et modèles étrangers sous l'Ancien Régime*, edited by Virginie Dufresne and Geneviève Langlois, 145–58. Québec: Presses de l'Université Laval, 2009.

Effertz, Julia. "The Woman Singer and Her Song in French and German Prose Fiction, 1780–1848." PhD diss., Oxford, 2009.

Ellis, Markman. *The Politics of Sensibility*. Cambridge: Cambridge University Press, 1996.

Emerson, Isabelle Putnam. *Five Centuries of Women Singers*. Westport, CT: Greenwood Publishing Group, 2005.

Encyclopédie, ou dictionnaire raisonné des sciences, des arts et des métiers, par une société de gens de lettres. Edited by Denis Diderot and Jean Le Rond D'Alembert. 35 vols. Stuttgart: Friedrich Frommann Verlag, 1966–1967.

Encyclopédie, ou dictionnaire raisonné des sciences, des arts et des métiers, etc., eds. Denis Diderot and Jean le Rond D'Alembert. University of Chicago: ARTFL Encyclopédie Project (Spring 2011 edition), Robert Morrissey (ed), http://encyclopedie.uchicago.edu/.

Encyclopedia of Diderot & d'Alembert Collaborative Translation Project. Ann Arbor, MI: MPublishing, University of Michigan Library, 2002. http://quod.lib.umich.edu/d/did/.

Erickson, Carolly. *Josephine: A Life of the Empress*. New York: St. Martin's, 1999.

Esterhammer, Angela. "The Cosmopolitan *Improvvisatore*: Spontaneity and Performance in Romantic Poetics." *European Romantic Review* 16, no. 2 (April 2005): 153–65.

———. *Romanticism and Improvisation, 1750–1850*. Cambridge: Cambridge University Press, 2009.

Explications des ouvrages de peinture, sculpture, architecture et gravure des artistes vivans, exposés au Musée Napoléon. . . . Paris: Imprimeur du Musée Napoléon, 1808.

Fabvre, Lucien. "La Sensibilité et l'histoire: Comment reconstituer la vie affective d'autrefois?" *Annales d'histoire sociale* 3 (January–June 1941): 5–20.

Fairweather, Maria. *Madame de Staël*. New York: Carroll and Graf, 2005.

Fars Fausselandry, vicomtesse de. *Mémoires de Madame la vicomtesse de Fars Fausselandry, ou Souvenirs d'une octogénaire*. 3 vols. Paris: Ledoyen, 1830.

Feldman, Paula. "The Poet and the Profits: Felicia Hemans and the Literary Marketplace." *Keats-Shelley Journal* 46 (1997): 148–76.

Ferris, Ina. *The Romantic National Tale and the Question of Ireland*. Cambridge: Cambridge University Press, 2002.

Festa, Lynn. *Sentimental Figures of Empire in Eighteenth-Century Britain and France*. Baltimore: Johns Hopkins University Press, 2006.

Finger, Stanley and David Gallo. "The Music of Madness: Franklin's Armonica and the Vulnerable Nervous System." In *Neurology of the Arts: Painting, Music, Literature*, edited by Frank Clifford Rose, 207–35. London: Imperial College Press, 2004.

Fitzpatrick, William J. *Lady Morgan: Her Career, Literary and Personal*. London: Charles J. Skeet, 1860.

Fontana, Biancamaria. "Madame de Staël, le gouvernement des passions et la Révolution française." In *Le Groupe de Coppet et la Révolution française. Actes du quatrième colloque de Coppet, 20–23 juillet 1988*, edited by Étienne Hofmann and Anne–Lise Delacrétaz, 175–81. Lausanne-Paris: Institut Benjamin Constant-Jean Touzot, 1988.

Franklin, Caroline. "Romantic Patriotism as Feminist Critique of Empire: Helen Maria Williams, Sydney Owenson and Germaine de Staël." In *Women, Gender and Enlightenment*, edited by Sarah Knott and Barbara Taylor, 551–64. Basingstoke: Palgrave Macmillan, 2005.

Fried, Michael. *Absorption and Theatricality: Painting and Beholder in the Age of Diderot*. Chicago: University of Chicago Press, 1980.

"Gabriel Byrne and the Art of Listening." Narr. Terry Gross. *Fresh Air*. Natl. Public Radio. WHYY, Philadelphia, April 30, 2009. Radio.

Genette, Gérard. *Narrative Discourse: An Essay in Method*. Translated by Jane E. Lewin. Ithaca, NY: Cornell University Press, 1983.

Gengembre, Gérard. *Le Romantisme en France et en Europe*. Paris: Pocket, 2003.

Genlis, Stéphanie-Félicité Comtesse de. *Hortense, or the Victim of Novels and Travels*. Translated by Archibald Haralson. Georgetown, DC: Richards and Mallory, 1813.

Gennari, Geneviève. *Le Premier voyage de Madame de Staël en Italie et la genèse de* Corinne. Paris: Boivin, 1947.

Gidal, Eric. "Civic Melancholy: English Gloom and French Enlightenment." *Eighteenth-Century Studies* 37, no. 1 (2003): 23–45.

———. "Melancholy, Trauma and National Character: Mme de Staël's *Considérations sur les principaux événements de la Révolution française*." *Studies in Romanticism* 49, no. 2 (Summer 2010): 261–92.

———. "Mme de Staël and the Sociology of Melancholy." In *The English Malady: Enabling and Disabling Fictions*, edited by Glen Colburn, 20–40. Newcastle upon Tyne: Cambridge Scholars Publishing, 2008.

Gillett, Eric. *Maria Jane Jewsbury: Occasional Papers. Selected, with a Memoir*. London: Oxford University Press, 1932.

Girard, Marie-Hélène. "Corinne collectionneur, ou le musée imaginaire de Madame de Staël." *Art et littérature*, 241–61. Aix-en-Provence: Université de Provence, 1988.

Giuli, Paola. "Poetry and National Identity: *Corinne*, Corilla, and the Idea of Italy." In *Germaine de Staël: Forging a Politics of Mediation*, edited by Karyna Szmurlo, 213–32. Oxford: Voltaire Foundation, 2011.

Goldberger, Avriel. "Introduction." In *Corinne, or Italy*, by Germaine de Staël, xv–liv. New Brunswick, NJ and London: Rutgers University Press, 1987.

Goldschmidt, Victor. *Anthropologie et politique: les principes du système de Rousseau*. Paris: Vrin, 1974.

Goodden, Angelica. *Madame de Staël: The Dangerous Exile*. Oxford: Oxford University Press, 2008.

Goodman, Dena. *The Republic of Letters: A Cultural History of the French Enlightenment*. Ithaca: Cornell University Press, 1994.

———. "*Le Spectateur intérieur*: Les journaux de Suzanne Necker." *Littérales* 17 (1995): 91–100.

———. "Suzanne Necker's *Mélanges*: Gender, Writing, and Publicity." In *Going Public: Women and Publishing in Early Modern France*, edited by Elizabeth C. Goldsmith and Dena Goodman, 210–23. Ithaca: Cornell University Press, 1995.

Gould, Cecil. *Trophy of Conquest: The Musée Napoléon and the Creation of the Louvre*. London: Faber and Faber, 1965.

Gramit, David. *Cultivating Music: The Aspirations, Interests and Limits of German Musical Culture, 1770–1848*. Berkeley: University of California Press, 2002.

Gray, Francine du Plessix. *Madame de Staël: The First Modern Woman*. New York; London: Atlas, 2008.

Grigson, Geoffrey. *The Harp of Aeolus and Other Essays on Art, Literature & Nature*. London: Routledge, 1947.

Grouchy, Sophie Marie Louise de, marquise de Condorcet. *Lettres sur la sympathie; suivies des Lettres d'amour*. Montreal: Étincelle, 1994.

Gueniffey, Patrice. *Le Dix-huit brumaire: L'épilogue de la Révolution française*. Paris: Gallimard, 2008.

Guerlac, Suzanne. "Madame de Staël et le discours féminin de la 'civilisation universelle.'" *Cahiers staëliens* 57 (2006): 77–88.

Guigoud-Pigalle, Pierre. *Le Banquet magnétique, comédie, en vers et en deux actes*. Londres [i.e., Lyons], 1784.

Gutwirth, Madelyn. "Forging a Vocation: Germaine de Staël on Fiction, Power, and Passion." *Bulletin of Research in the Humanities* 86 (1983–85): 242–54.

———. *Madame de Staël, Novelist: The Emergence of the Artist as Woman*. Urbana: University of Illinois Press, 1978.

———. "Madame de Staël, Rousseau, and the Woman Question." *PMLA* 86, no. 1 (1971): 100–09.

———. "Nature, cruauté et femmes immolées: Les *Réflexions sur le procès de la reine*." In *Le Groupe de Coppet et la Révolution française*, edited by Etienne Hofmann and Anne-Lise Delacrétaz. Paris: Touzot, 1988.

———. "Woman as Mediatrix: From Jean–Jacques Rousseau to Germaine de Staël." In *Woman as Mediatrix: Essays on Nineteenth–Century European Women Writers*, edited by Avriel H. Goldberger, 12–29. New York: Greenwood Press, 1987.

Gutwirth, Madelyn, Avriel Goldberger, and Karyna Szmurlo, eds. *Germaine de Staël: Crossing the Borders*. New Brunswick, NJ: Rutgers University Press, 1991.

Hadlock, Heather. *Mad Loves: Women and Music in Offenbach's Les Contes d'Hoffmann*. Princeton, NJ: Princeton University Press, 2000.

———. "Sonorous Bodies: Women and the Glass Harmonica." *Journal of the American Musicological Society* 53 (2000): 506–42.

Hamilton, Alexander, John Jay, and James Madison. *The Federalist Papers*. Edited by George W. Carey and James McClellan. Indianapolis: Liberty Fund, 2001.

Hamilton, Sir William, ed. *The Collected Works of Dugald Stewart*. 11 vols. Edinburgh: Thomas Constable, 1863.

Hankins, Thomas L., and Robert J. Silverman. *Instruments and the Imagination*. Princeton, NJ: Princeton University Press, 1995.

Hannin, Valérie. "Une ambition de femme au siècle des Lumières: le cas de Madame Necker." *Cahiers staëliens* 36 (1985): 5–19.

Haussonville, Gabriel Paul Othenin de Cléron, Comte d'. *Le Salon de Madame Necker, d'après des documents tirés des archives de Coppet*. 2 vols. Geneva: Slatkine Reprints, 1970.

Hawes, Clement. *Mania and Literary Style: The Rhetoric of Enthusiasm from the Ranters to Christopher Smart*. Cambridge: Cambridge University Press, 1996.

Hayley, William. "Epigram on this Question: 'Which Is the more eligible for a Wife, a Widow or an Old Maid?'" In *A Philosophical, Historical, and Moral Essay on Old Maids. By a Friend to the Sisterhood*. London: T. Cadell, 1785.

Head, Matthew. "Birdsong and the Origins of Music." *Journal of the Royal Musical Association* 122, no. 1 (1997): 1–23.

Heidegger, Martin. *Zollikon Seminars Protocols–Conversations–Letters*. Edited by Medard Boss. Evanston, IL: Northwestern University Press, 2001.

Hemans, Felicia, and Dorothea Browne. *Selected Poems, Prose, and Letters*. Edited by Gary Kelley. Peterborough, Ontario: Broadview, 2002.

Hensel, Sebastian. *Die Familie Mendelssohn, 1729–1847: nach Briefen und Tagebüchern*. Leipzig, Insel, 1924.

Herbert, Robert L. *David, Voltaire, Brutus, and the French Revolution: An Essay in Art and Politics*. New York: Viking, 1973.

Herder, Johann Gottfried. "Philosophei und Schwärmerei, zwo Schwestern." In *Sämtliche Werke*, edited by Bernhard Supha. Berlin: Weidmannsche Buchhandlung, 1893.

Herold, J. Christopher. *Mistress to an Age: A Life of Mme de Staël*. New York: Grove Press, 2002.

———. *Mistress to an Age: A Life of Mme de Staël*. Alexandria, VA: Time-Life Books, 1981.

Hersant, Yves. "Une lyre où il manque des cordes." In *Chateaubriand. Le Tremblement du Temps*, edited by Jean-Claude Berchet, 279–88. Toulouse: Presses universitaires du Mirail, 1994.

Heydt–Stevenson, Jill and Jeffrey N. Cox. "Introduction: Are Those Who Are 'Strangers Nowhere in the World' at Home Anywhere: Thinking about Romantic Cosmopolitanism." In *Romantic Cosmopolitanism*. Special Issue of *European Romantic Review* 16, no. 2 (April 2005): 129–40.

Hibbert, Christopher. *Napoleon's Women*. London: W. W. Norton, 2002.

Hoffmann, Bruno. *Music for Glass Harmonica*. Vox Unique, 1990.

Hoffmann, Freia. "Institutionelle Ausbildungsmöglichkeiten für Musikerinnen in der ersten Hälfte des 19. Jahrhunderts." In *Von der Spielfrau zur Performance-Künstlerin. Auf der Suche nach einer Musikgeschichte der Frauen*, edited by Freia Hoffmann and Eva Rieger, 77–93. Kassel: Furore, 1993.

———. *Instrument und Körper. Die musizierende Frau in der bürgerlichen Kultur*. Frankfurt: Insel, 1992.

Huber, Catherine Rilliet. "Notes sur l'enfance de Mme de Staël." *Cahiers staëliens* 60 (2009): 61–73.

Hume, David. "Of Superstition and Enthusiasm." In *Essays: Moral, Political, and Literary*, edited by Eugene F. Miller, 73–79. Indianapolis: Liberty Classics, 1985.

Hunter, Alfred Collinson. *J. B. A. Suard, un introducteur de la littérature anglaise en France*. Paris: Champion, 1925.

Isbell, John Claiborne. *The Birth of European Romanticism: Truth and Propaganda in Staël's* De l'Allemagne, *1810–1813*. Cambridge: Cambridge University Press, 1994.

Jacoubet, Henri. *Le Genre troubadour et les origines françaises du Romanticisme*. Paris: Société d'Édition "Les Belles Lettres," 1929.

Jamain, Claude. *L'Imaginaire de la musique au siècle des Lumières*. Paris: Honoré Champion, 2003.

Janaway, Christopher. *Images of Excellence: Plato's Critique of the Arts*. Oxford: Oxford University Press, 1995.

Jensen, Heather Belnap. "Diversionary Tactics: Art Criticism as Political Weapon in Staël's *Corinne, or Italy* (1807)." In *Women Against Napoleon: Historical and Fictional Responses*, edited by Waltraud Maierhofer and Gertrud Roesch with Caroline Bland, 161–85. Frankfurt: Campus, 2007.

———. "Modern Motherhood and Female Sociability in the Art of Marguerite Gérard." In *Reconciling Art and Mothering*, edited by Rachel Epp Buller. Burlington, VT: Ashgate, 2012.

———. "Portraitistes à la plume: Women Art Critics in Revolutionary and Napoleonic France." PhD diss., University of Kansas, 2007.

Jewsbury, Maria Jane. *The History of an Enthusiast*, in *The Three Histories*. Boston: Perkins and Marvin, 1831.

———. Review of *The Nature and Dignity of Christ* by Joanna Baillie. *The Athenæum* 187 (May 28, 1831): 337.

———. "Nobody's Happy Now: Verses by a Proser." *The Athenæum* 167 (January 8, 1831): 25.

———. *Phantasmagoria*. 2 vols. London: Hurst, Robinson, & Co., 1825.

Johns, Christopher M. S. *Antonio Canova and the Politics of Patronage in Revolutionary and Napoleonic Europe*. Berkeley: University of California Press, 1998.

Johnson, James H. *Listening in Paris: A Cultural History*. Berkeley: University of California Press, 1995.

Jones, William. "On the Aeolian Harp." In *Physiological Disquisitions, or, Discourses on the Natural Philosophy of the Elements*, 338–45. London: Rivington, 1781.

Kadish, Doris Y. "Narrating the French Revolution: The Example of *Corinne*." In *Germaine de Staël: Crossing the Borders*, edited by Madelyn Gutwirth, Avriel Goldberger, and Karyna Szmurlo, 113–21. New Brunswick, NJ: Rutgers University Press, 1991.

———. "Patriarchy and Abolition: Staël and the Fathers." In *Germaine de Staël: Forging a Politics of Mediation*, ed. Karyna Szmurlo, 63–78. Oxford: Voltaire Foundation, 2011.

Kant, Immanuel. *Critique of Judgment*. Translated by Werner S. Pluhar. Indianapolis: Hackett, 1987.

———. *Raising the Tone of Philosophy: Late Essays by Immanuel Kant, Transformative Critique by Jacques Derrida*. Edited and translated by Peter Fenves. Baltimore: Johns Hopkins University Press, 1993.

Kelley, Theresa. "Romantic Exemplarity: Botany and 'Material' Culture." In *Romantic Science: The Literary Forms of Natural History*, edited by Noah Heringman, 223–52. Albany: State University of New York Press, 2003.

Kiefer, Carol Solomon. *The Empress Josephine: Art & Royal Identity*. Amherst: Mead Art Museum, 2005. An exhibition catalog.

Kilgour, Maggie. *From Communion to Cannibalism: An Anatomy of Metaphors of Incorporation*. Princeton, NJ: Princeton University Press, 1990.

Klein, Lawrence and Anthony J. La Vopa, eds. *Enthusiasm and Enlightenment in Europe, 1650–1850*. San Marino, CA: Huntington Library, 1998.

Knee, Philip. "Les Mésaventures politiques de la sympathie chez Rousseau." In *Les Discours de la sympathie: enquête sur une notion de l'âge classique à la modernité*, edited by Thierry Belleguic, Eric Van der Schueren, and Sabrina Vervacke, 423–41. Quebec: Les Presses de l'Université Laval, 2007.

Kosofsky, Eve. *Touching Feeling: Affect, Pedagogy, Performativity*. Durham, NC: Duke University Press, 2003.

Kristeva, Julia. "Gloire, deuil et écriture. Lettre à un 'romantique' sur Mme de Staël." *Romantisme* 62 (1988): 7–14.

———. *Powers of Horror: An Essay on Abjection*. Translated by Leon S. Roudiez. New York: Columbia University Press, 1982.

Lacépède, Bernard-Germain-Étienne de. *La Poëtique de la musique*. 2 vols. Paris: L'Imprimerie de Monsieur, 1785.

Landes, Joan B. *Visualizing the Nation: Gender, Representation, and Revolution in Eighteenth-Century France*. Ithaca: Cornell University Press, 2001.

Landon, Letitia Elizabeth. *Letitia Elizabeth Landon: Selected Writings*. Edited by Jerome McGann and Daniel Riess. Peterborough, Ontario: Broadview, 1997.

Larg, David Glass. *Madame de Staël: La vie dans l'œuvre 1766–1800*. Paris: Champion, 1924.

Lawford, Cynthia. "Diary." *London Review of Books* (September 21, 2000): 36–37.

Law-Sullivan, Jennifer. "Border Crossings as a Gateway to Border Dwellings: The Case of the Novelogue." *Prism(s): Essays in Romanticism* 13 (2005): 47–62.

Le Brun, Charles. *Art in Theory 1648–1815*, edited by Charles Harrison, Paul Wood, and Jason Gaiger. Oxford: Blackwell Publishers, 2000.

Ledoux-Lebard, Guy, and Denise Ledoux-Lebard. "L'Impératrice Joséphine et le retour au gothique sous l'Empire." *Revue de l'Institut Napoléon* 92 (July 1964): 117–24.

Lepschy, Laura. "Madame de Staël's Views on Art in *Corinne*." *Studi francesi* 14 (1970): 481–89.

Les Français peints par eux-mêmes; Encyclopédie morale du dix-neuvième siècle. 8 vols. Paris: L. Curmer, 1841–42.

Levi, Anthony. *French Moralists*. Oxford: Clarendon Press, 1964.

Levitine, George. *Girodet-Troison: An Iconographical Study*. New York and London: Garland Press, 1978.

Lincoln, Abraham. "Address to a Young Men's Lyceum of Springfield, Illinois." In *Speeches and Writings, 1832–1858*. New York: The Library of America, 1989.

Lokke, Kari. "L'Enthousiasme, l'éternité, et les 'armes du temps' chez Madame de Staël." *Cahiers staëliens* 57 (2006): 63–76.

———. "Staël's Enthusiasm, Eternity, and 'les armes du temps.'" *Prism(s): Essays in Romanticism* 15 (2007): 33–49.

———. *Tracing Women's Romanticism: Gender, History and Transcendence*. New York: Routledge, 2004.

Lotterie, Florence. "Madame de Staël. La Littérature comme 'philosophie sensible.'" *Romantisme* 34, no. 124 (2004): 19–30.

———. *Progrès et perfectibilité: Un dilemme des Lumières françaises (1755–1814)*. Oxford: Voltaire Foundation, 2006.

Lubkoll, Christine. *Mythos Musik. Poetische Entwürfe des Musikalischen in der Literatur um 1800.* Freiburg im Breisgau: Rombach, 1995.

Lutz, Tom. *Crying: The Natural and Cultural History of Tears.* New York: W. W. Norton, 1999.

Luzzi, Joseph. "Tragedy without Society: Alfieri's Italian Theater and the Discourse of Value." *European Romantic Review* 20, no. 5 (2009): 581–91.

———. "Translator's Introduction: Italy in Translation," *Romanic Review* 97, nos. 3–4 (2006): 275–78.

MacFarlan, Robert. *The Poems of Ossian, in the Original Gaelic, with a Literal Translation into Latin.* 3 vols. London: W. Bulmer, 1807.

Machiavelli, Niccolò. *The Prince.* Translated by Harvey C. Mansfield, Jr. Chicago: University of Chicago Press, 1985.

Mareschal, Louis-Nicolas. *Le Magnétisme animal, Mesmer ou les sots. Comédie, en vers & en un acte, . . . Œuvre posthume d'une mauvaise digestion de Pierre Bouline.* London: James Flesher, 1786.

Marmontel, Jean-François. *Essai sur les romans, considérés du côté moral.* In *Œuvres complètes,* edited by Mathieu-Guillaume-Thérèse Villenave. Vol. 3. Genève: Slatkine Reprints, 1968 [1819–1820].

Marshall, David. *The Surprising Effects of Sympathy: Marivaux, Diderot, Rousseau, and Mary Shelley.* Chicago: Chicago University Press, 1988.

Marshall, James F. *De Staël–Du Pont Letters: Correspondence of Madame de Staël and Pierre Samuel Du Pont de Nemours and of Other Members of the Necker and Du Pont Families.* Madison: University of Wisconsin Press, 1968.

Marshall, Kimberly. *Rediscovering the Muses: Women's Musical Traditions.* Boston: Northeastern University Press, 1993.

Marso, Lori Jo. "Defending the Queen: Wollstonecraft and Staël on the Politics of Sensibility and Feminine Difference." *Eighteenth Century: Theory and Interpretation* 43, no. 1 (Spring 2002): 43–52.

———. *(Un)Manly Citizens: Jean–Jacques Rousseau's and Germaine de Staël's Subversive Women.* Baltimore: Johns Hopkins University Press, 1999.

Martin, Judith E. *Germaine de Staël in Germany: Gender and Literary Authority (1800–1850).* Madison and Teaneck, NJ: Fairleigh Dickinson University Press, 2011.

Martin-Fugier, Anne. *Les Romantiques: Figures de l'artiste, 1820–1848.* Paris: Hachette, 1998.

McClellan, Andrew. *Inventing the Louvre: Art, Politics, and the Origins of the Modern Museum.* Los Angeles: University of California Press, 1999.

McClellend, I. L. *The Origins of the Romantic Movement in Spain.* Liverpool: Liverpool University Press, 1975.

McGann, Jerome. *The Poetics of Sensibility: A Revolution in Literary Style.* Oxford: Clarendon Press, 1996.

McGinley, Paul. "On Crying." *Existential Analysis* 19, no. 2 (2008): 210–23.

Mee, Jon. *Romanticism, Enthusiasm, and Regulation: Poetics and the Policing of Culture in the Romantic Period.* Oxford: Oxford University Press, 2003.

Mellor, Anne K. and Richard E. Matlak, eds. *British Literature 1780–1830.* Fort Worth, TX: Harcourt Brace & Co., 1996.

Ménard, Jean. "Mme de Staël et la peinture." In *Madame de Staël et l'Europe,* edited by Simone Balayé, 253–264. Paris: Klincksieck, 1970.

Mercier, Louis Sébastien. *L'An deux mille quatre cent quarante. Rêve s'il en fût jamais.* Londres: Gale ECCO print editions, 2010.

———. *Tableau de Paris.* Edited by Jean-Claude Bonnet. 2 vols. Paris: Mercure de France, 1994.

Miller, Nancy K. "Performances of the Gaze: Staël's *Corinne, or Italy.*" In *The Novel's Seductions: Staël's Corinne in Critical Inquiry,* edited by Karyna Szmurlo, 84–94. Lewisburg, PA: Bucknell University Press, 1999.

———. *Subject to Change: Reading Feminist Writing.* New York: Columbia University Press, 1988.

Mitchell, W. J. T. *Iconology. Image, Text, Ideology.* Chicago: University of Chicago Press, 1986.

Moi, Toril. "A Woman's Desire to Be Known: Expressivity and Silence in *Corinne.*" *Bucknell Review* 45, no. 2 (2002): 143–77.

Mongrédien, Jean. *La Musique en France, des Lumières au Romantisme, 1789–1830.* Paris: Flammarion, 1986.

Montesquieu. *The Political Theory of Montesquieu.* Edited and translated by Melvin Richter. Cambridge: Cambridge University Press, 1977.

Moore, Fabienne. *Prose Poems of the French Enlightenment: Delimiting Genre.* Aldershot: Ashgate, 2009.

Moraud, Marcel Ian. *Lady Morgan, une Irlandaise libérale.* Paris: Didier, 1954.

Morton, Timothy. *Ecology without Nature: Rethinking Environmental Aesthetics.* Cambridge, MA: Harvard University Press, 2007.

Mueller-Vollmer, Kurt. "On Germany: Germaine de Staël and the Internationalization of Romanticism." In *The Spirit of Poetry: Essays on Jewish and German Literature and Thought in Honor of Géza von Molnár,* edited by Richard Block and Peter Fenves, 150–66. Evanston: Northwestern University Press, 2000.

Mullan, John. *Sentiment and Sociability: The Language of Feeling in the Eighteenth Century.* Oxford: Oxford UP, 1988.

Nancy, Jean–Luc. *À l'écoute.* Paris: Galilée, 2002.

———. *Listening.* Translated by Charlotte Mandell. New York: Fordham University Press, 2007.

Naudin, Marie. "Madame de Staël, précurseur de l'esthétique musicale romantique." *Revue des sciences humaines* 139 (Juillet–Septembre 1970): 391–400.

Necker, Suzanne. *Mélanges extraits des manuscrits de Madame Necker.* Edited by Jacques Necker. 3 vols. Paris: Pougens, 1798.

———. *Nouveaux mélanges extraits des manuscrits de Madame Necker.* Edited by Jacques Necker. 2 vols. Paris: Pougens, 1801.

———. *Réflexions sur le divorce.* Edited by Jacques Necker. Lausanne-Paris: Aubin-Desenne, 1794.

Neuls-Bates, Carol. *Women in Music: An Anthology of Source Readings from the Middle Ages to the Present.* Boston: Northeastern University Press, 1996.

The New Grove Dictionary of Music and Musicians. 3 vols. New York: Grove's Dictionaries of Music, 1995.

Nolan, Christopher, dir. *Inception* (film). Burbank, CA: Warner Bros. Pictures, 2010.

Nussbaum, Martha C. *Upheavals of Thought: The Intelligence of the Emotions.* Cambridge: Cambridge University Press, 2001.

Ockman, Carol. *Ingres's Eroticized Bodies: Retracing the Serpentine Line.* New Haven, CT: Yale University Press, 1995.

Ó Gallchoir, Clíona. "Germaine de Staël and the Response of Sydney Owenson and Maria Edgeworth to the Act of Union." In *France-Ireland: Anatomy of a Relationship*, edited by Eamon Maher and Grace Neville, 69–82. Frankfort, Germany: Peter Lang, 2004.

Oliver, Alfred Richard. *The Encyclopedists as Critics of Music*. New York: Columbia University Press, 1947.

O'Neal, John. *The Authority of Experience: Sensationist Theory in the French Enlightenment*. University Park, PA: Penn State University Press, 1996.

Orr, Clarissa Campbell. "Mary Shelley's Rambles in Germany and Italy, the Celebrity Author, and the Undiscovered Country of the Human Heart." *Romanticism on the Net* 11 (August 1998).

Owenson, Sydney, Lady Morgan. *Patriotic Sketches of Ireland*. 2 vols. London: Phillips, 1807.

———. *The Wild Irish Girl*. Oxford University Press, 1999.

Paccoud, Stéphane, and Léna Widerkehr, eds. *Juliette Récamier. Muse et mécene*. Paris: Editions Hazan and Lyon: Musée des Beaux-Arts, 2009.

Pange, Comtesse Jean de. *Auguste-Guillaume Schlegel et Mme de Staël*. Paris: Éditions Albert, 1938.

Pange, Victor de. "Madame de Staël and her English Correspondents." 2 vols. DPhil. diss., University of Oxford, 1955.

Pange, Victor de, and Norman King. "La Bibliothèque anglaise de Mme de Staël," *Cahiers staëliens* 14 (September 1972): 33–67.

Park, Suzie Asha. "Picturesque Interiority: Eliza Fenwick's *Secresy* and the Novel of Information." *Literature Compass* 7/8 (2010): 659–73.

Peel, Ellen and Nanora Sweet. "*Corinne* and the Woman as Poet in England: Hemans, Jewsbury, and Barrett Browning." In *The Novel's Seductions: Staël's* Corinne *in Critical Inquiry*, edited by Karyna Szmurlo, 204–20. Lewisburg, PA: Bucknell University Press, 1999.

Pendle, Karin, ed. *Women and Music: A History*. Bloomington: Indiana University Press, 2001.

Philo. *Every Good Man Is Free*. Vol 9 in *Philo*. Translated by F. H. Colson, 10 vols. and 2 supplementary vols. Cambridge, MA: Harvard University Press, 1941.

Plato. *The Republic*. Translated by Allan Bloom. New York: HarperCollins Publishers, 1991.

Plessner, Helmuth. *Laughing and Crying: A Study of the Limits of Human Behavior*. Evanston: Northwestern University Press, 1970.

Pollak, Michael. "Glass, Wet Fingers and a Mysterious Disappearance." The Arts/Cultural Desk E2 *New York Times*, December 12, 2001.

Pomeroy, Jordana, ed. *Royalists to Romantics: Women Artists from the Louvre, Versailles, and Other French National Collections*. New York: Scala, 2012. An exibition catalogue.

Potts, Alex. "Beautiful Bodies and Dying Heroes: Images of Ideal Manhood in the French Revolution." *History Workshop Journal* 30 (Autumn 1990): 1–21.

———. *Flesh and the Ideal: Winckelmann and the Origins of Art History*. New Haven, CT: Yale University Press, 1994.

Pougetoux, Alain. *La Collection de peintures de l'Impératrice Joséphine*. Paris: Éditions de la Réunion des Musées Nationaux, 2003.

Prasad, Pratima. *Colonialism, Race, and the French Romantic Imagination*. New York: Routledge, 2009.

Pratt, Mary Louise. *Imperial Eyes: Travel Writing and Transculturation*. New York: Routledge, 1992.

———. "Transculturation and Autoethnography: Peru, 1615/1980." In *Colonial Discourse, Postcolonial Theory*, edited by Francis Barker, Peter Hulme, and Margaret Iverson, 24–46. Manchester: Manchester University Press, 1994.

Prettejohn, Elizabeth. *Beauty and Art*. Oxford: Oxford University Press, 2005.

Prévost, L'Abbé. *Manon Lescaut*. Translated by Leonard Tancock. New York: Penguin Books, 1949.

Pupil, François. *Le Style troubadour, ou la nostalgie du bon vieux temps*. Nancy: Presses Universitaires de Nancy, 1985.

Queffélec, Lise. *Le Roman-feuilleton français au XIXe siècle*. Paris: Presses Universitaires de France, 1989.

Rafroidi, Patrick. *L'Irlande et le Romantisme*. Lille: Éditions Universitaires, 1972.

Rand, Richard, ed. *Intimate Encounters. Love and Domesticity in Eighteenth–Century France*. Hood Museum of Art, Darthmouth College. Princeton, NJ: Princeton University Press, 1997.

Reddy, William. *The Navigation of Feeling: A Framework for the History of Emotions*. Cambridge: Cambridge University Press, 2001.

Rée, Jonathan. *I See a Voice: A Philosophical History of Language, Deafness and the Senses*. London: HarperCollins, 1999.

Reich, Nancy. "Women as Musicians: A Question of Class." In *Musicology and Difference: Gender and Sexuality in Music Scholarship*, edited by Ruth A. Solie, 125–46. Berkeley: University of California Press, 1993.

Richardson, Alan. *The Neural Sublime: Cognitive Theories and Romantic Texts*. Baltimore: Johns Hopkins University Press, 2010.

Richter, Melvin. *The Political Theory of Montesquieu*. Cambridge: Cambridge University Press, 1977.

Ridell, Robert. "Lochaber." In *Scots Musical Museum*, pt.1, no. 95 (1787). http://chrsouchon.free.fr/lochaber.htm (accessed).

Rieger, Eva. *Frau, Musik und Männerherrschaft*. Kassel: Furore–Verlag, 1988.

———. *Frau und Musik*. Frankfurt: Fischer, 1980.

Robespierre, Maximilien. *Lettres à ses commettans*. In *Œuvres de Maximilien Robespierre*, edited by Albert Laponneraye and Armand Carrel. 3 vols. New York: Burt Franklin, 1970.

Robinson, Douglas. *Performative Linguistics: Speaking and Translating as Doing Things with Words*. New York: Routledge, 2003.

Roger, Joseph-Louis. *Traité des effets de la musique sur le corps humain, par Joseph-Louis Roger, . . . traduit du latin et augmenté de notes, par Étienne Sainte-Marie*. Paris: Brunot, an XI (1803).

Ronsin, Francis. *Le Contrat sentimental: Débats sur le mariage, l'amour, le divorce, de l'Ancien Régime à la Restauration*. Paris: Aubier, 1990.

Rosenblum, Robert. *Transformations in Late Eighteenth-Century Art*. Princeton, NJ: Princeton University Press, 1967.

Rossiter, Clinton, ed. *The Federalist Papers*. New York: Penguin Books, 1961.

Roulin, Jean-Marie. "Réflexions sur le procès de la reine: Du procès d'une femme au procès de la Révolution." *Cahiers staëliens* 57 (2006): 89–102.

Rousseau, Jean-Jacques. *Discourse on the Origin of Inequality*. Translated by Donald A. Cress. Indianapolis: Hackett Publishing Company, 1992.

———. *Discours sur l'origine et les fondements de l'inégalité parmi les hommes. Discours sur les sciences et les arts*. Edited by Jacques Roger. Paris: Flammarion, 1992.

———. *Du contrat social, écrits politiques*. In *Œuvres complètes*. Edited by Bernard Gagnebin and Marcel Raymond. Vol. 3, Paris: Gallimard, 1964.

———. *Ecrits sur la musique, la langue, et le théâtre*. In *Œuvres complètes*. Edited by Bernard Gagnebin and Marcel Raymond. Vol. 5. Paris: Gallimard, 1995.

———. *Émile, Education, Morale, Botanique*. In *Œuvres complètes*. Edited by Bernard Gagnebin and Marcel Raymond. Vol. 4. Paris: Gallimard, 1969.

———. *Essay on the Origin of Languages and Writings Related to Music*. In *The Collected Writings of Rousseau*. Edited by Roger D. Masters and Christopher Kelly. Translated by John T. Scott. Vol. 7. Hanover, NH: University Press of New England, 1998.

———. *The First and Second Discourses*. Edited and translated by Roger D. Masters and Judith R. Masters. New York: St. Martin's, 1964.

———. *Julie, or the New Heloise*. Vol. 6 in *The Collected Writings of Rousseau*. Edited by Roger D. Masters and Christopher Kelly. Translated by Philip Stewart and Jean Vaché. 11 vols. Hanover, NH: University Press of New England, 1997.

———. *Julie ou la Nouvelle Héloïse*. Edited by Henri Coulet. 2 vols. Paris: Gallimard, 1993.

Rutherford, Susan. *The Prima Donna and Opera, 1815–1930*. Cambridge: Cambridge University Press, 2006.

Sade, Donatien Alphonse François, Marquis de. *Les Crimes de l'amour, nouvelles héroïques et tragiques précédées d'une Idée sur les romans*, edited by Michel Delon. Paris: Gallimard, 1987.

Sadie, Julie Anne. "*Musiciennes* of the Ancien Régime." In *Women Making Music, The Western Art Tradition, 1150–1950*, edited by Jane Bowers and Judith Tick, 191–223. Urbana: University of Illinois Press, 1986.

Saint-Amand, Imbert de. *The Wife of the First Consul*. Translated by Thomas Sergeant Perry. New York: Charles Scribner and Sons, 1890.

Sainte-Beuve, Charles-Augustin. *Portraits of Women*. Translated by Helen Stott. London: D. Stott, 1891.

Saint-Just, Louis Antoine de. *Second discours concernant le jugement de Louis XVI*. Edited by Charles Vellay. Vol. 1. Paris: Charpentier and Fosquelle, 1908.

Sand, George. *Consuelo. La Comtesse de Rudolstadt*. Edited by Léon Cellier and Léon Guichard. 2 vols. Paris: Gallimard, 2004.

———. *Correspondance*. Edited by Georges Lubin, 26 vols. Paris: Garnier, 1964–1995.

———. [a.k.a. Jules]. *La Prima Donna. Revue de Paris* 25 (April 1831).

Scarry, Elaine. *The Body in Pain: The Making and Unmaking of the World*. New York: Oxford University Press, 1985.

Scher, Steven Paul. *Literatur und Musik*. Berlin: Erich Schmidt, 1984.

Schiff, Stacy. "The Woman Who Never Stopped Talking: The Secret of Madame de Staël's Success," *Slate*, October 6, 2008. http://www.slate.com/id/2201499.

Schlegel, Friedrich. *Dialogue on Poetry and Literary Aphorisms*. Translated by Ernst Behler and Roman Struc. University Park: Penn State University Press, 1968.

Schor, Naomi. "Corinne: The Third Woman." *L'Esprit créateur* 34, no. 3 (1994): 99–106.

———. *Reading in Detail: Aesthetics and the Feminine*. New York: Routledge, 1989.

Scognamiglio, Ornella. *I dipinti di Gioacchino e Carolina Murat*. Naples: Edizioni Scientifiche Italiane, 2008.

Scudo, Paul. *Critique et littérature musicales: Première et deuxième séries*. Preface by François Lesure. Genève: Minkoff, 1986.

Senancour, Etienne-Pivert de. *Obermann*. Paris: Garnier, 2003.

Seth, Catriona. *Marie-Antoinette: Anthologie et dictionnaire: textes choisis, présentés et annotés par Catriona Seth*. Paris: Editions Laffont, 2006.

Sheriff, Mary D. *The Exceptional Woman: Elisabeth Vigée-Lebrun and the Cultural Politics of Art*. Chicago: University of Chicago Press, 1996.

——. *Moved by Love: Inspired Artists and Deviant Women in Eighteenth–Century France*. Chicago: University of Chicago Press, 2004.

Shiner, Larry. *The Invention of Art: A Cultural History*. Chicago: University of Chicago Press, 2001.

Siegfried, Susan L. *Ingres: Painting Re-imagined*. New Haven: Yale University Press, 2009.

Simon, Sherry. "Germaine de Staël and Gayatri Spivak: Culture Brokers." In *Translation and Power*, edited by Maria Tymoczko and Edwin Gentzler, 122–40. Amherst: University of Massachusetts Press, 2002.

Smith, Adam. *The Theory of Moral Sentiments*. Edited by D. D. Raphael and A. L. Macfie. Oxford: Clarendon Press, 1976.

——. *The Theory of Moral Sentiments*. Edited by D. D. Raphael and A. L. Macfie. Indianapolis: Liberty Fund, 1984.

——. *The Theory of Moral Sentiments*. Edited by Robert L. Heilbroner. New York: Norton, 1986.

Smith, Marian. "'Poésie lyrique' and 'Chorégraphie' at the Opéra in the July Monarchy," *Cambridge Opera Journal* 4, no. 1 (March 1992): 1–19.

Solie, Ruth, ed. *Musicology and Difference: Gender and Sexuality in Music Scholarship*. Berkeley: University of California Press, 1993.

Solomon-Godeau, Abigail. *Male Trouble: A Crisis in Representation*. New York: Thames and Hudson, 1997.

Solovieff, Georges. ed. *Madame de Staël, ses amis, ses correspondants: choix de lettres, 1778–1817*. Paris: Klincksieck, 1970.

Sontag, Susan. "Notes on Camp." In *A Susan Sontag Reader*, edited by Elizabeth Hardwick, 105–20. New York: Farrar, Strauss and Giroux, 1982.

Soumoy-Thibert, Geneviève. "Les idées de Madame Necker." *Dix-Huitième Siècle* 21 (1989): 357–68.

Spalding, Paul. "Germaine de Staël's Role in Rescuing Lafayette, 1792–1797." In *Germaine de Staël: Forging a Politics of Mediation*, edited by Karyna Szmurlo, 35–46. Oxford: Voltaire Foundation, 2011.

Spera, Gianni. *Significati e Poetiche della Narrativa Italiana: Fra Romanticismo e Idealismo*. Firenze: Casa Editrice le Lettere, 1989.

Staël, Germaine de. *Les Carnets de voyage de Madame de Staël: contribution à la genèse de ses œuvres*. Edited by Simone Balayé. Genève: Droz, 1971.

——. *Considérations sur la Révolution française*. Edited by Jacques Godechot. Paris: Tallandier, 1983.

——. *Corinne, or Italy*. Edited and translated, with introduction by Avriel Goldberger. New Brunswick, NJ: Rutgers University Press, 1987.

———. *Corinne ou l'Italie.* Edited by Claudine Herrmann. 2 vols. Paris: Editions des femmes, 1979.

———. *Corinne ou l'Italie.* Edited by Simone Balayé. Paris: Gallimard Folio, 1985.

———. *Correspondance générale de Madame de Staël.* Edited by Béatrice W. Jasinski, vols. 1–4, Paris: Pauvert, 1960–78; vol. 5, Paris: Hachette, 1982–85; vol. 6, Paris: Klinksieck, 1993.

———. *Correspondance générale de Madame de Staël.* Edited by Othenin d'Haussonville and Béatrice W. Jasinski. vol. 7. Paris: Champion, 2008.

———. *De la littérature considérée dans ses rapports avec les institutions sociales.* Edited by Axel Blaeschke. Paris: Garnier-Flammarion, 1998.

———. *De la littérature considérée dans ses rapports avec les institutions sociales.* Edited by Gérard Gengembre and Jean Goldzink. Paris: Garnier-Flammarion, 1991.

———. *De l'Allemagne.* Edited by Simone Balayé. 2 vols. Paris: Garnier-Flammarion, 1968.

———. *De l'Allemagne.* Edited by Jean de Pange with an introduction by Simone Balayé. 5 vols. Paris: Hachette, 1958–60.

———. *De l'esprit des traductions.* In *Œuvres complètes de Madame la Baronne de Staël-Holstein.* 2 vols. Paris: Firmin Didot Frères, 1844.

———. *De l'influence des passions.* In *Œuvres complètes,* série I, *Œuvres critiques,* edited by Florence Lotterie, vol. 1. Paris: Honoré Champion, 2008.

———. *De l'influence des passions sur le bonheur des individus et des nations.* Paris: Charpentier, 1842.

———. *De l'influence des passions sur le bonheur des individus et des nations: suivi de Réflexions sur le suicide.* Introduction by Chantal Thomas. Paris: Rivages, 2000.

———. *Delphine.* Edited and translated by Avriel H. Goldberger. DeKalb, IL: Northern Illinois University Press, 1995.

———. *Des circonstances actuelles qui peuvent terminer la Révolution et des principes qui doivent fonder la République en France.* Edited by Lucia Omacini. Geneva: Droz, 1979.

———. *Essai sur les fictions.* In *Œuvres de jeunesse,* edited by Simone Balayé and John Isbell. Paris: Desjonquères, 1997.

———. *Essai sur les fictions,* suivi de *De l'influence des passions sur le bonheur des individus et des nations.* Paris: Editions Ramsay, 1979.

———. *Germany by the Baroness Staël Holstein. Translated from the French in three volumes.* London: John Murray, 1813.

———. *Lettres inédites de Mme de Staël à Henri Meister.* Edited by Paul Ustéri and Eugène Ritter. Paris: Hachette, 1904.

———. *Lettres sur les ouvrages et le caractère de Rousseau.* In *Œuvres de jeunesse,* edited by Simone Balayé and John Isbell. Paris: Desjonquères, 1997.

———. *Madame de Staël on Politics, Literature, and National Character.* Edited and translated by Morroe Berger. New York: Doubleday, 1964.

———. *Major Writings of Germaine de Staël.* Edited and translated by Vivian Folkenflik. New York: Columbia University Press, 1992. Reprint of *An Extraordinary Woman: Selected Writings of Germaine de Staël,* 1987.

———. *Œuvres complètes de Mme la Baronne de Staël, publiées par son fils, précédées d'une Notice sur le caractère et les écrits de Mme de Staël, par Madame Necker de Saussure.* 17 vols. Paris, Treuttel et Würtz, 1820–21.

———. "The Spirit of Translation." Translated and introduced by Joseph Luzzi. *Romanic Review* 97, nos. 3–4 (2006): 275–84.

———. *A Treatise on the Influence of the Passions upon the Happiness of Individuals and of Nations.* Anonymous translation. London: Gale ECCO print editions, 2010.

———. *Zulma.* In *Œuvres de jeunesse*, edited by Simone Balayé and John Isbell. Paris: Desjonquères, 1997.

Stafford, Barbara. "Toward Romantic Landscape Perception: Illustrated Travels and the Rise of 'Singularity' as an Aesthetic Category." *Studies in Eighteenth-Century Culture* 10 (1981): 17–75.

Starobinski, Jean. "The Authority of Feeling and the Origins of Psychological Criticism: Rousseau and Mme de Staël." *Yearbook of Comparative Criticism* 7 (1976): 69–87.

———. "Critique et principe d'autorité: Madame de Staël et Rousseau." In *Préromantisme. Hypothèque ou hypothèse?*, edited by Paul Viallaneix, 326–43. Paris: Klincksieck, 1975.

———. "Le Journal de Mademoiselle Necker: Réflexion et passion." *Cahiers staëliens* 28 (1980): 25–32, réédité dans une version remaniée sous le titre "Germaine Necker: les prémonitions du premier *Journal*." *Nouvelle revue française* 531 (1997): 45–52.

———. "Madame de Staël: Passion et littérature." In *Table d'orientation: l'auteur et son autorité*, 83–110. Lausanne: Éditions de l'Âge d'homme, 1989.

St. Clair, William. *The Reading Nation in the Romantic Period.* Cambridge: Cambridge University Press, 2004.

Steinecke, Harmut. "Die Liebe des Künstlers. Männer–Phantasien und Frauen-Bilder bei E. T. A. Hoffmann." In *Codierungen der Liebe in der Kunstperiode*, edited by Walter Hinderer, 293–309. Würzburg: Königshausen & Neumann, 1997.

Stevenson, Lionel. *The Wild Irish Girl: The Life of Sydney Owenson, Lady Morgan (1776–1859).* London: Chapman & Hall, 1936.

Stewart, Philip. *L'Invention du sentiment: Roman et économie affective au XVIIIe siècle.* Oxford: Voltaire Foundation, 2010.

Strauss, Leo. *Natural Right and History.* Chicago: University of Chicago Press, 1953.

Suddaby, Elizabeth, and P. J. Yarrow, eds. *Lady Morgan in France.* Newcastle upon Tyne, UK: Oriel Press, 1971.

Swiderski, Marie-Laure Girou. "Entre morale et politique: *De l'influence des passions* de Mme de Staël." In *Figures du sentiment: Morale, politique et esthétique à l'époque moderne*, edited by Syliane Malinowski-Charles, 65–76. Québec: Presses de l'Université Laval, 2003.

Szmurlo, Karyna. ed. *Germaine de Staël: Forging a Politics of Mediation.* Oxford: Voltaire Foundation, 2011.

———. ed. *The Novel's Seductions: Staël's* Corinne *in Critical Inquiry.* Lewisburg, PA: Bucknell University Press, 1999.

———. "Pour une poétique des langues nationales: Germaine de Staël." In *Le Groupe de Coppet et l'Europe*, edited by Kurt Kloocke, 165–79. Lausanne: Institut Benjamin Constant and Paris: Jean Touzot, 1994.

———. "Pour un état des lieux de la recherche américaine: Germaine de Staël dans le discours de la modernité." *Cahiers staëliens* 57 (2006): 15–34.

——. "Speech Acts: Staël's Historiography of the Revolution." In *Literate Women and the French Revolution of 1789*, edited by Catherine Monfort, 237–52. Birmingham, AL: Summa Publications, 1994.

Tenenbaum, Susan. "The Coppet Circle: Literary Criticism as Political Discourse." *History of Political Thought* 1, no. 3 (Autumn, December 1980): 453–73.

——. "Liberal Heroines: Mme. de Staël on the 'Woman Question' and the Modern State." *Annales Benjamin Constant* 5 (1985): 37–52.

Thellusson, Madame de. *Lucile, ou la cantatrice.* 2 vols. Paris: Fournier jeune, 1833.

Thomas, Downing. *Music and the Origins of Language: Theories from the French Enlightenment.* Cambridge: Cambridge University Press, 1995.

Thuente, Mary Helen. "Liberty, Hibernia and Mary Le More: United Irish Images of Women." In *The Women of 1798*, edited by Dáire Keogh and Nicholas Furlong, 9–25. Dublin: Four Courts Press, 1998.

Tocqueville, Alexis de. *Democracy in America.* Translated by Harvey C. Mansfield and Delba Winthrop. Chicago: University of Chicago Press, 2000.

Todorov, Tzvetan. *Théories du symbole.* Paris: Seuil, 1977.

Trumpener, Katie. *Bardic Nationalism: The Romantic Novel and the British Empire.* Princeton, NJ: Princeton University Press, 1997.

Tscherny, Nadia and Guy Stair Sainty. *Romance and Chivalry: History and Literature Reflected in Early Nineteenth-Century French Painting.* London and New York: The Matthiesen Gallery and Stair Sainty Matthiesen Inc., 1996. An exhibition catalog.

Tunley, David. *Music in the 19th-Century Parisian Salon.* Armidale, N.S.W: University of New England, Armidale, 1997.

——. *Salons, Singers and Songs: A Background to Romantic French Song 1830–70.* Aldershot: Ashgate, 2002.

Ulliac-Trémadeure, Sophie. *Contes aux jeunes artistes.* Paris: Didier, 1836.

Vallois, Marie-Claire. *Fictions féminines. Mme de Staël et les voix de la sibylle.* Saratoga, CA: Anma Libri, 1987.

——. "Old Idols, New Subject: Germaine de Staël and Romanticism." In *Germaine de Staël: Crossing the Borders*, edited by Madelyn Gutwirth, Avriel Goldberger, and Karyna Szmurlo, 82–97. New Brunswick, NJ: Rutgers University Press, 1991.

——. "Voice as Fossil: Germaine de Staël's *Corinne, or Italy*: An Archaeology of Feminine Discourse." In *The Novel's Seductions: Staël's* Corinne *in Critical Inquiry*, edited by Karyna Szmurlo, 127–38. Lewisburg, PA: Bucknell University Press, 1999.

Van Tieghem, Paul. *Le Préromantisme français.* 2 vols. Paris: Félix Alcan, 1924.

Vigée-Lebrun, Elisabeth. *Souvenirs.* Edited by Claudine Herrmann. 2 vols. Paris: Editions des femmes, 1986.

Vila, Anne C. *Enlightenment and Pathology: Sensibility in the Literature and Medicine of Eighteenth-Century France.* Baltimore: Johns Hopkins University Press, 1998.

Villoteau, Guillaume André. *Recherches sur l'analogie de la musique avec les arts qui ont pour objet l'imitation du langage, pour servir d'introduction à l'étude des principes naturels de cet art.* 2 vols. Paris: L'Imprimerie Impériale, 1807.

Vincent, Patrick. *The Romantic Poetess: European Culture, Politics and Gender, 1820–1840*. Hanover: University Press of New England, 2004.

Vincent-Buffault, Anne. *The History of Tears: Sensibility and Sentimentality in France*. New York: St. Martin's, 1991.

Voltaire, *Dictionnaire Philosophique*. Edited by Béatrice Didier. Paris: Imprimerie Nationale, 1994.

Walker, Lesley H. *A Mother's Love: Crafting Feminine Virtue in Enlightenment France*. Lewisburg, PA: Bucknell University Press, 2008.

Waller, Margaret. *The Male Malady: Fictions of Impotence in the French Romantic Novel*. New Brunswick, NJ: Rutgers University Press, 1993.

Wallon, Henri. "La vie mentale," *Encyclopédie française*. Vol. 8, 1–7. Paris, 1938.

Walsh, Linda. "The Expressive Face: Manifestations of Sensibility in Eighteenth-Century French Art," *Art History* 19 (December 1996): 523–50.

Weber, William. *Music and the Middle Class: The Social Structure of Concert Life in London, Paris and Vienna*. Aldershot: Ashgate, 2004.

Wharram, C. C. "Translation as Symptom: The 'Sickness' of the Romantic." In *Translation of Romantic Texts: Proceedings of the Association of Slovene Literary Translators*, edited by Martina Ozbot, 184–203. Ljubljana, Slovenia: University of Ljubljana, 2004.

Whatley, Janet. "Dissoluble Marriage, Paradise Lost: Suzanne Necker's *Réflexions sur le divorce*." *Dalhousie French Studies* 56 (2001): 144–53.

Whitford, Robert Calvin. "Madame de Staël's Literary Reputation in England." *University of Illinois Studies in Language and Literature* 4, no. 1 (February 1918): 1–62.

Wilhelm, Jane Elisabeth. "La Traduction, principe de perfectiblilité, chez Mme de Staël." *Meta* 29, no. 3 (2004): 692–705.

Wohlgemut, Esther. *Romantic Cosmopolitanism*. New York: Palgrave Macmillan, 2009.

———. "'What Do You Do with That at Home?': The Cosmopolitan Heroine and the National Tale." *European Romantic Review* 13 (2002): 191–97.

Wolfson, Susan. *Borderlines: The Shiftings of Gender in British Romanticism*. Stanford: Stanford University Press, 2006.

Woolf, Virginia. *A Room of One's Own*. Annotated and with an introduction by Susan Gubar. New York: Harcourt, 2005.

Zamboni, Giuseppe. *Die italienische Romantik: Ihre Ausenandersetzung mit der Tradition*. Krefeld: Scherpe-Verlag, 1953.

Ziolkowski, Theodore. *German Romanticism and Its Institutions*. Princeton, NJ: Princeton University Press, 1990.

Tili Boon Cuillé is an Associate Professor of French and co-coordinator of the Eighteenth-Century Interdisciplinary Salon at Washington University in St. Louis. Her area of specialization is eighteenth-century French literature, philosophy, and the arts. She is the author of *Narrative Interludes: Musical Tableaux in Eighteenth-Century French Texts* (Toronto University Press, 2006). She has contributed to *Forum for Modern Language Studies*, *Opera Quarterly*, and *Studies in Eighteenth-Century Culture* as well as the collected volumes *The Super-Enlightenment: Daring to Know Too Much* (Voltaire Foundation, 2010), *Operatic Migrations: Transforming Works and Crossing Boundaries* (Ashgate, 2006), and *Phrase and Subject: Studies in Music and Literature* (Legenda, 2006). She is currently working on a book-length project entitled *Divining Nature: French Ventures in Fiction, Imagery, and Stagecraft*.

Karen de Bruin is an Assistant Professor of French at the University of Rhode Island. Her most recent scholarship addresses how Germaine de Staël presents the concept of the "femme supérieure" as a better model of emulation than the "grand homme" for a future free republic. She examines this theme through the lenses of the passions, aesthetic education, the power of the feminine idealist novel, and the legacy of Staël's "femme supérieure" in nineteenth-century international women's writing. She has contributed to the collected volumes *Héroïsme au siècle des Lumières* (Champion, 2010) and *Femmes des Lumières et de l'ombre* (Editions Vaillant, 2011).

M. Ione Crummy is a Professor of French language, literature and culture and member of the Women's and Gender Studies program at the University of Montana, Missoula. Her articles on Owenson, Staël, Chateaubriand, Sand, Balzac, Flaubert, and Michelet have appeared in *Neohelicon*, *George Sand Studies*, and *Cahiers staëliens* and in the collected volumes *George Sand et l'écriture du roman* (Université de Montréal, 1996) and *Le Siècle de George Sand*, (Rodopi, 1998). Her essay on Sand's

Lucrezia Floriani as a rewriting of *Corinne* is forthcoming in *Écriture, Performance et Théâtralité dans l'œuvre de George Sand* (Université de Grenoble, 2013).

Catherine Dubeau is an Associate Professor in the Department of French Studies at the University of Waterloo (Ontario, Canada). She is specialized in eighteenth-century French literature and psychoanalytic criticism. Author of *La lettre et la mère: roman familial et écriture de la passion chez Suzanne Necker et Germaine de Staël* (forthcoming from the Presses de l'Université de Laval), she is currently working on a critical edition of the *Mélanges* and *Nouveaux mélanges* by Suzanne Necker.

Julia Effertz is a Comparative Literature scholar and an actress. Having written her Ph.D. thesis on women singers in French and German Romanticism, she specializes in European culture of the nineteenth and twentieth centuries with a focus on gender studies and female cultural representation. She is currently a researcher at Humboldt University, Berlin.

Christine Dunn Henderson is a Senior Fellow at Liberty Fund, Inc. She is contributing editor of *Seers and Judges: American Literature as Political Philosophy* (Rowman & Littlefield, 2002), and co-editor of *Joseph Addison's "Cato" and Selected Essays* (Liberty Fund, 2004). She is also editor of *Tocqueville's Voyages* and co-translator of *Encyclopedic Liberty: Political Articles from the Dictionary of Diderot and D'Alembert* (both forthcoming). Her research interests and publications include Addison, Pierre Nicole, Alexis de Tocqueville, Gustave de Beaumont, classical liberalism, and politics and literature.

Heather Belnap Jensen is an Assistant Professor of Art History and Curatorial Studies at Brigham Young University and specializes in women in post-Revolutionary French art and culture. She has published her work in *Nineteenth-Century Art Worldwide* and has contributed essays to several volumes, including *Plumes et pinceaux: discours de femmes sur l'art en Europe, 1750-1850* (Les Presses du réel, 2012) and *Vanishing Acts: Women Art Critics in Nineteenth-Century France* (University of Delaware, 2012). She is coeditor of *Interior Portraiture and Masculine Identity in France, 1789–1914* (Ashgate, 2011), currently working on a book manuscript on art, fashion, and the emergence of the modern woman in early nineteenth-century France.

Jennifer Law-Sullivan is an Associate Professor of French at Oakland University in Rochester, Michigan. Her research interests include travel literature, gender studies, post-colonialism, and genre theory. Her publications investigate how Germaine de Staël and Flora Tristan addressed questions of gender, slavery, and nation-building.

Nanette Le Coat is an Associate Professor of French literature and language and the interim Chair for the International Program at Trinity University in San Antonio Texas. She has published articles on Rousseau, Germaine de Staël, and the Ideologues. She is currently working on a book—*Modernity and the Quest for Autonomy: French Writers and the Académie Française (1791-1811)*—which weaves together the three primary strands of her research: French literature and philosophy at the turn of the eighteenth and nineteenth centuries; French women writers in the post-revolutionary period; and the intersection between literature and the nascent social sciences.

Kari Lokke is a Professor of Comparative Literature at the University of California, Davis. She is the author of *Gérard de Nerval: The Poet as Social Visionary* and *Tracing Women's Romanticism: Gender, History and Transcendence* (Routledge, 2004). With Adriana Craciun, she co-edited *Rebellious Hearts: British Women Writers and the French Revolution* (State University of New York, 2001). She has also written on the aesthetics of the sublime and the grotesque, fairy tales, and women poets of the Romantic era.

Fabienne Moore is an Associate Professor of French in the Department of Romance Languages at the University of Oregon, Eugene. Her field of research and teaching are the European Enlightenment and early Romanticism. She has published several articles on eighteenth-century poetry and a book on *Prose Poems of the French Enlightenment: Delimiting Genre* (Ahsgate, 2009). Her current book project is entitled *Chateaubriand's Lost Paradises. Discourse/Counter-Discourse on Colonialism.*

Lauren Fortner Ravalico is a Visiting Assistant Professor of French in the Department of Romance Languages and Literatures at Boston College. She recently completed a Ph.D. dissertation on representations of listening and the construction of receptive agency in the work of Germaine de Staël and George Sand that she is currently expanding into a book project. She has articles forthcoming on the poetics and politics of nonverbal communication in French Romantic writing and Impressionist painting.

Mary D. Sheriff is the W. R. Kenan, Jr. Distinguished Professor of Art History at the University of North Carolina at Chapel Hill. She is a specialist of eighteenth- and nineteenth-century French art and culture, and she has published widely on issues of gender and theories of representation. Among her books are *The Exceptional Woman: Elisabeth Vigée-Lebrun and the Cultural Politics of Art* (1997) and *Moved by Love: Inspired Artists and Deviant Women in Eighteenth-Century France* (2008), both published by the University of Chicago Press.

Karyna Szmurlo is a Professor of French in the College of Architecture, Arts and Humanities at Clemson University. She has published on eighteenth- and nineteenth-century women writers, and modern literature. Her research is strongly interdisciplinary, combining history, feminist theory, philosophy of language, and the arts. She is the editor of *Germaine de Staël: Forging a Politics of Mediation* (Voltaire Foundation, 2011), collaborating editor of *Madame de Staël et les études féminines/Autour de Madame Necker* (Champion, 2006), editor of *The Novel's Seductions: Staël's* Corinne *in Critical Inquiry* (Bucknell University Press, 1999), and coeditor of *Germaine de Staël: Crossing the Borders* (Rutgers University Press, 1991). She serves on the Executive Board of the Germaine de Staël Society for Revolutionary and Romantic Studies, an allied organization of the American Association for Eighteenth-Century Studies.

Susan Tenenbaum is an Associate Professor of Political Science at Baruch College, CUNY. She is the author of numerous articles on Germaine de Staël. Her publications have appeared in *Political Theory*, *Annales Benjamin Constant* and the collected volumes *Germaine de Staël: Forging a Politics of Mediation* (Voltaire Foundation, 2011), *The Novel's Seductions: Staël's* Corinne *in Critical Inquiry* (Bucknell University Press, 1999), and *Germaine de Staël: Crossing the Borders* (Rutgers University Press, 1991). She is presently completing a study of public policy and the arts.

C. C. Wharram is an Associate Professor of English at Eastern Illinois University. His writing has appeared in *Germanic Review*, *Gothic Studies*, *Nineteenth-Century Literature Criticism*, and the collected volume *Translations of Romantic Texts* (Slovenian Association of Literary Translators, 2004). He is currently finishing a book manuscript on the role of translation theories and praxis in Romantic movements.

www.ingramcontent.com/pod-product-compliance
Lightning Source LLC
Chambersburg PA
CBHW021456110726
47899CB00001BA/172